lge

STUDIES IN SOCIAL AND POLITICAL THOUGHT
Editor: Gerard Delanty, *University of Liverpool*

This series publishes peer-reviewed scholarly books
on all aspects of social and political thought. It will be
of interest to scholars and advanced students working
in the areas of social theory and sociology, the history
of ideas, philosophy, political and legal theory,
anthropological and cultural theory. Works of
individual scholarship will have preference for
inclusion in the series, but appropriate co- or multi-
authored works and edited volumes of outstanding
quality or exceptional merit will also be included. The
series will also consider English translations of major
works in other languages.

Challenging and intellectually innovative books
are particularly welcome on the history of social and
political theory; modernity and the social and human
sciences; major historical or contemporary thinkers;
the philosophy of the social sciences; theoretical issues
on the transformation of contemporary society; social
change and European societies.

It is not series policy to publish textbooks, research
reports, empirical case studies, conference proceedings
or books of an essayist or polemical nature.

Discourse and Knowledge: The Making of Enlightenment Sociology
Piet Strydom

The Moment: Time and Rupture in Modern Thought
edited by Heidrun Friese

Essaying Montaigne
John O'Neill

The Protestant Ethic Debate: Max Weber's Replies to his Critics, 1907–1910
edited by David Chalcraft and Austin Harrington

Discourse and Knowledge

The Making of Enlightenment Sociology

PIET STRYDOM

LIVERPOOL UNIVERSITY PRESS

First published 2000 by
Liverpool University Press
4 Cambridge Street
Liverpool
L69 7ZU

Copyright © Liverpool University Press 2000

The right of Piet Strydom to be identified as the author
of this work has been asserted by him in accordance
with the Copyright, Design and Patents Act, 1988

British Library Cataloguing-in-Publication Data
A British Library CIP Record is available

ISBN 0–85323–805–7 hardback
      0–85323–815-4 paperback

Typeset in Plantin by Koinonia, Bury
Printed and bound in Great Britain by
Bell and Bain, Glasgow

Contents

Acknowledgements

I owe an immense debt of gratitude to two colleague friends in particular. Klaus Eder not only encouraged me to publish more of my materials, but also confronted me with such a profusion of theoretical and methodological ideas that I could not but rethink my position in detail. Gerard Delanty was in regular contact, and in his tireless pursuit of various projects created stimuli and opened up possibilities from which I benefited both in terms of the preparation and the publication of the book. I wish to thank Gerard Delanty, Klaus Eder and Mike Featherstone for instructive comments prior to publication, the latter two on the first draft and the former on various drafts. Thanks are also due to graduate students Paulina Chiwangu, Marie Mater, Bridget McAdam-O'Connell, Gerard Mullally and Orla O'Donnell as well as graduate seminar participants and undergraduate students who shared various of the ideas in this book with me and responded constructively to them. Relieving friends, colleagues and students of all responsibility, the errors of fact and judgement that remain in the text are mine alone. I thank Maria Strydom for the invaluable work she did on the index. Finally, I wish to acknowledge a grant received from the Arts Faculty Fund, National University of Ireland, Cork, in support of research undertaken in the course of completing this book.

I dedicate this book to the memory of a mentor and very good friend of mine, John B. O'Malley, who tragically died in 1976 at the age of fifty while on the academic staff of the University of Liverpool.

Preface

This book was written against the background of the current problem of the legitimacy or collective validity of knowledge and the ironic phenomenon of a concerted attack against sociology from within sociology departments themselves. It is devoted less to a direct defence of sociology, however, than to an exploration, in the realms of theory, methodology and the history of sociology, of what I regard as one of the most profound implications of the problem of the legitimacy of knowledge. It concerns the breakdown of the link, first recognised by Plato and forcefully renewed by Karl Marx, between mind and power, between the cultural domain of ideas and symbols and the domain of physical or material compulsion, upon which the modern concept of authority and practices of authorisation depended. As Walter Benjamin (1980, 253–55) and Michel Foucault (1987a, 39) did earlier with reference to the tension between the victors and the victims of history, Zygmunt Bauman (1992) has drawn attention in recent years to this problem by highlighting the ambivalence of modernity. Utilisation research (e.g. Lau 1984; Evers and Nowotny 1987; Beck and Bonss 1989; Stehr 1996) has made matters still more complicated by demonstrating the untenability of the assumption that a direct relation holds between theory and practice or between scientific knowledge and its application.

In this book, which forms part of a larger project, the current challenge is met through an analysis in terms of a cognitivist communication and discourse theory of the discursive construction of Enlightenment sociology in the context of the early modern rights discourse. This focus can be justified by the fact that the problem of the legitimacy of sociological knowledge compels us to surrender the customary linking of sociology and modernity beginning with the French Revolution and the industrial revolution in favour of investigating the form sociology originally took. Rather than beginning the history of sociology too late, as is usually done, it is necessary to take a step back. Only then is it possible to free sociology from its pernicious identification through the concept of history and the philosophy of history with the dominant view of modernity and thus to regain, through the recovery of a pluralist and participatory concept of politics, the collective validity of sociological knowledge. For by considering its original construction, sociology can be seen in its embroilment in both cultural symbolism and power and its contradictory relation to both the victors and victims of modernity – including, to be sure, the possibility of distancing itself from this in a critical and self-critical manner.

This realisation, arrived at through an appreciation of the relation of sociology to practical discourse, today places before us the task of revitalising the public role of sociology. On this depends the meaningful survival of sociology in the new millennium.

PIET STRYDOM
Kinsale, Co. Cork, Ireland

CHAPTER 1

Introduction: Discourse and Sociology

As the title intimates, this book is in principle concerned with the role of discourse in the generation, utilisation and development of knowledge. Written as it is by an author professionally employed as a sociologist, this relationship will be investigated more specifically with reference to the process through which sociology arose, became established and is continuously being maintained, revised and developed. Despite this emphasis, however, knowledge is confined here neither to scientific knowledge created by paid professionals, such as myself, nor more generally to the systematised and formalised knowledge of academia. Rather it is broadly understood as the tools or instruments and the working materials used by people at all levels and in different contexts to make or construct their world. In this sense, it includes the widest variety of kinds of knowledge, from the informal, everyday knowledge of ordinary people, through the more formal, systematised knowledge of professionals, to public knowledge such as frameworks of meaning and cultural models that reach people through public communication, controversies and the media. At the centre of interest is precisely how discourse makes possible and facilitates the interrelation or interconnection of all these different kinds of knowledge in the course of the constitution of social reality.

Rather than embarking at this point on an outline of the theoretical and methodological positions and steps that will be taken in order to be able to pursue the intended investigation of the relation between discourse and knowledge, I want to provide the reader with as clear and substantive a point of access as possible to the material presented in this book. Such an access is to be found in the concern of the book with the history of sociology. What I propose to do is briefly to confront a number of more or less widely accepted conventional explanations of the rise of sociology and then, against that background,

1

to suggest an alternative account that will be presented in detail later in this book. This preliminary overview will make possible the introduction in an intelligible manner of the key theoretical, methodological and epistemological concepts adopted in the book for the purposes of analysing the relation between discourse and knowledge.

Explanations of the Rise of Sociology

It is well known that sociology as such was first institutionalised only as late as 1892 in the United States, followed by France in 1913 and Germany in 1918. It is relatively easy to determine precisely when university departments, courses in sociology and research institutions were first created. The question as to when sociology or, more generally, the social sciences arose, however, is more difficult to answer with certainty. Today, it is generally accepted that the social sciences came into being during the great transition in and through which modernity made its first appearance. Indeed, the social sciences are regarded as having been a part of the process of the formation of modernity. What makes them unique is that they take the very process and the societal arrangement to which they themselves belong – i.e., the process of formation and the structural features of modernity – as their object of study. This applies more to sociology than to any of the remaining social sciences. In other words, sociology came into being for the first time on the level of reflection attained when modern society became aware of its own processes of genesis and development. This is what Anthony Giddens (1984, 9) means when he writes that: 'Sociology came into being as those caught up in the initial series of changes brought about by the "two great revolutions" in Europe sought to understand the conditions of their emergence, and their likely consequences ... The climate of ideas involved in the formation of sociology in some part, in fact, helped give rise to the twin processes of revolution.' George Ritzer (1992, 5, 7) says precisely the same, if somewhat less acutely, when he submits that:

> All intellectual fields are profoundly shaped by their social settings. This is particularly true of sociology, which is not only derived from that setting but takes that social setting as its basic subject matter... The long series of political revolutions ushered in by the French Revolution in 1789 and carrying over through the nineteenth century was the most immediate factor in the rise of sociological theorising... At least as important as political revolution in the shaping of sociological theory was the Industrial Revolution, which swept through many Western societies, mainly in the nineteenth and early twentieth centuries.

There is no sense in amassing example upon example; the point has been made. Sociology is widely regarded as having arisen at the beginning of the modern period. Interpretations part ways, however, as soon as the more precise question of the approximate date of this occurrence is raised. In the quotations above, both Giddens and Ritzer accept that sociology came into being in relation to the changes brought about by the French Revolution and the industrial revolution. This implies that they regard sociology as having come into being in the period between the late eighteenth and the late nineteenth centuries, well before its institutionalisation. For Giddens (1976), this means that the leading figures responsible for the founding of sociology include Auguste Comte, Karl Marx and Herbert Spencer. In his account, Ritzer concentrates on the contributions of Karl Marx, Emile Durkheim, Max Weber and Georg Simmel.

The great emphasis commonly laid on the French and industrial revolutions as marking the start of the period in which sociology emerged, irrespective of which sociologists are singled out, owes a good deal to the dominating influence of Talcott Parsons during the middle decades of the twentieth century. In his theoretical work (Parsons 1966; 1977a), he made much of the caesura created by these two events, and in his historical interpretation (Parsons 1968) he depicted sociology, although recognising that it had been preceded by various theories of society, as having emerged for the first time in an emphatic sense in the nineteenth century, more particularly between 1890 and 1920. In this period, he focused especially on Durkheim and Weber to the exclusion of Marx – a judgement for which he was severely taken to task in later years (Dahrendorf 1959; Habermas 1969b; 1971; Gouldner 1970; Giddens 1976). Simultaneously, however, the emphasis on the two great revolutions was reinforced by Marxist interpretations of modernity and of social theory and sociology. E. J. Hobsbawm (1977, 11), for instance, introduced the influential thesis of the so-called 'Dual Revolution' of the period between 1789 and 1848, while Herbert Marcuse (1973), who distinguished Hegelian–Marxist social theory from positivistic sociology, traced sociology back to Claude Henri Saint-Simon and Auguste Comte in France and Friedrich Julius Stahl and Lorenz von Stein in Germany.

The generally accepted understanding that sociology has from the start been rooted in a structured social setting, however the latter may be interpreted, and that it takes that very setting as its object of study, had first been formulated explicitly by an early twentieth-century sociologist who exerted a pervasive, if not always acknowledged, influence and whose work has been experiencing a revival in the past few decades. He is Karl Mannheim (1972; Meja and Stehr 1982; Stehr and Meja 1984), who elaborated this reflexive insight into a sociological sub-discipline known as the sociology of knowledge. According to him, all knowledge is socially situated and therefore socially conditioned: 'every form of...thought is essentially conditioned by the life situation of the thinker and his group... behind every theory there are collective forces [and a] collective point of view' (Mannheim 1972, 111, 110). All knowledge is 'fundamentally collective knowing... it presupposes a community of knowing which grows primarily out of a community of experiencing...' (28). And as soon as people become aware of this fact and begin to process it reflectively, sociology makes its appearance: 'out of the investigation into the social determination of history arises sociology' (222). Given its reflexive nature, sociology is thus 'an adequate picture of the structure of the whole of society' (228). Despite the fact that he had been prompted by this reflexive turn to develop an admirably clear grasp of the communication revolution of the early modern period (7–11), Mannheim may also have contributed to the predominant tendency to locate the rise of sociology only in the nineteenth century after the French and industrial revolutions. He regarded the experience and recognition of the social realm and hence the appearance of the concept of 'the social', historically speaking, as a late phenomenon. Having been inhibited by the individualistic form of society in the early modern period when epistemology and psychology reigned, social reality was experienced and recognised as such only when society took a more social form. This occurred only in the nineteenth century when the socialist mentality succeeded the liberal and conservative worldviews. It is on this basis that 'sociology' and 'sociologist' later made their appearance.

While accepting the generally held assumption that sociology had originally arisen during the great transition, Jürgen Habermas takes a broader view than the above-mentioned authors. This allows him to date the emergence of sociology somewhat earlier. According to him, sociology originated as an intellectual concern whose

> theme was the changes in social integration brought about within the structure of old-European societies by the rise of the modern system of nation states and by the differentiation of a market-regulated economy. Sociology became the science of crisis par excellence; it concerned itself above all with the anomic aspects of the dissolution of traditional social systems and the development of modern ones (Habermas 1984, 4).

The formation of the system of nation states to which he refers, central to which was the absolutist state, started in the early sixteenth century and became formally established on the basis of the Treaties of Westphalia in 1648, but the absolutist state and the *ancien régime* themselves of course called forth a reaction in the form of a whole series of political revolutions starting with the Dutch Revolt and ending with the French Revolution. The formation of capitalism was closely intertwined with this political development, as is attested for instance by the relation between mercantile capitalism and the absolutist state, and it in turn benefited immensely from the political revolutions. Modern capitalism was possible only on the basis of the modern constitutional state.

Despite relating the rise of sociology to the long-term processes of the formation of the system of states and of the market-based economy, Habermas nevertheless locates this event only as late as the third quarter of the eighteenth century. Both in his early and his recent work (Habermas 1966, 2110; 1969a, 216; 1996, 43–44), he regards the moral philosophers of the Scottish Enlightenment, particularly Adam Ferguson and John Millar, as the first sociologists. In this, Habermas is followed by others (e.g. Radnitzky 1970, 129; Van Houten 1974, 14). Although he is less inclined to endorse the dogmatic distinction between Marxist social theory and bourgeois sociology, this interpretation of his does owe something to Marxism and its insistence on modern society being equivalent to bourgeois society. This is clear from the manner in which he introduces and evaluates the significance of Ferguson and Millar who, according to him, found themselves on the trajectory between Aristotle and Marx.

This would suggest that, although his position is more adequate than those of Mannheim, Parsons, Marcuse, Giddens and Ritzer, there is a certain tension in Habermas' understanding of the emergence of sociology. Whereas he on the one hand locates this event in the context of the formation of both the state and the market-regulated economy, he ties his identification of the first sociologists exclusively to capitalism. Two difficulties thus become apparent here. First, he seems to neglect the process of state formation, although from other parts of his work it is clear that the French Revolution is of the utmost importance to him. More serious is the related tendency to assimilate the early modern to the modern period. Rather than respecting the integrity of the early modern period, the contributions of Ferguson and Millar are dislodged from their context and appropriated from a nineteenth- and twentieth-century viewpoint. According to Habermas' understanding, they prepared the way for a theory of society which is based, if no longer on a Neo-Marxist philosophy of history, then at least on a developmental-logical theory of socio-cultural evolution. Like the philosophy of history, however, this particular version of the theory of evolution has become discredited because of its dependence on the progressivist or developmentalist assumptions so typical of the nineteenth and twentieth centuries (Strydom 1992a). But, perhaps, the major problem with Habermas' account of the rise of sociology is that he neglects to exploit the potential of his own acute insight into the revolutionary nature of the great transition. According to this insight, it would be more profitable to focus on the communication revolution of the early modern period[1] than to fix on the French and industrial revolutions alone.

Very recently, a commendable attempt has been made by Johan Heilbron, Lars Magnusson and Björn Wittrock (1998; see also Strydom 1998) in the context of the new historiography of the social sciences to go back behind the dual revolution in order to pinpoint the rise of the social sciences in relation to the formation of modernity. Instead of the economic-industrial and political revolutions, the authors seek to unearth the traditionally underestimated and openly neglected epistemic-conceptual transformation of the time. Operating with both the principle of continuity or gradual change, which allows the inclusion of the seventeenth century, and the principle of rupture, with the year 1795 marking the decisive caesura constitutive of the social sciences, however, the anthology does not succeed in resolving the question of when sociology first arose. Nor does it make much clearer the specific context in which this occurred. While the authors are inspired by Foucault's discourse analysis, Koselleck's historical semantic analysis, Skinner and Pocock's linguistic contextualism and the sociology of scientific knowledge, they by no means exhaust the potential of the means at their disposal. For one, although the theoretical concept of discourse is frequently mentioned, it is not developed and exploited. The same is true of the methodology of discourse analysis. It should be pointed out here that Foucault's work on discourse is both theoretically and methodologically far too unspecific to lead to fruitful results. More generally, the analysis would have benefited from embedding the epistemic-conceptual transformation in the communication revolution of the early modern period.

In his endeavour to identify what he calls 'the first formulation of sociology', Björn Eriksson (1993) undertakes explicitly to attend to a significant 'discursive innovation of the eighteenth century'. At the centre of his attention is the new 'discourse of sociology' to which the Scottish Enlightenment had given rise. He acknowledges that Comte is 'the father of the name of sociology', but insists that the corollary that he is the founder of 'the discourse or conceptual frame of sociology' (251) does not follow. He is adamant that the rise of sociology should rather be located in the context of the Scottish Enlightenment. Eriksson (1993, 253) argues forcefully, moreover, that the proposition that the Scottish moral philosophers had been the first sociologists should for once be taken seriously. It is a well-known one that is relatively often repeated, yet its incorporation into the history of the discipline remains a desideratum. His project, therefore, is to develop the necessary arguments to accomplish this.

Eriksson (1993, 253) sees the new discourse of sociology as having emerged on the basis of a new theoretical problem, a corresponding conceptual framework, and a major break with the common-sense understanding of social life and history prevalent at the time. Led on by Newton's spectacularly innovative theory of gravity, the Scots – i.e., Adam Smith in particular, followed by Ferguson and Millar – transposed 'subsistence' into a new conceptual category and thus provided sociology with its basis and framework. In his concentration on the discursive innovation of the eighteenth century in the sense of an epistemological rupture eventuating in the establishment of sociology, however, Eriksson assumes an unreflective internalist view that leads him to overlook the link between the discourse of sociology and the wider practical discourse of modernity taking place in the surrounding situation. A consequence of the screening out of the embedding societal discourse of the time is his predilection to link the emergence of sociology too closely to Smith's social scientific transformation of Newton. The end result is a scientistic interpretation of Enlightenment sociology that does not allow an adequate understanding of the contribution of the Scottish moral philosophers. His interpretation also militates against the relatively widely accepted view that, far from Smith, it was rather Ferguson and Millar who discovered civil society and made it as such into the object of study of sociology.

Given the close relation between sociology and modernity, it is obvious that an author's position on the rise of sociology correlates with his or her at least implicit interpretation and periodisation of modernity.[2] The most widely accepted interpretation links modernity with the political dispensation inaugurated by the French Revolution and the rise of industrial capitalism, and consequently locates the beginnings of the modern era in the late eighteenth and early nineteenth century. The only room left for sociology, then, is some time later in the nineteenth century or even the twentieth. This is the position of authors such as Parsons, Marcuse, Giddens and Ritzer. If an author is willing not to wait for the actual occurrence of the two great revolutions but rather to link up with developments leading up to them, then it becomes possible of course to see the rise of sociology as having occurred a little earlier. This is apparently what Habermas does. If, on the other hand, one identifies modernity with science, then the third decade of the seventeenth century during which both Galileo and Descartes made their signal contributions would seem to be the most important years for a periodisation of the beginning of the era. Although he does not trace sociology to this period, Eriksson extrapolates from this line of development to locate his Newtonian interpretation of the rise of sociology in the mid-eighteenth century.

Another possibility is to take the political claims of the territorial and nascent nation-state as one's reference point, in which case the beginnings of modernity can be located in the period between the late sixteenth and the mid-seventeenth century. One could further add to this the early modern social movement that reacted against the state and the European system of states, and bequeathed its political and social ideals to the French Revolution, thus helping to open the road to democracy, political participation and the judging of intentions and policies according to impartial universalistic standards. This interpretation seems to be intimated by Habermas (e.g. 1989b, 1996) in some of his more recent writings, but it is nowhere made explicit, not to mention brought to bear on the emergence of the social sciences. The neglected possibility that becomes apparent here obviously bears great promise.

The proposed study of the making of sociology in this book shares the general assumption that the rise of the social sciences, and sociology in parti-cular, is best understood in the context of the process of the formation of modernity. Rather than laying emphasis on the French and industrial revo-lutions as is commonly done, however, the investigation will go back behind the dual revolution, as is proposed by Eriksson and Heilbron, Magnusson and Wittrock.[3] It will be assumed that sociology originated as a concern focused on the changes brought about within the structure of pre-modern European societies not only by the emergence of the modern system of states and a market-based economy, as Habermas argues, but also by the early modern social movement that appeared in reaction to these developments and eventually passed on its ideals to the French Revolution and helped to clear the way for constitutional democracy. This means that the beginnings of modern-ity will be located in the period between the late sixteenth and the mid-seventeenth century. Such an interpretation of modernity opens the possibility of meaningfully incorporating into the history of sociology earlier develop-ments that are conventionally omitted or excluded. To reconstruct the rise of sociology in relation to the formation of modernity, the brilliant insight into the communication revolution of the early modern period will be taken up and pursued beyond Mannheim and Habermas. This decision has various implica-tions. An emphasis on communication and, by extension, discourse will allow one to avoid a purely internalist account of sociology, such as the one given by Eriksson, by bringing into play the wider public communication and practical discourse taking place in the surrounding situation. It will be possible to reconstruct the original formulation of Enlightenment sociology within the context of the embedding societal discourse of the time, the rights discourse. The advantage of this broad approach is that it allows the early modern period to be treated without violating its integrity in so far as the latter is represented by a central and perhaps the most important practical discourse of the time or, at least, one that put all the major dimensions of society in contact with each other. By following processes of communication and discourse that took place at the time and identifying the making of sociology within and through those very same processes, one can regard the rise of sociology in a gradual and unified way throughout the early modern period, without being compelled to exclude such significant events as the emergence of science and technology, the market-based economy, the early modern revolutions, and so forth, and their impact on sociology. More important is that inappropriate or anachronistic nineteenth- and twentieth-century points of view, such as progressivist or developmentalist assumptions which have contributed to the delegitimation of sociology in recent times, can then be given up.[4] At the same time, the focus on communication and discourse also makes possible the avoidance of the complementary contextualist error of becoming native. It will give us the means to develop an understanding of the role of both practical discourse and sociology, whether in the early modern period, the high modern period or at the beginning of the twenty-first century.

This is the interpretation of modernity and the interpretation of the rise of sociology that will be adopted for the purposes of the substantive historical-sociological analysis in this study. To develop a preliminary grasp of the communication and discourse theoretical approach that will be followed to fill out these interpretations, it is necessary now to introduce briefly a series of theoretical, methodological and epistemological concepts and considerations. A first step will be taken by offering a brief summary of the basic assumptions from which the study proceeds.

Basic Assumptions

The general theoretical approach that will be followed in the proposed analysis of the relation between knowledge and discourse through a study of the making of sociology is what may be described as a communication and discourse theoretical approach. The most basic assumption of this approach is that communication in general and discourse – as a specific form of reflective communication – in particular have become increasingly important in society.[5]

Since the communication revolution of the early modern period, all the major cultural innovations in modern societies have been achieved through this medium. Social processes were penetrated by communication and were henceforth steered through communication. The outcomes of social processes were made effective through communication. Isolated social groupings and communities were opened up and put in touch with one another through communication. Associations in which people could freely debate and engage

9

in dialogue were formed, and large national and international communication communities were created. Not only everything but also everybody became connected with one another through communication, and it became possible to change virtually anything, as long as there was an opportunity to communicate about it. The fact that everything has become a matter of communication does not mean, of course, that there is nothing but communication. Earthquakes or nuclear accidents happen, but it is through communication that people make sense of such events and deal with them. Or people mobilise through communication to create a mighty historical event such as the French Revolution about which they have to this day not yet stopped communicating. Through its innovative thrust, such mobilisation has spurred on further waves or cycles of mobilisation, even hundreds of years later.

Through communication, people create or construct the semantically rich, meaningful worlds or universes of the societies in which they live. The meaningfulness of the universes of these societies is audibly and visibly encapsulated in a variety of semantics. They stretch from the characteristic social and political language and vocabulary crystallising around significant historical events or serious collective problems to the many distinct, specialised languages and vocabularies of different cultural and intellectual pursuits, including religion, ethics, philosophy, the arts, architecture, the sciences, etc. Such semantics of course point to deeper classification schemes that not only organise experience, perception and interpretation, but also structure communication and are reflected upon, articulated, brought to awareness and even made into objects of conflict by discourse.

The upshot of all this is that modern societies are communication societies, and that discourse, the special form of communication through which problems are collectively identified, issues are collectively defined and actions are collectively coordinated, is a constitutive feature of the modernity of these societies.

Theoretical Approach

Based on assumptions such as these, which will be further explicated below, the communication and discourse theoretical approach adopted in this book is pre-eminently suited to deal with the question of how knowledge emerges from a social setting or develops in relation to historical events or social structural change. Judging by past and present contributions, however, the relation in question can be approached in a variety of quite different and more or less fruitful ways.

The oldest and best known approach is Karl Mannheim's (1972; 1993)[6] sociology of knowledge, which was briefly considered above. A less well-known yet very interesting approach is Reinhard Koselleck's (1985) sociologically informed historical semantic study of the rapid and radical transformation of political and social vocabularies in the course of the great transition leading to modernity. Another important approach is Niklas Luhmann's (1980) systems theoretical analyses of social structure and semantics, for instance the investigation of the language and vocabulary of the aristocracy in the transition from hierarchically structured to functionally differentiated societies. While all these approaches have some very interesting and commendable qualities, they nevertheless suffer from different theoretical and hence methodological limitations that make a lock, stock and barrel adoption of any one unattractive. Insights drawn from these approaches will nevertheless enrich the communication and discourse approach proposed here.

The sociology of knowledge, to begin with, needs a more explicit and elaborate theory of communication and discourse. Such an enhancement is necessary if one is to be able to establish relations of mediation between cultural products and their social carriers beyond the problems plaguing the traditional method of imputation.[7] Its presupposed theory of society also needs strengthening to enable the sociologist to locate both cultural products and social groups in their proper context. As regards later developments, not only the idea of the social construction of reality but also that of the broadening and abstraction of knowledge require a more stringent theoretically informed and analytical treatment. Historical semantic inquiries into the relation between conceptual history and social history have had a beneficial influence on sociologists of different persuasions, such as Habermas (1969a; 1989a), on the one hand, and Luhmann (1980), on the other, and therefore there is clearly much to be learned from them. As a historical approach rather than a sociological one, however, this does not command a theoretical foundation that will satisfy the sociologist. Methodologically, the introduction of a comprehensive communication and discourse theory also means that its meaningful focus on semantics can be integrated into a more sophisticated mode of analysis of communication and cultural products. Systems theory disposes over a well-developed theoretical apparatus embracing a communication, a differentiation, a complexity and an evolutionary theory, and is thus able to compensate some of the most pressing theoretical deficiencies of the sociology of knowledge and historical semantics. Yet this is true only up to a certain point, since its basic reliance on the theory of differentiation renders systems theory incapable from the start and throughout to deal with the genetic or constructive dimension of the production of society. This is apparent from its exclusion of any reference to the social carriers of ideas, which in addition results in an inadequate treatment of the communication dimension.[8] It is certainly the case that one can learn from systems theory, particularly in its autopoietic version, about the dynamics of meaning systems or culture, but it does not possess the means to provide the finely tuned cognitivist discourse analysis covering both the micro- and the macro-dimension needed to carry out the task before us.

Given the limitations of the approaches that one could have considered adopting, a different route is followed in this work. It is provided by a theory of the collective production and reproduction of society to which communication and discourse – and hence reflexivity – are central and that is of the genetic- or constructivist-structuralist type.[9] A suggestion of the direction in which this approach goes in the present context can be gleaned from a brief reflection on an interesting observation Wolf Lepenies (1977a, 345) once made. From Saint-Simon to Thomas Kuhn, according to him, the history of science depended on the parallelism between political and scientific revolutions as a substitute for a yet to be formulated social history of theory production. In his view, preliminary work towards such a social history could be accomplished by an approach that seeks to analyse the scientific community as some kind of link between the political and scientific systems. In a sense, this is what is envisaged here, yet with a number of differences. The political and scientific systems are dealt with in terms of socio-political and sociological semantics respectively, and the scientific community linking them is regarded as forming part of a larger set of communicative relations and approached in terms of pragmatics through the concept of a societal practical discourse. Rather than a social history of theory production, therefore, a preliminary social theory of the production of knowledge – in this case, sociology – is thus developed within the framework of a more encompassing theory of the production and reproduction of society.

The starting point of this theoretical approach is that society is a temporal and hence dynamic yet structured phenomenon that is suspended in a process of construction, of collective production and reproduction, formation and transformation, constitution and reconstitution or replication and transmuta-tion. Rather than representing an existing, more or less stable, institutional or social order, as for instance Parsons (1968),[10] who started from the so-called 'Hobbesian problem', taught sociologists to think, society is a matter of both order and disorder, continuity and change, that is best approached in terms of the ambivalent and contradictory process of its constitution and reconstitu-tion, the process of construction in which different collective actors through their conflict and cooperation, through their division and coordination, replicate and transform society. Central to this process is a mechanism or procedure that is both processual and structural, both processing and structuring, through which not only human beings but also social and cultural objects, as well as things and indeed nature itself, are brought into relation with one another in a variety of ways and thus rendered socially significant. Rather than being just on the product, the focus is also on the process or, better, rather than being just on the outcome or effect, the focus is also on the procedure whereby the elements of a dynamic structural totality are constantly being related and put together.

The micro-macro model is useful for developing an understanding of one aspect of the collective production and reproduction of society in the above sense. In sociology, the constructivist approach has been developed in, for instance, symbolic interactionism, phenomenology, dramaturgic analysis and ethnomethodology where it typically remained confined to the micro-dimension of action and interaction. What the theory of the collective construction of society calls for, by contrast, is that the macro-dimension be brought into purview. The perspective of the ambivalent and contradictory process of the construction of society must be extended so as to include also the macro-dimension. This takes the form neither of connecting system and action or lifeworld, as Habermas (1984; 1987a) does in the theory of communicative action, nor of linking agency and structure, as Giddens (1986) does in the theory of structuration. Whereas Habermas' boxer approach is too dualistic, Giddens' processual approach leaves too little room for the mediating role of discourse and culture. It is equally difficult, however, to follow Eder's (1988, 257) proposal to regard praxis as complementary to system. Apart from the problems lurking in the adoption of the concept of system, praxis for him involves the appropriation of Touraine's concept of historical actor in the sense of collective action taking the form of a social movement. This entails not only ascribing central theoretical significance to the concept of social movement, but at the same time also over-estimating the importance of social movements in society. It certainly makes sense to consider society from the perspective not of order but rather of movement or process, the theoretical thrust of the concept of social movement. Why remain attached to social order if it is abundantly clear that it is something dependent on the creation of order by means of the marshalling of interests, values or power, something derivative, contingent and awaiting empirical confirmation? And what is more, which kind of social order is most important: the market, the lifeworld, or the state? Yet this insight into the primacy of movement or process over order spearheaded by a cultural creator, however profound, should not be allowed to mislead one into focusing on social movements as the embodiment of the collective action or praxis that brings forth the social evolution of modern society.[11]

The theoretical approach advocated here instead draws collective actors of different types, not only social movements, to the centre of the stage and makes the interaction between the processes they give rise to as well as the outcomes thus produced the theoretical problem. Of central interest becomes the interaction between or the separation and coordination processes of collective action, the ensuing strategic interaction, attempts to regulate these processes and their observation and the emergent outcomes, effects or structural manifestations – interaction that is itself structured by discourse and hence intervening variables such as culture and power, which diversify and complicate the dynamics of both the construction of problems by the different actors and attempts to solve them.

Taking this path entails reservations about a number of more or less prevalent interpretations of the micro-macro model in sociology. It is neither a matter of accounting for micro-phenomena (e.g. social action) by reference to macro-phenomena (e.g. capitalism), nor of explaining macro-phenomena (e.g. large-scale events, processes or structures) by reference to other macro-phenomena (e.g. semantic, economic or technological change), nor even of making sense of macro-phenomena by reference to micro-phenomena, irrespective of whether the latter are seen to generate or create the former in such a way that unintended consequences follow (Mayntz 1990; 1992). The problem as envisaged here, which does not necessarily exclude the agency-structure relation (Giddens 1986),[12] is the more complicated one of the construction, through the mediation of communication and discourse, at the macro-level as socially significant phenomena of certain properties of aggregates of actors or events that are inserted into public communication at the micro-level.[13] For instance, a given event is evaluated, described and judged by different actors who then communicate their own distinct definitions according to their own particular identities in the public domain. Upon this follows the competition and conflict of the various definitions in public communication before a varied public of observers, commentators, sympathisers, opponents, and so forth. Due to the attention paid by the public to the issue and the widespread communication of its evaluation and judgement of what is involved, a certain collective understanding of the issue, the participating actors and the event referred to is discursively constructed in public communication and a certain social significance ascribed to them.[14] In a sense, Karin Knorr-Cetina (1988) is correct when she submits that the micro- and the macro-dimensions are one and the same. It is difficult to see, however, how a sociologist could sustain this position by persisting in proceeding from a purely phenomenological basis. A communication and discourse theory renders this constructive concordance more readily intelligible than her 'representation hypothesis of the macro-social order' (21) in that it makes clear that both the micro and the macro involve, at different levels of abstraction, the same mechanisms, structures or rules of coordination of social actions.[15]

A related aspect of the above-mentioned ambivalent and contradictory process of the construction of society needs to be mentioned at this juncture. It is related to the nature of this process as a genetic process that is on the one hand possible only within a structural framework and on the other again leads to another structural framework. This feature lies in the fact that every such process in principle transpires in two more or less clearly identifiable steps or phases: the breakdown and loss of a state of equilibrium and the recovery and build-up of a new one (Piaget 1973, 208–09; Swidler 1986).[16] These two moments, punctuated by a critical turning-point or discontinuity, follow each other permanently. In the case of human society, this shift can be regarded as a matter of uncertainty followed by certainty (Evers and Nowotny 1987), and so forth. The difficulty that this process poses to sociological understanding is attributable to the fact that its two sides affect three distinct aspects.[17] Whilst at the level of organised semantics it takes the form of the breakdown of a particular socio-political semantics and its replacement by a new one, it is manifested at the same time at two further dimensions: the cognitive foundations in the form of a cultural model that provides cultural orientations, and secondly the individual, groups and collective actors engaged in the construction of a collective identity. Considered from the viewpoint of these three different aspects, not only the normative order and the cultural form undergo change, but simultaneously also the awareness or knowledge society has of itself, its self-interpretation and ability to act and secure its sovereignty, is affected.

Currently, we find ourselves in a situation of change and uncertainty, comparable to at least two previous historical situations,[18] which is characterised by a loss of certainty and by an intensive attempt to compensate for it. On the one hand, the questioning of the cultural model of mechanical nature (Moscovici 1982a; 1990; Merchant 1989) has been accompanied by the breakdown of the optimistic trust in scientific-technological and social progress as well as the loss of the 'utopian energies' (Habermas 1986) propelling the project of state intervention and welfare. On the other hand, an intensive search is simultaneously under way for new guiding ideas and orientations, a whole new language, and ways of dealing with a dark future. A particularly disconcerting aspect of the current situation to many, however, is that it seems as though we have gone beyond the limit where the re-establishment of a full-scale certainty is possible. Both the concepts of 'postmodernity' (e.g. Lyotard 1984) and 'reflexive modernity' (e.g. Beck et al. 1994) serve to give expression to this new condition. It should be insisted against the extreme version of both these two positions, however, that the structural fluidisation observed today does not necessarily exclude a certain and, indeed, significant degree of structuration.[19]

Discourse and Discursive Dynamics

The permanently succeeding phases of breakdown and recovery that render the process of the construction of society all the more contradictory and ambivalent are most graphically visible at the level of discourse and the associated dynamics.

Various social groups communicate ideas and on entering public communication these ideas interrelate, compete and conflict with one another, and in the process give rise to a discourse in the sense of a historically specific, empirically identifiable form of structuring beyond the participants in the communication that is taking place. Not only does discourse activate the organised semantics and, more broadly, culture, but it also intertwines these dimensions with the action and communication of individuals, groups and collective actors in historically specific ways. By so doing, it unfolds in two more or less unambiguously identifiable phases. Pushed by conditions of dissolution and uncertainty, discourse in its earlier phase gives evidence of a collective attempt by the participants to identify and define the characteristic problem of the time and to find a way toward a solution to it. Pulled by recovery and the regaining of certainty once the first phase registers sufficient progress, discourse provides access in its later phase to the emergent common ground and new assumptions increasingly shared by the participants. It is here that it is possible to begin to see the new cultural model and socio-political semantics forming round the core provided by the problem definition and the proposed solution, but at the same time, to be sure, also the new conflicts among the participants. For the fact that the participants come to share new cultural orientations as well as concepts and theories does not exclude conflict between them but rather makes it more likely (see e.g. Blok 1998). As soon as common ground emerges, contradictions appear between them in their respective attempts to give direction to the development of society according to the new cultural orientations and in terms of the new socio-political semantics. Conflict ensues first of all within the framework of the new paradigm established on the basis of the collective definition of a common problem and possible solution, but it could also extend to struggles between the hegemonic and exclusionary paradigm and a potential alternative or alternatives.

The centrality of the identification and collective definition of problems and the opening up of approaches to their solution requires clarification of the theory of discourse accepted here. In brief, it is based on a synthesis of the positions of Habermas and Foucault.[20] While Habermas stresses the universalising logic of culture and Foucault the logic of power, with the implication that they hold diametrically opposed views, the fact of the matter is that their positions are in a strategic respect actually complementary to one another. Both regard discourse at bottom as a condition of the cultural and social construction of reality.[21] Given this relationship, the basic discourse theoretical assumption made in this work is that discourse can bring about symbolic universalisation only to the extent that power comes into play and, complementarily, that the discursive exercise of power is possible only to the extent that culture is opened up.

Possessing irreducible complementary sides, discourse brings about the structuring of communication in two distinct ways. On the one hand, it allows power to be brought into play to regulate and control communication and, on the other, it brings the compulsion of its own argumentative or symbolic logic to bear on communication processes. The two sides of discourse serve as an indication of the mediating position it occupies between social interaction or communication processes and culture. Emerging from and structuring communicative action on the one hand, discourse takes place on the other hand within the context of culture or, more particularly, of some historically shaped socio-political semantics or another. Here discourse plays a central role in replicating and transforming culture, yet at the same time its own logic is reconstituted by such a semantics.[22]

Semantics

Already since its original emergence in the second half of the eighteenth century, but more decisively still since its explicit naming by means of a neologism in the early nineteenth century, sociology represents a clearly identifiable and well-circumscribed semantic field. From early on, it not only exhibited an orientation towards the value principle of the integrity of a particular complex of meaning and the adherence to a corresponding standard of consistency, but from that very moment it also gave evidence of its own particular history. Since the late nineteenth century, and again with renewed vigour since the 1960s and 1970s, this history has been reconstructed in ever new versions. One can expect this process of historical reconstruction to be repeated again and again as the sociological semantic field, while maintaining its own integrity, historically shows unmistakable signs of more or less drastic periodic change. Rather marked changes are observable in three periods in particular: in the late eighteenth and early nineteenth century, the late nineteenth and early twentieth century, and again in the late twentieth century.

Given the fact that sociology, despite undeniable internal pluralism and contradictions, represents a more or less consistent semantic field with its own history, it is quite possible in a work devoted to the discipline to present a conceptual analysis of the field or even an extended historically informed version of such an analysis. Analyses of this kind, although typically only highly selective ones, are of course an essential ingredient of both pedagogical and creative work in the field. But this is not the approach that is followed here. An alternative becomes apparent when it is recognised that the change or development of a semantic field such as sociology, notwithstanding its own integrity and internal standard of argumentative and conceptual consistency, is not unrelated to changes and developments in the more general and culturally more potent socio-political semantics of the corresponding period, which in turn is of course again influenced and shaped by significant historical events and their interpretation.

Consider for example such concepts as 'violence', 'order', 'sovereignty', 'rights' and 'state', or such concepts as 'poverty', 'economy', 'growth' and 'justice', or such ones as 'ecological crisis', 'risk', 'sustainable development' and 'responsibility'. These three groups of concepts arose out of completely different historical and social situations. The first set emerged from the early modern revolutions (e.g. the Revolt of the Netherlands, the English Revolution, the French Revolution), while the second group followed in the wake of the establishment of industrial capitalism. The third set of contemporary concepts, in turn, was given rise to by such significant historical events as the Windscale, Three Mile Island, and Chernobyl accidents. In their respective times, these three sets of concepts proved to be politically, socially and culturally highly significant. Not only did they decisively stamp the socio-political semantics of their respective eras, the language and vocabulary that ordinary everyday people and politicians used to make sense of their world, but they also entered into a variety of more specialised semantic fields, including literature, the theatre, philosophy, and sociology itself. Indeed, the sociological semantic field, although by no means reducible to it, draws its lifeblood from the more general socio-political semantics, remaining dependent upon vital infusions from period to period. What sociology does, of course, is to translate practical discourses in society and their semantics into something different, i.e., into sociology, and in this way it provides a specialised language and vocabulary, a semantics, that makes possible the reflexive use of ongoing discourses.

Here, then, sociology is regarded as a semantic field governed by logical rules of consistency with its own continuous history that articulates closely with the wider and culturally important socio-political semantics characteristic of a given period. Rather than being simply reducible to some social carrier, whether a collective actor, social group or class participating in societal practical discourses, however, it is treated as a discrete part of culture that itself forms an independent and autonomous semantic order allowing distancing and reflexivity.

18

Crisis Discourses of Modernity

For the purposes of this book, the historically specific and hence empirically identifiable practical discourse that will serve as the central object of study is represented by what – following Habermas – may be called the discourse of modernity. The reason for this is obvious. In view of the fact that the interest here is in sociology as a specifically modern phenomenon manifesting itself as a particular internally consistent semantics that articulates more or less closely with the more encompassing and culturally significant socio-political semantics of the time, the general field within which sociology makes its appearance is provided by the discourse of modernity. The discursive construction of sociology emerges and unfolds in this field. Within its compass, certain social actors are identified by others and themselves in a publicly relevant way as carriers of a semantics that becomes explicitly defined and generally accepted as sociology. On the one hand, these carriers possess certain objective charac- teristics – e.g. a certain relation to historical events and historically important collective actors or movements, a particular concern with both disappearing and newly emerging conditions of existence, a certain way of perceiving reality, a certain vocabulary and language, a particular identity, a certain mode of communication – that are in accordance with and interpreted as meaningful within the public sphere as delimited by a particular discourse. On the other hand, they communicate and present an image to other actors, who in turn respond to such communication as sympathisers, adversaries, or by-standing observers. Through this intricate web of communications, which is given a particular profile in so far as it is orchestrated by the discourse of modernity, sociology is collectively defined and given an existence at the macro-level in the public sphere. In this way it is discursively constructed.

The discourse of modernity obtains its particular character from the fact that it addresses a certain problem. This is the very complex and virtually insurmountable problem of the constitution of society and the mutual com- patibility, reconciliation and consolidation of the different dimensions of society, the discovery of a common principle of social identification, and the most appropriate structuring under given conditions of identities, legitimately defensible interests, and differences. Although the discourse of modernity is a historically specific discourse, it nevertheless represents a master discourse, and although its problem is a particular one, it is nevertheless general enough to retain its relevance over the rather long time-span stretching from the sixteenth century to the present day. This circumstance is underscored by the fact that the discourse of modernity is produced and reproduced by a series of changing, still more historically specific discourses. These discourses are all about the persistent yet changing crisis faced by modern society. They may therefore be referred to as crisis discourses. All of these crisis discourses address the general problem articulated in the discourse of modernity, yet they do so under varying historical conditions where each faces the question of the specific definition of the problem and the corresponding collective political action that is required for its solution. Given the relation of the master discourse of modernity and the plurality of historically articulated crisis discourses, the construction of sociology is best investigated within the context of each of the latter discourses.

Three such historically specific crisis discourses can be distinguished, but in the present study an analysis is carried out in respect of only the first one. This is the early modern rights discourse that raged from the outbreak of the Reformation to the completion of the first phase of the French Revolution and was centred on the widely experienced problem of violence and disorder that was articulated in terms of a socio-politically and culturally significant semantics of rights. The second is the justice discourse that arose in late eighteenth-century England and continued unabated yet in a sublimated form until the second half of the twentieth century, focused on the problem complex of exploitation, pauperisation and loss of identity which followed in the wake of the market-based industrial capitalist economic system. The third and final historically specific crisis discourse that provides a context for the construction of sociology is what I propose to call the responsibility discourse. This title suggests that the theory of justice is today making way for another, still newer semantics in the form of the moral theory of responsibility which is crystallising around a number of intertwined debates about the problem of 'risk' (Beck 1992).

The sense of the proposal – only part of which can be realised in the present context – to analyse the construction of sociology within the context of each of the above-mentioned three crisis discourses should now be obvious. Each of these discourses, centred around a historically specific, collectively recognised problem as they are, unfolds concurrently with a historical attempt to overcome the crisis situation generated by the problem with a view to regaining autonomy and sovereignty. As such, each crisis discourse is closely related to a particular historical form of collective action. Indeed, it plays the role of producing and reproducing the collective political action deemed necessary to re-establish confidence and certainty. By allowing social actors to communicate with one another, to express their identities, to recognise each other, and to assert their interests and differences, the crisis discourses make possible the construction of collective action and collective actors but, by the same token, also the deconstruction of preceding movements (Eder 1993a, 187).[23] Within the context of each of these crisis discourses, then, the construction of sociology can be understood, on the one hand, as referring to the societal problem that becomes collectively defined and, on the other, as being related to the collective solution devised to overcome it. In the latter case, the sociological interest extends beyond the collective actors and the political action they take to resolve the problem to both the cultural and institutional implications of the solution, whether already historically realised or still sought. On the whole, then, sociology as a specific semantic field is suspended, against an increasingly articulable and changeable semantic background, between two major poles: on the one hand, the general socio-political semantics that develops around the principal problem of a given period and, on the other, the more formal and specialised moral-theoretical semantics that crystallises to lend coherence and consistency to and to govern the unfolding of the crisis discourse, thus encapsulating the reference point for identity formation and collective action as well as the institutional solution to the problem.

Constructivist Epistemology

A final observation that needs to be made here concerns some of the deepest assumptions underlying the proposed analysis.[24]

Recent epistemological developments at a general level as well as within sociology itself[25] confront one with a basic option today. If one is to live up to the contemporary state of the art, one either has to adopt a reflexive theory of the social sciences or is compelled to disprove it by introducing a novel perspective. Not having a new departure within my command at present, I propose for the purposes of this book to adopt a reflexive theory in its widely accepted yet by no means uncontroversial contemporary form. This is what has become known as constructivism.

Constructivism has its origin in the modern realisation that reality is the knowledge that we have of it. Whereas this insight previously led epistemologists to formulate an idealistic position that involved the claim that reality is only in the mind, twentieth-century constructivism focuses in the scientific context on our knowledge of knowledge of reality without finding it necessary to deny the existence of the latter. Any events or actions that constitute reality by giving rise to other events or actions and hence to knowledge of reality are empirical by nature. The social scientific endeavour, which is impossible without such events, actions and knowledge, is not to give a purely empirical or ontological realist account of these events and actions as such, which is in principle an unattainable and indeed impossible aim, but rather to construct in its own particular terms knowledge about the knowledge of the reality so constituted. Neither the full description of the events, actions and knowledge constituting reality, nor their full reconstruction, nor their full explanation is possible within the scientific (in this case the social scientific) context. The best that can be achieved is a construct, which is neither a reproduction nor a representation of reality. Being a remove away from reality, the social sciences can achieve access to reality for the purposes of building up a construct only via the knowledge that is attained in the course of the events and actions that constitute reality in the first place.

In this book, we enter this reflexive dimension, this '"hot" self-referential context' of sociology, as Luhmann (1992, 512) calls it. But rather than adopting Luhmann's autopoietic systems theoretical solution by regarding sociology as a closed semantic system, an attempt will be made to control this hothouse by means of the concept and theory of discourse. The aim is to give an account of this intellectual scientific commitment not purely in its own terms, nor in terms of the presumably one and only correct ontological view of it, but rather by reflexively constructing knowledge about the knowledge constructed by a host of authors who in different ways not only participated in the constitution of their own social reality, modern society, but also sought to make sense of it.

The Structure of the Book

In accordance with the outline offered in the present chapter, the book falls into two major parts. Part I is devoted to a statement of the theoretical and methodological approach adopted, and Part II, while also offering a constructivist account of the empirical basis of the making of sociology, consists of an analysis of the construction of sociology as such within the context of the discourse of modernity.

Part I is opened with introductory reflections on contemporary problems in the historiography of sociology. They are designed to lead from the so-called 'problem of presentism' via the historicist solution to a more adequate discourse theoretical approach to the history of sociology. The theoretical and methodological dimensions of this approach are the subject of the four chapters of which this part of the book consists. They range from an elaboration of the theory of discourse to an extrapolation of a corresponding methodology of discourse analysis. Chapter 2, which is devoted to the clarification of general theoretical and meta-theoretical considerations, substantively centres on a synthesis of the complementary contributions of Habermas and Foucault to the theory of discourse. Of overriding concern is Habermas' theory according to which discourse allows the coordination of action through reflexive communicative action. To be able to take into account the operation of power in discourse, however, Foucault's theory, according to which discourse controls feelings, thought, judgement and action, is also introduced. On the basis of the confrontation of Habermas' and Foucault's respective concerns with the logic of symbols and of power, Chapter 3 – the theoretical heart of the book – is taken up by the development of a sociological theory according to which discourse, in the sense of a collective mechanism for the identification of problems, the definition of issues and the coordination of action, is a central element in the dynamic process of the construction of society. In order to clarify the structure that this dynamic process nevertheless possesses, it is also given over to a presentation of a theory of cognitive structures or so-called 'frames'. Central here is the threefold distinction among micro-level frame elements or intellectual, moral and conative framing devices, meso-level identity and ideological frames constructed by each of the discourse partici-pants, and the macro-level master frame that is generated by and emerges from the competition and conflict of the actor frames. This theoretical exposition provides a point of departure for a theory of the discourse of modernity put forward in Chapter 4. It prepares the ground for distinguishing the early modern rights discourse, which is the focus of the analysis in this book, from the later justice discourse and the contemporary responsibility discourse. Chapter 5, finally, is devoted to a presentation of the discourse analytical methodology that makes possible the analysis of the cultural and social con-struction of reality from the micro- to the macro-level. Essentially, it outlines a methodology of frame analysis focusing on framing devices and actor frames that will be brought to bear on the violence communication of the participants in the rights discourse and later on the texts of a selection of early sociologists. This is followed by a projection of the methodology of discourse analysis that will be employed to analyse the emergence of the rights frame and later the construction of Enlightenment sociology.

Drawing on the theoretical and methodological preparation provided in the preceding part, Part II consists of four chapters covering the substantive concern of the book with the history of sociology. It presents a detailed analysis of the construction of sociology within the field of the discourse of modernity, concentrating in particular on the early modern rights discourse and the rise of Enlightenment sociology. Readers who are less inclined to begin with more abstract theoretical and methodological considerations could of course start with the substantive investigation of Part II and return to Part I as a reference guide on theory and methodology whenever the need arises.

In the first two chapters of Part II, an analysis is conducted of the early modern rights discourse. Chapter 6 opens with a brief review of the communi-cation revolution in order to clear the way for an extensive treatment of the characteristic early modern problem of violence and disorder. This problem is considered in the three important contexts of mercantilism, Absolutism and the Reformation. Chapter 7 follows the Europe-wide violence communication and debates, particularly their socio-political semantics, that accompanied the practices of the major actors in these contexts and in the medium of which the problem of violence was transposed into the issue of the survival of society in its political environment. The critical shift that occurred here from monarchical to popular sovereignty, from religion to politics and from hagiography to reason is considered in terms of the efflorescence of rights theories and the establishment of the rights frame. The exposition of the rights frame is of central theoretical significance in this chapter. Its structuring effect accounts for both identity formation and collective mobilisation against the *ancien régime* in Holland, England, the North American Colonies and France. The resultant legal and political achievements finally provide an occasion for considering the sense in which one can speak of the rights discourse as a crisis discourse. Despite the constitutionalisation of the state, problems remain to which certain persistent pathogenic features of modern societies can be led back. It is in the light of these same problems that the critical dimension of Enlightenment sociology will later become intelligible.

Having established the rights discourse as context, Chapters 8 and 9 are devoted to a frame and discourse analysis of the discursive construction of sociology. Chapter 8 takes the form of a finely grained analysis of the micro-level framing devices employed and the meso-level frames constructed at different phases in the rights discourse by such sociologically significant authors as Thomas More, Thomas Hobbes, Giambattista Vico, Montesquieu, Adam Ferguson and John Millar. This is followed in Chapter 9 by a consideration of the public discourse through which the construction of Enlightenment sociology was achieved. Here attention is paid to the incorporation of the discursive contributions of the above-mentioned authors and their elevation to the macro-level.

The thrust of the analysis is a differentiated concept of the Enlightenment that questions various conventional positions in the social sciences. It problematises not only the conventional understanding of the Enlightenment, which has been reinforced by postmodernist criticisms, but also some of the most familiar interpretations of the origin and meaning of the social sciences, sociology in particular. The latter include both liberal and Neo-Marxist interpretations that link sociology to a progressivist position as well as the new critical perspective of Foucault and Bauman according to which sociology from the start formed part of a new conceptual-theoretical system oriented towards social control. Given the relation of the present author to critical theory, however, a central place is given to Habermas' position, which is nevertheless subjected to a critical treatment. It is argued that whereas Habermas' understanding of sociology is predicated on a combination of the etatist rationalistic frame and the popular republican frame of the social, his recent concern with deliberative democracy harks back to the pluralist contestatory frame of the social that informed a central strand of Enlightenment sociology.

The loose ends of the analysis are finally tied together in Chapter 10 by a confrontation of Reinhart Koselleck's famous interpretation of the relation between critique and crisis with those of Habermas and Eder. The alternative interpretation offered of the crisis of early modern society and the critical function of Enlightenment sociology serves as a conclusion in that it completes the circle by relating Enlightenment sociology to the search for a solution to the contemporary problem of the authority, legitimacy or collective validity of sociology. This takes the form of linking sociology not to the philosophy of history and the theory of progress but rather to political theory – the aim being to make the generative principles of society central to sociology. The sense of this result of the analysis of the discursive construction of sociology is of the utmost importance. It underlines the relation between sociology and public debate or practical discourse, and exhorts us not only to incorporate an awareness of this relation into sociology itself, but to proceed in the practice of sociology in such a manner that its public role is retrieved, revitalised and kept alive.

PART I

Theory of Discourse and Discourse Analysis

Introduction: From Presentism and Historicism to Discourse

This part is devoted to a theoretical and methodological preparation for the discourse analysis of the construction of sociology carried out in the second part of this study. After introductory remarks aimed at clarifying the rationale for this approach by reference to the contemporary debate about the history of sociology, some of the most central theoretical and methodological considerations of the proposed discourse approach are presented.

The basic assumption here is that the construction of sociology takes place within the context of the discourse of modernity. It is thus a matter of discursive construction. The discourse of modernity opened up the space or field and thus made and, indeed, still makes possible the construction of sociology. It provides the framework within which societal problems are first collectively identified and defined, and then addressed from the point of view of finding a collectively acceptable solution. The identification, definition and solving of societal problems involve the production of knowledge of various kinds. The participants – social actors, collective agents and social movements, but also social scientists, particularly sociologists – take part in the production of collective interpretations and definitions, explanations and theories, and orienting knowledge, thus carrying the process of the self-interpretation and self-diagnosis of society. The societal discourse produces general, collectively shared social knowledge as well as more systematic and specialised moral philosophical and social scientific or sociological knowledge. These different types of knowledge all play a part in structuring and organising the experience of the participants and providing cultural resources, such as a horizon of expectations, orientations and goals.

The rationale for considering the construction of sociology as being related to the production of social knowledge within the framework of the discourse of modernity can be highlighted by reference to the lively debate of the last twenty years about the history of sociology and our sense of its past. This is what has been called the 'presentist-historicist' controversy (Baehr and O'Brien 1994, 67).[1] Presentism refers to the traditional approach to the history of sociology (or more generally science) and the classics, while historicism represents a family of 'new perspectives in the historiography of sociology' (Lepenies 1981, iii). The latter emerged in the 1970s against the background of the turn in philosophy from mentalistic to linguistic categories (e.g. Apel 1963; 1980; Rorty 1967; Derrida 1972) and the work of such people as Thomas Kuhn (1970) and Stephen Toulmin (1972) in the history and philosophy of science. Presentists take an internal point of view and thus focus on the inner form of sociological knowledge which they see as having been created and carried forward by past sociologists and as representing a continuous development linking up with contemporary sociologists. They assume not only that there is some set or another of categories, problems, concerns or dilemmas that is definitive of sociology and gives the discipline its coherence, but also that the great sociologists of the past recognised them as such and dealt with them in enduringly significant and authoritative ways. Historicists, by contrast, take an external or contextual view of sociological knowledge. Accordingly, they insist on the application of historical methods to sociology's past, are critical of a cumulationist or progressivist interpretation of its development, exhibit a sensitivity for culturally excluded or eclipsed and, hence, unrealised alternative concepts, theories and arguments, and finally emphasise the importance of taking into account pervasive background ideas not necessarily consciously entertained, in addition to explicitly held ideas, concepts and themes. The discourse approach is of course more closely related to the historicist than to the presentist position, yet as it is conceived here it goes beyond both.[2]

Although presentists and historicists have entered into a productive dialogue promising to relativise their respective viewpoints and moving them to a more adequate position, limitations and unclarities are still in evidence. For instance, although Peter Baehr and Mike O'Brien (1994, 3–32) introduce the concept of discourse, they continue to understand it in the sense of what one may call the discourse of sociology rather than seeing that there are different levels of discourse which may be related to one another. What they variously refer to as 'the structure of intentions' (22), 'presuppositional frameworks' (23), 'the extant universe of problems and assumptions' (70), 'ramifying ideas in the background' (72), and so forth, cannot be confined to the sociological discourse alone but requires to be clarified in relation to the collective identification, definition, discussion and solution of pressing societal problems or issues through practical discourse. All of these expressions contain a significant reference to the more encompassing culturally shaped, practical or socio-political discourse of modernity that provides the context within which the cultural and social scientific discourse of sociology unfolds. It would be better, therefore, to understand discourse as a dynamic mediation between a more general societally relevant socio-political semantics, on the one hand, and the more specialised, internally more or less coherent and consistent sociological semantics, on the other. Stephen Turner (1983, 276–77),[3] in turn, does not overlook the macro-level of discourse, as is shown by his concern with the tradition of Western philosophy as the framework of sociological argumentation. But by fixing on philosophy, he renders himself incapable of identifying a high-level yet historically specific macro-discourse such as the discourse of modernity. Tending to reduce discourse to all too specific common conventions or common substantive policy concerns, he consequently finds instead of a discourse only an agglomeration of mutually regarding viewpoints put forward by people who hold contrary positions and talk past one another. What should be appreciated, however, is that discourse mediates a framework, or more specifically a cognitive macro- or master frame, within which a variety of more specific, competing and even conflicting viewpoints or, rather, cognitive structures or frames, including socio-political and sociological frames, take on shape and interrelate. Missing not only in Baehr and O'Brien but also in Turner, and this is by no means untypical, is the concept of public societal discourse.

It should be clear from these examples that the present proposal to regard the discourse of modernity as the field within which the construction of sociology takes place is aimed at bridging the gap between the internal presentist and the external historicist perspectives and, thus, at providing a coherent theoretical and methodological position beyond them. The constructivist-structuralist approach of which it forms a part allows not only the elimination of certain general problems sometimes shared by presentism and historicism, but also the elaboration of a theoretical and methodological model that avoids the specific pitfalls of these alternatives deriving from their internal and external perspectives respectively.

A set of related problems present in the way sociologists generally deal with the history of the discipline includes the myth of the creation or founding of sociology, often regarded in a serial fashion, and the myth of a lineage. A product of this kind of thinking, for instance, is the notion of the 'father of sociology', whether Auguste Comte, as is widely maintained, or more esoterically Ibn Khaldun (Conyers 1972; Restivo 1991, 25; Ritzer 1992, 8), or the baseless debate about 'the first real sociologist': Montesquieu (Gay 1969, 323), Ferguson (MacRae 1969, 27), Millar (Habermas 1969b, 216), Comte (e.g. Therborn 1977, 115–16; Seidman 1994, 330), or Durkheim and Weber

(Parsons 1968, iii)? Recent analyses of the rhetoric of sociology have shown that these conceptions possess not only religious, political and masculine connotations, but still more revealingly that they rest on the assumptions of an unscientific monogenetic theory of procreation (Delaney 1986; Pateman 1988, 77–115; Baehr and O'Brien 1994, 46–51). The significance of this latter point is that this kind of thinking is incapable of recognising the competitive, collaborative and conflictual nature of the process of intellectual innovation. This is typically the case with presentism, while the opposing historicist approach has made great strides towards grasping this process. What the latter tends to lose sight of, however, is the relation of such intellectual innovation to a comparable but much more pervasive discursive process. Or at least, it remains uncertain as to the level at which this process is to be located: for instance, the Western intellectual tradition, or historical events such as the Franco-Prussian War? The discourse theory proposed here takes both these dimensions into account and locates the discursive process at the level of the public societal or practical discourse of modernity.

The Discourse Theoretical Approach

Rather than being based on monogenetic assumptions, the constructivist-structuralist approach to which the concept of discourse belongs is what may be called a polygenetic approach. It regards its object of investigation, the process by means of which both modernity and sociology are produced and reproduced, as a pluralistic (Heller 1982; Arnason 1988) or polyphonic (Höffe 1995) one. According to this view, both modernity and sociology have a number of different sources or origins and, hence, also beginnings. Modernity can be traced to diverse developments in the economic, the political and the cultural domains, and far from having one single founder, sociology was promoted by a number of people who came from different cultural back-grounds and had different economic and political interests. Norman Birnbaum's (1953) suggestion that Marx and Weber's respective interpretations of the genesis of modernity are not contradictory but rather complementary is a well-known example that bears out both of these points.

The interesting thing is now that, while the proposed constructivist-structuralist approach is polygenetic, this does not lead it to deny that the variety of sources and representatives at some stage or another somehow became related to one another. On the contrary, as an approach based on communication theory, it assumes that all these elements are related to one another through communication, more precisely communication in the form of a historically specific practical discourse of a collective or societal nature. Lack of recognition or denial of mutual relations is the problem of for instance Turner (1983, 276–77) who, when considering 'mid-nineteenth century social thought', sees only people with 'different exclusively valid philosophical and theological frameworks' who 'talk past one another'.[4] If this were the case, then how could Saint-Simon, Comte, Marx, and others ever have been taken to have made a contribution not only to the understanding of their time but also to sociology? This is Giddens' (1987b, 182)[5] puzzle of how two men so different as Weber and Durkheim could have come to be regarded as the principal founders of sociology. However, neither his (Giddens 1987b, 188) solution of 'contextual association through disassociation', nor Baehr and O'Brien's (1994, 19) appeal to 'later generations' comes to terms with the problem. In the former case, the reference to the Franco-Prussian War and the First World War as providing the context for Weber and Durkheim is too specific and confining; in the latter, although this is closer to the truth, too much is surrendered to the later history of the reception of the work of these two classical sociologists. What both Giddens and Baehr and O'Brien fail to appreciate is the discursive construction of sociology[6] and, hence, the overarching framework provided by the discourse of modernity which allows both for a structure or commonality of intentions and divergent approaches to their realisation. The question, however, is how discourse, more specifically the discourse of modernity, and the framework provided by it should be conceived.

CHAPTER 2

Theory of Discourse

Introduction of the Concept

The theory of discourse became a possibility as a result of the so-called 'linguistic' (Rorty 1967) or 'pragmatic turn' (Apel 1963, 10; Böhler et al. 1986) in twentieth-century philosophy and the philosophy of the sciences which also affected the human and social sciences.[1] This change took hold of the major French, German and Anglo-American traditions on the basis of the contributions of Saussure, of Hamann, Von Humboldt and Dilthey, and of Peirce respectively. In its initial phase, it was most decisively carried out by Claude Lévi-Strauss in France, Martin Heidegger and Hans-Georg Gadamer in Germany, Bertrand Russell and Ludwig Wittgenstein in England, and by Charles Morris in the United States.[2] These developments made available two major points of departure for the elaboration of the theory of discourse, one French and the other German.[3]

It was the anthropologist Lévi-Strauss who first introduced the relatively widely used French substantive *discours* into the social scientific context and thus provided the starting point for the development of the structuralist and post-structuralist theory of discourse. In his book *Structural Anthropology* (1977, 209–10, 229),[4] he made a case for the use of the concept for the purposes of the structural analysis of myths. Myth he conceived of as a second-level linguistic order or an order of the second degree occupying a third or inter-mediate position between what his predecessor Saussure called the language system (*langue*) and speech (*parole*). Rather than being made up of timeless structures or particular events, therefore, this second-level order consisted of complex linguistic units which are accessible as discourse. It came to form the basis of the structuralist programme to which Roland Barthes (1967; Frank 1990a, 413–14) gave the name *linguistique du discours*. But it was Michel

Foucault whose name became internationally famous as a result of the transposition of the French word *discours* into the central concept of an ambitious theoretical programme.[5]

The second major starting point for the development of the theory of discourse was provided by the German tradition of transcendental hermeneutics, particularly as represented by Karl-Otto Apel (1950; 1973) against the background of Heidegger compared and contrasted with Wittgenstein. Already in his work from the 1950s and early 1960s, Apel exhibited a fascination with language in that it not only unlocks and opens up particular worlds in which human beings live and maintain corresponding dogmatic or orthodox views, but at the same time also allows transcendence of such specific concrete world views. Language is the unique and irreducible medium in and through which it is possible for human beings to constantly integrate a universalistic and hence eccentric viewpoint with their bodily-bound, perspectival world views (Apel 1973, I, 132, 196). From a hermeneutic point of view, language as medium in this sense is captured by the humanist notion of the conversation of history, what the poet Hölderlin called 'the dialogue which we human beings are' (Apel 1963, 166; 1973, I, 183; 1967, 57),[6] in the course of which the different worlds and world views are related to one another. From a more critical point of view, however, language can be regarded as 'meta-institution' or the 'institution of institutions' (Apel 1973, I, 197–221, here 217) in the sense of the 'last institution of reflexion' (Apel 1973, I, 218) by means of which human beings can critically distance themselves from existing institutions. While it takes the form of what Apel (1973, I, 217, 218, 219, 221) variously refers to as 'rational discourse' (*vernünftige Gespräch*), 'dialectical discussion' (*dialektische Diskussion*), or the 'rational conversation of all people' (*vernünftige Gespräch aller Menschen*), concrete examples would be democratic discussions, the provision of justifications for the concrete obligations of religious belief or political action, and clarification and justification in the scientific context (Apel 1973, I, 217, 219). Apel (1976; 1998) later systematised this position under the title of 'transcendental pragmatics of language'. Although not actually using the term 'discourse', it was on this basis that Apel was able through his critique of Habermas' notion of critical theory in 1969 to impress on the latter the importance of the concept (Apel 1973, II, 128–54).[7] Subsequently, Habermas' name became synonymous with the theory of *Diskurs*.

Michel Foucault

Foucault's employment of the concept of discourse dates from the first of the three phases of his intellectual development, his quasi-structuralist 'archaeological' phase. During this phase, based on a critique of the subject-centred human sciences, he investigated social forms of knowledge as autonomous cultural textual structures. His central idea was the linguistic nominalist one according to which 'things attain to existence only in so far as they are able to form the elements of a signifying system' (Foucault 1970, 328). The substantive correlate of his archaeological method was represented by what he significantly called 'discourse' in the sense of an autonomous, rule-governed, signifying system which organises social practices and historical epochs (Dreyfus and Rabinow 1982, xx; Honneth 1991, 136–37; Rabinow 1987, 9–10; Hoy 1987, 4–5), for instance, the discourse of the modern period in his sense of 'the Age of Man' beginning with Kant (Foucault 1970), or the discourse of the human sciences (Foucault 1972). By contrast with the nominalistic and idealistic tendencies of his first phase, however, Foucault's 'genealogical' phase is characterised by a certain distancing from structuralism under the influence of the late nineteenth-century German philosopher Friedrich Nietzsche and the development instead of what some commentators call a 'post-structuralist' position (Hoy 1987, 4; Dreyfus and Rabinow 1982, xxi). Rejecting the idealistic structuralist idea that the purely linguistic phenomenon of discourse is autonomous and constitutive of reality, he shifted in the direction of social analysis and linked discourse to social practices (Foucault 1971)[8] in the sense of placing it in the context of concrete economic, technological, political or administrative activities. By means of a number of further modifications which gave centrality to a monistic concept of power (Honneth 1991, 151–75), he sought to show that discourse does not constitute reality but rather that discursive knowledge is actually produced in the service of an expanding social power which increasingly penetrates modern institutions like prisons, armies, schools, factories and so forth. This is the period during which he is regarded as having been concerned with the analysis of power and with the elaboration of the foundations of such an analysis. Foucault's third so-called 'ethical' phase is a continuation of his post-structural stance adopted at the outset of the second phase, but it entails a shift from a direct concern with power to the question of sexuality and the implied historically changing relation to self. Although it appears as though Foucault's development follows a linear path in which the initial concern with discourse progressively weakens, it is actually retained, albeit in modified form, together with power and ethics as an essential level of social reality in his later works (Foucault 1981; Hoy 1987, 3).

Discourse for the first time played a crucially central role in *The Order of Things* (1970), originally published in 1966, but Foucault systematically theorised his historical discourse analysis later in *The Archaeology of Knowledge* (1972). In these early works, he applies the concept to what he refers to as the *episteme* in the sense of the characteristic system of thought or classification scheme of particular historical epochs, such as the Renaissance, the Classical Age, and the modern Age of Man. What he intends by 'discourse', however, is something still more specific. 'Discourse' refers not so much to schemes and systems of thought themselves as to the context of an order of symbols within which the thought of a particular epoch moves. It is the space or symbolic order by virtue of which the world of the participants in a particular community is unlocked and opened up in a linguistically and culturally specific way. Like Lévi-Strauss, Foucault here regards discourse as a second-order symbolic order which occupies an intermediate position (Dreyfus and Rabinow 1982, 58; Frank 1990a, 415) between what Lévi-Strauss' predecessor Saussure called *langue*, the static language system, and *parole* or speech. By means of his archaeological method, Foucault analyses discourse in this sense as a framework-like complex made up of elements which are individual and unique rather than typical. These elements are called *énoncés* (Foucault 1972, 50–55, 107), enunciative statements or serious speech acts (Dreyfus and Rabinow 1982, 48) that distinguish themselves from merely conventional linguistic units such as propositions, statements, phrases or ordinary speech acts in that they have been transformed into knowledge by institutional rules or argumentation. Enunciative statements are ordered into an autonomous network of discursive practices or a 'discursive formation' (Foucault 1972, 31–41) by discourse as a rule-governed system. There are different, vertically organised discursive formations, each of which is ordered according to institutional domain and field of use or application. The order of the elements points towards the fact that discourse has a constraining character. Foucault speaks of a 'dispositive of torture' (cited in Frank 1990a, 423) which does not tolerate subjects, intentions and meanings.

Foucault initially developed his concept of discourse along these quasi-structuralist lines for an entirely plausible critical purpose. His aim was to counter intellectual tendencies, particularly humanistic hermeneutics, that not only level the richness and variety of history by making it uniform by means of such notions as universal history or a homogeneous spirit of the time, but also find subjects, intentions and meanings everywhere, without appreciating the discontinuous unities giving structure to history (Dreyfus and Rabinow 1982; Frank 1990a, 418, 424). This led him to take the position that, while there is always a symbolic order of discourse, there is never just one or even an over-arching discourse connecting the others in some way or another. Rather there is a plurality of historically relative discourses, each with its own particular institutional reference and field of application. Although the attention is thus directed towards a variety of more or less circumscribed cultural symbolic orders such as, for instance, scientific discourse, clinical discourse, economic discourse or psychiatric discourse, it should be emphasised that Foucault was here less interested in specific bodies of knowledge than in the boundary conditions of discourse.

Foucault's early theory of discourse and the archaeological method based on it, as the critics virtually unanimously hold,[9] proved to be a failure, compelling him to change tack and thus to inaugurate the second phase in his intellectual development. In the course of time, therefore, many of the characteristic features of his position have attracted criticism. Among those worth mentioning are the following four. First, various critics (Dreyfus and Rabinow 1982, 79; Hoy 1987, 4; Fink-Eitel 1989, 57) pointed out that the concept of discourse as an autonomous rule-governed system that is not merely immanently intelligible but actually unifies the whole system of practices amounts to an idealistic illusion. Second, some critics (Frank 1990a, 424) have shown that Foucault's definition of discourse as a singular, systematically uncontrollable and multiple element complex, if not contradicts, then at least stands in a relation of extreme tension to his method of structuralist, i.e. non-hermeneutical, discourse analysis. In a related vein, others (Dreyfus and Rabinow 1982, 12) have argued that he overreacted to hermeneutics or that he pushed his ethnology of European society too far when he denied the estranged social world all intentionality and meaning whatsoever (Honneth 1991, 147–48). Third, many critics have attacked Foucault's historically relativist conception of discourse, to which is tied a critique of his consequent inability to deal with the problem of truth or, more broadly, validity (Habermas 1987b, 238–65; 1987c, 108; Taylor 1986).[10] Habermas' strong disagreement with Foucault on this point, as will become clear later, corresponds to his important contribution to the theory of discourse. In the fourth place, various critics have demonstrated that, although Foucault's discourse analysis appears to be pervaded by a critical animus, he is actually not able to develop any critique at all, not only because his relativism prevents him from establishing normative criteria making critique possible (Habermas 1987b, 266–93), but also because he regards discourse ultimately as in principle impenetrable (Frank 1990a, 425). People are and remain unaware of discourse operating behind their backs or over and above their heads in so far as Foucault portrays them as lacking reflexivity.

The transition that difficulties such as these compelled Foucault to make from a semiological analysis of cultural knowledge systems to a power-oriented social analysis involved not merely a radical reversal of position, as many critics hold (Dreyfus and Rabinow 1982, 102–03; Rabinow 1987, 9–10; Hoy 1987, 4–5), but also a profusion of concepts of discourse (Honneth 1991, 141–42,

144–45, 151, 152, 169–70). The reversal of the relation between discourse and social practices, or between theory and practice, is undoubtedly of the utmost importance, yet for a proper assessment of Foucault's contribution to the theory of discourse it is essential to consider the theoretical models on which he based his changing concept of discourse.

In their influential interpretation, Dreyfus and Rabinow (1982, 102–03)[11] have shown that in all his later works Foucault conceives of social practice on all levels as preceding or being more fundamental than cultural systems of knowledge. Instead of discourse organising itself and unifying social practices and historical epochs, it is seen as part of a larger set of organised and organising practices. Social practices both give rise to and condition cognitive discourse. Although this reversal rested on a shift from historical discourse analysis to the social analysis of power and involved a change in the concept of discourse, it did not entail a reduction in the importance of discourse. On the contrary, Foucault emphasises that discourse is one of the essential components through which organising practices operate (Dreyfus and Rabinow 1982, 103). His general aim remained to pinpoint exactly when a particular discourse emerged from social practices and techniques and came to be seen as true (Foucault cited in Rabinow 1987, 7).

After tentative suggestions in *The Archaeology of Knowledge* (1972, e.g. 41–42, 45, 67–68),[12] Foucault started to make this drastic move in his inaugural lecture of 1970 entitled 'Orders of Discourse' (1971)[13] which, not surprisingly, remained ambivalently suspended between archaeology and genealogy. Being interested, under the influence of Nietzsche, in the social effects of societal processes, he pushed the institutional conditions of knowledge production and more generally the societal context to the foreground. All discourse, particularly the rules of formation of discourse, was now seen as linked to the operation of social power. Discourses indeed have immanent principles of intelligibility, but they are more importantly bound by regulations enforced through social practices of appropriation, control and policing. Through institutional strategies, such as the cultural control of topics, the scientific study of discourse contents and the social regulation of participation in discourse, a social system controls, selects, organises and channels the production of discourses. It is only in later works such as *Discipline and Punish* (1979) and the first volume of *The History of Sexuality* (1981), however, that Foucault's new position was worked out in detail. From now on, power would be his major theme until his last investigations into sexuality. And within this context, discourse was recognised as being a social practice itself (Foucault 1979, 26–28; Hoy 1987, 5) or, at least, an essential component through which organising practices operate (Dreyfus and Rabinow 1982, 103).

Insisting on the indissoluble relation between discourse and power, Foucault (1979, 27–28; 1981, 92–98) now regarded knowledge of all sorts that get articulated in discourses as being thoroughly caught up and enmeshed in the everyday conflicts, the larger struggles and the institutional strategies constituting the social world. Initially, he regarded the articulation between discourse and the social practices of power as being negative, but typical of the later phases of his development is an appreciation of the fact that power is not just a matter of repression, exclusion, limitation and prohibition since it also makes things possible and is productive (Foucault 1979, 23–24; 1980, 118–19; 1981, 15–49; 1987b, 60–62).[14] In Western society of the past three centuries, accordingly, he discovers various discourses that construct programmes for the constitution or construction of social reality – discourses about science, medicine, the prison, sexuality, and so forth, all of which help to shape and form modern society. Although modern society does not follow any programme, we nevertheless live in a society of programmes, a world shot through with the effects of discourses of various kinds, all of which have the aim of making reality transparent, programmable and rationalisable.

At a certain point in *The Archaeology of Knowledge*, Foucault (1972, 107)[15] admitted that instead of making the concept of discourse clear, he had actually multiplied its meaning many times. As Honneth (1991, 105–202)[16] has appreciated, unlike many of Foucault's interpreters, this remained the rule in a serious theoretical sense throughout Foucault's career. At the outset, he conceived of discourse in terms of structuralist semiology as a purely linguistic phenomenon, a special case of a system of statements forming an objective cultural framework. By means of the concepts of discursive practice and discursive formation, however, this stable cognitive order was soon after transformed into a dynamic system of statements. As regards the latter, in turn, Foucault could not make up his mind but operated with two distinct models. The first consisted of the idea of a regulated combination, achieved by some anonymous synthesis, of institutional techniques and cognitive processes (e.g. Foucault 1981, 134–43). The second was an economic model according to which discourse is a scarce resource whose possession social actors compete for (e.g. Foucault 1979, 26–27; 1980, 90–91; 1981, 92). The latter model provided Foucault with a vehicle to make the transition to the second of the phases in his intellectual development. Initially, it became infused with the spirit of late nineteenth-century vitalism which reached Foucault through Nietzsche,[17] with the result that he conceived of discourse as a continuous and omnipresent stream of unstable, contingent and unmediated linguistic events. As such, it represented a social medium in which both power and desire could express themselves and which thus becomes an object of strategic competition. Due to the difficulties implied by this dualistic conception based on an unclear synthesis of theoretical components deriving from vitalism and the theory of power, however, Foucault (e.g. 1981, 139–43) felt himself compelled to adopt a monistic concept of power. The resulting notion of society as a social complex of power in which cognitive constructions assume the function of increasing power proved decisive for the concept of discourse. Once more it underwent a transformation, now referring to socio-cultural systems of knowledge that, on the one hand, owe their existence to the strategic requirements of an established power complex and, on the other, again work in upon that complex. The precise content given to the concept of discourse, however, in turn depended on the way in which the concept of society as a power complex was conceived. Although often unappreciated by his interpreters (e.g. Gordon 1980, 237, 243; Hoy 1987, 6–7; Poster 1991, 127, 129), there are two models for doing so available in Foucault's later works, with the latter of the two strongly tending to predominate. They are an action theoretical and a systems theoretical model (Honneth 1991, 151, 175). According to the former (e.g. Foucault 1979, 26–27; 1980, 90–91; 1981, 94), power is generated by and emerges from a continuous process of strategic action between social actors who entertain opposing goals and conflict with each other about their implementation. The predominance of the systems theoretical model derives from Foucault's (1979, 28; 1981, 139–43) real interest that lies in the complex of strategic power relations emerging from conflictual action situations. Through the historically new productive character of power in modern society, a subjectless, intentionless and centreless system of societal power relations emerges which becomes increasingly more effective and efficient in discursively overpowering reality, disciplining the body or normalising behaviour and administratively controlling the population. The crucial sociological question here is, of course, how such a system emerges. Despite the fact that he himself speaks of 'the theoretical and practical search' (Foucault cited in Dreyfus and Rabinow 1982, 193) for mechanisms of organisation of society, despite the fact that normalising technologies pre-suppose the collective identification of a problem and collective agreement on a corresponding solution (Dreyfus and Rabinow 1982, 198), Foucault (1979, 23; 1981, 140–41) is adamant that society is a permanently unstable complex of power relations which is given a direction only by the modern technologies of power. Moral orientations, legal norms, the practical dimension of norm-ative agreement, all of these are so many illusions and cultural delusions that only serve to cover over the systemic process of the increase and totalisation of power. What precisely discourse amounts to in Foucault's later work becomes clear in these two theoretical contexts. In terms of the action theoretical model, according to which power is the outcome of social conflicts, discourse relates to the competition and conflict of social actors who engage in strategic action; in terms of the systems theoretical model, according to which power is the product of a systemic process of adaptation, it is a purely systemic instrument by means of which reality is cognitively overpowered.

At this stage, it is abundantly clear that, were one to render Foucault's contribution useful for the development of a theory of discourse, he or she would be required to make an informed theoretical selection from the variety of concepts of discourse he elaborated throughout his career and to assign it its proper place within a larger theoretical framework. A consideration of Habermas' contribution would be helpful in achieving this.

Jürgen Habermas

In 1971, at the outset of the second phase in his intellectual development, Habermas introduced the concept of discourse on the basis of the linguistically or communicatively transformed transcendental hermeneutic tradition. This language-pragmatic or communicative starting point explains why he conceives of it in terms of the conceptual pair 'communicative action/discourse' (Habermas and Luhmann 1971, 114–22; Habermas 1974a, 16–19). He draws a sharp distinction between action and discourse or, differently, between communication which remains embedded in a context of action and communication which is uncoupled from and thus transcends the compulsions of action, yet the two terms of the distinction remain related to one another.

Habermas' employment of the concept of discourse and, more broadly, of communication should first of all be seen in the light of his concern with the revitalisation of the moral-practical or political dimension within the framework of critical sociology. In his early work (Habermas 1969a; 1989a), he introduced this dimension under the title of the 'public sphere', but since the late 1980s he has recast it in the form of radical pluralist democracy (e.g. Habermas 1989b). In the latter case, the emphasis is on active citizens who are engaged in a plurality of public spheres forming a whole network that carries the collective identity of society.[18] In this context, discourse is of the utmost importance. Habermas envisages that, were adequate institutional underpinnings for discourse to be developed, democracy would be deepened and broadened, and autonomy, freedom, equality and justice would be advanced. This potential of discourse has its basis in the nature of culture and its role in society.

Generally speaking, culture has to do with the universalisation of the framework of social action through the construction of symbols shared by the members of society (e.g. Habermas 1976, 108–17). The construction of common symbols is achieved through symbolic understanding and agreement in the medium of social interaction. Habermas, like his friend, colleague and collaborator Apel, regards discourse in terms of such symbolic understanding. It is the special institutionally secured yet meta-institutional form of symbolic understanding through the medium of communication by means of which human beings construct common cultural systems. As a meta-institution, discourse allows the introduction of radical rationality into existing institutions, and thus the breaking up of their particularism and closure in favour of opening them up and making them more universalistic or communicatively shared. It is possible to accomplish this through discourse in so far as it entails the search for and creation of new ideas, meanings and symbols that are compelling, convincing and acceptable to a significant number and then played out against the status quo. Discourse places the existing institutions under pressure to change and open up in a more universalistic direction. This pressure, however, is of a particular nature. Discourse is a form of communication that allows strictly only one single means through which the participants may influence and convince one another to the exclusion of bribery, psychological pressure, violence and so forth, namely arguments. An argument consists of a conclusion drawn from premises and a given set of initial conditions and it is oriented towards the preservation of the integrity of symbols, the criterion or standard applying being the consistency of symbolic systems.

Basic to Habermas' critical evaluation of modern Western society is the conviction that discourse has not been provided with the necessary, let alone adequate, institutional underpinnings to become fully operative. Historically, science, which serves as the institutional vehicle for theoretical discourse, has indeed been well institutionalised. Admittedly, legal and political institutions such as parliamentary democracy, important carriers of practical discourse, are also in existence, but there is a crucial sense in which Habermas holds that this institutionalisation, particularly in the political domain, has proved deficient. The reason for this he discovers in the pronounced tendency in modern society to narrow down symbolism or, more generally, rationality to a single level – what he refers to as purposive and by extension functionalist rationality (Habermas 1984; 1987a). In opposition to this tendency, he insists that human action and interaction, far from being just a matter of the choosing of means for the attainment of goals, involve a comprehensive concept of communicative rationality. This means that, depending on context, action displays both moral-practical or normative rationality and aesthetic-expressive rationality over and above purposive or cognitive-instrumental rationality. Each of these three dimensions of action relates to a different world and involves a different value standard or validity claim. Habermas' (1984, 8–43, 75–102) position on this is clearly worked out. Goal-oriented actions and constative speech acts, first, incorporate technical or empirical-theoretical knowledge that relates to the objective world and implies a truth claim. Normatively regulated action, secondly, embodies moral-practical knowledge that pertains to the social world and implicitly makes a claim to correctness in the sense of being in accordance with the rules. Thirdly, dramaturgical actions contain self-representations that apply to the subjective world and advance a claim to truthfulness, veracity or authenticity. On a larger scale, but parallel to this personal level, there are cultural products such as works of art that invoke the subjective world and are evaluated according to the collective, cultural standard of appropriateness or propriety. To this must be added, finally, that communicative utterances such as speech and written language implicitly contain the meta-validity claim of comprehensibility.

Although these different types of action are comparable in so far as each at least implicitly raises a validity claim which can be argued about, they differ in that the argumentative justification by the provision of good grounds or reasons is more stringent in the case of the redemption of truth claims in theoretical discourse and of correctness claims in practical discourse than in explicative discourse and therapeutic and aesthetic criticism. Ordinary everyday communicative actions rest on implicit validity claims which for the most part remain unproblematic in the action situation and are thus not argued about. But when problems of understanding arise as a result of the breakdown of meaning contexts of action, the validity claims contained in action are problematised and consequently become the object of discourse in which the rules of argumentation alone apply. When mutual understanding or consensus is shaken, the presupposition that validity claims are for all practical purposes satisfied is suspended, and through discourse the participants embark on the task of seeking a mutual interpretation, bringing about mutual understanding or agreement and thus achieving a new definition of the situation which can be shared by them. If this is not achieved, communicative action cannot be continued. In Habermas' (Habermas and Luhmann 1971, 115; Habermas 1979, 3) view, then, discourse refers to the dynamic process of bringing about or re-establishing a broken-down mutual understanding or agreement.

Habermas' unique contribution to the theory of discourse resides in linking discourse to universalisation and in bringing this nexus in a critical manner to bear on modern society. Discourse concerns the universalisation of symbols in such a way that the existing institutions are opened up, changed and improved in line with the rationalisation of communicative action. Communicative action is rationalised through the problematisation and explanation of its implicit validity claims, the re-establishment of a consensus about them by means of discourse and finally the drawing of conclusions from that for the organisation of social relations and society. Discourse is the special form of communication that is carried out through yet in opposition to communication so as to make explicit its implicit assumptions and thus to bring about or re-establish a shaken mutual understanding and agreement. Here lies the strength of Habermas' position, but also its weakness. His contribution to the theory of discourse has therefore attracted its share of criticisms – the most systematic from Herbert Schnädelbach (1977),[19] a representative of the Frankfurt tradition and thus sympathetic to Habermas.

Schnädelbach identifies a number of ambiguities and difficulties in Habermas' position that could be interpreted as pointing in the direction of a more adequate sociological theory of discourse. To begin with, Habermas is ambivalent about the relation between communicative action and discourse in that he conceives of it according to two quite different models (Schnädelbach 1977, 144–45), the latter of which is preferable to the former misleading one. In terms of a model of different levels, on the one hand, discourse is presented as distinct from communicative action. It is a type of communication in which everything that is characteristic of primary communication, such as pressures emanating from the situation, the exchange of information or experience and the call upon motivation, is excluded and virtualised. Discourse is distinguished from communication in that it occupies the level of meta-communication. According to a competing model of different domains rather than levels, on the other hand, discourse and communicative action are depicted as intrinsically connected to each other. Discourse is a special case of communicative action that is distinguished from naive language games only by certain pragmatic features, such as theme and boundary conditions. It is a form of communication that embraces both communication and meta-communication, and hence it remains subject to certain pressures and constraints, as for instance in the case of argumentation. It is in this dual form alone that discourse is at all able to thematise the meta-communicative elements of primary communicative action.

Habermas' tendency to emphasise the former model is related to his pre-dilection for questions of grounding or validity and his consequent confinement of discourse to consensus problems concerning the validity of the assumptions of communicative action (Schnädelbach 1977, 163–64). Although he himself regards the general goal of discursive communicative action as being mutual understanding and agreement, whether bringing about a new consensus or re-establishing an existing one, he subsumes all consensus problems under questions of validity. Yet problems of mutual understanding and agreement given rise to by the breakdown of the meaning contexts of action extend further than this and therefore do not admit of being circumscribed in this way. For this reason, McCarthy (1992, 68) regards Habermas' concept of practical discourse as too restrictive to serve as a model of will-formation and decision making in a democratic public sphere. As against Habermas' obliteration of the difference between these two cases, Münch (1984, 110–13) proposes a distinction between rational discourse and consensus-building discourse. A number of errors seem to be responsible for Habermas' reductive approach. On the one hand, he too closely identifies discursive understanding and anticipated freedom from domination, and thus not only utopianises reflexive communication, but also moralises empirically possible discourse situations (Schnädelbach 1977, 156–58, 161–62). On the other hand, by restricting discourse to a special range of problems, he simply assumes that it is already intersubjectively clear in what the disagreement about validity consists, and thus brushes aside the primary problem of arriving at an intersubjectively shared identification of the common problem (Schnädelbach 1977, 167). If one eliminates these tendential difficulties exhibited by Habermas, then discourse theory acquires a much greater attraction for the social scientist. Discourse not only confronts the existing institutions with a meta-institutional, universalistic perspective, as Habermas argues, but conversely the unconditional questioning also has to find its place within the concrete limits of a real meaning context.[20] The discursively developed cultural knowledge or symbolic material is in and through discourse also integrated with the assumptions or the unquestionable consensus of the participants. It is noteworthy that, in his theory of the lifeworld, Habermas (1987a, 124) himself argues that only a limited segment of the background assumptions provided by the lifeworld can be questioned at any one time, but never the lifeworld as a whole.

The avoidance of the utopianisation and moralisation of discourse opens up a whole field of possible empirical discourses beyond the pure form of discourse about validity. It becomes clear that discourse does not concern strictly only questions of validity, but could have any of a number of objects and hence a plurality of themes. Rather than being confined to a pure form, there are different types of discourse.[21] Of particular importance is the fact that consensus problems, far from arising only in relation to validity claims, more often than not appear in conjunction with the disturbance or breakdown of contexts of meaning in which action is embedded. It is only once this is recognised that the general goal of discourse, the bringing about or the re-establishment of mutual understanding and agreement, can be fully appreciated. In this way, room is created for approaching discourse in terms of the sociologically significant question of the collective identification and collective definition of a common or societal problem prior to the strict concern with validity.[22] Another sociologically indispensable dimension of discourse likewise neglected by Habermas is at the same time brought into view. It is not only that all language games in which mutual understanding and agreement are at stake may be called discourses, but also that strategic intentions and functional imperatives are in some degree present in all discourse (Schnädelbach 1977, 161). It is not possible, nor is it sociologically acceptable, to exclude power from discourse.[23] In this respect, Foucault's theory of discourse is a necessary corrective to Habermas' position. What is true of power also holds in the case of conflict. While Foucault's theory also makes room for the latter, it is the merit of Max Miller (1986; 1992) to have worked this dimension out most clearly in a sympathetic critique of Habermas.

Meta-Theoretical Assumptions beyond the Discourse Theorists

The respective contributions of Foucault and Habermas to the theory of discourse contain comparable yet quite different suggestions as regards the elementary meta-theoretical assumptions that need to be made for the development of a sociological theory of discourse which will be useful for the purposes of analysing the construction of sociology within the context of the discourse of modernity. A comparison of the two also shows up conspicuous gaps or blind spots in the contributions of both. On close inspection, however, it becomes apparent that there is a certain complementarity between Foucault and Habermas that possesses much interest from the point of view of a sociological theory of discourse.[24]

The most promising line of approach that Foucault takes to social reality, including both power and discourse, is to be found in his action theoretical model and the complementary notion of the unintended consequences of action – what may be called his theory of the production and reproduction of society. In terms of this theoretical approach, society or the existing complex of power is regarded as the outcome of the competition and conflict of social actors, the product of the process of social conflict. Representing the concurrent dimension of signification, discourse coincides with this process, its product and their cognitive organisation. On the other hand, Foucault's contrasting systems theoretical approach must be rejected since it goes much further than depicting the complex of power and the discourse accompanying it as a supra-intentional reality. If it did this, it would have been acceptable, but power and discourse are conceived as part of a systemic process of adaptation that is devoid of intentionality even at the level of its generation. Even if one rejects this systems theoretical conception of society as a possible meta-theoretical basis for a sociological theory of discourse, however, a marked limitation remains. The action theoretical component involves an exclusive emphasis upon competition and conflict, which means that society is reduced to a process of ongoing strategic confrontations. Non-strategic action, or what Habermas calls communicative action, is in principle excluded. By the same token, it is impossible for Foucault to conceive of discourse as the coordination of actions of different social actors or agents by way of an agreement or even a 'rational dissent'[25] about a common problem and its potential solution.

Habermas' contribution centres on his idea of discourse as a problematisation that brings about or re-establishes a shaken mutual understanding and agreement through the development of symbols and, further, his conviction that all this has consequences for the publicly relevant organisation of society. His insistence on this practical dimension of the search for and establishment of a normative agreement is of the utmost importance for the development of a sociological theory of discourse. It is striking that this dimension corresponds exactly to the gap left by Foucault in his theoretical foundation by focusing exclusively on strategic action. Here is thus an instance of complementarity between the respective positions of Foucault and Habermas. But it is quite possible to pursue it further in the opposite direction. Disregarding his recent self-corrective attempts, Habermas' conceptual pair of lifeworld and system as developed in *The Theory of Communicative Action* (1987a) is relevant here. While the former of these two concepts is confined to forms of the coordination of action through mutual understanding and agreement, the latter concerns only forms of external action coordination. A close inspection reveals that this means that the socio-cultural lifeworld is conceived as a power-free zone of communication, whereas all power and practices of the exercise of power are externalised to the system. The implication is that Habermas overlooks or ignores the processes of the generation and reproduction of power prior to the coordination of action by political means and the state. This conspicuous blind-spot on his part is precisely what Foucault avoids when he for his part insists on the significance of strategic confrontations and conflicts between social actors who pursue competing goals in everyday social life. In addition, it should also be pointed out that Habermas' emphasis on mutual understanding and agreement (*Verständigung*) entails a concern with consensus that leads him, at least sociologically, to seriously understate the significance of dissensus or conflict.[26] Miller (1992, 13–14) has proposed the important distinction between communicative understanding and collective acceptance that allows for the situation where a contrary position is perfectly well understood yet not accepted. This is what he calls rational dissent. The crucial point is now that mutual understanding and agreement or consensus is not the only possible rational outcome of discourse: rational dissent is equally possible.

The complementarity between the positions assumed by Foucault and Habermas respectively clearly signals not only the inadequacy of both positions, but also the fact that they are by no means mutually exclusive or completely incompatible. They can and should be brought together within a more encompassing and more adequate meta-theoretical framework. It must make room for both communicative action in Habermas' sense and strategic action in Foucault's sense, and over and above this action theoretical dimension it also needs to accommodate the outcome, result or product of such action beyond the intentions and the control of the actors. The complementarity between the positions of Foucault and Habermas at the meta-theoretical level leads one to suspect also a complementarity at the level of the theory of discourse itself.

The characteristic feature of Habermas' theory is the conception that discourse is a mode of raising and dealing with problems, a form of problematisation. It entails distinguishing discourse from communication or communicative action, yet without separating them from one another. Whereas the latter is embedded in the context of an action situation and thus rests on implicit counterfactual assumptions or validity claims, discourse is a reflexive form of communication that allows an explicit treatment of counterfactual assumptions or validity claims on a meta-communicative plain. As such, it is a problematisation of the taken-for-granted presuppositions from which communicative action proceeds. Although discourse can thus be said to be a special form of communication in the sense that it takes place in the medium of communication, it nevertheless stands in a relation of opposition to communication in so far as it stops communication in its tracks, breaks it open, induces reflection on its implicit assumptions, makes the latter explicit and thus clarifies and explains communication by reference to those assumptions. From the broader point of view of discourse as a cultural meta-institution concerning the universalisation of cultural symbols, such problematisation and eventually explanation introduce radical rationality in the form of new ideas, ideals or standards into the existing institutional arrangement in order to break up the particularism of institutions and open them up in favour of rendering them more universalistic or communicatively shared. The theoretical base-line for Habermas is thus the conception of discourse as a condition that makes possible the counterfactual explanation of communicative action and thus allows the logic of symbols or culture to take hold of, put pressure on, and guide the unfolding of communicative action. With Miller, one should insist here that discourse is able to play this significant cultural role not only through the mechanism of consensus but likewise also through dissensus or conflict.

Habermas' idea finds its counterpart in Foucault's theory of discourse. Like his German contemporary, he conceives in general of discourse as an important factor in the cultural and social construction of reality. This is borne out by his contention that modern society is shot through with the effects of discourses, all of which are constructions of programmes for the constitution and formation of social reality (Gordon 1980, 245). Rather than the universalising logic of symbols, however, he stresses the logic of power – yet power not just as a matter of repression, exclusion, limitation and prohibition, but also as something that is productive and makes things possible (Foucault 1979, 23–24; 1981, 141; 1987b, 60–62).[27] In this context, discourse is regarded as a condition that facilitates the exercise of power. Ideas, ideals, standards, criteria and symbols constructed in discourse and propagated through discourse are structures of power that operate in both positive and negative ways. On the one hand, discourse allows the construction of programmes that aim at opening up reality, making it transparent, rationalisable and programmable. On the other, it facilitates the regulation and control of action and communication.

Emphasising the logic of power as he does, Foucault's position is obviously diametrically opposed to Habermas' concern with the universalising logic of culture. Yet the fact that both regard discourse at bottom as an essential factor in the cultural and social construction of reality makes it possible to appropriate their respective contributions as complementary aspects of the theory of discourse – complementary in the sense of simultaneously excluding and presupposing each other. On this basis, the twofold assumption from which a more adequate theory of discourse can proceed can be formulated. Following Habermas, discourse is on the one hand regarded as a matter of symbolic universalisation, yet – as Foucault insists – it cannot attain this effect without bringing power into play. Following Foucault, discourse is on the other hand seen as the discursive exercise of power, but – as Habermas equally strongly insists – this necessarily involves the opening up of culture which unfolds according to its own logic.

Here this theoretical position is methodologically interpreted to mean that every historically specific discourse is a socio-cultural form that is generated by the action of social actors yet possesses its own dynamics beyond the privileged access or ultimate disposal of the participants and is therefore able to structure the relevant communication processes in two necessary but complementary ways. Both of these forms of structuration of communication and action need to be taken into account in the course of concrete analysis. On the one hand, discourse must be analysed in terms of the competitive and conflictual strategic actions whereby it is generated as well as in terms of the symbolic violence and structural force that it allows to come into play in the form of dominational or hegemonic relations in the construction of programmes and the regulation and control of communication. Three different types of relations or social processes are of theoretical importance here.[28] Power comes into play in discourse first through the competition and discursive conflict of several collective agents occupying different public arenas, e.g. the Enlightenment *philosophes* supporting absolutism in its enlightened despotic form, the *philosophes* opposed to the state, and the supporters of classical republicanism. In parts of his work, Foucault (1979, 26; 1981, 94) operates explicitly with this concept, although in other parts he evidently proceeds from contrary assumptions. By contrast, it is a concept that Habermas, despite his action theoretical starting point, found virtually impossible to accommodate in his theoretical architectonic. Secondly, power can manifest itself in the case where competing social agents represent a dominant or hegemonic discourse or public space which overwhelms or suppresses another one, e.g. the hegemonic aristocratic-bourgeois discourse in seventeenth-century England suppressing the plebeian or radical culture represented by the Levellers, Diggers and others. Although his interest is in power in so far as it is productive, Foucault (1979, 23; 1981, 141) does recognise the significance of modern techniques of power for domination and hegemony. Habermas' writings themselves are of course replete with references to and analyses of these phenomena under such titles as 'ideology' (1971), 'cultural impoverishment' (1987a, 355), the 'fragmentation of everyday consciousness' (1987a, 355), 'the colonisation of the lifeworld' (1987a, 355), 'the aestheticising, or the scienticising, or the moralising of particular domains of life' (1987b, 340), 'social power' (1996, 364), 'administrative power' (1996, 39–40) and the 'power of the media' (1996, 376). The third possibility is that of the exclusion of a constitutive other, the most typical case being that of women. It is this form of power and especially its exposure by the recent 'insurrection of subjugated knowledges' (Foucault 1980, 81) that inform Foucault's (1976; 1979) studies of the asylum and the prison. What is at stake here, according to Foucault (1980, 81–82), is what has been 'buried and disguised' or 'disqualified as inadequate' in such a way that it is 'present but disguised'. This concept of power is one that does not figure in the work of Habermas. Finally, then, these three dimensions of power all need to be observed in the course of the proposed discourse analysis, and Foucault has the merit of sensitising us to them in an inimitable way.

However important the observance of the different ways in which power enters discourse, a different approach is nevertheless equally indispensable. There are different reasons for this. As the paradigm of power tends to lead to a descriptive rather than an explanatory or reconstructive account (Heller 1986, 158),[29] it is sociologically unavoidable to bring in its complementary paradigmatic viewpoint. Related to this is the fact that Foucault's strategic action theoretic model with its Hobbesian 'Nietzsche's hypothesis' (Foucault

1980, 91) of a hostile engagement of forces or a perpetual war of all against all is incapable of resolving the problem of accounting for moments of stabilisation or institutionalisation (Honneth 1991, 160–61). Conceiving of power simply as success in a situation of ongoing struggle, this means that he lacks all awareness of the philosophical and sociological necessity of a theory of the normative recognition of power. Considering his emphasis on communicative power, agreement or normatively motivated consent, this latter problem is precisely Habermas' strength. On the other hand, therefore, discourse analysis needs to focus on the structuring effect that a given historically specific discourse exerts on communication processes and action by means of its argumentative, cultural or symbolic logic. It is only at this level, and emphatically not at the one stressed by Foucault, that the integrity and consistency of a particular discourse for the first time become visible. Historically speaking, this takes the form of a specific semantics, for instance, the semantics of a moral theory of rights, or of a theory of justice, or – as currently in the late twentieth century – of a theory of responsibility (Apel 1988; 1990; 1991b). Behind such a development lies a generative process that can more appropriately be conceived of in terms of Habermas' concepts of 'illocutionary force' (1979, 59) or 'communicative power' (1996, 147).

CHAPTER 3

Sociological Theory of Discourse

Points of Departure

The German sociologist Richard Münch has undertaken to undo the category mistake – as Schnädelbach calls it – that Habermas commits by reducing all discourse possibilities to validity discourse, and thus to widen the range of types of discourse. His assumption, which is in line with Schnädelbach's analysis, is that discourse needs to be located within the context of society. As a neo-Parsonian venture, Münch's (1984, 117–19) proposal is based on the fourfold LIGA- or AGIL-scheme.[1] First, rational discourse, in the sense of Habermas' pure type of theoretical and practical discourse about validity, is regarded as a subsystem of society, the rationalised cultural subsystem ('Latency'). Three further types of discourse are identified as fulfilling a mediation and integration function: consensus-building discourse between culture and the communal lifeworld ('Integration'), decision-building discourse between culture and the political subsystem ('Goal-attainment'), and finally unity-building discourse between culture and the economic subsystem ('Adaptation').[2] This attempt to arrive at a sociological conception of discourse is by no means without interest, but severe limitations are imposed upon it by the systems theoretical or functionalist approach preferred by its author.

Its concern with society as a system betrays its neglect of the process of construction of society in favour of society as a product of that process. Discourse is seen from the point of view of the maintenance of society as a system rather than as a factor in the process of the construction of society. As regards the latter, Habermas' much wider conception of discourse as a meta-institution and of the general goal of discourse as being mutual understanding and agreement in the sense of bringing about a new consensus (or rational dissent), or re-establishing an interrupted one, is much more helpful than the functionalist notion of discourse as an institution of the cultural subsystem. As such, it provides a ready starting point for a sociological theory of discourse. Compared to Foucault, Münch's proposal exhibits also another limitation. Unlike Foucault, who seeks to go beyond the discourses and practices of modern society as simply expressing the way things are, Münch follows Parsons in adopting a basically uncritical attitude and hence taking a more or less harmonious view of modern society in which the different dimensions inter-penetrate each other. The different forms assumed by discourse depending on its relation to the societal community, the polity and the economy, as con-ceived by Münch, on the other hand, point towards the societal embeddedness of discourse.[3] In a sense, this is closer to Foucault than Habermas. Over and above conceiving discourse in relation to breaches of existing understandings and agreements, the notion of embeddedness allows one to link discourse to the everyday level of social practices as well as the experience and processing of social change or transformation and ensuing societal problems.[4]

Language-Pragmatic or Communication Dimension

The sociological theory that emerges from the foregoing considerations locates discourse within the context of society which is itself conceived as a communi-cative phenomenon. To make clear what it entails, this latter concept can be contrasted with a mistaken but once widely-held view of society. Traditionally, society has often been conceptualised in analogy to an individual subject which has knowledge of itself and its world, relates to itself, and takes appropriate action to realise itself. Society appeared as a self-relating subject on a higher or macro-level and was thought of as forming a whole or totality with both a reflexive and an executive centre. This idea was contained in Hegel's (e.g. 1967, 216–20) concept of the world spirit and found expression also in Durkheim's (1964, 152–56) concept of collective consciousness, but it was theoretically most clearly formulated in the Marxist tradition from Karl Marx (1977) himself through Georg Lukács (1971, 46–82) to Alain Touraine (1977; 1981; 1988), all of whom proceeded from praxis philosophy. Being in crisis and knowing itself to be in such a state, society organises itself as a subject capable of making history in the guise of the proletariat, revolutionary workers' councils or the new social movements in order to lead itself out of the debili-tating situation. Although it has been under attack for a considerable time, it is only in the past three decades or so that the conception of society as a macro-subject has been discredited as an unfounded metaphysical notion serving as a repository of secularised messianic hopes.[5] Spearheading the attack are, on the one hand, action or agency theories (e.g. Coleman 1990) and, on the other, system theoretical approaches (e.g. Luhmann 1985).[6] Whereas the former approaches reduce society individualistically, the latter portray society as a differentiated system without a centre and thus exclude the possibility of identifying a societal crisis and a corresponding critique of society. The communication theoretical concept of society adopted here, which is inspired by Habermas (1974b; 1987b, 357–67; 1989a; 1996), steers a genuinely sociological course between these alternatives.

It is assumed that, even though one has to admit that society can no longer be centrally steered, not even by the state or the political system, it is still possible to locate a virtual centre of reflexive knowledge and self-understanding on the part of society. A sense of society as a whole exists and can be identified. This virtual centre, this sense of a whole, is a projection with real effects which obtains its existence in the public sphere or the sphere of public communication (Habermas 1987b, 359–60; 1990; 1996, 329–87).[7] It is thus better thought of as a dynamic but fragile network than as a stable core, and least of all can it be identified with a collective actor or social movement. Within this context, a variety of processes take place at the same time. Ordinary everyday communication, which is anchored in bodily centres, serves as the basis for spontaneous processes of self-understanding and identity formation on the part of a plurality of collectivities. Each of these collectivities forms something like a public sphere in which a local discourse takes place. The self-understanding and identity formed at this level allows the different collectivities at least potentially to enter into cooperative and competitive relations with one another. This typically occurs in so far as they make their own culturally and socially specific contributions to public communication around specific themes. As cooperative and competitive relations are established, a highly differentiated network of public spheres, involving a variety of technologies of communication, comes into being at the macro-level and points toward a comprehensive public sphere in which society as a whole forms knowledge of itself through a societal discourse. It is in this sphere of public communication that society is able to obtain distance from itself, to collectively process experiences and perceptions of problems and crises, to collectively identify and define them and find generally acceptable solutions to them within a horizon of projected expectations.

In contradistinction to the traditional sociological approach, the concept of society outlined above does not depend on an idealised model of social order. The public sphere or the sphere of public communication spanning society like a network, unlike a social order based on values, interests or power, is a highly dynamic, fragile, impermanent and transient phenomenon. It can be grasped only in the course of the process of the generation of collectively shared interpretations, definitions, meanings and knowledge. It forms part of the process of the construction of society, an ambivalent and contradictory process marked by phases of order and disorder, continuity and change, in which society is constituted and reconstituted or produced and reproduced. According to the sociological theory represented here, therefore, discourse finds its place not only within the context of society conceived as a communicative phenomenon, but by the same token also within the framework of the process of the construction of society.

In the course of the production and reproduction of society, times of relative stability and order are followed by times of instability and disorder, times of certainty by times of uncertainty, and so forth *ad infinitum* (Evers and Nowotny 1987, 17–25).[8] The unexpected takes people by surprise and brings a new world into being that causes pain or pleasure, demands to be attended to and compels them to reflect on and to rethink their most cherished assumptions, their anxieties and fears, hopes and expectations. Normally, such reflection and thought is not required as the social world is so structured and its members dispose over such strategies and recipes that people are confident and sure about how to deal with any eventuality within the familiar run of things (e.g. Schutz and Luckmann 1973). But when something that disrupts the normality of everyday life unexpectedly occurs, it could constitute a serious turning point for society.[9] Breaks between stability and instability, order and disorder, certainty and uncertainty can retrospectively be identified more or less clearly with reference to changes in institutional arrangements (e.g. the constitution), the demographic profile (e.g. famine), or national production figures (e.g. economic crisis or boom). The fact that no break or turn-about in the continuity of society goes without interpretation, however, confirms that change does not simply affect the form of society but at the same time also the knowledge that society has of itself, of its principal problem and its ability to organise itself and to autonomously determine itself.[10] Those involved seek to interpret and ascribe meaning to the event in question and to provide an explanation for it. Even more important is their attempt, by extension, to find new orientations fitting to the unexpected situation to which the event has given rise. The participants engage in processes of societal self-interpretation and self-diagnosis by means of which societal knowledge is produced about what the problem amounts to and how it could be dealt with. The participants themselves, the social actors, the collective agents and the social movements who take part in such practical discourse, play a central role in this process of the production of knowledge. The social sciences, sociology in particular, also play their part in such processes of societal self-interpretation and self-diagnosis, making a contribution, although in a more distanced and systematic manner than the immediate participants, to the development of societal knowledge.

The processes of societal self-interpretation and self-diagnosis are what we refer to as discourse or, in the present case, practical discourse at the societal level. By means of such public discourse, the members of a society seek to make sense of their experience and to find a collective interpretation, to develop an explanation and to establish new orienting knowledge. Discourse, as Habermas (e.g. 1974a, 18–19; 1996, 357)[11] makes clear, is a problematisation in the sense that it involves the breaching of a hitherto taken-for-granted understanding, the attempt to collectively identify a problem, to define it in a collectively shared way and to find a collectively recognised solution to it.[12] It is a way of dealing with the uncertainty that accompanies problems and of building up a new certainty. Discourse in this sense not only allows us to gain access to society and to grasp the process of its construction. At the same time, its phase structure and the cognitive elements and structure of which it is composed also enable us to gather what the members of a society select from among a variety of changes and ruptures as their principal contemporary problem or challenge, how they define this problem, how they think it is best dealt with, what kind of actions and measures they deem most appropriate to overcome the problem, and how they hold they should orient themselves so as to re-establish and maintain continuity, stability, order and certainty.

As Max Miller (1986, e.g. 23–26; 1987, 203–10)[13] has shown, the problem addressed by discourse concerns at bottom a problem of social coordination. In order to identify, define and solve a given problem, the orientations and actions of individuals and collectivities need to be coordinated by bringing about, even if only temporarily, a collectively shared interpretation. Ultimately, only one form of communication fulfils the conditions for achieving this, namely discourse or collective argumentation. It is the final and irreducible method for dealing with social coordination problems. It presupposes that the participants perceive a social coordination problem and it represents the attempt to develop a collective solution to it, irrespective of whether this is done in an explicit manner or is approached only implicitly. If it does not succeed, a limited range of alternatives is available, stretching from breaking off communication altogether, reverting to strategic action, engaging in conflict or civil war, or embarking on a new round of constructing a temporary consensus or, at least, rational dissent by means of discourse.

The fact that discourse is conceived as forming part of a dynamic process and is itself transient, however, does not contradict its organised or structured nature (Evers and Nowotny 1987, 19, 23–24; Eder 1993a, 9).[14] At the concretely observable level accessible by means of the print and today also the electronic media, discourse can take any of a variety of forms in the public domain. It can range from statements and arguments through conflicts and protests to negotiations and searches for interpretations.[15] Over and above the concrete forms it assumes, however, discourse as a special form of communication focusing on problematisation consists of cognitive structures and hence contains knowledge of various kinds. On the one hand, there is the social knowledge of the participants who experience the situation at first hand, observe it and attempt to regulate it. This knowledge, moving as it does between experience and everyday expectations as well as political visions, is of an experiential and conceptual kind and finds expression in a historically specific socio-political vocabulary and language or semantics. On the other hand, discourse contains expert knowledge ranging from – depending on the problem at issue – natural scientific and technical knowledge, which today is no longer thought to be as 'hard' as was thought earlier, to social scientific knowledge which articulates more or less closely with the interpretation of the situation developed by the participants and their observers. These different types of knowledge, expert knowledge and social knowledge, stand in a relation of dialectical exchange and mutual correction to one another. When this relation is activated and rendered dynamic, potentialities for collectively shared knowledge in the form of anticipatory orienting knowledge is generated. Interpretative schemes are developed in response to questions posed by actors, observers, regulators, experts and social scientists, and on the basis of their competition, conflict and integration, such structures as ethical guidelines, rules of political behaviour, a vision of the future, expectations, and a credible foundation for institutional solutions become established. All in all, then, discourse thus produces a new collective orientational framework that structures the experience and serves as a repository of collective knowledge. In so far as it gives rise to such a historically specific collective cognitive frame, discourse organises communication processes and follows its own specific logic.

From a more comprehensive point of view, it may be submitted that discourse takes place within the context of culture[16] or, more particularly, of some historically shaped semantic world or another.[17] The clearest index of this context is represented by the cultural or cognitive structures or frame dominant in relation to the issue at stake at the time. Looking at discourse in terms of its twofold phase structure punctuated by a critical turning point, however, it typically moves between two semantic worlds. On the one hand, there is the old semantic world that is being reproduced yet left behind and, on the other, the new semantic world that is in the process of being constructed in and through the discourse. Discourse thus plays a central role in replicating and transforming culture by reproducing an existing semantic world and producing a new one. At the same time, to be sure, its own logic is reconstituted by such a semantic world as the latter undergoes a change that is apparent from the shift from one frame to another.[18]

Cognitivist Theory of Frames

The proposal to conceive of cognitive structures as so-called 'frames' was first introduced into sociology by Erving Goffman (1986),[19] leaning on Durkheim (Collins 1994, 277–83), within the context of symbolic interactionism. If not the word, the concept of such structures of course goes back to a long tradition that started with Kant and culminated in late twentieth-century cognitivism. The names of such well-known thinkers as Lukács (1968), Mannheim (1972; 1993), Schutz (1976), Goldmann (1964; 1975), Piaget (1970; 1973), and Bateson (1973) could be mentioned here, and to them could be added relatively recent developments in the cognitive sciences (De Mey 1982), including linguistics, cognitive psychology, cognitive anthropology and cognitive sociology.[20]

Frames are complexes of rules that structure interaction situations in such a way that the participants are able to interpret and thus make sense of actions and their effects as well as the responses of others. Rather than the particular interpretations or meanings themselves at which the different participants arrive, frames are the rules or structures that define the cognitive foundation of the situation. Since the participants have in common a knowledge of these rules, a knowledge that is mostly implicit yet sometimes explicit, the relevant frames can be regarded as representing a cognitive order (Eder 1992c, 3).[21] As such, frames are the cultural-structural forms that make possible the generation of interpretations of reality by the participants and the ascription of meaning to it by means of symbolisation. Frames allow the framing of reality, as it were. Given that it is a set of cognitive structures that organises experience, a single frame allows a whole range of potentially competing and even conflicting interpretations or framings, yet the range is restricted in so far as it necessarily remains within the structural bounds of the frame.

While Goffman in true symbolic interactionist vein focused the attention on frames structuring the interactive relations of individuals, contemporary American authors shifted the emphasis from the micro-level to the meso-level of organised collective actors. David Snow and the group around him (Snow et al. 1986; Snow and Benford 1988; 1992),[22] for instance, concern themselves with collective action, social movements, and the interaction between and among organised collective actors. Here the coordination problem is of a different order than that relevant to individual actions. Thus frames are considered in relation to the shared knowledge and orientations that structure and coordinate collective actions. Accordingly, Snow and Benford (1992) analyse the so-called 'collective action frames' that structure and guide social movement activities and campaigns.[23] Although upgraded one level, frames remain both structurally and functionally the same as at the micro-level. They are structural forms in the guise of rules that make available a cognitive order that structures and coordinates actions and interactions.

It is quite possible to go a step further still by redirecting the attention to the macro-dimension. This is what Gamson and his associates (Gamson 1988a; 1988b; 1992a; Gamson and Modigliani 1987; 1989; Gamson and Stuart 1992) began to do by locating collective action, movements and the construction of issues within the framework of mass media discourse in particular and public discourse in general. Eyerman and Jamison (1991, 45–65, 99–102) have also moved in this direction by focusing on what they call the 'cognitive praxis'[24] of social movements and locating it in the context of the 'societal mode of communication'. But it is Klaus Eder (1992a; 1992b; 1992c; 1993a; 1996) who has developed theoretically the most advanced position on frames and the cognitive order at the macro-level.[25]

Although it is conceptually clear that there are micro-, meso- and macro-dimensions to frames, matters are complicated by the fact that a distinction can be made, as does Goffman (1986, 21–39), between primary and secondary frames. Whereas the former refer to deep-seated anthropological frames common to all people, the latter concern historically, culturally and socially specific cognitive structures. For current purposes, however, it is assumed that the sociologically relevant frames are all of the historically, culturally and socially specific kind. But even if this assumption is made, the problem remains that frames can be interpreted at different levels. For instance, while Bourdieu (1986) has a highly sophisticated understanding of the different dimensions as well as levels of cognitive structures, his emphasis on the habitus as a system of schemes operating below the level of awareness leads him to focus on frames closer to the primary or deep end. In this book, by contrast, I am concerned with frames that are closer to the secondary end of the spectrum than Bourdieu's are. To me it seems that Bourdieu's approach is too rigid today in our reflexive age in which cognitive structures or cultural models have increasingly shifted and are still shifting to the level of awareness.[26] A further problem resides in the fact that the whole area of frames is terminologically in disarray. Recently, Snow and Benford (1992)[27] have introduced the notion of 'master frame', but contrary to expectations continued to apply it below the highest level. Following the American authors in certain respects, Eder (1992a; 1992b, 18; 1992c, 4) has also run up against terminological difficulties. In the following, the term 'macro-frame' or 'master frame' will be reserved strictly for the macro-level, with due regard for the fact that it is manifested on different levels of generality (see Figure 3.1).

The frames located on the macro-level together constitute the cognitive order of society that structures and guides the experience of reality, both social and natural. As cognitive structures, these macro-frames in the first place take the form of general principles or rules that allow people to generate interpretations of reality and to act accordingly.[28] General principles or rules of this kind do not apply in their pure form, however, but become articulated in more specific forms in particular contexts. The macro-frames making up the cognitive order can therefore be identified on two distinct yet closely related levels of abstraction. Given our basic reference point for the analysis of the discursive construction of sociology, i.e. the modern age, the macro-frame in its most general form relevant here is the master frame of modernity that emerged during the early modern period, became established in the seventeenth century, and predominated for a considerable period afterwards, at any rate until relatively recently. It is 'the frame of free, equal and discursively structured social relations', as Eder (1992c, 3, slightly modified) describes it, the most general manifestation of the cognitive order underpinning and structuring modernity. This liberal-egalitarian-discursive master frame of modernity was in turn articulated in specific ways, depending on the particular historical context. At a less general level, therefore, historical master frames forming part of the cognitive order of modernity can be identified. During the early modern period when the modernity master frame was articulated in terms of the question of rights, sovereignty, the constitution and democracy, the rights frame structured the experience and expectations of those living at the time. In the subsequent period, which was animated by the social question or the question of society, a corresponding shift occurred in the historical master frame from rights to justice. From the sixteenth to the twentieth century, then, the general master frame of modernity took the more historically specific form first of the rights frame and next of the justice frame.[29]

Recently, it has become apparent that the general master frame of modernity has undergone a marked modification. Indications of this change are contained in the emphatic twentieth-century concern with the question of nature in a broad sense and related cultural and social phenomena (e.g. Touraine et al. 1976; Moscovici 1982a, 13–32; 1990). Among the latter, the late twentieth-century environmental crisis is of much importance, but still more fundamental is the sobering realisation that society, far from being the discoverer and master of nature, is the creator as well as the subject of the historical state of nature in which it finds itself (Moscovici 1982a, 15, 27, 31). This realisation, which radicalised reflexivity, led to the addition of supplementary principles or rules to the master frame of freedom, equality and discursivity, which had the effect of relativising to a certain extent the emphasis on the form of social relations yet by no means doing away with it. To this day, experience in modern society continues to be structured by the liberal-egalitarian-discursive frame, yet society itself is now understood in a new way, and this understanding has its own particular structuring effect on experience. The general cognitive order of late modernity, the master frame of our own time, consists of what Eder (1992c, 3, slightly modified) calls 'the frame of an order inherent in nature, the frame of a natural order of modern societies'. It should be pointed out, however, that here it is not a matter of returning to the pre-modern frame, according to which trust was put in nature to form human nature, to produce a political order and to provide solutions for human problems. Intended is rather the twentieth-century insight that the relation between society and nature has grown closer, that the interdependence between the two has reached a critical point, and that society has to accept, consciously and deliberately, both the duty and responsibility for its relation to nature. It could therefore be referred to as the society-nature nexus. This general frame of late or postmodernity, which has started to take effect for the first time only recently, is at present specifically articulated in the form of what I propose to call the responsibility frame. Eder (1992b, 18) speaks of 'the risk frame' instead, but this is too partial in view of the fact that it qualifies as a more specific variant of the responsibility frame as historical master frame of our time.[30] In proportion as the responsibility frame is becoming effective in structuring experience in contemporary society, it is taking the place of or, at least, is recontextualising and thus reconstituting the preceding modern historical master frame, the justice frame.

In the light of the above discussion of the cognitive order of modern society, the complex of macro-frames of which it consists can be represented diagrammatically as shown in Figure 3.1. Although the macro-frames of which the cognitive order is composed are themselves cognitive structures that give form to or structure the experience of the social and natural world, they are neither static nor given once and for all. Rather they are structures that include rules for their own transformation, structures that entail their own genesis or construction, structures suspended in a process of constitution and recon-stitution (Piaget 1973, 207–09; Bourdieu 1986, 467). These macro-frames therefore include a reference to structuring activities through which they come into being, are constructed and reconstructed, while they themselves can be regarded as the structured result or outcome of such constructive activities. Through its structuring force, discourse in turn is the organised form of such constructive activities. The genetic or constructive achievement of such activities is always a matter of a transition from one structure to another, from a departure structure to a destination structure.[31] Discourse is thus suspended between a preceding structure that is losing its structuring effect and breaking down and a new structure that is in the process of coming into being and

Figure 3.1: The modern cognitive order

LEVEL I: GENERAL MASTER FRAME

1	2
Modernity Master Frame: free, equal, discursively structured social relations	Late Modernity Master Frame: society-nature nexus

LEVEL II: HISTORICAL MASTER FRAME

1	2	3
rights frame	justice frame	responsibility frame

becoming established as the predominant macro-frame. It typically embraces two phases, the first characterised by the gradual increase of uncertainty, and the second by the gradual regaining of certainty. The critical discourse moment resides at the point of discontinuity between the two phases.

The cognitivist theoretical point of view that was brought to bear on micro-, meso- and particularly macro-frames above can be extended also to the construction of macro-frames. While this is available as a suggestion in Piaget (1973)[32] and as a not entirely clear project in Merchant (1989, e.g. xvi-xviii), it has been worked out most systematically in the neo-Kantian tradition as represented by Habermas' threefold scheme of the cognitive, normative and aesthetic spheres of value and validity.[33] Eyerman and Jamison (1991, 66–93)[34] appropriate it via his older notion of three so-called 'knowledge interests' as representing the different dimensions of what they call 'cognitive praxis', whereas Eder (1992a; 1996, 167)[35] does so via his later conception of so-called 'validity claims'.[36] Using it for classificatory purposes, he takes it a step closer to potential empirical indicators by speaking, with Gamson, of 'framing devices'.[37] Correlating with the differentiated dimensions of modern culture, they refer to the factual, the social and the subjective worlds respectively, and are therefore called the framing devices of 'empirical objectivity', 'moral responsibility' and 'aesthetic judgement'. These objectifying, moral and aesthetic or conative framing devices are the basic cognitive instruments or means used by actors to construct frames.

Merchant (1989, xvi) intuitively captures the sense of framing devices by way of three questions. How do people 'conceptualise' the world? How do they 'behave' in relation to the world? How do they 'give meaning' to the world? It could be accounted for, however, in a more analytical and systematic manner

(Eder 1996, 167). Employing the factual or objectifying framing device, actors rely on empirical knowledge of the world in order to form a concept of it. The moral framing device is a cultural tool by means of which actors lay down certain principles according to which they behave towards the world. By means of the conative framing device, actors organise their subjective experience and perception of the world in a way that makes it meaningful to them. The above-mentioned structuring activities through which macro-frames are generated or constructed consist of framing activities in which these three basic types of device are applied to reality. What the actors do within a specific discursive context is to use these cognitive framing devices in such a way that they delimit or define the problem at issue in the discourse.

Different actors frame reality or, rather, the basic problem at issue in different and, at any rate, competing or even conflicting ways. Actors (e.g. the absolutist monarchy, aristocracy, bourgeoisie and the people, or the state, industry and social movements) who differ from one another due to the fact that they come from distinct socio-cultural forms of life and represent different institutional cultures (e.g. hierarchies, markets, collectives or networks), arrive at their own particular framings since they employ the three framing devices for constructive purposes in different combinations. For instance, either the objectifying device is given priority over the other two, or the moral device is treated as the most important, or the others are subordinated to the conative device. The framing devices are differently bundled in symbolic forms or symbolic packages (Eder 1992c, 4; 1996, 168), most typically presented through narratives (Eder 1996, 168),[38] which lend the propositions, principles and motivations involved a coherent form and allow actors to construct collective identities for themselves and to communicate those identities. Examples of such symbolic forms are meso-frames or ideologies such as enlightened despotism, classical constitutionalism or classical republicanism from the early modern period, or twentieth-century conservationism, environmentalism, ecologism and deep ecology. The symbolic forms transform framing devices into frames that can be communicated. They not only bundle framing devices in a symbolically significant way, but also link them to actors and the social situation and insert them into public communication or discourse. Actors therefore do more than merely frame the problem at issue by packing framing devices into symbolic forms. At the same time, they also employ their symbolic forms as framing strategies (Eder 1996, 168) so as to communicate their particular frames and hence identities in the public communication or discursive context in their own distinctive ways.

Whereas political actors typically communicate ideological consent so as to obtain the support of those sections of the population who are perceived as counting, economic actors seek to convince the members of society of their potential to improve the present situation. In contradistinction to these orthodox strands in the discourse, movement actors characteristically pursue an oppositional stance which is communicated in the form of an alternative or counter-position.[39] In the earlier phase of the discourse when a new macro-frame is still taking on form, a variety of frames are present, relentlessly competing and conflicting with one another to establish their dominance. Eder (1996, 169) introduces the concept of 'frame competition' which implies 'an analysis of the way in which frames mediate between collective actors'.[40] The concept of competition, which takes us beyond Habermas' account of discourse, can be regarded as acknowledging a particular way in which power enters into discourse. As such, it is in accord with Foucault's emphasis in parts of his work on the strategic action of a diversity of actors engaged in the conflicts of everyday social life. The nature of the discourse, which organises the framing and communication activities of the different actors and, in particular, the nature of the nascent macro-frame, provides conditions for such competition and conflict.

Discourse is an open complex of communication, mutual interpretation, understanding, agreement and rational disagreement possessing its own logic and dynamic, which, while being generated by the actions and communication of social actors, allows no privileged membership rights and ultimately is withdrawn from the disposal of any participant, individual or collective. Above and beyond the participants, the public forms a constitutive component of such a generalised communication process. Since it plays a more or less decisive role in rendering determinate what at first appears indeterminate in public communication, the public introduces a dimension of contingency into discourse that does not admit of easy mastery by the competing or conflicting participants.[41] The emergent macro-frame forms an inherent part of this elusive discursive reality beyond the reach of the intentional action of the participants. Due to the fact that the symbolic or cultural logic of the discourse carried by the collective argumentation can go unpredictably in any of a number of directions, depending on the evaluation and judgement of the public, no actor can be sure how a particular framing of a problem will resonate nor, indeed, whether it will resonate at all. Here, of course, power enters discourse too. It could secure competitive advantage in the struggle over the control of frames, in Foucault's (1980, 118–19) sense of suppressing some and of leading others in a certain direction by opening up new programmes or vistas as well as in his sense of exclusion. But the logic of power is as elusive as the cultural logic of discourse. Power, which in principle flows in a circuit (Foucault 1980, 98; Habermas 1996, 354–58),[42] can unpredictably shift in a discursive context where ideological and legitimation struggles are fought out (Bourdieu 1997, 242; Dietz et al. 1989) within view and earshot of the public (Strydom 1999a). Actors often delude themselves about their disposal, not only over resources of the situation, but also over definitions. Under such conditions, the constructive activities of the participating actors give rise to a range of frames from the competition and conflict of which in the critical phase of the discourse emerges a single frame that is discursively defined as being collectively valid (Miller 1986, 29–30, 258–80; 1992). An overarching frame emanating from a public discourse as possessing collective validity is a macro-frame, such as any of those specified in Figure 3.1. It is a master frame since it lays down the limits that circumscribe whether what the participating actors seek to communicate in the public communication context is audible, makes sense, and sounds like music to the ears of those involved, particularly the public.

Miller's concept of collective validity is of great importance here. It forms part of Habermas' correction of the one-sidedness and sociological untenability of Foucault's position. On the one hand, Foucault (1980, 114) proceeds from the model of perpetual 'war and battle' in his conceptualisation of strategic action, and consequently he is incapable of solving the problem of the temporal stabilisation or institutionalisation of the occasionally achieved outcomes of social action. Power is simply success in a situation of struggle (Honneth 1991, 161). From a sociological point of view, by contrast, institutionalisation invariably involves some degree of mutual recognition, agreement, rational disagreement, compromise and the normative acknowledgement of power. The outcome of social struggle is thus more than a matter of sheer power; moral orientations and legal norms are more than mere illusions and deceptions. In this respect, the Gramscian concept of hegemony (see Eley 1992; Cohen and Arato 1992, 142–59), which includes a normative dimension over and above sheer power, would seem to be more appropriate for the conceptualisation of institutionalisation. It is the case, of course, that Foucault surrenders this action theoretic approach without having resolved the problem of institutionalisation in favour of concentrating on the novel modern mode of power – the main theme of his theory of power. In this context, as Honneth (1991, 173–75) has convincingly demonstrated, he conceives of social stabilisation in terms of a power-wielding, institutional order that involves a one-sided rule by force which is carried along by a systemic process of the continuous perfecting of technologies of power.

From this it can be concluded, finally, that a macro-frame emanating from discourse, as something to which pertains collective validity, cannot be conceived in the terms made available by Foucault. It is neither simply success in a social struggle nor merely the one-sided rule of an institutional order. As the mutable or more or less fragile outcome of the strategic competition and conflict of social actors, a discursive macro-frame certainly involves power. But as a set of structures that becomes cognitively and normatively institutionalised, it also involves an intersubjective dimension that is best conceived in terms of the model of language rather than the model of war and battle.

CHAPTER 4

Discourse of Modernity

The Opening of the Discourse

In 1984, in one of the last courses he offered at the Collège de France, Foucault (1987a, 38)[1] presented Kant as the one who opened the discourse of modernity. Kant was the first to focus on modernity in its own right, free from its usual contrast with the Ancients, and to conceive of the significance of his own work as a reflection on and analysis of the present. In the lecture course he held at the University of Frankfurt in 1983–84, Habermas (1987b, 43)[2] by contrast submitted that the discourse of modernity was opened by Hegel. The modern age, of course, had already begun at an earlier point in time. Thus he would agree with Foucault that Kant represents modernity in so far as he emphasises that critical reason replaces the search for substantive truths about human nature, and that the breakdown of religion and metaphysics makes necessary not only a consideration of society, social bonds and moral action but also the mature acceptance of responsibility for the organisation of our own lives (Dreyfus and Rabinow 1987, 110). Yet, in Habermas' view, Kant's successor Hegel was the first for whom modernity became a problem. In his work an explicit relation was for the first time established among modernity, the new time-consciousness and the problem of rationality. Kant was undoubtedly modern, but it was Hegel who initiated the discourse of modernity.

What both Habermas and Foucault have in mind when they refer to what Habermas often calls 'the discourse of modernity' is not the discourse of modernity representing the central object of study of the present book, however, but rather a partial aspect of it. Both men are concerned with what in Habermas' (1985 and 1987b, title) more precise terminology is called 'the philosophical discourse of modernity'. Their object of attention, which is admittedly analysed in their own peculiar ways, is a particular semantics, namely a philosophical discursive semantics, that has been and is still being generated by the more encompassing practical discourse of modernity. The beginning of the discourse of modernity that is of interest here does not lie in the late eighteenth or early nineteenth century. It can be traced to the sixteenth century, particularly to what Arnold Hauser (1979, 6–11, 23–43) has called 'the crisis of the Renaissance'.[3] During this period, a discourse ensued in response to the failure of the hitherto taken-for-granted understanding of reality to provide a shared background against which people could orient themselves and justify their activities. In contradistinction to a philosophical discourse, this was a society-wide practical discourse that provided the context for the development of a broad socio-political semantics in relation to the significant historical events of the time as well as a variety of more specialised semantics, including a social scientific and a philosophical one.[4]

The meandering course of this discourse, the discourse of modernity, can be followed from the sixteenth century to the present day.

Discourse of Modernity

The assumptions on which the sociological idea of the discourse of modernity is based admit of brief restatement. Modern society is spanned by a permanently live network of public communication in the medium of which collectively shared interpretations, definitions, meanings, knowledge and even rational disagreements are developed and revised throughout the process of its construction. This network becomes particularly activated when, in the course of this ambivalent and contradictory process, the shared background of taken-for-granted assumptions is interrupted, so that order gives way to disorder, continuity to change, or certainty to uncertainty and the need arises to collectively identify, define and resolve some societal problem. The discourse of modernity formally refers to this feature, so characteristic of modern society, of agitated public communication around a societal problem in which the collective activities of identification and definition are discursively coordinated with a view to resolving it. It thus links up with the experience and processing of social change and transformation and the ensuing problems. In contradistinction to the many local discourses continually under way, however, it does so at the macro-level of fragile public communication where society forms knowledge of itself as a whole, organises itself and takes action to determine itself. The discourse of modernity is a practical discourse of societal scope, the discourse of modern society, that is generated by public communication at the macro-level and, in turn, coordinates and organises that very communication.

Generally speaking, the problem at issue in the discourse of modernity is the complex and only temporarily resolvable one of the constitution as well as the mutual compatibility, coordination, reconciliation and consolidation of the different dimensions of society. How could society be brought into being? How could identities, legitimately defensible interests and differences most appropriately be organised under prevailing conditions? What is the most appropriate common principle of social identification for achieving this? How could deep-seated conflicts be transformed into mutual understanding, rational disagreement or even agreement? What collective political action is necessary to realise it? How could the new arrangement be justified or rendered legitimate? The central problem of modern society could thus be expressed in the form of the simple question, 'What should we do?' The resolution of the problem requires creativity, cooperation, conflict resolution, collective opinion- and will-formation – in short: permanent discourse (Habermas 1996, 37, 158). This problem made its first appearance in the sixteenth century and in its general thrust has since become a defining characteristic of modern society.[5]

The manner in which this general problem has become collectively defined in the context of the discourse of modernity as one that is in principle resolvable is of particular interest here. It can be gauged from the cognitive structures that underpin the modern perception and experience of the social and natural world and give direction to action, thus in turn structuring the discourse of modernity itself. Since the beginning of the modern period, as argued above, this cognitive order has taken the form of the macro- or master frame of free, equal and discursively structured social relations. It has allowed social actors from different cultural forms of life to approach the problem of the construction of modern society from their own particular angles and to interact with one another and to act upon each other in the pursuit of their points of view and interests. Some emphasised freedom and pursued individual interests, others emphasised equality and pursued collective needs, and yet others emphasised the division of powers and their interrelation through public discussion. It is only recently that the discourse of modernity has taken such a course that the liberal-egalitarian-discursive master frame of modernity has been modified and supplemented by additional principles or rules. Instead of organising perception, experience, action and communication in terms of social relations or society alone, the discourse of modernity was increasingly compelled through historical developments, events and concomitant experiences to incorporate phenomena that have a bearing on the relation between society and nature. Among these phenomena are the scientific objectification, the technological manipulation and the industrial exploitation of external nature, the relation of modern human beings to their emotions and bodies, gender, and so forth. The general problem addressed by the discourse of modernity thus became collectively regarded in terms of the society-nature master frame of the late twentieth century.

Crisis Discourses

The general problem of the constitution and organisation of society at issue in the discourse of modernity first made its appearance in the sixteenth century in the wake of the Reformation, the Counter-Reformation and the ensuing general crisis of the time. In the seventeenth and eighteenth centuries, it became increasingly acute as a result of the establishment of the absolutist state. This was the case to such an extent, indeed, that it reached crisis proportions in the early modern period. At the root of this crisis was the contradictory rationalisation or civilisation of power entailed by the absolutist state's monopolisation of all resources, from force to knowledge. In proportion as power was subjected to regulation and control, its excessive use also grew. This crisis was still further exacerbated by the peculiar relation that developed between the absolutist state and the different collective actors taking action in relation to or against it. Of particular importance here are the different actors who are as a rule indiscriminately taken together under the title of the Enlightenment. The self-deceptive or illusory ideals projected by most of these actors, their moralisation and utopianisation of social and political relations in response to the confinement of politics to the state, further contributed to placing an impediment in the way of appropriate collective political action being taken. As a result, society's capacity to regulate the course and direction of its own development was severely fractured. These developments set the scene for the peculiar way in which the discourse of modernity has ever since been produced and reproduced. From historical period to historical period, it was carried by a crisis discourse.

The problem at stake in the discourse of modernity, being of a general nature as it is, never presents itself to be addressed as such. As a problem that repeats itself periodically in modern society as a collectively relevant one under particular circumstances in a novel form, it can be collectively identified, defined and dealt with only in the context of distinct, historically specific discourses. The discourse of modernity is therefore produced and reproduced by a series of historically specific yet changing discourses. Under varying historical conditions, each discourse addresses the general problem articulated in the discourse of modernity, focusing on the specific societal problem and the collective political action necessary for its solution. Given that modern society was born in and through a societal crisis that, far from having been properly resolved, placed an impediment in the way of the development of society which reasserts itself time and again, however, these historically specific discourses typically take the form of crisis discourses. The discourse of modernity is thus in fact produced and reproduced by a series of historically specific but changing crisis discourses.

By considering the historically specific cognitive structures or historical macro-frames constructed in the course of the production and reproduction of the discourse of modernity, one can grasp the particular problems addressed in the context of the crisis discourses marking the different phases in the discursive construction of modern society. Earlier the argument was put forward that three historical master frames forming part of the modern cognitive order can be distinguished. They are the rights frame, the justice frame and the responsibility frame. In turn, they serve to provide a structure for the crisis discourses of modernity. They are the sixteenth-, seventeenth- and eighteenth-century rights discourse, followed by the late eighteenth-, nineteenth- and twentieth-century justice discourse, and finally the late twentieth-century responsibility discourse.[6]

The first crisis discourse, the early modern rights discourse, emerged in the sixteenth century in relation to the Reformation, the Counter-Reformation and the ensuing Wars of Religion. It continued parallel to the Dutch struggle against the Spanish Crown and the English Revolution, and essentially ended with the completion of the American War of Independence and the first phase of the French Revolution in the late eighteenth century. The central institutional factor in this context was the absolutist state or, more broadly, the *ancien régime*.[7] The rights discourse was carried by a series of debates that concentrated on the widely experienced problem of violence and disorder and unfolded in terms of the concepts of domination, sovereignty, resistance against tyrannical government, and formally recognised rights (Skinner 1978; Saage 1981; Willke 1992, 216–39). In the deployment of this discourse, a socio-politically and culturally significant semantics was developed that was lent coherence and consistency by a moral theory of rights,[8] which had been given its most important initial formulation by the Huguenot Philippe du Plessis-Mornay in his *Vindicae contra Tyrannos* of 1579 (Skinner 1978, II, 316–18, 332–35; Elton 1985, 237). Subsequently, it was carried forward by a whole series of both conservative and radical authors and pamphleteers (Tuck 1979). This theory, which gave explicit formulation to the frame structuring the discourse, provides the justification for giving it the name of the rights discourse. In addition to forwarding a solution to the collectively defined societal problem, the rights discourse also contributed to identity formation and the mobilisation of the collective political action necessary to realise the proposed solution. While also mobilising other actors such as the state, it particularly assumed the form of the early modern social movement, what is commonly called the classical emancipation movement. Having negotiated its course via a protracted series of exchanges and conflicts, the rights discourse eventuated, on the one hand, in the guarantee of basic rights or liberties and, on the other, in the establishment of a new law-based institutional infrastructure which was assigned the task of taming violence and creating order in society. The latter took the form of the constitutional state.

The second of the three crisis discourses of modernity, structured by the justice frame as it is, may be called the justice discourse.[9] It arose and developed in response to the market-based industrial capitalist economic system and the effects it generated. It appeared for the first time in late eighteenth-century England, rapidly spread throughout the Continent in the nineteenth century, and was reproduced in a sublimated form under the conditions of the welfare state until the second half of the twentieth century when this institutional arrangement started to break down. The justice discourse was activated by a series of debates often collectively referred to as the poverty debate (Polanyi 1957; Evers and Nowotny 1987, 88–184; Willke 1992, 239–62; Winch 1996). The reason for this is that the problem complex that provided the focal point of this discourse was the exploitation, pauperisation and loss of identity that affected a significant number of people in the wake of industrial capitalism. Initially, all the participants accepted that the objective laws of the new system are unalterable, yet in a drastic turnabout in the discourse during the latter part of the nineteenth century the problem was collectively defined as being manageable by means of state intervention on the basis of scientific-technical progress. This solution took the form of state-supported industrial capitalist production and welfare through the redistribution of the fruits of growth. On the one hand, this crisis discourse gave rise to a socio-politically and culturally significant semantics that was lent coherence and consistency by the logical rules of a new moral theory, the theory of justice.[10] On the other, it contributed to appropriate identity formation and collective political action by making possible the construction of the working-class or labour movement as a collective actor. The impact of the justice discourse can be gleaned from the guarantee of compensatory claims to a just share of social wealth and the significant degree to which the existing institutional arrangement, the constitutional state, was modified and supplemented by a new departure, namely the money-based institutional infrastructure known as the welfare state.

The third and final historically specific crisis discourse producing and reproducing the discourse of modernity is the responsibility discourse, as I propose to call it.[11] This proposal is based on the conviction that the historical master frame of the preceding period – the justice frame – is making way for

Table 4.1: Crisis discourses of modernity

PERIOD	C16th–18th	late C18th–mid-20th	late C20th
SOCIETY	early modern	industrial capitalist	risk or cultural?
DISCOURSE		discourse of modernity	
CRISIS DISCOURSE	rights	justice	responsibility[*]
PROBLEM	violence	poverty	risk
QUESTION	political	social	nature[†]
ISSUE	survival of society in its political environment	survival of society in its social environment	survival of society in its natural environment
MASTER FRAME	rights	justice	responsibility
COLLECTIVE ACTORS	monarchy aristocracy bourgeoisie classical emanicipation movements	capitalists state functionaries labour movements	industry state functionaries new social movements
INSTITUTIONAL INFRASTRUCTURE	constitutional state	welfare state	neo-corporatism or postcorporatism(?)
MEANS	law	money	knowledge

[*] It is of course the case that considerations of justice pertain also to rights and to responsibility. In the case of the former, for instance, early representatives of the modern theory of rights such as Suarez and Grotius explicitly discussed questions of justice in connection with rights (see, for example, Tuck 1979, 56–57, 59–60). Similarly, questions of so-called 'environmental justice' have begun to capture the contemporary imagination (see, for example, the special issue of the journal *Social Problems*, 40 (1) February 1993, edited by Judith Perrolle). The second crisis discourse is nevertheless referred to here as the 'justice discourse' since justice is what gave coherence to this discourse in the same way that rights did in early modernity and responsibility does today. It concerned a just share of social wealth.

[†] Schäffer (1985, 269–70) speaks of the 'political question...or the question of the form of the state, the social question...or the question of the form of society, and the... ecological question or the question of the interaction with nature...'. Following Schäffer, Eder (1988, 228) refers to the 'political (constitutional) question', the 'social question' and the 'nature question' (my translations).

another – the responsibility frame – and that, consequently, the theory of justice is being displaced, or at least recontextualised, by a new semantics. The latter takes the form of the moral theory of responsibility.[12] This moral theoretic or philosophical semantics gives expression to the new master frame and articulates the internal coherence and consistency of the currently emerging crisis discourse. Since the 1970s, the responsibility discourse has been generated by a variety of intertwined debates that all in one way or another deal with what has become known as 'the problem of nature', that is, with some aspect of the relation between society and nature. They range over a series of apparently disparate problems, including technology and science, industry, armaments, collective decision-making, the status of collective goods, the environment, the modern relation to external nature, the modern relation to the body and emotions, and gender. Given that it has played a part in the discourse from the outset and that it has progressively assumed increasing significance, risk (Beck 1992) has gained currency as a concept by means of which to make sense of these problems. This concept not only captures the dangers and disadvantages that culturally defined social processes harbour for collective forms of life, but at the same time also invokes its complement, the responsibility that needs to be taken for the collective definition and social organisation of such processes.[13] As far as collective political action aimed at redressing these problems is concerned, the responsibility discourse has made possible the deconstruction of older forms of collective action such as the labour movement and the construction of novel identities and forms of collective action collectively known as the 'new social movements'.[14] As a result of the exchanges, conflicts and negotiations forming part of the responsibility discourse, a new society with a knowledge-based institutional infrastructure is at present coming into being which would seem to possess some novel features. No agreement has as yet been reached as to how this society and its new institutional order should be characterised. The 'risk society' (Beck 1992) or 'cultural society' (Moscovici 1982a, 446; Lash 1994, 208)?[15] 'Neocorporatism' (Willke 1992, 78–79) or 'postcorporatism' (Eder 1996, 209–11)?[16]

In view of the fact that Habermas' communication theory of society and particularly his theory of discourse serve as an important reference point for the ideas developed above, the view of a concatenation of crisis discourses put forward here is open to misunderstanding. The three crisis discourses centred on corresponding historically specific societal problems, it should be emphasised, do not form a logical sequence, as one might expect from Habermas' (1979) developmental-logical theory of social evolution, and hence do not stand in some necessary relation to one another. But rejecting Habermas' notion as being based on an untenable assumption, what has been called 'the ontogenetic fallacy' (Strydom 1992a), does not prevent one from recognising that such a concatenation is empirically justifiable in the case of the discourse of modernity providing the context for the construction of sociology. At the same time, it should also be pointed out that the above account does not imply that the societal problems on which the crisis discourses focus are mutually exclusive. Rather, they are coeval and hence coexist in all the historical periods, but through the constructive effect of discourse a particular one is given a special weighting and thus predominates over the others in a specific historical context. The question of nature, for instance, had already been present in the early modern period, yet it remained subordinated first to the political or constitutional question and secondly to the social question, only to be brought to the fore by the responsibility discourse in the late twentieth century. Likewise, even though the concern with risk and responsibility enjoys priority today, the older issues of violence and rights and of poverty and justice by no means disappear from the scene.[17] They remain relevant in a recontextualised form. This is abundantly clear from such contemporary concerns as 'technological citizenship' (Frankenfeld 1992; Zimmerman 1995) and 'environmental justice' (Perrolle 1993).

CHAPTER 5

Sociological Discourse Analysis

Context and Background

The outline of the sociological theory of discourse developed in the preceding two chapters has the purpose of preparing for the discourse analysis of the construction of sociology within the context of the discourse of modernity to be carried out in Part II of the book. The theoretical account given thus far already contains some methodologically relevant considerations, but before embarking on the proposed analysis it is necessary to elaborate independently on the methodology of discourse analysis adopted here. To do so in an intelligible way, it is necessary first to place this approach within the broader context of contemporary discourse analysis and to clarify its particular background.

Being informed by Habermas' theory of communicative action and discourse and entailing the introduction of some of Foucault's ideas to strengthen its concern with power, the discourse analysis represented in this book belongs most closely to the theoretical and research tradition of critical theory, particularly the philosophical and sociological space opened up by the second generation of critical theorists in Frankfurt, Habermas and Apel. It is therefore a form of discourse analysis in which emphasis is placed on critique as well as on the cognitive or, more fully, the socio-cognitive dimension. As such, however, it needs to be distinguished from a number of other varieties of discourse analysis that have been developed and applied more or less successfully in the past decade or so. Five different approaches are most directly relevant here.

Not only in France, but also in Germany and Britain, Foucault's impact on the conceptualisation of discourse analysis seems to outweigh that of every other author.[1] In all these cases, Foucault's concept of 'discursive formation' is taken on board, while he is nevertheless interpreted as having imbued his theory of discourse with a critical intent.[2] The work of Michel Pêcheux (1982;

1988) and his associates, representing the major tradition of discourse analysis in France, retains a dominant position for Foucault's theory of discourse, despite a shift of emphasis from Althusser's theory of ideology to a more text-oriented approach displaying the influence of Bakhtin's linguistic and literary theory. The predominant German tradition of discourse analysis, represented by Utz Maas (1989) on the one hand and Siegfried and Margreth Jäger (1993; 1996) on the other, exhibits an equally strong adherence to Foucault's conception of discourse. Although the British critical discourse analysts (Kress and Hodge 1979; Fowler 1991; Dant 1991; Fairclough 1995) apparently give somewhat less weight to the concept of discursive formations in an attempt to leave greater scope for a critical linguistic dissection of textual materials, Foucault is still able to make his presence remarkably strongly felt here. By contrast with the French, German and British traditions, Dutch critical discourse analysis represented by Teun van Dijk (1997, I, 1–34) has a cognitive focus in that it examines everyday talk and news coverage by means of a threefold model according to which social structures and discursive structures are mediated by individual and social cognition. The Austrian school of critical discourse analysis led by Ruth Wodak (Wodak et al. 1998) combines Bernstein's socio-linguistics, on the one hand, and Habermas' critique of formal linguistics and emphasis on communication barriers, on the other, with van Dijk's socio-cognitive concern with schemata for the production and reception of texts. Given the difficulties plaguing Foucault's theory of discourse reviewed previously, these latter two traditions of discourse analysis thus make theoretical assumptions that go well beyond the above-mentioned French, German and British varieties.

Finally, I wish to introduce the sociological tradition of American frame and discourse analysis. What is immediately apparent is that it differs from the Continental approaches in various respects. It was spearheaded by William Gamson (1988a; 1988b; 1992a; 1992b; Gamson and Modigliani 1987; 1989; Gamson and Stuart 1992) and applied and developed in social movement studies by Snow and his associates (Snow et al. 1986; Snow and Benford 1988; 1992) and lately also by Johnston (1995). Not only does this approach show little or no Continental influence, but it does not claim to be critical either. It is nevertheless instructive in so far as it develops symbolic interactionism by means of Goffman's (1986) concept of 'framing' in a direction that converges with the Dutch and Austrian – as well as of course Habermas' – concern with the cognitive dimension. In all these cases, therefore, it is possible to conceive of discourse with reference to what subjects bring about intersubjectively, although not entirely intentionally, through their action-based cognitive achievements. These approaches are thus able to avoid both the semiological-structuralist notion of context-free linguistic events or symbolic structures and the systems theoretical notion of a subjectless, non-intentional, rule-governed system of signs specialised in the function of control and domination.

Critical, Socio-Cognitivist, Public Discourse Analysis

The critical, socio-cognitivist approach to discourse analysis put forward in this book differs more or less sharply from the French, German and British as well as from the Dutch, Austrian and American traditions. In contradistinction to the French, German and British schools, the present approach gives priority to Habermas' theory of discourse. The reason for this option resides in Habermas' emphasis on the problematisation of and reflection on taken-for-granted assumptions as well as on the opening up, expansion and communicative sharing of the symbolic foundations of social action. Equally important is the critical intent of Habermas' theory of discourse, which is so often forgotten by critics who focus on his assumption that communication is basically informed by idealisations and who are typically unable to distinguish between philosophical and sociological arguments. An attempt is nevertheless made to incorporate Foucault, in addition to compensating for a certain weakness in Habermas' position, not only because critical theorists are seeking to build bridges between Habermas and Foucault, but also because the present author is working in the English-speaking world where the question of Habermas' relation to Foucault invariably arises.

Comparable to the Dutch, Austrian and American versions, the present approach to discourse analysis has a cognitive focus. This is apparent from its abiding concern with cognitive structures, schemata or frames that play a central role not only in the production and reception of culture but also in the structuring of identity and social action. It differs from the Dutch, Austrian and particularly the American traditions, however, in that this cognitive focus is deliberately cultivated and theoretically elaborated. Through the cognitive component of Habermas' work, it further links up with the rich and varied classical sociological tradition in both its European and American strands. This allows it to conceive of the cognitive dimension theoretically in a clearer and sharper way than the other approaches. In a characteristic move, it differentiates the structural sense of this dimension along cognitive (in the narrow sense) or intellectual, normative or moral, and aesthetic or conative lines. In addition, it regards this dimension as being manifested from the micro- to the macro-level and as dynamically developing along the diachronic axis. The approach adopted here accepts, like the Austrian school, that discourse is at one and the same time socially constitutive and socially constituted. While it also analyses texts according to these theoretical guidelines, it is willing to reduce discourse analysis neither to formal textual analysis, as in linguistics, nor to micro-discourse or frame analysis, as proposed by American authors (e.g. Johnston 1995). The present approach undertakes both frame and discourse analysis, each at its appropriate level. By contrast with the Americans, who plausibly focus the symbolic interactionist concern with the objective structures of situations by means of Goffman's cognitive predilection but stop short at the level of organised action systems, it pursues the matter right up to the macro-level, as Touraine (e.g. 1981; 1988) has insisted by way of his concept of 'totality' or 'cultural model'.[3] The present approach further observes the historical dimension of discursive practices – understood in a Habermasian (e.g. Eyerman and Jamison 1991) rather than in a Foucauldian sense – and follows the diachronic changes in discourse, comparable to the Austrian school's concern with a discourse-historical method, but unlike the latter it takes a stronger sociological view of discourse. This means that it is willing not merely to register such macro-effects of discourse as societal production and reproduction or formation and transformation, but to go beyond particular discursive arenas in everyday life, institutions, politics and the media focused on issues such as prejudice, racism and sexism in order to consider equally real manifestations of discourse on a societal macro-scale of long duration centred around more deep-seated issues.

The version of critical, socio-cognitivist, sociological public discourse analysis adopted for the purposes of this book is a development of a methodological approach first devised by Klaus Eder (1992a) at the beginning of the 1990s – what he refers to as 'a methodology for public discourse analysis' (Eder 1996, 166). Through Eder, who worked closely with Habermas during the 1970s and early 1980s in the Max Planck Institute in Starnberg, this approach has a direct connection with some central ideas of the eminent German author. Due to Habermas' cognitive emphasis, Eder also came to regard van Dijk's socio-cognitive contribution as an instructive way of methodologically operationalising discourse analysis. Through one of Eder's collaborators at the European University Institute in Florence, Paulo Donati (1992), who in turn studied with Gamson in the United States, the American concern with frame analysis became available for incorporation into this methodological development. The resulting sociological methodology of public discourse analysis was extensively applied in a sophisticated computer-based version to newspaper reports during the first half of the 1990s as part of a comparative study of the framing and communication of environmental problems in six European countries – Germany, Italy, Spain, France, Britain and Ireland (Eder et al. 1995; Eder 1996).[4]

For the purposes of the present study, this methodology is applied in a much broader socio-historical context than it had been used for originally. While it is employed for the close analysis of textual materials of various kinds, particularly in so far as it is aimed at the analysis of frames and their construction, its application is much less intensive than in the original case. Instead of the original computer-based version, a more traditional hermeneutical approach is adopted. Since the historical and societal scale of the analysis undertaken here ultimately requires a macroscopic concept of discourse, the present study engages in a stronger sense in macro-discourse analysis. Other differences between the original and the current conception concern the cognitive dimension and the critical orientation of the methodology. As regards the first, the cognitive dimension is emphasised more strongly and made more explicit in this book than in the original application,[5] and whereas the original application lacked a critical orientation, both the theoretical and methodological conception of the present study are expressly designed to highlight it. This, after all, is the sense of the incorporation of a modified Foucauldian concept of power into a Habermasian framework.

Methodological Assumptions

Discourse analysis in the sociological sense intended in this work is aimed at grasping the dynamic process of the construction of reality that takes place within the field opened up by a historically specific, structured or organised discourse. Discourse analysis thus serves the clarification of the discursive construction of reality. Its starting point is provided by a historically specific discourse that is in principle empirically identifiable. This discourse is understood as a phenomenon that coincides with the context of public communication or the public sphere. This means that it is taken to be located at the macro-level represented by society. As such, discourse is from a sociological point of view the ultimate condition of the social and cultural construction of reality. This reference to the macro-level is what gives discourse analysis its particular character and what entitles us to speak of discourse analysis in an emphatic sense. It is a macro-analysis that involves the decomposition and reconstruction of the relations among micro- and meso-phenomena by reference to a master frame.[6]

Since reality is both socially and culturally constructed within a discursive field, sociological discourse analysis is required to traverse two dimensions at one and the same time. Discourse analysts have these same two dimensions in mind when they characterise discourse, whether spoken or written, as a form of 'social practice' (Fairclough and Wodak 1997, 258; Wodak et al. 1998, 42).

The first dimension consists of the social processes by means of which reality is generated, particularly the discursive strategies of the social actors involved, and the second is made up of the semantics or texts by means of which reality is represented. In the case of the former, the analyst must dispose over some knowledge of the relevant historical events and the related collective actions, but of particular importance are the definitions of the situation and the strategies of the participants in the discourse. In the case of the latter, it is necessary to delve into the discursive contributions of the various actors, their ideas, statements and communications, which eventually compete and conflict with one another and thus come to form a discursive or textual reality structured by a macro- or master frame.

The analysis of the dual-level process of construction within its discursive field is carried out in terms of the cognitive structures or frames that are produced and reproduced in the course of the discourse. Starting from the discourse as context, and since there are three levels of cognitive structures, as argued earlier, the analysis moves from the micro-frame elements of the actors, through the meso-frames of their identities or the ideological streams to which they belong, to the macro- or master frame produced by and in turn structuring, directing and guiding the discourse. While discourse analysis is a form of macro-analysis proceeding by reference to a master frame, it is thus made up of frame analyses of different orders.[7] In contradistinction to frame analysis, however, discourse analysis[8] entails the more complex endeavour of analysing frames that have to such an extent become interrelated through communication that they form something like a text or what is here more often called semantics. It is only by going beyond frames as largely intentional constructions to discourse as an unintentional, emergent construction bringing into play objective structuring features of the situation that it is possible to grasp the unintended consequences of social action, to appreciate the reality of society, and to develop a critique of society.

Methodology

The discourse analytical methodology that emerges from these assumptions focuses on a discourse or discursive field in the sense of the structured context of the constructive activities of collective actors who produce and reproduce reality. This methodology provides the framework for the analysis of the construction of sociology within the context of the discourse of modernity in the remainder of this study. It can schematically be conceived as progressing through two phases that involve five distinct yet related steps. The first preliminary phase is designed to identify the historical dimension of discursive actions and to embed the discursive events in their proper historical context. The second phase represents the methodology of discourse analysis proper.

The first two closely interrelated steps that make up the first phase of the methodology to be followed here are intended to secure the stereoscopic orientation of the proposed sociological discourse analytical methodology. It establishes a link with the social processes and discursive practices generating reality, on the one hand, and with the semantic or textual representation of reality, on the other. The first step consists of the initial identification and circumscription of the object of analysis, namely a particular process of the cultural and social construction of reality. This step requires the isolation of significant historical events and the identification of social actors involved in and responding to them by way of discursive action. The second step calls for the location of the chosen object of analysis within its appropriate macro-conditional context. It entails the selection of the corresponding context of public communication or public sphere in which the historical events appear as topics of discussion and in which the social actors act and interact. This step eventuates in the identification of the appropriate discourse or discursive field.

These two initial methodological steps are not carried out in a systematic manner in this book. To fulfil the requirements of the first one, descriptive historical information is included throughout the chapters where appropriate with the aim of clarifying the significant historical events at the root of modern society and the collective actors who were involved in them. Since the subsequent analysis is confined to the construction of Enlightenment sociology, however, under the historical events are included only the Renaissance, the Reformation, and the democratic revolutions, such as the Revolt of the Netherlands, the English Revolution, the American War of Independence and the first phase of the French Revolution, as the historical conditions of early modern society. Among the most important collective actors who were involved in these various historical events were the aristocracy and monarchy, the church, the bourgeoisie, the humanists, the Reformers, the scientific movement and the Enlightenment. Besides information provided in the text itself about events and actors, recourse is taken to the inclusion of chronological tables (e.g. of the Dutch Revolt or the French Revolution) as well as of important historical documents (e.g. the *Declaration of Independence* of 1776 or the *Declaration of the Rights of Man and of the Citizen* of 1789). In addition to such descriptive information, remarks are also included where appropriate which are aimed first at placing the historical events and collective actors in the context of modernity, more particularly the discourse of modernity, and secondly at giving an indication of the emergence of sociological semantics from this context.

Theory of Discourse and Discourse Analysis

The remaining three steps constituting the second methodological phase of the proposed analysis, which will be carried out in a somewhat more systematic manner, concern the actual analysis of the selected discourse or discursive field as the context of the constructive process of interest. They are intimately related and consist of the analysis of the cognitive structures or frames involved in the discursively organised constructive process at the micro-, meso- and macro-levels respectively. These methodological steps direct and guide the analysis presented in Part II of the book concentrating on the discourse analysis of the construction of sociology. While the construction of sociology is placed within the general context of the discourse of modernity, the process is actually analysed only in one of the historically specific contexts provided by the three crisis discourses, namely the rights discourse. An analysis of the construction of sociology within the framework of the justice and responsibility discourses cannot be presented in the present book. In the case of the rights discourse, the analysis of the process of the discursive construction of sociology passes through all three of the methodological steps in question here – from the micro- and meso-level frame analysis to the macro-level discourse analysis.

The smallest units of discourse analysis are the cognitive structures by means of which social actors construct frames in the sense of building up definitions of the situation in which they find themselves and of the problem they are facing. These micro-frame elements are what Eder (1996, 167, 172–76), following Gamson, calls 'framing devices' in order to convey the fact that they make sense only in relation to constructive activity. They are the instruments or tools drawn from culture, as suggested by Swidler (1986), and used by actors to construct frames that can be communicated publicly. The first step in the second methodological phase consists of the analysis of these micro-units. It proceeds by analysing the intellectual, moral and aesthetic or conative cognitive structures by means of which actors conceptualise their world, behave in relation to it, and give meaning to it in order to arrive at an overall definition or frame. Although it is not possible rigorously to apply this methodological instrument to all the participants in the rights discourse presented in Chapter 7, a detailed analysis is carried out in Chapter 8 of a selection of major authors who had contributed to the construction of sociology in the early modern period, including Thomas More, Thomas Hobbes, Giambattista Vico, Montesquieu, Adam Ferguson and John Millar.

The next step in discourse analysis involves a shift from the micro- to the meso-level with a view to analysing middle-range cognitive structures and their insertion into public communication. The focal concern here is thus communicative or, at least, communicable cognitive structures. Important from an analytical point of view is the way in which actors put together the different frame elements in a symbolic form, Eder's (1996, 168, 177–80) Gamsonian 'symbolic packages', typically embedded in a narrative. Then the question is how such forms are used as framing strategies by collective actors to communicate their peculiar frames and hence identities, thereby distinguishing themselves from others. For example, here it would be crucial first to identify the ideological variants making sense within the confines of the rights frame and represented by different actors in the early modern discourse. Most important among them are the absolutist ideology of monarchical sovereignty or later enlightened despotism, the republican ideology of virtuous civic moralism, and the constitutionalist ideology of conflict, contestation and the balance of powers. In the second instance, it would be necessary to establish the precise variant with which the identity of each of our major authors is associated. As will become apparent, frame analysis of this kind is essential to correct the inadequacies of previous far too rough and undifferentiated analyses. Most important in this respect is what is customarily and, indeed, quite indiscriminately called the Enlightenment.

Macro-level discourse analysis, or what Eder (1996, 169) calls 'public discourse analysis', the final methodological step, presupposes that a number of collective actors have obtained identities through the communication of their particular meso-frames in the public domain and that they got entangled in competition and conflict through the communicative exchange of their frames. The competition and conflict of the collective actors through their frames take place before the eyes of the public, who evaluate and thus either support some frames, turn against others or compel the alignment of a number of them. Over and above the intentional construction of frames by collective actors, the public context, which represents a new level of contingency (Strydom 1999a), introduces an unintentional reality beyond the reach and control of any of the actors. It constitutes a process of selection in which some frames are eliminated, others subordinated or assimilated, and still another emerges victorious as the master frame. In the case of the rights discourse, the period between 1572 and 1640 is of great interest as it represents the critical turning point that allowed the transition between its two major phases, during which the shift from religion to politics occurred and the rights frame became unequivocally established. As such, it is comparable to the third quarter of the nineteenth century and the 1980s when the justice frame and the responsibility frame respectively became established on the basis of macro-level processes of frame competition and selection.

As regards the actual analysis, the collectively binding master frame emerging from the discourse is obviously central to discourse analysis at the macro-level. Yet the dynamics or competition of frames that on the one hand produces it and on the other is reproduced by it claims most of the analytical attention. In Chapter 7, dealing with the rights discourse, attention is given to the rights frame per se as well as the varied dynamics leading up to and deriving from it. Presupposing the twofold phase-structure of the rights discourse and the establishment of its master frame, the emphasis in the analysis of Enlightenment sociology in Chapters 8 and 9 is more on the dynamics as it affects the construction process. What this involves becomes clear when one recognises that frames are mediated through any of a number of different language-based media of communication providing a foothold for power. While frames are made up of structures filled with cultural or symbolic content carried by verbal, typographical and electronic media, it is the case that culture or symbols, as Foucault insists,[9] are themselves saturated with power. This means that the discursive dynamics or competition of frames consists not only of ideological struggles over the control of frames, but, in so far as frames imply command over any of a range of resources such as money, political support, or public concern (Dietz et al. 1989), also legitimation struggles. The argumentative, cultural or symbolic logic of discourse, which determines whether and how convincing or compelling frames are to the public because of their consistency and coherence, intertwines with the logic of power of discourse which determines whether and what amount of compelling force is accumulated and wielded by frames.[10] A proleptic example involving a whole sequence of shifts can be given. Whereas the concept of society, supported by the nascent rights frame, first arose in opposition to the absolutist state, the representatives of the *ancien régime* were able to appropriate it on the basis of their spectacular and resource-rich court-based culture, yet in the wake of identity formation and collective mobilisation in the Netherlands, England, the American Colonies and France made possible by the established rights frame, a definitive differentiation between society and state was introduced in the eighteenth century. That society successfully established itself in the medium of the rights discourse does not diminish the fact, however, that it involved both the suppression of radical movements of relatively deprived men and the exclusion of women who nevertheless were constitutive of it.

The relationship among the three steps comprising the second methodological phase of discourse analysis is, at least by implication, the object of much disagreement in the social sciences.[11] What is largely overlooked, paradoxically, is that it is precisely here that one of the most significant examples of contemporary theoretical and methodological advancement is to be found. The sense in which this relationship is understood here allows the privileging neither of macro-phenomena nor of micro-phenomena as *explanans* of their opposite. It rather consists of the genetic-structuralist or constructivist-structuralist insight that, while a discursively established, collectively valid macro- or master frame is a product of constructive activities at the micro- and meso-levels, features of actors or events located at the micro- and meso-levels only admit of being constructed as socially significant phenomena at the macro-level through communication and discourse structured by a master frame. The latter three methodological steps therefore stand in a much more complicated dialectical relation to one another than the sequential presentation would at first sight lead one to believe.[12]

Constructivism and Critique

The theoretically informed methodology outlined above has been designed for the purposes of an analysis of the discursive construction of sociology in the early modern period to be presented in Part II. As is apparent from the emphasis on constructive activities and processes within the context of the discourse of modernity, this discourse analytical methodology is assumed to be in accordance with the constructivist epistemology adopted for the purposes of this book. The critical, socio-cognitivist, public discourse analytical method-ology, in other words, is at the same time also of a constructivist kind. This obviously requires some clarification. But there is still more. Since traditional or conventional concepts of critique are not easily reconcilable with construc-tivism, the question arises as to the precise sense in which this methodology can be said to be critical. Let us take these two issues in turn.[13]

The central position given to the cognitive dimension in the methodology developed in this chapter may lead the reader to suspect that the basic concern of the analysis is with social actors and cognitive action competences. On the contrary, however, discourse analysis as accepted here is understood to focus on the relational setting or structured situation within which actors find themselves and within which their actions take their course.[14] The theory of discourse informing this methodology is taken to make available a situation theoretic model, the model of a structured situation, which is both relational and structure-oriented. While it takes a plurality of actors, value-orientations, motives, rational calculations and actions into account, it proceeds from the assumption that there are structuring factors or rules operative in social situations which coordinate action events independently of the motives, intentions and goals of the actors. Such objective situational structures can be linked to what are variously called 'frames' (Goffman 1986), 'cultural models' (Touraine 1981; 1988), 'classificatory schemes' (Bourdieu 1986), 'social repre-sentations' (Moscovici 1982b), 'symbolic codes' (Giesen 1991b, 13) or 'cultural codes' (Eder and Schmidtke 1998, 428), the structuring force of which is reproduced in social situations through communication.

Social action that makes a difference depends for its effect not on the subjective meanings, intentions or goals of the actors involved but rather on being objectively defined in the social situation as significant action. The constructive context provided by the relational setting or structured situation creates a web of relations that makes it possible for those observing the actors involved and commenting on them to make a decisive contribution to the definition of the meaning of their actions. This context takes the form of public communication or discourse. The actors and observers are all components of this public domain, and these components are all related to each other through the communication that takes place within that context. This occurs by being made a medium of communication or being thematised and thus being coordinated with one another. A characteristic effect of this tendency, which helps to account for the crucial role played by the public, is that in proportion as actions and relations are coordinated by communication, power becomes dependent on the acceptance of definitions of reality (Eder 1993a, 12). The more communication becomes the mechanism of coordination, the more power accrues to the public, who are in the most propitious position to accept or reject the meanings communicated by the participants and thus to fix the collectively accepted definition of reality. What is collectively accepted, however, is a consensus only in the ideal case. The frames that are communicated, struggled over and finally accepted are shot through with power, with the result that what is collectively accepted amounts to a significant degree to a dominant definition of reality, what was earlier called a macro-frame. Although it is the case, as Habermas (1979) and Apel (1976) plausibly maintain from a philosophical point of view, that a final consensus is necessarily and unavoidably presupposed, communication processes or discourse cannot be sociologically analysed directly and exclusively in terms of such a consensus. Neither the participants nor even the observing public, who have the power to define the meaning of the actions of the participants, know beforehand what the final collectively accepted agreement will be (Miller 1992, 15–6). The fact that the observing public is itself divided into competing counter-publics (Fraser 1997, 75) or into supporters, sympathisers, opponents and bystanders (Neidhardt and Rucht 1991, 457) exacerbates this condition of indeterminacy and uncertainty. The definition of reality that is eventually accepted in the wake of an observed process of communication and struggle over meanings, which overcomes this indeterminacy and uncertainty, is a construction achieved not only by the participants but in particular also by their audience, the observing public.

Having clarified the sense in which the proposed discourse analytical methodology relates to constructivism, we now come to the question of critique. According to Habermas, critique is possible only on the basis of a normative reference point provided by the validity dimension of the organisation of society. Rather than regarding it as an ideal opposed to reality, as he did in his earlier writings, he now sees such normative import, in the sense of existing reason, as being partially inscribed in ongoing social practices (Habermas 1996, 287–88). While such a normative reference point is philosophically to be found in the aspiration to objectivity and impartiality, Habermas (1998, 98) therefore also locates it within society itself. It is the moral point of view embodied in those social movements that engage in a critique of modern society.

By contrast with this proposal by Habermas, it should be pointed out that constructivism, by its very nature, forbids the social scientist to adopt an identificatory procedure. It requires that the whole plural range of participants relevant to a given constructive context be taken into account without any tendency to favour one and hence to identify with it. To do so would be to subvert the very constructivist perspective that the social scientist claims to be upholding. It would be tantamount to taking a legitimationist rather than a constructivist position.[15] Taking a legitimationist position, the social scientist identifies with the intentions, goals, values and identity of one of the participants and interprets the constructive process in terms of the normative code preferred and communicated by that participant, rather than standing back to consider the dynamic interplay of the normative codes of all the participants within their common setting and the outcome of this dynamic as settled by what is eventually collectively accepted. The demands of constructivism, however, are very different. Although the social scientist might tend to want to identify with a social movement struggling for a worthy cause, in the constructivist perspective the movement is only one among a plurality of participants all of whom warrant equal attention. Constructivism even requires that disagreeable social agents be included in social scientific research. From a constructivist point of view, the moral point of view or the normative reference point making critique possible admits neither of being projected beyond society nor of being tied to any one social actor or agent. It is rather treated as forming part of and being carried by the communicative or discursive process. The normative reference that serves as the foundation of critique is thus to be located in the objective features structuring the situation within which the different communication partners or discourse participants relate to one another.

Although constructivism operates at a certain distance from the participants, this approach is not simply morally neutral or devoid of any normative foundation for critique. Rather than maintaining an immediate relation with a transcendent normative standard, as though the social scientist knows what ought to be the case, it is a more indirect approach. Given the nature of language and communication, a constructivist analysis undeniably presupposes by pragmatic necessity a reference to an indefinite and unlimited community, but its more immediate concern is the public. From this it seeks to grasp what is collectively accepted in the particular situation. This neither entails measuring existing reality against a necessary and unavoidable presupposition stylised as a normative standard, nor identifying with a particular point of view that is immanent in the situation. The adoption of a transcendent normative standard tends to cast theory and analysis in the form of abstract moralisation, i.e. stating what ought to be and pointing out that reality does not measure up to this standard. The constructivist approach, by contrast, is more concerned with locating starting points for a new constructive learning process that could possibly move in the direction of an unlimited and indefinite public. This requires that the normative codes or frames of all the participants, not just that of a preferred one, be investigated as possible presuppositions for furthering constructive learning. By singling out a social movement, for instance, and linking a normative standard to it, one not only identifies with the movement but also renders any critique of it impossible. What one effectively does in such a case is to engage in a form of partial or partisan moralisation in terms of an unreflexive epistemology of conviction.[16] Instead, all the participants, social movements included, must be subjected to a critique that focuses on the particular illusion that each entertains in its strategic communication in relation to the other participants. Constructivism neither merely holds up the picture of a transcendent normative standard to the participants so that they can begin to appreciate how far short their own ideals fall, as does the moral philosopher, nor does it simply adopt the point of view of a particular social actor as its normative standard, as does the partisan social scientist who holds to an epistemology of conviction. The constructivist sociologist, by contrast, seeks out the illusory side of the ideals projected in the situation in order to expose the errors that need to be corrected. The aim pursued here is critique in the sense of the uncovering and exposure of illusory ideals about reality and their effects on what becomes collectively accepted in the course of public communication within a particular situation.[17] What becomes collectively accepted is, in turn, only a particular cross-section of a range of competing, contradictory and conflicting cultural models that is itself open to critique.

PART II

Discourse of Modernity and the Construction of Sociology

Introduction: Crisis Discourse
and Sociology

The aim of Part II is to develop, at least in a first outline, an analysis of the construction of sociology within the context of the discourse of modernity.

The discourse of modernity emerged in the sixteenth century against the background of the breakdown of the medieval feudal order and the religious-metaphysical worldview. It was a response to the failure of the understanding of reality taken for granted until then to provide a shared stock of cultural and social assumptions on the basis of which people could orient themselves and justify their activities. The discourse addressed the general problem of the loss of common foundations and the need to come to terms with the new historical situation that emerged as a consequence. At issue in it were matters such as moral action and social bonds and the need on the part of the people of the time to organise their own lives and relations in a conscious way. The appearance of the discourse of modernity coincided with the emergence of reflexivity, with the growing awareness that, far from being fixed beforehand as unchangeable, all the constituent elements of social relations and their organisation could be different and indeed are open to challenge. All the constituent elements of society are related to one another in and through communication, and by way of discourse any of these components could be thematised and even be problematised with a view to changing it. Rather than problematising everything all at once, however, the discourse of modernity since this reflexive turn provided the context for addressing the general problem of how society could be constituted and how its different elements or dimensions could be brought into relation with one another, be rendered mutually compatible, reconciled and consolidated so as to form a discursively justifiable societal arrangement. How could different communities with their own particular identities and different social actors pursuing competing yet legitimate interests be brought together, and around which common principle of social identification could this be achieved, if not by agreement then at least by rational disagreement? Most pressing was the issue of how to bring society into being, how to organise it, and what collective social and political action was required to push it through. Since the sixteenth century with the emergence of conditions of a reflexive relation to society, the discourse of modernity has taken its course as the field in which constituent elements, components or dimensions of modern society are thematised and problematised with a view to resolving, at least for the time being, the general problem of its creation and organisation.

The general problem of the creation and organisation of modern society takes on a different, historically specific form in each epoch. What is remarkable about European or Western modern society, however, is that as early as the sixteenth century there had already been a failure to find an adequate solution to this problem. In spite of an astonishing and most promising development in the cognitive order, the collective political action necessary to find a common definition of the problem under historically specific conditions, as well as measures or institutional arrangements to resolve it, was impeded. The result was that modern society was incapable of regulating the course and direction of its own development. The problem assumed crisis proportions, and the discourse of modernity acquired the form of a historically specific crisis discourse. Ever since the early modern period, through the consequent pathogenesis of modernity, the discourse of modernity has taken its course in the form of a crisis discourse. Considering the macro-level of historically specific societal problems collectively identified and defined in the course of the discourse of modernity, it may be submitted, as was done earlier, that there are three crisis discourses: discourses generated by communication about the problem of violence, about the problem of poverty, and finally about the problem of nature. If one takes cues from the cognitive frames that emerged from these discourses and in turn gave coherence and consistency to them, they may more properly be referred to as the rights discourse, the justice discourse, and the responsibility discourse.

Discourse Analysis of Enlightenment Sociology

In the four chapters that make up Part II of this book, the construction of sociology is investigated within the context of the discourse of modernity with special reference to the first of the three crisis discourses producing and reproducing it. Chapters 6 and 7 are devoted to a presentation and analysis of the early modern rights discourse, centred on the problem of violence, that covered the period from the sixteenth to the late eighteenth century. Chapter 6 opens the analysis with the identification of some historical starting points for the perception of the problem of violence as a societal problem and its shifting into the issue of the survival of society in its political environment. Of central importance in this context is the early modern state, particularly the absolutist state, but neither early capitalism nor religion can be excluded. The rights discourse generated by the Europe-wide debates about violence and the political survival of society is then presented in Chapter 7. To make intelligible the identity formation, collective mobilisation and institutional innovation rendered possible by the discourse, brief consideration is given to such crucial historical events as the Revolt of the Netherlands against Spanish absolutism and the English Revolution as well as the American War of Independence and the French Revolution.

The clarification of the rights discourse achieved by these analyses, although not much more than an outline, is sufficient to provide a context for the discourse analysis of the discursive construction of sociology in its initial form, the sociology of the Enlightenment, in the next two chapters. Chapter 8 consists of an analysis of the constructive steps represented by early authors such as Thomas More, Thomas Hobbes and Giambattista Vico and later Enlightenment *philosophes* such as Montesquieu, Ferguson and Millar. The construction of Enlightenment sociology by the incorporation of these discursive contributions into a macro-level discourse is analysed in Chapter 9. Here the implications of the theoretical innovation of emphasising construction through public communication in a historically specific discourse become apparent.

The conclusion, Chapter 10, is devoted to an attempt to draw out some of the implications of the preceding analysis for a more precise grasp of the crisis of early modern society and hence the basis of the pathogenesis of modern society. This provides the opportunity to clarify the sense in which sociology can be said to be a critique of modernity and, by extension, to consider the relation between social theory and political theory. This latter aspect is of much importance. It allows a link to be established between Enlightenment sociology and contemporary sociology which is not only embattled because of its past relation to the theory of progress and the philosophy of history, but also in need of reconstituting itself and finding a new way of legitimising its knowledge. As is suggested by the approach adopted in this analysis, I am convinced that sociology will be able to renew itself only if it grasps its relation to public practical discourse and, accordingly, recognises its public role, its role in public communication or discourse.

CHAPTER 6

The Early Modern Problem of Violence

Communication and the Monopolisation of Force

Whether one investigates primary sources, intellectual products or works of art from the early modern period, or whether one reads secondary materials about it, the most striking feature is the perception of violence by the early moderns as the predominant problem of the time. Although violence can be assumed historically to have been ubiquitous, it had not always been perceived as a problem. Under the conditions of the warrior society of the feudal period, violence had not been made and, in fact, could not have been made into the widely recognised problem it became in the early modern period. This is attributable to at least two factors. On the one hand, a worldview had still been in place here that precluded violence from being addressed as a problem; on the other, the social strata had still been so isolated that they were incapable of communicating and thus playing conflicting forms of thought and experience off against one another (Mannheim 1972, 5–11; Giesecke 1992, 74–76). Given the nature of feudalism, a discourse about the problem of violence was simply not a possibility. In addition to this, however, a starting point for the construction of violence as a problem did not exist under these conditions. This is the case, paradoxically, because of the fact that violence in a crude and undifferentiated form pervaded the whole complex of feudal relations. In the struggles of the feudal lords against one another, physical and non-physical forms of military and economic violence were not only present in the relationship of warrior to warrior, but also combined to shape both the social and psychological structure (Elias 1982, 150–51, 235–37, 261). With the warrior nobility locked in mutual struggles, feudal relations were continually under the threat of the sudden irruption of direct physical violence. Violence was personalised, part of everyday life and omnipresent.

It was only once communication had penetrated the whole of society, so that different interpretations could be publicly aired (Mannheim 1972; Habermas 1979; Hill 1992; Giesecke 1992, 77), and once the use of force had become circumscribed and controlled, that violence could be perceived as a problem and be made into an issue. Both of these conditions started to apply at the beginning of the modern period. First, the religious-metaphysical world-view collapsed and the clergy lost its monopolistic control over intellectual matters and, hence, over the official interpretation of the world. As a result, a free intelligentsia deriving from different social strata emerged who produced different and even conflicting interpretations that competed with one another for the favour of various public groups. Among this intelligentsia were the humanists, who were the first authors to address their work to a broad and increasingly anonymous public (Hauser 1951, II, 79, 81),[1] and, succeeding them, the representatives of the scientific movement, all of whom were in search of the so-called 'New Science' (Van den Daele 1977).[2] At this very point, secondly, the long-term process of the formation of the state, which in the seventeenth century culminated in the absolutist state as the first form of the modern state, had reached a stage where it was able to monopolise both the means of physical force and financial resources in the form of taxation and thus to pacify a large population within a particular territory (Elias 1982, 235–40).[3] Physical force was monopolised in the sense that arms and armed men were forged into an army (and, important in Europe, a navy) placed under a single authority which regulated the use of violence in a calculated and controlled way. This is what is known as the 'Military Revolution' of early modern times (Mann 1987, 453–58). Concurrently, the rest of the population was compelled to move into pacified social spaces and to forestall or restrain their own use of force through foresight and reflection. The fact that violence was now more or less clearly circumscribed, so that its unauthorised or unjustifiable use could become visible, provided the condition for it to be perceived as a problem and to be made into a publicly relevant issue.

In early modern Europe, the opportunities for perceiving violence as a problem and making it into a publicly relevant issue multiplied exponentially. The long-term process of the monopolisation of force by the state ran parallel to and intertwined with the equally protracted process of the development of capitalism which, in the crucible of mercantilism, at this stage took the violent form of what Marx (1977, 667) discussed under the title of 'the so-called primitive accumulation of capital'. At the same time, the Reformation and subsequent Wars of Religion provided a historically concrete, socio-political context characterised by an extraordinary degree of conflict and violence within which these developments obtained a further impetus and became linked. Both the state and capitalism as well as the Reformers and Counter-Reformers generated violence, and each of these social agents regarded the violence of the other as a threat or imposition that could be countered or mastered only by violence. Not only was violence perceived as an all-pervasive problem in the early modern period, but it was also constructed as a societally significant issue from different points of view and in varying yet frequently overlapping contexts.

In the following, it will not be possible to trace in detail the changes from historical situation to historical situation in terms of the resulting rather complex configuration of relations made up of the monarchy or state, its loyal and critical supporters, and the moderate and radical opposition. The major starting points for the perception of violence as a problem and its construction as a societal issue in the early modern period will be identified and then, in the next chapter, the emergence of the rights discourse from the Europe-wide debates about violence will be reconstructed in outline with reference to a selection of central historical reference points. The general framework within which the starting points of violence communication are identified relates to the broad range of changes and conflicts connected with the large-scale disintegration of medieval feudalism and the transition to modern society. These changes first began visibly to assert themselves in the incredibly fecund and dynamic decades around the year 1500, associated with the Renaissance,[4] and then in the mid-sixteenth century eventuated in what has been called 'the crisis of the Renaissance' (Hauser 1979, 6–11, 23–43),[5] which in turn marks the beginning of the so-called 'general crisis' of the seventeenth century (Hobsbawm 1954; Aston 1980; Rabb 1975; Maravall 1986). The framework in question embraces at least five dimensions:

(1) economically, new financial and mercantile capitalistic practices, increasing trade connected with the age of discovery and overseas expansion, and soaring prices;

(2) demographically, a sharp rise in the population from approximately 55 million in 1450 to 100 million in 1600 (Braudel 1985, I, 46–47);[6]

(3) politically, the centralisation of power and the emergence of the Renaissance absolutist monarchies and states, and – starting with the Italian wars in the late fifteenth century – endemic unrest and conflict at international level;

(4) socially, a new fluidity and mobility in social relations due to the breakdown of village life and the ties of traditional localisation; and

(5) culturally, the breakdown of the religious-metaphysical worldview and the stimulation of the dynamics of culture through the revitalisation of the

classical heritage, on the one hand, and innovation in the intellectual (e.g. science), artistic (e.g. mannerism), and religious and legal (e.g. universalistic moral principles) domains, on the other.

Capitalist Violence

The perception and collective definition of the problem of violence in the early modern period obtained a foothold not only in developments centred on concerns such as religion and the monarchy brought to the fore by the collapse of the traditional ecclesiastical and feudal order. A strong dynamic force such as capitalism[7] likewise served as a vehicle of events and processes that provided a starting point for the construction of violence as a serious societal problem. One of the most important aspects of capitalism from the early modern period which directly raised the problem of violence is the phenomenon of so-called 'enclosures' discussed by writers from Thomas More (1989, 18–20) through Karl Marx (1977, 671–85) to Barrington Moore (1987, 9–29). To this internal aspect may be added a second external aspect of the more general phenomenon of the 'primitive accumulation of capital' (Marx 1977, 667), namely overseas expansion, conquest, imperialism and colonialism.

The enclosure was the major mechanism by means of which big landowners and large tenant farmers in the early modern period brought about a basic structural change which led to the commercialisation of agriculture. In its classical form it was unique to Britain, but in some guise or another it also made its appearance on the Continent. Marx (1977, 671) described the enclosure movement formally as the 'expropriation of the agricultural population from the land', and his predecessor Thomas More (1989, 18–19) conjured up the graphic image of 'sheep...that...have become so greedy and fierce that they devour men themselves'. Through the application of legal and semi-legal methods, landlords deprived peasants of their rights to use common lands for agricultural purposes, and forcibly cleared manors, estates and cottages of the resultant surplus population. Once this had been done, they were then free to encroach upon those lands and to consolidate them into privately owned commercial sheep walks oriented towards the export wool trade.

In Marx's (1977, 669) judgement, the forcible tearing and sweeping of masses of peasants from the soil, which was essentially the divorcing of the producer from the means of production, formed the basis of the process of the primitive accumulation of capital, which in a historically significant manner prepared the way for the establishment of the modern capitalist economic system. As it entailed 'massive violence exercised by the upper classes against the lower' (Moore 1987, 29) over an expended period, the 'shameless violation of feudal rights' by way of the 'grossest acts of violence' (Marx 1977, 680), it does not constitute an overstatement to submit that the history of the enclosure movement, as of primitive accumulation more generally, is written 'in letters of blood and fire' (Marx 1977, 669). The extent to which this is true of the external aspect of primitive accumulation can be demonstrated by an endless series of examples drawn from the history of the age of exploration and discovery and the subsequent colonialist and imperialist policies and practices of the European states. Hernán Cortes' conquest and genocide of the Aztecs in 1521, Francisco Pizarro's destruction of the Inca civilisation a decade later, and the transatlantic slave trade – the biggest enforced emigration in history – are only some of the most graphic of these examples.[8]

At least in its earlier phases, the process of the primitive accumulation of capital indicated by these examples in turn presupposed the formation and functioning of the early modern state or, more generally, the characteristic yet variable set of political and institutional arrangements that arose in sixteenth-century Renaissance Europe and marked the institutional beginning of the modern period.[9]

Absolutist Violence

Since the end of the Middle Ages, as Norbert Elias (1982) has shown,[10] a process of the consolidation of royal power through the monopolisation of military, financial and administrative resources and the pacification of a territory has gradually taken its course and eventually culminated in the absolutist state. The states of France, England and Spain had been the first to become established. During the sixteenth and early seventeenth century, Spain had been the most powerful yet its place was soon taken by France, only to be rivalled and surpassed by England. In fact, three different types of the early modern state can be distinguished (Williams 1988, 34): the strong version combining absolutist monarchy and corporative institutions, as in France, Spain, Austria and Prussia, and the two weaker versions of absolutist monarchy without corporative institutions in Russia, and of corporative institutions with constitutional rather than absolutist monarchy in England and the Netherlands.[11] The absolutist state, as Giddens (1987a, 83–103) has shown, is nevertheless a novel political order distinct from the preceding traditional state as well as, it may be added, from the later modern nation-state.

At a crucial juncture, the religious conflicts and ideological confrontations following in the wake of the Reformation made a decisive contribution to this process by strengthening monarchical power and preparing the ground for the establishment of a system of absolutist states and, more generally, the consolidation of the *ancien régime* or old order.[12] In the wake of the Reformation's shattering of the religious and ideological unity of Christendom based on the ideas of *Societas Christiana* and universal empire, a fundamental rift, roughly marked by the Alps, appeared in Europe. The forces of the Counter-Reformation initially sought a reunification by means of the Holy Roman Empire under the Hapsburg Emperor, Charles V, but it soon became apparent that the establishment of a whole series of territorially based yet often ethnically diverse states, assisted by the fragmentation of Protestantism, made a reconstituted Roman Catholic Europe impossible. In fact, Europe as it had existed up till then in the guise of Christendom at this point made way for Europe in the modern sense of the word (Delanty 1995a, 66–69; 1995b). Both inter-state relations and intra-state relations provided an impetus for the Europe-wide establishment of absolutism. On the one hand, the Wars of Religion enforced an alliance between church and state in both Protestant and Catholic countries, as reflected by the so-called confessionalisation of the state (Schilling 1991), which nurtured the consolidation of centralised government authority and hence the emergence of sovereign territorial-confessional states. On the other hand, problems were experienced within both Protestant and Catholic states as a consequence of a discrepancy between territorial organisation and ethnic or confessional diversity which could be solved only by the introduction of a centralised state capable of monopolising, among other things, legitimate force. In the majority of cases, despite examples of religious toleration, this development was accompanied by political authoritarianism. The Catholic countries spearheading the Counter-Reformation in particular placed a high premium on orthodoxy and authoritarianism, and correspondingly exhibited a defensive reaction against the extension of popular political participation and citizenship. The absolutism that resulted from these diverse external and internal pressures and, as a result, was predisposed toward war and repression, was captured in the writings of authors of different persuasions such as Jean Bodin, John Calvin, and Thomas Hobbes.

Agreements such as the Peace of Augsburg of 1555, the Edict of Nantes of 1598, the Peace of Westphalia of 1648, the Stuart Restoration in 1660 and the Glorious Revolution of 1688, all in varying degrees ensured religious peace by consolidating political sovereignty. Particularly, the congress of Westphalia, which brought the first European war – the Thirty Years War – to a peaceful conclusion and thus in effect took the form of the first European meeting (Parker 1990, 281–93),[13] proved to be decisive for the consolidation of absolutism. A whole series of treaties involving virtually all the European states was negotiated to distribute territorial state authority and regulate relations among them. Not only was the legitimacy of individual states acknowledged in terms of the new concept of sovereignty, but an overarching inter-state framework, the European system of states, which mitigated the volatile spontaneous relation between states, was established at the same time. In writing his well-known book on the *ancien régime* in Europe, the English historian E. N. Williams (1988) was therefore able to start his account in 1648 – perhaps the most significant date in the political development of early modern Europe at the institutional level.[14]

Once this stage had been reached, once it had successfully monopolised all legitimate force on the basis of the already achieved level of military, fiscal and administrative centralisation and the modern concept of sovereignty, the abso-lutist state set about the task of centralising and expanding the administrative apparatus. This involved the development of an officialdom as well as a sur-veillance and repressive apparatus, the rationalisation of fiscal management, the tax system and revenue collection, linking up with regional and local government, and the development of both the formulation and the application of law (e.g. Giddens 1987a, 93–103). Central to the consolidation of a central administration was the monopolising of all knowledge production (Van den Daele 1977; Mandrou 1978, 213–27, 259–65, 273; Eder 1988, 207), particu-larly knowledge important to the newly developing institutional arrangements and thus having a bearing on the future (Koselleck 1989, 26–27). It is this systematic regulation and control of knowledge in the absolutist state, accord-ing to Eder (1988, 100, 206–07), that provided the starting point for the characteristically modern attempt to civilise power by making it communicatively manageable as well as, to be sure, the equally characteristic excessive resort to power when this fails.

One way of highlighting the different starting points that the early modern state provided for the perception of violence as a problem is to consider somewhat more closely certain institutional features of the new centralised monarchical states of the time.

Militarism and Warfare

The absolutist state, as Karl Mannheim (1993, 500) showed and Perry Anderson (1980, 15–42) later again affirmed, was the perpetuation in a new political form of the class-domination of the land-owning aristocracy that had existed under feudalism. The absolutist monarchies indeed introduced modern features, such as a standing army, a permanent bureaucracy, diplomacy, national taxation, codified law, trade and a market, which led Marx to think that the absolutist state was a bourgeois phenomenon. Yet these Renaissance states remained feudal at bottom, as is attested by the retention of and emphasis on a range of typically aristocratic concerns. Conspicuous among these are the centralisation of power, the consolidation of property in land, *imperium* in the sense of a drive towards expansion and universal domination, and – Trevor-Roper (1980) would add – outrageously extravagant and exhibitionist courts. All of these were underpinned by a subterranean yet characteristically aristocratic archaic rationality: violence and bellicism, an emphasis on the necessity and profitability of constantly acting forcefully, even aggressively, and engaging in warfare (Anderson 1980, 32, 37).[15]

Of the institutional features of the absolutist state, the army, bureaucracy and trade are particularly relevant from the current perspective. The professional, administratively well organised and disciplined army made its appearance for the first time in the context of the absolutist state (Anderson 1980, 29–33; Giddens 1987a, 103–16).[16] Approximately a century after its establishment, its numbers exceeded a quarter of a million men, as in the case of the Spanish army, and at the beginning of the eighteenth century approached half a million men, as in the case of the French army (Giddens 1987a, 109). What is remarkable about the Renaissance state army, however, is that it fulfilled the same function as it did in feudal times for the dominant aristocratic class (Anderson 1980, 31). To supplement the low level of agricultural productivity and trade, it was used for the maximisation of wealth by territorial invasions and conquests. Territory had been the object of aristocratic rule and warfare under feudalism and it remained so in the early modern period. It is unsurprising to find, therefore, that under absolutism different aristocratic dynasties were virtually permanently engaged in armed conflict and warfare. At most twenty-five years in the sixteenth century and seven years in the seventeenth century did not witness large-scale military operations or major wars in Europe (Anderson 1980, 33).

During the early modern period, war proved to be the major mechanism by means of which power was centralised and consolidated. This is clear from the centrality and development of the taxation regime and its associated bureaucratic infrastructure. Tax was collected mainly to maintain the army and to finance warfare, while the necessary bureaucratic machinery, which was developed between the sixteenth and eighteenth centuries, played a unifying role presupposed by the modern nation-state. The first regular territory-wide tax to be imposed in France in the mid-fifteenth century was designed to finance the first permanent military units in Europe (Anderson 1980, 32). As the absolutist army grew and its commitments increased, the demand for military expenditure as a proportion of state revenue shot up dramatically. The mid-sixteenth century saw the Spanish army consuming a massive 75 per cent of state revenues, and a century later this amounted to 80 per cent in France (Anderson 1980, 32–33).[17] In order to mobilise the required revenues and other resources, the state had to acquire the capacity to extract resources from its subject population by developing an appropriate bureaucratic as well as coercive infrastructure (Tilly 1975, 42; Held 1992, 95). Of overwhelming importance from the point of view of the population were the demands made on them in the course of the process of resource extraction. As the exaction mounted and the controls tightened, virtually every section of the population was affected, yet the burden was very unevenly spread. At one end of the social scale, the nobility had some reason to object to royal centralisation and increased taxation, to manipulate restive social groups below them to protest, to register insubordination or even to attempt rebellion themselves, as for example the *Frondes* (1648–53) in France. At the other end, the majority of the population of the absolutist states, the artisans, labourers, domestic servants and innumerable peasants, were permanently weighed down by the burden of taxation.

The fact that the absolutist state had been designed to pursue bellicose intentions externally or internationally, however, did not mean that internal pacification was achieved in the smooth complementary way that Elias' (1982)[18] formal evolutionary model seems to suggest. The army was extensively used for these internal purposes, too. One of the most characteristic features of the army of the absolutist state, the mercenary element (Kiernan 1980; Anderson 1980, 30), facilitated the fulfilment of this particular function. Unlike the later national conscript force, the army of the absolutist state was a mixed force in which foreign mercenaries, usually from outside the territories covered by the new monarchies, occupied a central position. Up to two-thirds of an army could be made up of hired troops from Switzerland, Albania, Hungary, Turkey, Ireland, and so forth. The mercenary phenomenon is explained by the fact that not only the nobility, who were affected by the centralisation of power, but also the rulers themselves were reluctant to put arms into the hands of the people. It was highly unlikely that peasants or yeomen and burghers who acted aggressively abroad would be docile at home. Another important consideration, however, was that troops neither belonging to the local population nor speaking their language could be relied upon to root out and crush social strife and rebellion. This is borne out by numerous historical examples, such as the employment of Germans or Italians in England or Swiss troops in France to stamp out peasant uprisings, rural revolts and guerrilla activities. The complete crushing of the peasantry was prevented only by the presence of partially autonomous urban communes (Giddens 1987a, 97) which observed rather than received the kind of coercive treatment meted out to the lower classes. Thus the subject population of the absolutist state, particularly its lower end, bore the brunt not only of providing the means for the upkeep of the army and financing warfare, but also confronting the mercenary face of the coercive machinery of the state. Already the sixteenth century, but particularly the seventeenth, was rife with violent scenes around the issue of taxation (Anderson 1980, 35; Williams 1988, 169, 197). In rebellion upon rebellion, the poor desperately sought to ward off taxes imposed upon them. In other instances, provincial aristocrats sought to safeguard their own chances of collecting local dues by leading their peasants against the tax collectors. In turn, the state responded by protecting fiscal officers working in the country-side by units of fusiliers.

Parasitic Bureaucracy

Like the army in both direct and indirect ways, the administrative structure of the absolutist state also provided a ready starting point for the perception and definition from different points of view of violence as a pressing societal problem. It involved a central plank of the multi-layered bureaucracy of early modern times, the so-called 'offices' occupied by the 'officer' class (Trevor-Roper 1980, 72–78; Anderson 1980, 33–35, 94–95; Williams 1988, 166–67). This layer was created by Renaissance monarchs in the first wave of centralis-ation in order to overcome feudal fragmentation and to make administration more efficient and effective. A relatively limited number of offices were initially staffed by a skilled stratum of lawyers drawn from the bourgeoisie, but by the seventeenth century, after a process of inordinate expansion, the most important offices were in the hands of nobles. This administrative layer had now become a parasitic bureaucracy. The chronic dearth of money experienced by all the monarchs of the time encouraged this development. To raise funds, offices were not only offered for sale, but even allowed to become hereditary. The absolutist state was thus an ever-expanding bureaucracy, with much of the apparent power of the monarchy actually inhering in the thousands of privately owned hereditary offices surrounding it. On the one hand, the Crown had become the prisoner of its servants, but on the other it was able to externalise by far the larger proportion of the cost of the royal bureaucracy. At most, one quarter of the cost fell directly on the monarch, while the population was required to foot the bill for the remainder (Trevor-Roper 1980, 73–74).

Officers of state received only a small fee and could therefore perfectly legitimately supplement their income, as they universally did, by exploiting the office for profit. It was quite possible for an officer to increase his income legitimately by between fifteen and twenty times. By the addition of profits from improper practices, which themselves became increasingly acceptable in the course of time, many of the top officers were able to emulate the extravagant tastes of their masters. The casual profits of office, both legitimate and corrupt, were of course garnered at the expense of the client. Services cost the client at least four times what the state received from them, but on the whole they cost far more (Trevor-Roper 1980, 76). In effect, the system of offices was an indirect means of raising revenue from the nobility and bourgeoisie on terms profitable to them and at the same time imposing a further tax on the poor who could not bear it (Anderson 1980, 34–35). The already over-exploited subject populations of the European absolutist states were thus further exploited, while the state itself profited from a system it encouraged or acquiesced in.

Bellicist Mercantilism

The typical economic policy pursued by the absolutist state, mercantilism (Gay 1969, 345–47; Williams 1988, 177–80; Anderson 1980, 35–37; Wuthnow 1989, 159–79), which reached its perfection under Louis XIV's chief minister Colbert, also reflected the archaic aristocratic rationality evident in other institutional spheres. France and England were the dominant mercantilist states, while the German states, Sweden, Spain and Russia were drawn into the system. Although the Dutch Republic, which rivalled France and England, followed a free trade policy rather than mercantilism, it nevertheless engaged in various practices in the economic field which were typical of mercantilism. 'Mercantilist policies', writes Peter Gay (1969, 346), 'were the continuation of warfare by other means'.

Mercantilism was a doctrine of state planning of the economy for growth with a view to ensuring and increasing the power of the state relative to all other states. In so far as it demanded the creation of a unified domestic market for commodity production and stimulated corresponding barrier-free trade within the realm of the state, it anticipated the modern economy. Its encouragement of the export of goods, however, was qualified by protectionist measures, particularly restrictions on dealings in bullion and coins in the belief that the wealth of a state measured in gold and silver was proportional to the poverty of its competitors. This zero-sum model of international politics reveals the aggressive and indeed bellicist underside of mercantilism. In theory, it emphasised the economic and political advantages of warfare, and in practice it took every opportunity to appropriate neighbouring territory or even trade by military force. This conquest-oriented foreign policy of the early modern state found especially pointed expression in foreign expeditions, conquests, the appropriation on the high seas of valuable cargoes carried by enemy fleets, genocide, colonisation and imperialism which were often undertaken by one of the characteristic inventions of the time, chartered companies.

106

Paternalistic Culture

The absolutist state's drive towards centralisation did not cease with the monopolisation of force and fiscal resources together with the concomitant pacification and unification of a territory, but penetrated right into the inner core of culture and the symbolic structures of society. On the one hand, this was indirectly achieved by the state interventionism that accompanied the creation of a domestic market and the stimulation and regulation of commodity production. On the other hand, it was pursued in its own right. Another significant institutional innovation of absolutism, therefore, consisted of the monopolisation of the production of culture and control over cultural products (Mandrou 1978, 213–27, 246–65; Williams 1988, 180–83). Of the critical technical innovations of the period, all of which significantly related to communication (Habermas 1979; Anderson 1980, 22), language and printing[19] in particular, but also ballet (Theweleit 1987, 315–18), theatre (Benjamin 1978) and the visual arts (Maravall 1986, 251–63), played a central role in making this possible. The state founded a wide range of academies, colleges, schools, and courses, ranging from science, administration, architecture, and language and literature, through painting and sculpture, music, opera and theatre, to crafts such as glass-blowing and weaving, and it laid down and controlled the standards.

A central and perhaps the crucial prong of this paternalistic cultural tutelage was the monopolisation of knowledge production and control over knowledge. Not only was the content of publications and courses rigorously controlled and censored in order to prevent the dissemination of information or views that might undermine tradition and authority, but forms of knowledge that did not fit in with the state monopoly of knowledge were systematically and ruthlessly excluded. Among them were different strands of the so-called 'New Learning', including Baconianism in England and Cartesianism in France (Mannheim 1993, 412; Van den Daele 1977; Williams 1988, 182), as well as forms of knowledge of which Jews (Geiss 1988, 114–27) and women (Mandrou 1978, 114–17, 143–48; Theweleit 1987, 308; Merchant 1989, 127–48) were the carriers.[20] While many intellectuals suffered insecurity, exile, persecution and death, while the Jews were expelled from Spain and Portugal in a ruthless act that bred modern racism and slavery, some 80,000[21] women appeared in witch-trials in the various European countries and were put to death.

The monopolisation of knowledge occurred against the background of the breakdown of the religious-metaphysical worldview and the clergy's loss of intellectual monopoly, in general, and of the Ptolemaic geocentric model of the universe which pictured the earth as a divine female organism, in particular.

107

The absolutist drive towards cognitive monopoly was therefore intensified, on the one hand, by the demand of the Counter-Reformation for intellectual discipline. On the other, it constituted an attempt to overcome the uncertainty generated by the shift towards the Copernican heliocentric model that placed the masculine sun at the centre of the universe (Merchant 1989, 127–48). The sixteenth- and seventeenth-century image of nature was that of a disorderly, chaotic and violent realm that might collapse at any moment, and correspondingly social relations also appeared as wildness, fraught with violence and more potential violence. Like the wild and savage indigenous tribes of distant lands, women came to symbolise the unruliness and violence of nature. This was irrespective of whether they were lustful women from the lower social orders, witches contriving disorder, or royalty such as Mary Tudor alias Bloody Mary, Mary of Lorraine or even Queen Elizabeth I, all of whom persecuted religious non-conformists. Such wildness, disorder and violence could not be left to go untamed, but required to be mastered by aggression, cunning and manipulation. Alongside war and the subjugation of the mass of the population, therefore, the absolutist state resorted to the cognitive mastery of nature and social relations and the manipulation of the symbolic structures of the interpretation of reality. Central to cognitive mastery was the laying of the institutional foundations for the development of science. The manipulation of symbolic structures included the employment of such symbolic devices as the title 'Sun King' (*roi soleil*), capitalising on the new centre of the universe (Benjamin 1978, 247; Merchant 1989, 128), the eroticisation of the image of the noblewoman in conjunction with the violent de-eroticisation of the common woman as witch, and the monogamisation of the relation between the sexes, the latter two both by means of literature and ballet (Theweleit 1987, 324–27). In the following paragraphs, a brief overview is given of the monopolisation of scientific knowledge and of the eroticisation of the image of the noblewoman.

Monopolisation of Scientific Knowledge

While the cognitive programme of science depended on a certain degree of differentiation and autonomisation, the laying of its institutional foundations called for an adaptation to the conditions of Restoration in England and absolutism on the Continent (Van den Daele 1977; Mandrou 1978, 213–27, 265–83).[22] The process of the institutionalisation of science took place most vigorously in England in the period between 1640 and 1662, but was paralleled in France. It assumed the form of the establishment on a secure footing in these two countries of academies that emerged through a protracted gestation from the meetings of informal learned societies that had been held on a more or less regular basis during the preceding period. The Royal Society, the more important of the two, was founded in London in 1662, followed by the establishment of the *Académie des Sciences* in Paris in 1666. Theoretically, the institutionalisation of science can be regarded as a threefold process: first, the generation of cultural potentialities taking the form of a variety of competing ideas of the 'New Science'; second, the selection of one or two of these potentialities by way of the taking of a decision; and finally the establishment of the institution of science as such.

England assumed the leading role in the institutionalisation of science for a variety of extra-scientific reasons (Groh and Groh 1991, 37). For one, the point of gravity of Europe shifted increasingly towards England from the Mediterranean as it tended to become the location of the most important political, economic and cultural events. For another, the succession in Protestantism of pessimistic Lutheranism by the more optimistic strain of Calvinist Puritanism, after the loosening of the grip of the Counter-Reformation and the destruction of the Spanish Armada, manifested itself in England in particular and served as a powerful stimulus for its already strongly developed millenarianism to embark on the establishment of the new science as an essential part of God's plan (Webster 1975). Here in Puritan England during the revolutionary decades of the 1640s and 1650s, the different groups carrying the scientific movement were actively busy devising and advancing a diversity of ideas, schemes and programmes, each representing a different variant of the new science. Amongst these culturally creative groups, the most important were: the Baconian Puritan reform movement conceiving the 'New Learning' as intrinsically possessing moral, educational, social and political dimensions; the chemical philosophy movement proposing a Christian version of magical-religious knowledge of nature; the experimental philosophy movement and the mechanical philosophy movement, each of which put forward its own reductionist concept of science; and the so-called Virtuosi, such as Boyle, Petty, Henshaw, Digby, Winthrop and Ray (Van den Daele 1977, 38–39; Groh and Groh 1991, 45–46). All these groups accepted the importance of experimentation, experience, reasoning according to constructive models and the universalistic evaluation of propositions, but they emphasised these assumptions differently and combined them with different and even antagonistic ideas.

The introduction of alternative conceptions of the new science by these competing groups thus gave rise to controversies in which they were confronted with one another and played out against each other in a symbolic and cognitive contest. While this contest stretched over decades, in the absence of a scientific tradition, an institutional forum or established criteria, none of these variants could gain the upper hand over the others by demonstrating its cognitive superiority. This was achieved in a way that for the first time created the social structures required for establishing science and providing a basis from which it could rise and develop. A selection from amongst the variants of the new science was made and a corresponding set of criteria rendered cognitively binding by a momentous historical decision in the form of a royal edict issued by King Charles II. The Charter of 1662 entailed the political incorporation of the experimental and the mechanical philosophy to the exclusion of the variants of the new science defended by the remaining groups representing the scientific movement. On the basis of the historical choice made by way of this decision, the first formal and permanent scientific institution, the Royal Society, was established. Within the framework of this institution arose institutional features such as libraries, laboratories, observatories, publications, regular meetings, defined scientific standards, procedures of social control, gate-keepers evaluating the work of scientists – in a word, a whole infrastructure that made permanent the unbroken generation of scientific knowledge.

Of crucial importance for the social structure that science acquired through this process of institutionalisation was the particular social context within which the process occurred and, hence, the way in which science was socially constructed (Van den Daele 1977, 40–44; Mandrou 1978, 265–83; Hill 1988). While the culturally creative period of the generation of a plurality of concepts of the new science coincided with the unsettled years of the Puritan Revolution and Civil War, the historical selection of the experimental and the mechanical concept of science by a royal decision and the establishment of the Royal Society took place after the return of Charles II under the conditions of the Restoration in England. This was a period characterised by a conservative reaction in all fields, from religion, culture and education to law and social policy. As a consequence, the price that the new science envisaged by the scientific movement had to pay to become institutionalised was high, and the implications for many of the excluded representatives of the scientific movement were severe. Far from separating religion, morality, politics and education from science as was done later, the scientific movement of Puritan England prior to the Restoration, in keeping with Baconianism as the official philosophy of the Revolution, explicitly and actively linked the new learning or the new science to a programme of radical political, social and educational reform. Being anti-authoritarian, progressive, anti-elitist, educationally ideal-istic, humanitarian in orientation and in favour of a unity of theological and philosophical knowledge (Van den Daele 1977, 32–39), the movement devised programmes for universal education, agricultural innovation, experimental medicine, free health care, employment for the poor, economic reform oriented toward general prosperity, and state intervention in various areas with a view to social amelioration (Webster 1975). The Restoration of 1660 marked not only the end of the Puritan Revolution, but also the curtailment of the reform programme associated with the new science.

Together with the rescinding and revocation of the laws, legal reforms, social and educational policies and religious institutions of the Puritan era, Charles II at the same time purged the educational institutions of those representatives of the scientific movement who held views unacceptable in the new atmosphere of conservative reaction. In order to gain royal recognition, protection and support, and thus to become institutionalised and incorporated into Restoration society, the scientific movement had to demonstrate its conformity by renouncing all cultural, social, political and educational goals and claims that could be regarded as subversive of the new dispensation or could lead to conflict with the regime. The high price of cutting science loose from its normative goals and social meaning, of separating science from emancipation and human social progress, was paid. Science was given a social structure that established it as a neutral concern involving the pursuit of tightly circumscribed explanatory goals and the growth of knowledge, while the potential value of scientific knowledge was identified with the objectivity of knowledge itself and its progressive potential confined to its technical potential. Concomitantly, the scientific movement purged itself of those of its representatives who entertained undesirable views. In this it was assisted by the repressive machinery of the absolutist Stuart state (Mandrou 1978, 259–61), particularly during the rule of Clarendon. By means of police measures rather than legislation, all kinds of supporters and sympathisers of the previous regime, including representatives of the scientific movement, were hunted down during the first years of Charles II's reign, many of whom had to seek safety in exile, either in the United Provinces or the American Colonies.[23] The theoretician providing a justification for Stuart absolutism and who criticised the intelligentsia was nobody less than Thomas Hobbes (1588–1679), tutor of Charles II during his stay in France and famous author of *Leviathan* (1651).

In France, a comparable yet qualitatively different process of institutionalisation of science took place (Mandrou 1978, 261–65, 271–74). Here, too, we see a multiplicity of informal learned societies meeting regularly over a long period of time, a royal decision giving formal recognition to a certain variety of ideas to the exclusion of others, and the establishment of a scientific institution – the *Académie des Sciences* founded in 1666. But whereas the Royal Society, notwithstanding the royal edict of Charles II, was to a significant degree the outcome of an initiative of the scientific movement itself, the French institution was almost completely created by intervention from above, particularly by Colbert who was leading the government under Louis XIV. The Academy was founded with the specific intention of exalting the Sun King's glory[24] while regulating, controlling and disciplining the scientific movement in France. As such it should be seen in the context of strict censorship, active surveillance, firm repression and control over intellectual life.[25] Encouragement was given to right-thinking savants by pensioning them, but at the same time the freedom of research was strictly circumscribed, Colbert giving directives to guide their work in areas useful to the absolutist state. Government tutelage was accompanied by the banning of unacceptable points of view, which included Cartesian philosophy and physics as well as the Copernican heliocentric position. As in England, yet more decisively and more completely, the new institution of science was overlaid with an authoritarian institutional form in so far as the absolutist state, often hand in hand with the Church, more or less successfully monopolised the production of knowledge through the exercise of force (Koselleck 1989, 26; Eder 1988, 207). The range of possibilities opened up by the scientific movement as well as the traditions upon which it drew were made palpable and manageable by, on the one hand, founding a new institution as the hub of a whole network of communication and, on the other, hunting down, suppressing and rooting out the carriers of all those forms of knowledge that did not admit of being smoothly incorporated.

Eroticisation of the Image of Women

Besides the monopolisation of knowledge by the early modern state in order to gain control over the public interpretation of reality, there are various examples of the pursuit of the same goal by the manipulation of the symbolic structures available for the interpretation of reality. One of them is the eroticisation of the image of women. In dealing with this topic, one should keep in mind the particular nature of seventeenth-century Baroque culture. As Benjamin (1978, 235–36) and Maravall (1986, 251–63) showed in some detail, it was a guided culture that pursued propagandistic ends and therefore was driven by the objectives of dissemination and effective action. Its most characteristic feature was thus the deliberate manipulation of symbolic materials. In the linguistic field, neologisms proliferated and adjectives were incorporated into substantives to form overpowering images,[26] and in art, politics, religion and morality priority was given to the visual image and emblems of all sorts in order to facilitate the spectators' or public's captivation.

The age of absolutism, which had been centred on the court and the aristocratic salon (Hauser 1951, III, 3–9; Elias 1983, 79–80), was thought of as 'the gallant age' or 'the women's century' (E. Fuchs and H. Mayer cited in Theweleit 1987, 332). Louis XIV himself embodied the mastery of gallantry and the new form of privatised free social interaction that developed in the court (Williams 1988, 172).[27] Women, who attained a degree of social power approximating that of men, were able to contribute decisively to determining social opinion and to coordinate a network of extramarital relations from their suites (Elias 1978, 184). But while women enjoyed an unprecedented degree of emancipation, their bodies were nevertheless deliberately used for political purposes (Theweleit 1987, 332–46). Sexuality or, rather, the sexualisation or eroticisation of women, involving what Luhmann (1986b) calls 'love as passion', served as a medium of communication and hence social bonding.

The sexualisation or eroticisation of women rested on a number of practices that were deliberately advanced by the manipulation of symbolic materials. They ranged from dance forms, such as the *Circe* ballet staged at the French court of Henry III (Theweleit 1987, 315–18), to instruction manuals addressed to female readers. Whereas the dance forms were designed to communicate desirable dispositions and relations, the manuals instructed women in sentimental love, in the construction of an appropriate image by constant comparison with an ideal, in the cultivation of beauty by rearranging the body, posture, movements and speech, and in the nurturing of lasciviousness in the sense of a continuous desire and constant appetite for lovemaking. Beyond and above communication and social bonding, such manipulation of symbolic materials simultaneously allowed the advancement of the interests of the nobility, including the monarchy, and eventually also of the bourgeoisie – two classes that came increasingly into contact with one another in court and salon. The problem for the nobility was to absorb the ascending bourgeoisie and thus to secure their own positions and privileges, while the bourgeoisie in turn sought opportunities to move upwards. In order to preserve their privileges, noblemen on the one hand allowed their women to become accessible to bourgeois men, and displaced the discussion of political questions relative to their privileges with stories of love and passion. To achieve this, Colbert prohibited witch trials in 1672 to dissociate eroticism and evil, and instead propagated a new cult of beauty, while Louis XIV set an example by exhibiting a truly royal appetite for the opposite sex (Theweleit 1987, 342; Williams 1988, 172). On the other hand, the bourgeoisie sought to move closer to the nobility by training their daughters through sexual pedagogy to function sexually, thus preparing them for marriage to noblemen. The eroticisation of the image of women through the manipulation of symbols embodied in dance and literature, which was nothing but a thinly veiled form of symbolic violence, thus led to the sacrifice of both noblewomen and bourgeois women.

The conflict between the mutually hostile classes was played out between noblewomen and bourgeois women as they encountered one another in the social arena of the court and the salon. Confronting one another at the level of ideals, they carried out the conflict in relation to their sexuality as the common stake. The female body became the site of competition in the life and death contest of the nobility and the bourgeoisie. At the outset, noblewomen enjoyed a certain advantage due to the freer nature of their sexuality as a result of its long-standing role as an instrument of both pleasure and power in the court, but by the eighteenth century bourgeois women had become the embodiment of male ideals of beauty.

In the above, we have seen that the monopolisation of culture and knowledge, including the manipulation of the structures for the interpretation of reality, was central to the process of absolutist centralisation. At the same time, it also became apparent that some of the most critical inventions of the epoch, which all turn on communication, provided the technical basis for this centralisation. I take these considerations to point to what was actually occurring in the context of the early modern state and thus what served as the basic condition for the construction of violence as the most pressing collective problem of the time. Marking the beginning of the modern period, both institutionally and as the first European state system, the absolutist state served as the point of departure of a long-term process that runs like a golden thread through modern society and has to this day not yet come to a close. Absolutism centrally involved the endeavour[28] to civilise and socialise as yet unavailable potentialities of power and to make them manageable through communication. The remarkable thing is that this attempt failed at the very outset and, as a consequence, gave rise to a pathogenic process to which we can trace the continuing crisis of modern society. While the absolutist state succeeded in increasing power in an unprecedented manner through various epochal technical innovations which are all communication-based, the concurrent attempt to make such increased power communicatively manageable, to link the exercise of power to the rational and formal agreement of all those concerned, came to grief. Technical innovations in communication such as war, travel, money, language and typography were used in such a way that, far from serving to civilise and socialise the increased power, they actually stimulated its inordinate or excessive application. This is borne out not only by absolutist inter-state aggression and bellicism, but also by the exploitation and decimation of subject populations, the persecution of intellectuals, the expulsion of Jews, witch-hunts and burnings, and the exploitation, enslavement and genocide of colonial populations. An investigation of these phenomena ultimately leads to the discovery of the characteristic early modern 'cultural trauma' (Eder 1988, 207) centred on the failure to regulate power through communication and corresponding collective action.

Both the manipulation of symbolic materials typifying early modern culture and its dark underside, the cultural trauma of the times, asserted themselves even within the framework of legality – in the form of regulated yet utterly disgusting violence in the administration of justice itself.

Sovereign Torture

In his famous book entitled *Discipline and Punish*, Michel Foucault (1979) made a study of two contrasting penal styles. The one takes the form of public execution centred on the body in pain, the 'art of unbearable sensations', and the other the form of prison surveillance centred on the self-related soul or mind, the 'economy of suspended rights'. The process of change leading from the former to the latter, registering itself unmistakably in the various European countries between 1769 and 1810, entailed the disappearance of torture as a public spectacle and a shift away from the production of bodily pain as the major aim of punishment. The early modern period, more specifically the absolutist state, was the context of the perfecting of the first penal style, what Foucault (1979, 32–69) in his inimitable style calls 'the spectacle of the scaffold'. This was possible since the administration of criminal justice had been rendered thoroughly political by being tied to the very person and power of the absolutist monarch. To this should be added, once again, the belief in the efficacy of visual resources in baroque culture, the centrality of the sensible image to it, and the persistent pursuit of socio-political objectives through the use of visual media (Maravall 1986).

The ceremony of punishment, the final stage of the judicial process, was the only public part of the criminal procedure. The procession, halts at crossroads and at the church door, the reading of the sentence, kneeling, repentance of the offence to God and to the king, followed by the execution by torture – all of this was deployed as a spectacle in public. Typically in European countries under absolutism, the criminal procedure prior to the sentence and execution took place behind closed doors, being the absolute prerogative and exclusive power of the monarch and the royal judges (Foucault 1979, 35–42). Following strict rules of evidence yet with little involvement of the accused, the case was first built up and then corroborated by way of subjecting the accused to judicial torture, a cruel but regulated form of physical violence, aimed at extracting a confession from him or her. This 'torture of the truth' (Foucault 1979, 40), which was originated by the Inquisition and refined by the absolutist state, finally led to the ceremonial of public punishment. Citing at length from contemporary eyewitness accounts, Foucault (1979, 3–6, 12, 45, 51) describes in grisly detail the unspeakably violent and utterly disgusting way in which criminals were publicly tortured so as to suffer the most horrific agonies, which could be drawn out for as long as eighteen days, before actually meeting their death.

The public execution constituted not merely a judicial but also, and in particular, a political ritual (Foucault 1979, 47–54). Over and above punishment, it was a ceremony aimed at manifesting and renewing power. Since the law represented the will of the absolutist monarch, since the force of the law was the force of the king,[29] a criminal offence was seen not merely as affecting the victim, but as a direct attack against the monarch personally. The administration of justice was thus above all oriented towards redressing the injury done to the kingdom, the disorder created, and allowing the monarch to revenge the affront to his person. The public ritual restores the sovereignty of the absolutist monarch and state, which are identical, by reasserting the asymmetry in the power relationship. The ceremony therefore takes the form of an exercise of terror that was calculated to impress the presence and power of the monarch upon everyone. It was the application of violence in order to master violence, and indeed an excess of violence so as to annul the violence done to the law and the king. The prerogative to punish was one aspect of the absolutist monarch's prerogative to engage in war against his enemies. Rather than a legal one, therefore, the ceremony took a military form. It was a show of arms, a manifestation of force, of physical violence, an excess of violence, a war against the internal enemies of the state. The power mobilised by the absolutist state asserted itself directly on the body of the convict and, not hesitating to butcher the body and reduce it to pulp, exalted, renewed and strengthened itself by the visible manifestation of its excessive physical violence.

The fact that the execution, besides its judicial function, could generate this political effect underlines the centrality of the people to the whole ritual. Without the immediate presence of the public and the arousal of horror and feelings of terror in the spectators, the proceedings would have been devoid of all meaning whatsoever. Foucault (1979, 56)[30] is thus correct to see the public ceremony as a medium of communication. It communicated both truth and power, both the justifiability of the punishment and the legitimate power of the absolutist monarch and state.[31]

As suggested earlier, the ritual of public execution becomes intelligible in the context of the failure of the endeavour of the absolutist state to civilise and socialise as yet unrealised potentialities of power and to regulate and control them through communication and collective political action. What it amounted to was an attempt to manifest the power that had been mobilised so spectacularly by the absolutist state and to make it manageable by establishing a particular form of social relations: Foucault's spectacle of the scaffold, with its characteristic cultural intention of overwhelming and captivating the audience. The power inherent in the complex of relations connecting the monarch, the institutions of the state, and the people was given an asymmetrical structure, and was regulated and controlled through the symbolically pregnant communication of power-saturated yet ostensibly legitimate violence.

Religious Violence

The Reformation,[32] followed by the Counter-Reformation and the Wars of Religion, immensely complicated and exacerbated the conflicts, campaigns, wars, exploitation and repression characteristic of European Absolutism.[33] These events of the period between 1517 and 1648 thus intensified the widespread perception of the problem of violence in the early modern period. The historian Theodore Rabb (1975, 116–45, here 118),[34] for instance, gives special weight to the 'revulsion against the brutal excesses of the Thirty Years War' as an impetus toward the general perception of violence as a societal problem and the search for a 'resolution'.[35] It is quite possible, of course, to go back to any of a number of much earlier more or less shocking events, such as Henry VIII's execution of leading Catholics in the 1530s (Elton 1985, 178) or the Massacre of St Bartholomew's Eve of the 1570s led by Catherine de Medici and the Guises (Elliott 1985, 215–27). The religious conflicts generated by the antagonistic Reformation and Counter-Reformation forces and powers were superimposed on absolutist relations for a considerable period. The result was a hybrid type of religious-political conflict that unfolded both within states and at the international level between states.[36]

At the inter-state level, it was in evidence for at least the century between Charles V's first armed struggle against Lutheranism in the 1540s and the end of the Thirty Years War in 1648.[37] The Peace of Westphalia (Parker 1990, 281–93), which proved to be decisive for the consolidation of both absolutism and the European system of states, brought to a close the most encompassing and intense but also the last of these hybrid struggles. At the intra-state level, political-religious conflict continued until late into the seventeenth century. In Spain, the Inquisition had been used since 1478 as a weapon against both Jews and Muslims, but it was given a new lease of life by the Counter-Reformation, in the context of which it was extended beyond the *auto da fé* within Spanish borders to become part of the machinery of the violence of empire (Geiss 1988, 116–19; Elton 1985, 107–09). In France, it progressively intensified until the eventual revocation of the Edict of Nantes in 1685, which deprived the Huguenots of the legal recognition their form of Protestantism had enjoyed since 1598 (e.g. Labrousse 1983, 1–10); and in England, religious dissenters were persecuted from the Restoration in 1660 until state paternalism was made impossible by the Glorious Revolution of 1688 and the Toleration Act of the following year (e.g. Williams 1988, 494).

That the Reformation had the effect of rendering antagonisms irreconcilable and exponentially intensifying violence is in the first place to be explained by the relations between religion and politics. While the Church on the one hand depended in various ways on the state, on the other the monarch and the state, and hence political power, required the sanction of the Church for their legitimacy. The state was given a religious definition and the monarch ruled according to the Divine Right of Kings. In keeping with the absolutist conception of publicness as being directly represented by the ruler (Habermas 1989a, 7–9), furthermore, there was no distinction between the monarch and the state. Consequently, the monarch's personal faith was also taken to coincide with the interests of the state. Not only were religion and the persecution of heretics the monarch's personal concerns, but brutal repression could be justified by reference to the religious foundations of the state. Irrespective of whether it was Protestants or Catholics who were the objects of persecution, and irrespective of the country where it took place, this amalgam of political and religious considerations is without exception to be seen throughout the sixteenth and seventeenth centuries. Many instances of religious bloodletting had an intrinsic religious motivation, such as for instance the late example of the Revocation of the Edict of Nantes, yet at bottom also stood on a political foundation. Similarly, the persecution of intellectuals, the expulsion of Jews, and witch-hunts and burnings, which were by no means unrelated to an anxious religiosity and hence often cast in a religious idiom, can be fully understood only in the light of the absolutist pursuit of political centralisation and unity. The characteristic confrontations, conflicts, brutality and devastation flowing from this amalgam of intense religious-political inspiration and motivation provided some of the most concrete and potent starting points for the collective identification and definition of violence as a societal problem in the early modern period and its construction into a collectively recognised issue. At the same time, they also pointed in the direction of the kind of solution that was collectively devised to this most pressing of early modern problems.

There can be no doubt about the integrity of the religious principle and the efficacy of religious motivation. The purification of theological orthodoxy and doctrines, inspired by purely religious considerations, indeed took place in the medium of human blood. Yet the most basic factor eventually turned out to be politics. The clarification of religious doctrine and the consolidation of the institutional basis of religion in the three major churches actually meant the monopolisation of religion (Schilling 1991, 202–03) as a significant step in the early modern process of state-formation. This was first secured by the principle of *cuius regio, eius religio* (Koselleck 1989, 24) or *hujus regio, cujus religio* (Labrousse 1983, 7), agreed upon at the Peace of Augsburg in 1555 (Elton 1985, 265–66), which sought to resolve religious conflicts on a regional basis. It allowed only rulers to have freedom of conscience, and thus provided a basis for the achievement of political unity through religious uniformity. This dispensation, also mirrored in a refracted form in the 'French solution' (Mandrou 1978, 166–69) contained in the Edict of Nantes of 1598, was finally ratified and extended to the international level by the division of Europe into Catholic, Lutheran and Calvinist states in terms of the Treaties of Westphalia of 1648 (Parker 1990, 290–93). There is good reason to conclude, therefore, that the ideological and military confrontations of the Reformation and Counter-Reformation's forces and powers in a certain sense subserved the strengthening of a form of power and the consolidation of a type of state (Koselleck 1988, 15–22; Mandrou 1978, 104–05, 137) that exemplified a violence-saturated use of force.[38]

Raison d'État: Formal Universalism and the Body Politic

When one considers the above-mentioned aspects of absolutism and their interaction with and strengthening by religious schism and conflict, the deepest root of the early modern problem of violence becomes visible. It may be submitted that it is to be found in the way that the concern with the collective interest and the common good, or universalism, became institutionalised in the early modern state. Through various means, a state had been built that was represented by the body of the monarch – a body that embraced all the bodies within the territory.[39] The means employed were reviewed above and included the centralisation of power, the monopolisation of force, the pacification and unification of a territorially-bound population, the monopolisation of culture and knowledge, and the administration of the monarch's law through sovereign torture. At the time of the formation of the absolutist state, a universalistic foundation was thus laid down according to which social relations should be organised. It provided the basis for deciding how those bodies that did not fit into the body of the monarch should be dealt with.

The universalism that became institutionalised in the early modern period had earlier already been realised in the Church, supervised by the Inquisition, and was only then carried over into the absolutist state. When the religious-metaphysical worldview or the unifying force of the 'Christian *ecumene*' (Mann 1986, 301–40) collapsed, a transfer of certain achievements of the Church to the state took place at the institutional level. At its core was what at the time was first called *ragione di stato* (Skinner 1978, I, 248)[40] and later became generally known as *raison d'État*.

Raison d'État, as a literal translation would suggest, refers to the delineation and establishment of an area or space to which solely the matters of state and the kind of reasoning appropriate to the state are admitted.[41] It is an area or space in which politics, freed from all encumbrance, could unfold regardless of normative considerations, overriding the ethical, moral and legal norms of society (Koselleck 1988, 16; Skinner 1978, I, 248–54; Tuck 1993, xiii, 62–63).[42] It was occupied by the absolutist monarch and state and excluded the subjects of the monarch or members of society. Within this domain, the representatives of the state could exercise power in an unlimited manner. The rationality or reason of the absolutist state was thus based on a purely formal conception of universalism, what Max Weber (1978, 85–86, 225, 656–57, 809–38)[43] later called 'formal rationality'. It allowed the state to do anything, whether good or evil, as its great theorist Machiavelli (1975) made clear, without justification in order to advance what was deemed to be in the interest of the common good.[44]

That good may come of it, the absolutist monarch was more than willing and prepared to do evil. Those bodies that were not in accord with the monarch's, irrespective of whether they were competitor states or traders, restive subjects, intellectuals, Jews, witches, criminals, or the indigenous populations of colonies, were severely dealt with or eliminated. This is why it could with some justification be submitted that the presupposition of modern universalism was killing and genocide (Eder 1988, 208).

This was the single most important starting point for the perception, collective identification and definition of the deep-seated and all-pervasive phenomenon of violence as the most pressing societal problem of the early modern period.

CHAPTER 7

The Rights Discourse

Early Modern Debates about Violence

The most immediate background of the cultural malaise of the early modern period in the context of which violence first became a problem was provided by the Reformation and Counter-Reformation as they broke in upon and disrupted the Renaissance. This is what makes the so-called 'crisis of the Renaissance' (Hauser 1979, 6) so central to any account of this period. But other correlative events, forces and ideas deriving from economic and political developments also offered a challenge to the ability of the already bewildered early moderns to comprehend and assimilate what is new, strange and disconcerting. The dissolution of Italian humanism, for instance, was inaugurated by the invasion of the country by Charles V, the brutal and devastating sack of Rome,[1] and sealed by the outcome of the Council of Trent, particularly the Inquisition under Carafa. Of importance were also the Mediterranean economic crisis induced by pressures emanating from the Arab and especially Turkish presence on the eastern frontiers, the reorientation of the trade routes, and the transformation and globalisation of the economy. These developments in turn entailed the shift of political power northward and westward, and the facilitation of the process of the centralisation of power and the formation of the state. The consequent religious, ideological, political and economic rivalries and conflicts, the surveillance, repression, exile and burning of humanists and scholars, and the ruthless hunting down and extermination of witches, all continued to render conditions exceedingly uncertain throughout the rest of the century and well into the next. Even the Peace of Augsburg (1555), which did make a certain difference, was not able to create a new climate. That this was the case is explained by the fact that '[n]o succession of events so disruptive of safe and comfortable suppositions had occurred for hundreds of years' (Rabb 1975, 37).

Discourse of Modernity and the Construction of Sociology

The late sixteenth century was a time of ideas, values, dispositions and actions that ran counter to the humanism of the Renaissance. It was a time of the anti-humanism of Luther, Zwingli, Calvin and others, but also a time of the sceptical philosophy of Montaigne and Lipsius, the political double morality of Machiavelli and the Tacitists,[2] the decentring of the human-centred universe by Copernicus, the exposure of the ambivalence of human affairs by Shakespeare, the anti-intellectualism of *Don Quixote*,[3] and of the anti-classical, reflexive mannerist art of Pontormo, Parmigianino, Tintoretto, Greco and Brueghel.[4] In one way or another, these various dramatic cultural expressions point to the characteristic feature of the age: bewilderment, disquiet, unease, anguish, uncertainty, and doubt as to whether dignity and depravity, free will and helplessness, spiritual and corporeal needs, the concern with salvation and the pursuit of earthly happiness, the good and evil sides of human nature admit of being reconciled with one another (Hauser 1979, 6–11, 23–43; Rabb 1975, 37–48; Eder 1988, 92–97, 206–09). It is this feature that such designations as the 'crisis of the Renaissance' (Hauser 1979, 6), the 'failure of nerve' (Clark 1967, title) or, more broadly, the 'general crisis of the seventeenth century' (e.g. Aston 1980), seek to capture. Maravall (1986, 19–53) focuses on the epoch of the Baroque as one divided by social tension, representing a social situation of conflictive relations, and manifesting a generalised consciousness of crisis. Eder (1988, 207) speaks of this period in the emergence of modern society as a time of 'cultural trauma' when the modern symbols of good and evil were constructed, which at one and the same time allowed the institutionalisation of a universalistic morality and the ruthless persecution and extermination of Jews, witches,[5] and – more globally – such strange cultures and forms of life as those of the Aztecs, Incas, Native Americans, Khoi and San. The unease and hesitancy, the uncertainty and anxiety that had taken hold of European culture, expressed in widely differing yet equally dramatic ways by major writers and artists between the mid-sixteenth and the mid-seventeenth century, derived from the more or less acute sense of incoherence and disorder of the age, of a world that was out of joint, and the complementary impulse to grope toward mastery, control, confidence and certainty.

If one considers less the objective characteristics of the out-of-joint world of the early modern period than the crisis-consciousness and communication of contemporaries about them, then a most striking feature of the age comes to the fore. The suffering of brutal repression, the spectacle of public executions, the incessant wars and conflicts, the brutality and destruction that dominated the early modern period in the wake of the breakdown of the feudal order and the religious-metaphysical worldview, accompanied by the crack of arms, the fury of embattled fighters and the destructive resentment of mutineers – all these produced and reproduced situations that led those involved as well as those observing to set about communicating about them. They articulated their bewilderment, disillusionment, uncertainty and anxiety, they clarified their attitudes and motives, elaborated their analyses and theories, and expounded their conceptions of possible peace or order. Throughout Europe, one series of debates incessantly followed upon or branched out from another related series. This very period, then, was the time of the raging of a whole series of inter-related, searching, anguished Europe-wide debates (Mandrou 1978, 133–36, 252, 257; Maravall 1986, 20–21) in which an attempt was made to collectively identify and define the perceived central problem of the age. At first, these debates were conducted in France, but then with special vigour in Germany and England, followed by France again, then the Netherlands and Scotland, and still later once more England and France. Their basic theme was violence[6] and, by extension, the concomitant disorder as well as the use of power – from one point of view the use of power to quell violence and create order, from another the arbitrary use of power or the opaque power relations underlying it. The necessary means for properly addressing the problem of violence and for making it into an issue admitting of resolution started to become available only in the late sixteenth and early seventeenth centuries. Only very gradually, therefore, did the violence debates penetrate the legitimation foundations of the age,[7] clarifying such notions as sovereignty, toleration, resistance and ultimately rights and thus making available some structure where previously none seemed possible for a considerable time.[8] The communication and debates provided the medium not only for the collective identification and definition of the characteristic early modern problem of violence, but also for its trans-position into a collectively recognised issue admitting of resolution.

In the course of focusing the problem of violence, the debates dealt with a variety of phenomena in such a way that the latter at times appeared as indis-tinguishably intertwined and at other times as more or less distinct. Among them were political and religious phenomena, but legal and economic considerations often entered as well. Simultaneously, the debates took place at a number of distinct levels that often became likewise interwoven with one another. The arguments of theorists, lawyers and theologians were part and parcel of debates which raged through whole communities and across communities, carried and spread by pamphlets accessible to virtually everyone. From approximately 1515, debates about the novel and little understood power, the centralising territorial state or nascent absolutism, not only led to the revival of an older tradition but also gave rise to, and were in turn stimulated by, a number of new categories of contributors. On the one hand, there were the so-called 'legists', who included the older Roman lawyers as well as a new type of legal expert looking in a more abstract manner at the implications of the emerging monarchs and states. On the other hand, there was the new strain of historians who reconstructed their people's past with a view to clarifying power relations and the seat of sovereignty. On the whole, these various contributors to the debates developed some variety or another of a theory of royal supremacy and defended the absolutist state (Rabb 1975, 53–54; Skinner 1978, II, 259–67; Tuck 1979; 1993). Religious considerations frequently entered these arguments, for instance, through the notion of the divine right of kings. The legists and historians were in turn confronted or opposed by those who were compelled to recognise and justify the existence of minorities. For them, the people or, at least, their representatives were supreme. In this case, religion proved to be a potent weapon in the debates, particularly in so far as it combined with demands for the toleration of minorities. As indicated by the contribution of Thomas More (1989), for instance, the violence of landlords against the peasantry in the enclosure movement was similarly a topic of discussion already in the early sixteenth century, and it remained so until the eighteenth. In the seventeenth century, the same theme was carried forward by the Levellers who, as opponents of enclosures, sought to level all hedges (Mandrou 1978, 254). Most important of all, however, were the distinct concrete contexts within which the debates took place. Depending on the particular theatre of war, conflict, atrocity, massacre, tax extortion, repression, execution or whatever, they were the most dramatic events of the time – all more or less graphically telling the story of violence and its dreadful consequences – that were decisive in providing a focal point and giving a distinctive tone to the debates in the different countries.

Profile of the Debates

A rough historical schematisation is sufficient at this stage to provide an idea of the most dramatic events and, hence, of the nature and vicissitudes of the debates. A fairly clear profile of the early modern violence debates emerges when a few nodal points – i.e., three coinciding with the sixteenth, seventeenth and eighteenth centuries – are distinguished, and the peaks created by the increase in communication – i.e., seven coinciding with major dramatic historical events – are ranged around each of them (see Figure 7.1). At the same time, it serves to indicate just how complex the early modern European situation was and, to be sure, how perverted by cross-currents of interest and cross-purposes. One thing is beyond doubt, however, and that is that Europe as a whole was implicated in all this.[9]

An abiding contextual factor, to begin with, was the centralisation of state

Figure 7.1: Profile of the early modern violence debates

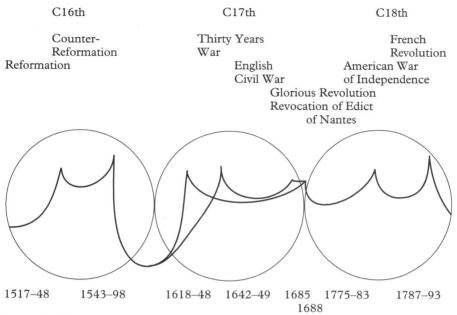

C16th   C17th   C18th

Counter-   Thirty Years   French
Reformation   War   Revolution
Reformation   English   American War
                             Civil War   of Independence
                         Glorious Revolution
                         Revocation of Edict
                             of Nantes

1517–48   1543–98   1618–48   1642–49   1685   1775–83   1787–93
                                             1688

Other significant events:
- Massacre of St Bartholomew's Eve (1572) and death of the Duke of Anjou (1584): culmination point of the second peak
- Edict of Nantes (1598) and Truce of Antwerp (1609): cut-off point of the sixteenth-century debates
- Peace of Westphalia (1648), end of the Thirty Years War, and the Regicide (1649), culmination of the English Civil War

power and the formation of absolutism, epitomised by Charles V's conquest of Italy and victory over the pope in the 1520s. Highly visible and significant events that generated violence communication and drove the debates to a first peak included such occurrences as the Reformation, which was itself exacerbated by the Peasants' War (1524–25), the failure of peace talks at the Diet of Augsburg (1530), the brutalities of Henry VIII against Catholics in the mid-1530s, and the affair of the Protestant *placards* denouncing Catholicism in France and their bloody persecution by Francis I, followed by the Edict of Fontainebleau (1540). The dashing of all hopes of reconciliation at the symbolically highly charged Diet of Regensburg (1541) called forth a twofold violent response: on the one hand, the Counter-Reformation reaction (1540–63) which began to put Protestantism under severe pressure, and Charles V's war against the Schmalkaldic League and the decisive battle of Mühlberg in Saxony (1547), which 'brought out some unpleasing savagery and unreasonable

Table 7.1: Chronology of the Reformation, Counter-Reformation, Wars of Religion and Absolutism

1517	Martin Luther nails his *Ninety Five Theses* to the church door, Wittenberg
1520	Luther publicly burns Leo X's papal bull, excommunicating him
1521	Luther clashes with Charles V, King of Spain and Emperor of the Holy Roman Empire, at the Diet of Worms, being condemned and outlawed as a heretic by the Edict of Worms
1524	Peasants' War
1527	Sweden adopts Lutheranism
1529	Reformation Parliament under Henry VIII, continuing until 1536
1530	Diet of Augsburg, ending in the failure of peace talks
1531	Battle of Kappel, Switzerland, between Zwingli's Protestant forces and a Catholic army
1534	The affair of the *placards*, and the persecution of Protestants by Francis I in France
1535	Henry VIII beheads Bishop John Fischer and Thomas More
1536	Closure of the monasteries in England and Ireland; Denmark adopts Lutheranism
1540	Pope Paul III approves the founding of the new order of the Jesuits to spearhead the campaign against Protestantism
1541	Diet of Regensburg dashes all hopes of reconciliation and overcoming of religious schism; John Calvin's twenty-three-year rule over Geneva begins
1542	Pope Paul III revives the centuries-old *Court of the Inquisition* to try heretics
1543	Outbreak of war of religion in Germany between Charles V and the Lutheran princes
1545	First session of the Council of Trent, meeting over an eighteen-year period to reform the practices of the Catholic Church and define its doctrine
1546	Henry II persecutes the Huguenots in France
1547	England under Edward VI becomes a Protestant country
1553	Queen Mary ('Bloody Mary') leads England back to Catholicism, dispossessing 2,000 clergy, and burning 300 Protestants as heretics
1555	Peace of Augsburg, bringing to an end the war of religion between Charles V's Catholic forces and the German Lutheran princes
1557	Henry II of France promulgates the Edict of Compiègne, stipulating the punishment of heresy by death
1558	Queen Elizabeth I, determined to lead England back to Protestantism, establishes the Church of England or Anglican Church, eventuating in the persecution of both strict Catholics and Puritans
1559	The Guises, regents of Francis III, unleash vicious persecutions of the Huguenots, thus pushing France towards religious war
1560	Scottish Reformation Parliament adopts Calvinism as represented by John Knox; Huguenot conspiracy of Amboise

1562   Outbreak of the first war of religion in France between the Huguenot Duke de Condé and the Catholic Guises

1567   Deposition of Mary Queen of Scots

1572   Massacre of Huguenots on St Bartholomew's Eve, under Catherine de Medici

1584   Death of the Duke of Anjou, and the Protestant Henry of Navarre becomes heir to the French throne

1588   Destruction of Philip II's Great Spanish Armada, sent against England, by the English fleet

1598   Promulgation of the Edict of Nantes, recognising the legal existence of the Reformed Church in France

1610   Assassination of Henry of Navarre, King Henry IV of France

1618   Revolt of Bohemia; outbreak of the Thirty Years War

1648   Treaties of Westphalia bring to an end the Eighty Years War between Spain and the Netherlands as well as the Thirty Years War, thus providing a consolidated basis both for the absolutist state and the European system of states

1661   The English Parliament passes the Corporation Act, an anti-Presbyterian measure

1664   The English Parliament passes the Conventicle Act, an anti-Catholic measure

1685   Revocation of the Edict of Nantes by Louis XIV, stimulating a stream of *émigrés* from France and the formation of the *Refuge* abroad

1689   The English Parliament passes the Toleration Act, establishing freedom of worship

---

stubbornness' in the victorious emperor (Elton 1985, 250). These various developments, which stimulated and, in fact, immensely increased communication and debate all over Europe due to their more or less dramatic quality, were closely intertwined with intra-dynastic, inter-dynastic, church–state, and inter-state rivalries, conflicts, and wars. Particularly important here were the relations between the Hapsburg and Valois dynasties. In addition, the effect that the conflicts and wars between Europe and the Ottoman Empire and Islam had on relations in Europe should not be underestimated.

This first peak in the unfolding of the violence debates was followed by a second that began to build up around the middle of the century.[10] Crucial here was the spread of Protestantism after Luther's death (1546) under the aegis of Calvinism, which gave the Reformation a new aggressive and expansive impetus driving it well beyond the mid-century mark. The major countries affected were France, the Netherlands and England, where the Reformation had not yet succeeded. Given that those in power in those countries had no intention of capitulating before Geneva, and given further that Calvinism now encountered both a reformed and re-invigorated Catholic Church and pendulum swings between Catholicism and Protestantism, as in England, events during this

127

period took on an even more dramatic character. Relentlessly, the Calvinists were compelled into the role of rebels and revolutionaries, pitting themselves against both ecclesiastical and civil authorities. As regards the latter, despite the dynastic peace signalled by the treaties of Cateau-Cambrésis (1559), matters were exacerbated by the interaction, overlapping or coincidence of religious convictions and dynastic concerns – as in the cases of, for example, Mary Tudor, Philip II of Spain, Catherine de Medici, and Queen Elizabeth I. The build-up was supported by a further series of violence debates that took off with the persecution of Calvinists in Scotland (1546–58), Henry II's persecution of the Huguenots in France (1547–59), and Mary Tudor's persecution and burning of more than three hundred Reformers between 1553 and 1558. The civil war in France that began in 1562 and Philip II's repressive decrees, together with the Duke of Alba's atrocities in Holland, which marked the start of the Eighty Years War against Spain, provided the basis for the strengthened reproduction of the debates. They were then forced to a culmination point and a significant redirection by such dramatic and symbolically pregnant events as the ruthless and bloody slaughter of thousands of Huguenots under Catherine de Medici in the Massacre of St Bartholomew's Eve (1572); governor Alexander Farnese's proscription of William of Orange (1580) and his assassination (1584); and the death of the Duke of Anjou in 1584, which left Catholics with the frightening prospect of the avowed Huguenot Henry of Navarre being the direct heir to the French throne. The promulgation of the Edict of Nantes (1598) by Henry IV, which gave legal existence to the Reformed Church in France, and the Truce of Antwerp (1609), which obliged Spain to recognise the United Provinces, were among the events that inaugurated a period of twenty years of armed neutrality in Europe which saw a certain subsidence of the violence debates – until the eruption of a European war and civil war in England.[11] This trough, as will become clear later when the new cognitive structures of the time are considered, proved to be a fecund period of reflection and redirection for Europe.

The historical framework within which the violence debates developed in the seventeenth and eighteenth centuries was set by the three events that proved to have had the most decisive impact on the shape assumed by Europe. These three events mark the peaks reached in the violence debates during the seventeenth century, just as the American and French Revolutions did for the eighteenth. The first is the barbarous and devastating European war known as the Thirty Years War (1618–48), which a well-known historian described as follows:

Neither in scale nor in brutality, neither in geographic reach nor in indiscriminacy yet ferocity of partisanship, had armies behaved in this fashion before. The minimum of one-third of the population of Central Europe that died as a direct or indirect result of the war stands as mute testimony to its unparalleled devastation. Wallenstein's 'living off the land' and Gustavus Adolphus' 'swath of destruction' were tactics whose far-reaching viciousness had never been equaled in a thousand years of Western history (Rabb 1975, 76).

Although the shifting networks of alliances were rather complex, it could nevertheless be said that while dynastic and state rivalries were an important ingredient of the war, religious or confessional differences were of overriding significance and, as often in the past, served as the principal stimulus to violence.[12] The second major seventeenth-century event or, rather, series of events in relation to which the violence debates were deployed was the English Revolution, involving the Civil War, the Regicide, the Restoration and eventually the Glorious Revolution. To this series should also be added both the concurrent repression of Levellers and Diggers and other radical elements,[13] and the institutionalisation of science in the 1660s.[14] The third event that immensely increased violence communication in the seventeenth century and, combining with the effects of earlier events, stretched into the eighteenth century, was the revocation of the Edict of Nantes by Louis XIV and the resultant flow of *émigrés* out of France and the phenomenon of the *Refuge* in cities such as Amsterdam, Rotterdam and London.

An idea of the significance of these three major historical events for the development well into the eighteenth century of the European debates about the central problem of early modern society and its possible resolution can be formed by considering their respective relevant impacts. The Peace of Westphalia of 1648, which brought the Thirty Years War to an end, laid the definitive foundation for the consolidation of the typical European absolutist state as well as the European system of states. A core aspect of this new dispensation was the *ancien régime* that provided the essential foil against which the Enlightenment formed.[15] The Glorious Revolution of 1688, in turn, brought the English revolutionary period to a more or less felicitous close which, through the constitutional arrangements it represented, came to exert a wide and penetrating influence. The most central figures in the diffusion of this impact were the English Enlightenment figure John Locke and, even more importantly, the leading French *philosophe* Montesquieu. Finally, considering its intention, the revocation of the Edict of Nantes had the ironic effect of providing, through the *Refuge* and outstanding *émigrés* such as Pierre Bayle (1995; Labrousse 1983), all of Europe with Enlightenment ideas, often in the form of clandestinely printed, banned reading materials.[16]

The dramatic events that fill out the framework of the historical scheme sketched above each served to some extent as a flash-point,[17] as it were, in the course of the development of the violence debates that raged all over Europe during the early modern period. As such they not only immensely increased communication, thus allowing hitherto taken-for-granted matters to be articulated and hitherto isolated matters – and people! – to be divided, classified and related to one another. By the same token they also formed the ever-changing foci of the violence communication as it followed the vicissitudes of its own dynamics, thus giving the historical debates their peculiar profile.

Settings, Media and Genres

Concentrated by such events and focusing on violence, the debates were conducted in different settings, both institutional and non-institutional as well as anti-institutional, while the different points of view, the polemics and the results were communicated through a variety of genres. Of special importance was the new typographical or print medium,[18] but this should not be allowed to obscure the centrality of the sensible image and visual media to the Baroque culture of the time. Particular audiences were addressed, yet the publications – themselves taking many different forms – were read in war-torn or violence-ridden countries and, indeed, throughout Europe where similar phenomena had occurred or were still expected to happen.

Forums or Arenas

Meticulously worked-out arguments, very often with a clearly conceived strategic purpose, were not only put forward and considered in detail at meetings of the churches, such as the Council of Trent (1545–63) or the Synod of Dordrecht (1618). Beginning with forums of pre-modern estate politics, such as the Diets of Augsburg (1530) or Regensburg (1541), they increasingly also became the object of more secular or political congresses, frequently involving costly delegations and risky negotiations. The peace negotiations at Augsburg (1555) and especially those at Westphalia (1648) are paradigmatic examples of the latter.[19] Parliamentary Commissions, such as those appointed in 1548 or 1638 to investigate the violent destruction of the peasantry and the spread of enclosures (Marx 1977, 674), represented another high-level institutional context from which crucial contributions to the violence debates emanated.

In contradistinction to institutional or official forums, however, the debates had also been generated and carried by both non-institutional and anti-institutional forums. A great variety of different publics all over early modern Europe provided informal contexts for the unfolding of the debates of the time. In seventeenth-century England, the Protestants represented such a public (e.g. Zaret 1992). Elizabeth Labrousse's (1983) biography of Pierre Bayle contains many descriptions showing how the *Refuge* served as a non-institutional forum of violence communication and the production and reproduction of the typical debates of the time.[20] Finally, movements such as the revolutionary chiliastic Hussite and Anabaptist movements in Bohemia and Germany (Mannheim 1972, 190–97), the Levellers and Diggers and other radicals in England (Hill 1988), or the Ormeé in France (Mandrou 1978, 258–59) provided anti-institutional settings for the assertion of popular voices in the debates.

Printing and Visual Media

To appreciate the principal medium through which the violence debates were conducted, it should be recalled that the Reformation was a cultural revolution that produced cultural resources which supported its own more specific aims and achievements yet possessed a far wider significance. Luther as well as other Reformers played an important role not only in extrapolating the cultural implications of the new technological medium, the printing press, but also in extending the new culture beyond the confines of the essentially elitist groupings of the Renaissance, consisting of learned clergy, courtiers, jurists and scientifically oriented scholars, to the laity and public more generally. Involved here were simultaneously the globalisation of culture via the media (Giddens 1991, 77) and what Moscovici (1982a, 201) calls 'the laicisation of society'. The Reformation provided the context for the spread of literacy throughout the population and included a campaign specifically directed towards realising this aim (Giesecke 1992, 122–85). The new technology, which was subjected to a decisive test in the religious arguments and struggles of this period, represented the most advanced medium through which polemical and ideological points of view – in the form of pamphlets – as well as developed theological arguments – in the form of books – could be transmitted to the public. The impact of Luther's *Ninety Five Theses* depended on being distributed widely and rapidly, while he authored a third of the printed output of Germany between 1518 and 1523 (Hauser 1979, 66). The Reformation could not have achieved what it did without both writing for the printing press and the reading of printed text having been upgraded to the level of a general cultural competence and activity.

Statistics are useful in conveying an idea of the immense impact of printing.

Immediately after the invention of the movable-type printing press between 1440 and 1450, the number of books in Europe increased dramatically from 30,000 to a few million, and by 1500 some 20 million books had been available (Mann 1986, 446). At this point, the population of Europe amounted to approximately 70 million. Like the Reformation later, the Renaissance would have been impossible without this expanding communications infrastructure. At a more general level, the cultural efflorescence that accompanied these developments was manifested in the emergence of the modern European vernaculars (Giesecke 1992, 73–121) and, by extension, the development of national literatures and literary genres (Mandrou 1978, 127–30). On closer inspection, we see here the beginnings of a thorough-going process that transformed the fragmented, estate-bound communication relations of the medieval and early Renaissance period, including the elitist learned Latin communication system, into comprehensive national communication communities based on the modern standard European languages (Giesecke 1992, 74–77; Mandrou 1978, 131; Bourdieu 1997, 46–48). Although the use of Latin in the learned world continued throughout the next century, the number of works published in this language had already shown a decline in the second half of the sixteenth century in proportion as the new phenomenon of translation between vernaculars became a growing feature not only of literary activity but also of scholarship.

While considering the media through which the early modern violence debates had been conducted, one should keep in mind that the culture of the time was one of the sensible image (Maravall 1986, 251–63). The early moderns appreciated that direct vision was important beyond measure, and thus emphasised the efficacy of visual resources. It is not surprising, therefore, that visual media of various kinds played a central role in the debates. Etches and prints, produced in large numbers, were of particular importance. Often pamphlets and even sermons were accompanied by hieroglyphics, i.e. etched or printed pictures to be deciphered, that were calculated to move the audience and to capture its attention and imagination. By these various means the different voices in the debates sought to advance their socio-political objectives and accomplish their propagandistic ends.

Learned Treatises, Novels, Pamphlets, and Literature of Crime

Made possible and stimulated by the movable-type printing medium, the points of view and polemics of the different participants and observers were communicated through distinct and often new genres. Beginning with the Reformation and the religious-political conflicts and wars of the first half of the sixteenth century, and continuing unabated even after the signing of peace treaties, a spate of publications of all sorts became the order of the day. They were frequently published in their thousands and even tens of thousands, and in many cases enjoyed new editions for years and even decades after the original publication date. These publications stretched from comments on current affairs in broadsheets and pamphlets, through occasional manifestos and vindictive pieces called 'admonitions', to substantial books and learned treatises. They came in waves. A spurt of manifestos, pamphlets and comments, which at times took cues from or were guided by learned treatises, typically accompanied the dramatic historical events, sometimes proliferating in their thousands.[21] Inspired by and drawing upon the debates so generated, further admonitions, substantial works and learned treatises as a rule followed in the wake of dramatic events, in turn providing a starting point or even guidance for the next round in the debates.

Among those making use of the learned treatise (Tuck 1979; 1993; Skinner 1978, II; Randall 1962, 89–167), which both stimulated and summarised debates while reacting to and learning from the Wars of Religion, was the line of authors who developed a theoretical justification of the absolutist state. These authors included those who did so more or less directly, such as Claude de Seyssel, Charles du Moulin, Pierre Rebuffi and Jean Bodin, as well as those who did so with reference to a theory of rights, such as Luis de Molina, Francisco Suarez, Hugo Grotius,[22] John Selden and Thomas Hobbes. Introducing new topics of discussion, such as royal supremacy and the state, and thus opening a new perspective on the historical situation, these works occasioned an enormous number of publications. The latter were typically of a substantial nature and belonged to the general category of political writings produced not so much by philosophers as by legally trained authors such as magistrates, chancellors and bureaucrats. In France, Germany and England in particular, but also elsewhere in Europe, these authors addressed a wide range of questions. They included such topics as the nature of the state, the monarchy, the implications of civil war for the state and the monarchy, the desirable degree of absoluteness of the monarchy, the rights of princes, royal genealogies, royal ceremonies, relations with the Emperor of the Holy Roman Empire, the secularisation of Church property, and so forth. The authors of these learned treatises differed in their conceptualisation of the nascent and as yet obscure power of the centralising territorial state. Whereas some sought to revive the divine rights of kings, others developed a secularised version of the same principle, and still others moved to a more abstract plane to deal with the questions of rights and of sovereignty. Notwithstanding the presence of polemics, however, the majority of these authors were representatives of princes or monarchs whose primary purpose was to secure, strengthen and improve the established order.

This absolutist or quasi-Tacitist tradition called forth criticism from various sides. At an early stage, humanist opponents such as Thomas More and Erasmus articulated critiques (Skinner 1978, I, 221–28), but the most sustained criticism came from constitutional authors entertaining a variety of points of view. Tuck (1993, xiv, 120–53)[23] speaks of the 'resistance' against the 'new culture...of *raison d'État*' put up on the basis of 'constitutionalism'. Constitutional points of view ranged widely. At the one extreme were authors such as Estienne Pasquier and Bernard de Girard, the Seigneur du Haillan, who were not entirely willing to give up the absolutist position. The other extreme was occupied by Calvinists and Jesuits who, despite their deep-seated confessional differences, both salvaged constitutional ideas from medieval sources and combined them with theological or religious arguments in favour of constitutional remedies for the social problems of the time. As attested by the major treatises of the so-called *Monarchomachi*, Theodore Beza, Philippe du Plessis Mornay and George Buchanan, the radical Calvinism of the 1550s became so radicalised after the St Bartholomew's Eve Massacre of 1572 that it approached a theory of popular sovereignty allowing a justification of the tyrannicide of a legally recognised monarch. Catholicism arrived at a comparably radical position by way of the work of Jean Boucher, Guillaume Rose and Juan de Mariana. The effective uncoupling of the theory of popular sovereignty from religion by this inadvertent agreement between Calvinists and Jesuits opened the way for the great treatises on constitutionalism[24] first of Johannes Althusius (1603) and, via Samuel Pufendorf, of Matthew Hale and Richard Cumberland, then importantly of John Locke (1970).

The novel was a new genre of the time that differed from the learned treatise. An example of a popular and very influential work in this category, which was related to the absolutist tradition, is the then widely read novel entitled *Argenis* (1621) by John Barclay (Koselleck 1988, 17–19). The son of an *émigré* family, he popularised an idea or, rather, a set of arguments that was familiar not only to moderate Huguenots. Starting from the violence of the Wars of Religion, he challenged the monarch to assume responsibility for bringing about peace between the embattled parties and to assure domestic tranquillity for all those who subjected themselves to the sovereign. In effect, he provided a justification for the monarchy and the absolutist state by means of a sequence of argumentation that became a commonplace at the time among groups entertaining divergent points of view. They included a powerful politician such as Cardinal Richelieu and an influential philosopher and royal tutor such as Thomas Hobbes, both of whom would later advance this argument strongly and effectively.

Contrasting sharply with learned treatises and substantial books developing intricate arguments as well as novels, the other end of the print medium scale gives evidence of a considerable amount of pamphleteering concerned with religious and political perspectives on the problem of violence. Going back to the Lollards, an English-language movement, the radical wing of Protestantism produced a mass of cheap, illustrated pamphlets during the liberal reign of Edward VI (1547–1553) spreading both a religious and social revolutionary message (Hill 1992, 102–04, 106). In England, pamphleteers had been suppressed and exiled in various historical periods, for instance, under Mary Tudor (1553–1558), for a number of years under Elizabeth I (1588–1589), and again from the reign of James I in 1603 to the outbreak of the Civil War in 1642. Yet men such as Martin Marprelate and Thomas Scott succeeded against all the odds in distributing illegal pamphlets, thus continuing a tradition that linked the period of Edward VI to the revolutionary 1640s (Hill 1992, 109). In France, the Massacre of 1572 called forth a range of famous anonymous tracts describing and analysing the event (Skinner 1978, II, 304–05, 309, 324). The Revolt of the Netherlands, which was influenced both by English and French materials, was likewise accompanied by the production and distribution of numerous pamphlets (Saage 1981, 23–112). Once again, statistics provide an idea of the extent and significance of pamphleteering. The so-called 'pamphlet war', which had been waged during the Civil War in England, gave rise to the astounding number of approximately 22,000 pamphlets (Mandrou 1978, 258; Saage 1981, 115–237). The five troublesome years between 1648 and 1653, the period of aristocratic insubordination in France known as the *Frondes*, also produced a few thousand titles (Mandrou 1978, 258; Williams 1988, 157–62). According to Christopher Hill (1992, 117), a direct line of pamphleteering runs from the sixteenth through the seventeenth to the eighteenth century. The revival of radicalism in America and Europe in the late eighteenth century, also supported by the wide distribution of pamphlets, occurred by recourse to the pamphleteering of the English Revolution, which in turn fed on the communication practices developed during the reign of Edward VI (1547–1553).

The pamphlets, most typically deriving from moderate and radical oppositional points of view, often sent out a different message from that of the learned treatises and books, and did so in their own particular way. Harping on treason and dangers, often cast in vitriolic terms, numerous pamphlets were no more than just a few pages in length. On the other hand, however, they could also serve as vehicles of powerful and sustained arguments. In revolutionary England, we come across sophisticated pamphleteers on the side of the parliamentary revolutionaries who developed a theory of inalienable natural rights, including such men as Henry Parker, Henry Ireton and Anthony Ascham

(Tuck 1979, 143–53). The pamphlets of extreme radicals such as the Levellers and Diggers, which culminated in the great manifesto entitled the *Agreement of the People* (1647, 1649), demanded popular sovereignty on the basis of inalienable individual rights, and they did so in a language that struck terror into the hearts of the establishment (Hill 1988, 66–69, 107–50). With the exception of the Ormeé movement, which demanded popular freedom, the French pamphlets were neither as critical nor as demanding as their English counterparts (Mandrou 1978, 258). Against the background of the violence engendered by the centralisation of state power and by the Religious Wars, they concentrated on a variety of questions, from the limits of monarchical power and the duties of the nobility, through the rights of *parlements* to the abuses of the taxation system. Occasionally, they also veered off into personal attacks on the ruling elite.

Given that the explosion of pamphlets during the early modern period is at least partially explicable by reference to the fact that a public had come into being who required to be persuaded and won over in support of different points of view, it is not surprising to find that pamphlets were used also for the purposes of propaganda. In any case, this propagandistic orientation was endemic in a culture that tirelessly pursued the objectives of captivating and guiding the public (Maravall 1986). During the reign of Henry VIII, for instance, his chief minister deliberately employed pamphlets – as well as ballads and theatre – in a propaganda campaign against the so-called 'Papists' (Hill 1992, 104). In the seventeenth century, this pamphlet propaganda became standard practice, particularly during the Civil War when the propagandists of the Parliamentarians resorted also to sermons and tracts in addition to pamphlets (Hill 1992, 112–13).

The administration of criminal justice produced yet another literary genre by means of which the early modern debates were given form and the problem of violence was approached and delimited. Starting from the reciprocal relations or, rather, strategies and counter-strategies of the super-ordinate and subordinate agents in the context of the public execution, a debate erupted about the violence and the implied relations entailed by the public ceremony. In turn, these debates gave rise to a literature that became quite varied in the course of time. Foucault's (1979, 57–69) analysis of the public execution contains interesting observations that go in this direction. The violent form of public penal justice practised by the absolutist state called forth a reaction on the part of the people which showed itself in the state of permanent unrest accompanying executions. From here, the conflicting interpretations and reciprocal relations intensified in a spiral-like fashion. To ensure order, the authorities had to take steps that were at least potentially distressing to the people and humiliating to themselves. Once this potential took on reality, once legal violence was stripped of all restraint, the people felt more threatened than impressed and, as a consequence, the solidarity of the people rather than the sovereign power of the monarch was strengthened. In proportion as it became apparent that the public execution was a ceremony that rather inadequately channelled the relations of super-ordination and subordination it sought to ritualise, debates sprang up in which the violent confrontation of criminal and justice, but also people and state, became the object of attention. On the one hand, the authorities, fearing the effects of such inherently ambiguous rituals, saw the political problem posed by the intervention of the people in the public ceremony. On the other hand, the redoubled violence as well as the gallows speeches, the frequently defiant last words of the condemned, aroused the indignation of the people or even their opposition to the established order. The condemned could even be transformed into a hero of the people or call up a whole memory of struggles and confrontations. The criminal often appeared in this guise in a wide range of media and genres, from the broadsheets through pamphlets and almanacs to adventure stories and later literature of crime. Beginning with the celebrated case of Massola, who was tortured and executed in an utterly disgusting way in late sixteenth-century Avignon (Foucault 1979, 50–51), the moral indignation aroused by judicial violence in those involved and in observing contemporaries further gave rise to a whole tradition of writings which culminated in the Enlightenment's critical analysis of the law and the legal system (Gay 1969, 423–47; Hufton 1985, 90–92).

The Logic of the Debates: Violence and Order, or Division and Coordination[25]

If one assumes a communication and discourse theoretical perspective on the early modern violence debates, then it becomes apparent that the widespread communication about violence and disorder provided the medium for the collective identification and definition of the central societal problem and its transposition into perhaps the most important issue of the time. This means that these debates in effect also served as the medium for the generation of a wide-ranging and all-embracing discourse. In the wake of glacial societal changes, including the collapse of the medieval cognitive order in the form of the religious-metaphysical worldview, the hitherto taken-for-granted background of assumptions and understandings broke down, with the result that by the sixteenth century Europe found itself in a deep-seated and thorough-going crisis. Incoherence, disorder, disarray, disorientation, anomie and above all violence – capitalist, absolutist, and religious violence – were the order of the day. That the world was out of joint was dramatically apparent from a pervasive cultural malaise, the crisis of the Renaissance, which itself assumed the proportions of a cultural trauma and in a more generalised form continued well into the next century. European cultural documents of the time attest to widespread bewilderment, unease, anxiety and uncertainty. Everywhere violence represented the central object of concern. Violence was the most immediate experience and, hence, the problem around which the arguments and conflicts, a whole semantics, crystallised and developed.

Amidst this atmosphere of disquiet and uncertainty, however, there were in evidence, at least as time went by, anguished attempts to re-establish confidence and certainty. Groping efforts were made to master the chaotic situation and to gain control over the various forces operative in it. They were accompanied by searching attempts to establish new ideas, symbols, standards, norms or rules of conduct, and cultural orientations that could guide action and allow appropriate justifications. From a communication and discourse theoretical perspective, this latter aspect of a search for the recovery of certainty indicates that the collective identification and definition of the problem of violence as a collectively shared issue involves not merely social conflict but at the same time also coordination.[26]

On the one hand, the problem of violence called forth different and even antagonistic definitions that divided their respective proponents and brought them into conflict with one another. On the other hand, the establishment of the problem as a shared or common issue, i.e. the fact that all the conflicting social actors were oriented towards this one major issue, means that their disparate actions became coordinated with one another. These two perspectives respectively bring into view the dynamics and the logic of the early modern discourse about the problem of violence. While the various debates served as vehicles of processes that divided people into antagonistic groups yet at the same time brought them to focus on one and the same issue, the discourse thus generated manifested itself in the logic of division and coordination. The dynamics can be described by means of an adequate empirical approach, but were one to objectify and account for such processes over and above their mere description, then one would be required to have recourse to the discursive logic of division and coordination. The logic of the discourse makes it possible to use the vocabulary and language, or the semantics, of the debates as a means to grasp the structure of the discourse, which in turn is indispensable for an adequate account of its dynamics.

138

Semantics of the Debates: From Name Calling to Concepts

On inspection, the vocabulary and language, or semantics, characteristic of the early modern Europe-wide debates about violence exhibit two clearly identifiable features. On the one hand, the semantics of the debates referred to historical events pregnant with confrontation, conflict and struggle as well as to experiences of violence and disorder associated with those events. In this context, the naming of events stands out. Names were sought that were appropriate to a given event, but the actual naming or nominative act was often shaped by the culture of the time which, as one oriented toward the sensible image and the captivation of the public, was given to exaggeration, escalation and aggrandisement (Benjamin 1978, 235–36; Maravall 1986, 254). This latter aspect of the semantics of the debates becomes especially clear from the names by which agents or opponents were called, often combining sarcasm and blaming with an intention to disparage. A selective scanning of the violence communication of the time yields examples such as the following: 'seditious rebels', 'the so-called reformed religion', 'reformers', 'protestants', 'the anti-Christ party', 'papists', 'Bloody Mary', 'the Machiavellian Catherine', the 'Powder Treason', 'the Popish Plot', 'tyrants and idolaters' or 'the feverish faction' which exhibits 'a pernicious heresy', engages in 'a violent and ambitious enterprise' and 'a monstrous war', hatches 'terrible designs' or shows 'a propensity to malignity and violence' (see e.g. Skinner 1978, II; Williams 1980). The application of disparaging names in the debates was supported and made even more poignant by the use of the visual image. By exaggeration and the distortion of reality, etchings and prints served as a widely employed means to indelibly engrave demonising and disparaging names in the imagination.

The semantics of the early modern debates about violence, however, was by no means exhausted by such emotive and often vitriolic name giving and name calling. Whereas such hot language use reflected the division of people into antagonistic and conflicting groupings, the semantics of the debates clearly also took on a more formal character. In proportion as the more formal aspect of the semantics developed as the debates unfolded, the emotive and vitriolic name calling, which predominated during the earlier phases of the debates, declined. What is remarkable about the semantics of the debates is the gradual development of concepts by means of which the conflicting parties tried to make sense of the historical situation by theorising and explaining it or proposing solutions to its problems. Such concepts represented the epistemic character of the practical discourse (Habermas 1998, 81) generated by the debates and were therefore the common property of the opponents. Some of the most important concepts constituting this aspect of the early modern semantics include 'sovereignty', 'state', 'people', 'contract', 'toleration', 'rights', 'citizen', 'society', 'civil society' and so forth. Rather than starkly dividing the social actors and antagonistically opposing them in a situation of pervasive uncertainty, as did the former set of names, this second set of concepts opened up the possibility of overlap, of shared assumptions, new cultural orientations, and agreement between the antagonistic or conflicting actors – despite their propensity to interpret what they agreed upon in contrary ways. In a word, the semantics of the early modern debates about violence did not reflect only the division of the participants, but also the coordination of their orientations and actions. The interests and values that were initially brought into the practical discourse from particularistic points of view were in the course of the discourse sifted and selected so that the generalisable value orientations acceptable to all the participants became part of the durable semantic outcome.[27]

The Rights Discourse: The Issue of the Survival of Society in its Political Environment

The shift in the early modern debates from particularistic semantic contents to generalised epistemic structures is indicative of the development according to which groups, who are at first counter-posed and placed in antagonistic relations of conflict, are brought closer together through emergent shared assumptions, cognitive structures or cultural models. This is the process of division and coordination, mentioned earlier, in which inheres the logic that is character-istic of discourse. If the semantics of the early modern debates about violence reflects this process or logic, it means that this semantics is sufficiently elaborate, rounded and coherent to be taken as confirming the existence of an encompassing discourse. The debates in fact generated a practical discourse. This can be further corroborated if it is possible to trace the logic of division and coordination at the more concrete level of the construction or making of a problem into a collectively acknowledged issue. There is sufficient evidence to argue that this can be done.

It is possible to follow the process of the collective identification and definition of the problem of violence in the early modern period up to the point where it was made into a collectively recognised issue possessing general or public significance. Transcending the specific details and plurality of the debates, the problem of violence was transformed into a general concern with power and the structures of power or with domination and the structures of domination of the time. Analysed in a more thorough and comprehensive way, however, the issue into which the problem of violence was transformed can be circumscribed as the collectively accepted concern with the survival of early modern society in its political environment. The central issue was how society could be secured within the volatile and unpredictable political context of the time. How could the political environment be brought to a state of rest and be sufficiently stabilised so as to allow the survival and continued existence of society? Or perhaps more properly formulated: how could society be brought into being and how could it be organised so as to take care simultaneously of its political framework?[28]

In the course of collectively identifying and defining violence as a problem, the different social actors or collective agents constructed it as a major societal issue of the time. This they did by bringing cognitive instruments or framing devices of an objectifying, moral and conative nature to bear on their situation and thus generating their own particular narratively presented symbolic packages. The first framing device focused on power as a requirement for the creation and maintenance of order, and allowed variation between a stress on the top or the bottom of the social scale. The second brought into play social relations and mutual recognition as a factor in the mastery of violence and disorder, and allowed variation on a continuum of closed and open social relations. The final micro-framing tool dealt with the pervasive need for meaning, which could be differently understood in terms of Catholicism and Protestantism as well as of different orientations toward power, wealth, prestige, and social interaction. Prioritising and combining these devices differently in narratively embedded symbolic forms, the social actors created distinct identities and ideologies for themselves in the form of cultural frames. The monarchy, the state and its varied supporters, engaging in narratives of the necessity and centrality of the monarchy and state, gave rise to a frame that allowed pride of place to the ideology of absolutism or Tacitism.[29] Its opponents, depending on the degree of recognition they were willing to give the state, related narratives or constructed symbolic packages in which the division of power or the people played a more significant role, and thus advanced either a constitutionalist[30] or an anti-statist populist or even fundamentalist frame.[31]

It is through identifying and defining or, rather, framing and communicating the problem of violence by means of these competing and conflicting narratively presented frames that the concerned social actors collectively established the survival of society in its political environment as perhaps the most pressing collective issue of the time. By which ideas or principles and forces could violence and unlimited competition be avoided in social life? What was needed to create, organise and maintain social life? What institutional conditions were necessary to assure the existence and development of an autonomous society? Indeed, through generating the early modern discourse in this way, the violence communication and the framing of the issue raised by the problem of violence gave rise to a novel, characteristically modern macro- or master frame – what will later be analysed as the rights frame.[32]

Sovereignty, Resistance, and Toleration

One way of uncovering the frame or cultural cognitive structure of the early modern discourse, which emerged from the construction of the problem of violence into the issue of the survival of society but remains hidden in the semantics of the violence debates, is to consider a bit more closely the primary sets of relations that were at stake at the time.

In the process of the formation of the absolutist, monarchical, territorial state during the Renaissance, the monarch fought on two fronts at one and the same time. One front was represented by feudalism, including feudal lords, corporatist institutions such as cities, diets and estates or *parlements*, and feudal customs and common law; the other was represented by the spiritual authority claimed first by the pope on behalf of the Catholic church and later also by Luther and Calvin. The concept of the absolute sovereignty of the territorial monarch was a weapon against feudalism, while the notion of the divine right of kings was used against the pope, the clergy and the new spiritual authorities. The success of the state in the battle for secular absolute sovereignty, which was due in part to support from many different quarters, led to three further crucial sets of relations. They found expression in the three structurally most important concepts of the early modern socio-political semantics, namely: sovereignty, resistance and toleration (Saage 1981) which were closely inter-related.

The first of these concepts, sovereignty, gave expression to the problematic relation between the absolute monarch and the people, and found formulation in the question as to who represents the seat of power or sovereignty, and whether domination is an acceptable form for power to take. In the discursive situation following on the disintegration of the religious-metaphysical world-view and the breakdown of the established order, this aspect of the issue compelled the different social actors to develop and put forward a justification or legitimation of public political power. The relation between the potentially tyrannical ruler and the people, highlighted by the abuse of monarchical power and the prevalence of state violence, often combined with economic and religious considerations, gave rise to the second concept, resistance. Its discursive articulation involved the determination and justification of the limits of state coercive force. Toleration, the last of the three concepts, sprang from the relation between the state and people as well as between different sections of the population with their own particular – both religious and economic –

concerns. Relating closely to the question of the limits of state power, on the one hand, it touched on spheres of autonomy carved out by the subjects of the state or citizens of the political community. Concerning different sections of the population, on the other hand, toleration had a bearing on the production and reproduction of distinct cultural, social and confessional groupings and relations between them.

The construction of the problem of violence into the issue of the survival of society in its political environment, and the concomitant articulation of relations in terms of such concepts as sovereignty, resistance and toleration, took place within a discursive process which became structured in a more or less clearly identifiable way. It is here that the emergent macro- or master frame of the time begins to loom large. The question is now what concept encapsulates most appropriately this overall discursive framework within which the aforementioned concepts found their place in the sixteenth and seventeenth centuries during the period of the complexly interrelated struggles among the array of early modern collective agents. If one employs an expression suggested by Anthony Giddens (1987a, 94),[33] one could speak of the early modern discourse generated by the debates about violence and disorder as the 'discourse of sovereignty' and, by extension, of its cognitive structure as the sovereignty frame. In this case, however, not only monarchical and state sovereignty must be included, as does Giddens, but popular sovereignty must also – indeed, in particular – be kept in mind. Alternatively, it could be referred to as the 'rights discourse' structured by the 'rights frame'. I prefer the latter nomenclature and will adopt it in the rest of this work. This choice may be hard to justify, since rights and sovereignty are conceptually equiprimordial. Rights and sovereignty necessarily form part of the constitutive conditions of a justifiable organisation of the public exercise of power.[34] But if a conceptual or logical justification is difficult to establish or perhaps even impossible to find, then there are other reasons that can be called upon. One is a historical semantic reason and another a thematic and eventually theoretical one.

Empirically, historical materials show that the development of the early modern discourse beyond its hegemonic determination by the absolutist state entailed an increasing and preponderant emphasis on rights. This is abundantly clear not only from the semantic trajectory that leads from the Revolt of the Netherlands through the English Revolution to the late eighteenth-century revolutions, particularly the French Revolution, but in particular from the development of the modern rights theory.[35] This reason alone is sufficient to justify the preference given in the present context to the expressions 'the rights discourse' and 'the rights frame', but there is also an important thematic reason for taking the concept of rights as a major reference point. It resides in the need to recognise the presence of two distinct dimensions at one and the same time. In the past, the dominant tendency has been to operate with the conceptual strategy of sovereignty and, as a consequence, to allow only the political dimension to come into view.[36] The opposite conceptual choice is made here with the specific intention of bringing out the social dimension, yet without suppressing the important political dimension. Even though the political question had been the primary one in the early modern period, it had nevertheless been posed in such a way as to make sense only in relation to the survival and autonomy of society. The rights discourse, together with its particular cognitive or cultural structure, turns on no less and no more than the issue of the survival of society in its political environment.

Two-Phase Structure of the Discourse

To be able to pinpoint the emergence of the rights frame, it is necessary to clarify the two-phase structure of societal discourse. Particular attention has to be paid to the crucial turning point or discontinuity at the heart of discourse that marks the cross-over from the first to the second of its two phases – the first of which is marked by a semantics of division, and the second by a semantics of coordination. In addition to the fact that it is discursively clearly identifiable, historical evidence drawn from different areas, all having a bearing on the important question of historical periodisation (e.g. Rabb 1975),[37] can be mustered to support the analysis.

An analysis of the violence debates and the discourse generated by them shows that a momentous shift had taken place in the early modern period. The analysis reveals a remarkable discontinuity in the period between 1572, the Massacre of St Bartholomew's Eve, and the 1640s, the Civil War in England and the Thirty Years War on the Continent. This discontinuous period, in which a drastic change took place, marks the transition between the two major phases of the rights discourse. The first was characterised by the breakdown of the religious-metaphysical worldview and, consequently, the prevalence of a high degree of uncertainty and unregulated or at best diffusely directed conflict between irreconcilable worldviews and antagonisms in all spheres of life. In the second phase, foundational assumptions were reconstituted and a new certainty slowly re-established, with the result that disagreement and conflict could be channelled in a more directed manner. Between the two phases a change of the greatest moment took place in that the cognitive order was reconstituted by the establishment of a new cognitive structure, cultural model or frame. A grasp of the early modern discourse depends on an appreciation of the precise nature of this phase-bound development from a loss of certainty to an intensive attempt to compensate for it.

Historically, the shift that occurred in the late sixteenth and the early seventeenth century in the early modern discourse can be descriptively supported by evidence drawn from a variety of fields. When one adopts a comparative perspective on the mid-sixteenth century and the late seventeenth and eighteenth centuries, one cannot but be struck by the stark contrast between the age of Reformation or the crisis of the Renaissance, on the one hand, and the age of Reason or the age of Enlightenment, on the other. Whereas the former had been a period of collapse, chaos, bewilderment, anxiety and destructive and self-destructive conflict between irreconcilable worldviews and antagonisms, the latter was a period of a recovery of nerve, clear ideas, potent guiding ideals, directed mobilisation and action, constructive conflict, and emancipation. In the historiography of the early modern period (e.g. Aston 1980; Rabb 1975), it is widely accepted that Europe had undergone a profound change in the course of the seventeenth century. This deep transformation occurred through a general crisis in the seventeenth century which, on the one hand, was triggered by a long period of change and decline which came to a head in the sixteenth century and, on the other, started to be resolved in the first half or so of the seventeenth century. At some time during the middle third of the seventeenth century, perhaps in its third quarter (Rabb 1975, 4, 116), Europe entered a new era in which a new sensibility as well as new social and political relations made themselves felt.

The contrast between the two eras in European history gains a sharp profile when one considers the difference in taste, standards and orientations as expressed by the visual arts, literature, music, religion, science, government, and so forth. Rabb (1975, 4) draws a line between:

> the taste of Rubens and the taste of Claude [or Vermeer]; between the commitments of Milton and the commitments of Dryden; between the aspirations of Charles I and those of his son, Charles II; between the ambitions of Condé in the 1640s and then during the last few years before his death in 1686; between the career of Wallenstein and the career of Eugène; between the reception of Galileo and the reception of Newton; between the angst-ridden striving for order of a Descartes or a Hobbes and the confidence of a Locke; between the image of Gustavus Adolphus, 'the champion of Protestantism', and Charles XII, the defender of Sweden's 'great-power position'; between the policies of Paul V and Innocent XI; between a society vulnerable and then relatively impervious to witchcraft panics.

To this illuminating list could also be added, perhaps, something more about painting as well as the caesura in music. As regards painting, it should be pointed out that the mannerism of the sixteenth century, which preceded the Baroque art of Rubens, Velázquez and Bernini, is one of the best sources for an insight into the way in which the early moderns processed the out-of-joint time in which they lived. The art of painters such as Pontormo, Parmigianino, Tintoretto, El Greco and Brueghel did not just exude restlessness, discomfort and imbalance, but it was the first form of reflexive art (Hauser 1951, II, 97–106; 1979).[38] As regards music, one could mention the big contrast between Palestrina, the leading Counter-Reformation composer of church music, for whom harmony was a by-product of counterpoint, and Bach, a composer of a wide range of music in Protestant north Germany, who considered harmony and counterpoint on equal terms and thus created a new balance between the harmonic and the polyphonic.

The profound change that had come over Europe in the seventeenth century can hardly be made more graphic than by reference to sources such as those mentioned above. A period of disorder, unease, conflict, destruction and the attempt to subdue uncertainty by grandeur and immensity was replaced by a period in which people started to regain their confidence and certainty and set out to bring some order and harmony into their world. It is of course the case that, despite this resolution of the crisis of the seventeenth century, certain differences and antagonisms remained and even became more acute, and that conflict did not simply disappear from the scene. Both the American War of Independence and the French Revolution still lay in the future.[39] The decisive battle against the *ancien régime* had still to be fought. Yet a fundamental change had taken place which draws a clear line between a period of the failure of nerve, collapse of identity, destructive and self-destructive conflict, and a period of the recovery of nerve, the formation of new identities, directed collective mobilisation and action aimed at building a new world – in short, between a period of uncertainty and a period of the regaining of certainty.

Interpretations of the Seventeenth-Century Change

The shift that occurred in the late sixteenth and seventeenth century in the early modern discourse has received different yet not necessarily mutually exclusive interpretations. Those of Giddens, Koselleck, Skinner, Hill and Toulmin, for instance, concern but different aspects of the same phenomenon.[40] A brief review of these interpretations could shed some light not only on the seventeenth-century change but also on the new emergent structuration factors.

146

From Monarchical to State Sovereignty

In his interpretation, Anthony Giddens (1987a, 94) focuses on the concept of sovereignty. He identifies a development, the turning point of which he locates in the work of Jean Bodin, published in 1576 as a critique of the Huguenot Revolution.[41]

Prior to this date, sovereignty was a quality that was associated with any individual of rank. Bodin, by contrast, gave the concept a more specific sense by arguing that there can be only one sovereign. Giddens, however, sees his characteristic contribution as residing less in the assertion of the transcendent or supreme authority of the individual monarch than in his proposal of a more generalised interpretation of state power. Although various of Bodin's followers pursued his argument so far that they were willing to defend the 'divine right' of a king to rule over a particular realm (Skinner 1978, II, 301), Bodin's concern with an absolute form of legislative sovereignty leads Giddens to conclude that he adopted a broader perspective. What makes Bodin's work so significant is that he was the first to argue for a concept of sovereignty that applies not merely to the authority of the monarch but rather to the power of the absolutist state. Sovereignty denoted the impersonal form of a coordinated system of administrative rule. Bodin thus contributed decisively to the transformation of sovereignty into a principle of government.

From Religion to Politics

Giddens arrives at his interpretation by confining himself to the intellectual level represented by the philosophers or political theorists of the time. If one adopts instead a broader discursive view that makes room for the debates among the social actors of the day which gave rise to the theories of the philosophers and political theorists, such as do for example Reinhart Koselleck (1985; 1988) and Quentin Skinner (1978), then the shift in question presents itself in a different yet complementary light. In this case, the change in question assumes the form of one from religion to politics.[42]

The dimension highlighted by Giddens, which is obviously embedded in what Tuck (1993, xiv) calls the 'culture of raison d'État', is doubtless of great importance in the present context. Yet if it is a matter of grasping the early modern discourse and its cognitive structure, if it is a matter of clarifying the relation between society and state, then a wider lens needs to be screwed on. That it is essential to adopt such a wider view over and above the one offered by Giddens is underlined by the fact that religion did play an important and perhaps even crucial role in the early modern discourse in a number of ways.

Not only did it serve as a potent stimulus towards violence, but it also provided one of the starting points for the establishment of rights.[43] It could be submitted, therefore, that the shift was not simply from monarchical to state sovereignty, but from the latter to popular sovereignty (see e.g. Habermas 1997, 177; 1998, 147).

After the Massacre of St Bartholomew's Eve of 1572 and the perceived threat of complete annihilation, and convinced of the necessity of winning support from the non-Protestant majority, the Huguenots found themselves under severe pressure. They had to find a generally acceptable theory of legitimate public political power that allowed a justifiable limiting of the coercive force of the state as well as resistance against a state power overstepping those bounds. Under these circumstances, they were compelled to begin to abandon their sectarian point of view together with the conviction that resistance could be legitimated solely on the grounds of religious uniformity. Although they were not yet able to be as clear and unequivocal as John Locke[44] more than a century later, instead of their religious position they adopted a specifically political theory of resistance or rather revolution, rooted in a clearly modern, secular assumption of the primacy of the sovereignty of the people (Skinner 1978, II, 334–43; Mandrou 1978, 135). Instead of theology and religion or the sacred tradition, they began to embrace politics; instead of sectarianism, they began to move in the direction of constitutionalism; instead of acting out of religious duty, they allowed themselves to be motivated by universalistic principles or rights;[45] instead of seeing sovereignty as being vested in the monarch as the potential protector of their faith, they began to realise that the only legitimate carrier of sovereignty can be the whole body of the people as a collectivity.

An unexpected turn in the tide of the Wars of Religion in France led the Catholics to make a comparable move. Faced in the wake of the death of the Duke of Anjou in 1584 with the prospect of an avowed Huguenot – i.e., Henry of Navarre – succeeding to the throne, they felt themselves compelled to take self-protective action. Their pamphleteers and some leading authors campaigned for a general insurrection against the Valois dynasty, and in this context they took a radical and decisive step. Their campaign was justified by recourse to the people as a whole (Mariana 1993; Skinner 1978, II, 345; Mandrou 1978, 136). Prior to the turn of the century, therefore, both the major religious groupings had arrived at a theory of popular sovereignty that was independent of religious creed yet simultaneously principled in the sense of avoiding capitulation before the type of cynical power politics represented by the Machiavellians and Tacitists.[46]

From History to Reason

Christopher Hill (1969, 158) adds another perspective on the shift, or what he calls 'a momentous transference', marking the development of the early modern discourse from its first to its second phase. For him, it was a shift from history, or rather 'bogus history', to reason.

Although Hill introduces it in relation to mid-seventeenth-century events in England, it would seem to apply equally well to what was happening in France, Scotland or Spain during the late sixteenth century. In these countries, the massive national histories of authors such as Hotman (*Francogallia*, 1573), Buchanan (*History of Scotland*, 1582) and Mariana (*History of Spain*, 1592)[47] were designed to serve systematic arguments, with the result that a change in reasoning was inaugurated. Historical argumentation was eventually overtaken by theoretical argumentation. In England, according to Hill's account, the situation was essentially similar. As against James I (1603–25) who still insisted on precedents as the only justification of arguments, the radical opponents of the Crown in the Civil War appealed instead to reason. Not only did reason have no precedent, according to their argument, but it was in fact the very origin of all legitimate precedents. Like the systematic theory of Hotman, Buchanan and Mariana, reason here meant a modern theory of the political organisation of society.

'Scaffolding of Modernity' or the Rights Frame?

Stephen Toulmin (1992) offers a very different interpretation of the seventeenth-century change – one that is both broader and more abstract than those reviewed above. While considering the disputes of early modern philosophers and scientists within the broader rhetorical context or discourse of the time, its focal point is what was earlier called the cognitive order of modernity. This concern gives it a particular relevance in the present context, for what I have proposed to call the rights frame represents a conception of this same cognitive order. The question then is which of the two conceptions is the more appropriate: Toulmin's 'scaffolding of modernity' or the rights frame?

Toulmin traces the emergence of the modern cognitive order to a radical turning point in European history between the years 1590 and 1640. In the wake of such disillusioning experiences as the assassination of Henry IV of France in 1610 and the Thirty Years War, the early moderns, including Galileo, Descartes, Grotius, Hobbes, the progressive clergy and the educated oligarchy who organised the education system and enjoyed access to printing and publishing, set about finding a new comprehensive system of ideas and shared presuppositions. This framework for the perception, experience and interpretation of reality in all its dimensions embraced both natural and socio-political ideas. On the one hand, the notion of nature was understood in terms of the well-ordered, stable, rationally comprehensible, heliocentric world of astronomy and, on the other, the notion of society and the system of sovereign states were regarded as ordered in a planned manner according to the principles of stability, hierarchy and paternalism. Toulmin (1992) variously refers to this new cognitive order as 'the modern world view' (108), 'the framework of modernity' (108, 116, 123), 'the scaffolding of modernity' (116–17, 128) or as 'the modern cosmopolis' (105–15).

The fact that Toulmin (1992, 118) is willing to give priority to a conception of the cognitive order of modernity as being equivalent to what he calls 'the Newtonian framework', however, reveals the real thrust of his interpretation. He approaches modernity from the point of view of natural philosophy and the natural sciences and conceives of the modern cognitive order accordingly. This means that he adopts a narrow perspective that excludes crucial developments which occurred during the late sixteenth and seventeenth century. Central to these developments is the discursive and hence cultural and social efflorescence that began in the 1570s and 1580 and provided the basis for the emergence of new cognitive structures in the form of a macro-frame, the rights master frame.[48] In addition to historical data of various kinds suggesting that this change occurred during the late sixteenth and the first part of the seventeenth centuries, this is supported by a historical analysis of rights theories. Having been preceded by an earlier spurt in the development of rights theories between the years 1350 and 1450, the modern rights theory began in the 1580s and enjoyed a huge efflorescence between the years 1590 and 1670 (Tuck 1979, 50, 177). The ideas of Du Plessis-Mornay, Mariana, Grotius, Selden, the Radicals and Locke gave expression to and helped to shape feelings, thinking and evaluations, so that social actors became motivated in a new way, acquired new concepts, and changed their behaviour accordingly. These cognitive structures forming the rights frame were encapsulated in the social and political ideals and moral standards that were carried forward by the struggles against the old order from the late sixteenth to the late eighteenth century. This interpretation of course does not entail an outright rejection of Toulmin's view of the modern cognitive order as the 'Newtonian framework', but it does bring into play a crucial complementary dimension overlooked by him. This dimension proved to be historically highly efficacious and of much significance for the emergence of modern society – indeed, so efficacious and significant that the social scientist cannot afford to ignore it.

Excursus: Violence, Power and Society in Early Modern Art

To explore the pervasiveness of the modern cognitive order, the following excursus presents a brief foray into early modern art, an area well beyond Toulmin's intellectualist confines.

Pieter Brueghel, *The Massacre of the Innocents*, c. 1565–67 (Kunsthistorisches Museum, Vienna)

During the sixteenth and the first third of the seventeenth century, a major trend in the painting tradition was to idealise kings and rulers, to eulogise courage and prowess, to immortalise imperial and monarchical aggression and military successes, and to glorify the court, state or empire. Artists such as Botticelli (1445–1510), Titian (c. 1487/90–1576), Tintoretto (1518–94), Rubens (1577–1640) and Velázquez (1599–1660) provide numerous excellent examples of this painterly preoccupation. It reached its dizzying heights in the grand and arrogant Baroque court art that developed concurrently with the Counter-Reformation. It is interesting to note (Rabb 1975, 128) that in the 1630s and 1640s a radical change occurred in the orientations and commitments of

151

European artists – a change, I submit, in keeping with the establishment of the rights frame during the same period. Being graphically the clearest from the oeuvres of precisely such leading later Baroque artists as Rubens and Velázquez, it consists of disillusionment with those very qualities that they had for so long eulogised and glorified. The works from their later years thus unequivocally display a resolute rejection of heroism and militarism and their misery-creating and devastating consequences, violence and war.

A mannerist artist of the sixteenth century, particularly of the time of the crisis of the Renaissance, indeed one of the greatest representatives of this style, Pieter Brueghel (c. 1525/30–69), was the only major painter who took a resolute stand against the current. During his career some three-quarters of a century earlier, he opposed the glorification of power and force, and especially the grandiose dressing-up of their dreadful consequences, by criticising political oppression, militarism, bellicosity, religious intolerance, persecution and, above all, violence. In many of his paintings, particularly those dating from the 1560s, he powerfully develops these commitments in the reflexive – i.e., thought-through, self-conscious and self-referential – manner typical of mannerism. Perhaps the best examples include *The Triumph of Death* (reproduced in Roberts 1992, 51), *The Massacre of the Innocents* (reproduced in Deinhard 1970, 39; Roberts 1992, 101; Gibson 1993, 140), and *Census at Bethlehem* (reproduced in Roberts 1992, 98).

Brueghel's famous painting, *The Massacre of the Innocents*, is of particular interest in this respect. It brings the painter's orientations and themes together and displays them in a way that articulates directly with the central concerns of this book, especially the present part. The painting works on three distinct levels.

To begin with, the overt theme of the painting is violence. This is indicated, first of all, by the age-old Biblical theme encapsulated by its title. In the wake of the breakdown of the religious-metaphysical worldview, however, it is dealt with in the secularised version of an event in a snow-covered, sixteenth-century village in the Netherlands. Although a contemporary scene, the representation of the event is unspecific inasmuch as it could equally well be taken to refer to any one of the following: the coercive imposition of state or imperial authority on the recalcitrant populace by a ruthlessly acting military unit, or the forcible gathering of taxes by a collector supported by an armed extortion unit, or the rigorous enforcement of the *placards* against heretics by the local Inquisition, or the persecution of religious dissidents. As regards content, secondly, the painting unequivocally depicts numerous acts of violence of various kinds, from the persecution of a fleeing mother and child in the lower left-hand corner, through the axing of shutters and ramming of doors on the right, to the abuse and brutal killing of children in the centre foreground of the picture.

Second, the overt acts of violence and the suffering of the victims point to a deeper dimension. This is achieved by the fact that both the violence and the misery turn on a causal agent – i.e., the unarmed commander clad in black at the head of the armed troop – who remains unidentified and undefined. What this indeterminacy or ambiguity at the visual centre of the picture evokes is the issue of power and power relations and, hence, the issue of the survival of the social in its political environment. By leaving the central agent of power unidentified and the contemporary event unspecified, moreover, the painting suggests that this issue is at the core of every significant historical event in the early modern period.

In a genial move, finally, the painting posits the existence of a critical third person point of view or a reflexive relation to the confusing plurality of differences constituting the social dimension. This it achieves in two steps: first, by making everyone in the picture a participant, whether active or passive, and thus allowing no onlookers within its frame; and second, by extending the pictorial space so as to include the viewer of the picture in a slightly raised position within the pictorial space itself. By compelling the viewer to confront the problem of violence and the issue of the time in this unavoidable way, the painting stimulates the viewer to take an evaluative stance towards the whole and to engage in a discourse in the course of which a critique of the different worlds can be developed – a critique of, for example, the detached indifference of those in power and the brutality of the henchmen, but also of the uncomprehending and resigned passivity of the victims. Through projecting such a discursively activated third point of view, Bruegel thus indicates toward a socially and politically relevant set of considerations or rules that could take his contemporaries beyond the contemporary situation.

(This interpretation draws on Deinhart [1970, 38–55], Hauser [1951, II, 97–143, 172–82], Rabb [1975, 124–39] and Giesen [1991, 243–47]; see also Stechow [1990], Roberts [1992] and Gibson [1993].)

The Rights Frame

Above, the argument was put forward that the early modern rights discourse was characterised by two phases that were separated yet linked by a transitional phase. The first phase of breakdown, disorder and uncertainty started in the years around 1500, and the second phase of the recovery of confidence and certainty came to an end in 1793 together with the first phase of the French Revolution. The transitional phase covering the period between the 1570s and the 1660s, which harboured the radical turning point between the first and second phases, marked a caesura or discontinuity in which a momentous change occurred. While the latter has been interpreted variously as having involved a shift from monarchical to state sovereignty (Giddens), from religion to politics (Koselleck, Skinner) or from history to reason (Hill), the suggestion was made that a more fundamental shift had taken place. I proposed that this shift could be understood best in terms of the cognitive order of modernity. For this is what is presupposed by all these interpretations. If there was a break with the old and the beginning of the new, what emerged from the discontinuity in the late sixteenth and the early seventeenth century? What stemmed the tide of breakdown, disorder and uncertainty? What provided the basis for renewed confidence and certainty? It was suggested that the answer is to be found in a new set of cognitive structures or a cultural model – what I proposed to call the rights frame, rather than Toulmin's 'scaffolding of modernity' in the sense of the Newtonian worldview.

The question that arises now is what an analysis of the rights frame would reveal.[49] Following the lead given in Part I above, the rights frame will here be analysed briefly as a cultural cognitive structure that makes possible the organisation of experience, the structuring of communication and, eventually, also identity formation and collective mobilisation and action. For this purpose, I make use of the cognitivist theory of frames put forward earlier.[50]

Cognitive Structures or Rules

To begin with, a frame is a set of cognitive structures or rules that allows human beings to classify the various objects in their world, thus organising their experience and making possible interpretations of nature, society and themselves. This it does by enabling them to give meaning to their world, to think about or conceptualise it, and finally to regulate their behaviour in relation to it. In this sense, a frame consists of aesthetic or conative, objective and moral cognitive structures (Eder 1996) or, differently, of evaluative, descriptive and prescriptive rules (Burns 1986; Burns and Flam 1990).

In the case of the rights frame, this basic structure turns on a classification according to which the constitution and organisation of society is best achieved by means of legitimately constituted politics. In the later justice frame, by contrast, it turns on society as such, and in the contemporary responsibility frame nature occupies the central position. As such, the rights frame consists of the following cognitive structural elements or rules: (i) human beings as individuals who mutually attribute rights to each other by virtue of their active nature; (ii) a complex or system of rights that specifies the conditions for the legal and political organisation of society and calls for realisation; (iii) the self-organisation of the sovereign associated individuals; (iv) collective legislation of the norms that will regulate the associated individuals, thus creating a juriscommunity; (v) an objective framework for the juriscommunity taking the form of the state; and finally (vi) a constitution in the sense of both an act of founding the politically organised society and the constant reinterpretation and further realisation of the rights of individuals as persons and as citizens.[51]

The rights frame consisting of these various components emerged and became established in the late sixteenth and early seventeenth century at the critical turning point towards which the preceding phase of breakdown and loss of certainty had been steering relentlessly. As a new master cultural cognitive structure, it provided a set of new assumptions, a new mode of classifying reality and a new approach to the interpretation of the situation. At the same time, it also made possible the projection of a collectively accepted vision of a solution to the societal problem of violence. The rights frame was thus the major factor in enabling early modern society to weather and pass through the debilitating crisis that had been staring it in the face. On this basis arose a new confidence and a slow process of the build-up of a new certainty. It is thus that the rights frame enabled the early moderns not only to form a new identity, or rather, a range of different yet closely related identities, but also to mobilise collectively for social change and to engage in collective action in an attempt to actually bring about the envisaged change.

Identity Formation

It was within the symbolic space opened up by the new cultural cognitive structure that the early modern social actors constructed new identities for themselves which were not merely recognisably but indeed characteristically modern. The central reference point shared by these identities, as we have seen, was the newly recognised matter of rights, the rights of persons and citizens, which in turn made possible the constitution of a sovereign association, of law, a juriscommunity, a state and hence a political community. The general structuring force, the general limits of identity construction, that emanated from the rights frame is what retrospectively came to be called 'liberalism'.[52] What is intended here, to be sure, is not liberalism in the nineteenth-century sense, particularly not the economic liberalism which came to displace the broad legal-ethical-moral doctrine of the preceding period.[53] Rather, the emphasis is on liberalism in the broad sense of a basic concern with a general right to freedom or liberty[54] which in the first place makes possible legitimate law and hence the political constitution of society. It is within the symbolic space of liberalism in this sense, sustained by the rights frame, that the early modern social actors were able, by bringing into play quite different experiences and interpretations, to discursively form or construct a variety of distinct and even opposing yet closely related identities.

Three of these identities proved to be of particular importance. The first, at the one extreme, is the Tacitist, etatist or absolutist identity constructed by royalty, patricians, and their supporters and sympathisers which gave priority to the state over the other dimensions of the rights frame. Thomas Hobbes, who is often regarded not merely as an apologist for absolutism but as the theorist of the constitutional state without democracy and hence as the real founder of liberalism,[55] in the course of time came to give paradigmatic expression to this identity. At the other extreme, secondly, critics and opponents of the king, monarchy or the state constructed a republican identity. This involved a selection from among the dimensions of the rights frame that gave pride of place to the juriscommunity as a self-organising society which absorbed the state. Between these two extremes, finally, a space opened up for the construction of constitutionalism as a distinct identity. This was undertaken by those who opposed the absolutists and the republicans and, hence, were critical both of the state and of the people to the extent that full and undivided sovereignty and power were claimed on their behalf. The rights frame was drawn upon in such a way that the emphasis was on the division or separation of powers and their balancing through regulation in terms of a constitution.

Had it not been for the enabling impact of the new master frame and its stimulation of activities aimed at the construction of a modern identity, collective mobilisation and eventually collective action in early modern society would simply not have been possible. It is through identity formation that the rights frame was able to effect collective mobilisation and action. All over Europe, and indeed beyond, people began to understand the society of which they formed a part as an arrangement that not only required but in fact itself constituted collective mobilisation and action in order to solve collective problems. If it is possible to pinpoint the moment of birth of modernity, the emergence of this self-understanding of society as depending on and indeed coinciding with collective mobilisation and action is the closest one could get to it. In one form, which initially tended to predominate with much ill effect, this mobilisation of collective action took place in relation to the state, organised around an impersonal, centralised and unifying system of government, based on law, bureaucracy, and a monopoly of force. In another increasingly potent form, however, the early modern mobilisation of collective action took place for the first time on a significant scale in the Netherlands and then in England, followed by the eighteenth-century developments in the British Colonies in

North America and finally in France. In this case, the early modern social movement comes into view. Given the considerable elapse of time between the years 1600 and 1789, however, it is only to be expected that the structuring effect emanating from the rights frame differed qualitatively quite sharply as between the Revolt of the Netherlands and the French Revolution. Between those two events, the frame itself underwent development and became consolidated, so that its own structuring force became enhanced in the course of time.

At this juncture, another important factor should be mentioned that started to come into play during the very period of the emergence and establishment of the rights frame and had the effect of reinforcing the second phase of the rights discourse – the phase of the gaining of confidence, the building up of a new certainty, of identity formation, and of collective mobilisation and action towards social change. This factor concerns the philosophical revolution of the seventeenth century and its most conspicuous product, science. Seventeenth-century science[56] contributed to the attempt to compensate for and overcome the loss of certainty that had occurred with the breakdown of the religious-metaphysical worldview[57] by supporting in various ways the unequivocal establishment of the rights frame. This had been the case already in the first two-thirds of the seventeenth century, as is attested by the publications of Grotius, Hobbes and Pufendorf, all of whom brought scientific insights to bear on the development of the modern theory of rights. The impact of science, while being refracted by social, political and moral concerns, showed progressively more strongly in the course of the seventeenth and especially the eighteenth century, as the centre of gravity shifted from England to France. Grotius, a contemporary of Galileo, was the fountainhead of seventeenth- and eighteenth-century rationalism in political and moral matters (Randall 1962, 159), but it was Hobbes who first proposed a 'social physics' (Randall 1962, 940) or a 'physics of sociation' (Habermas 1974a, 72) aimed at contributing towards the creation of order by the state (Merchant 1989, 192–215).

As regards the rights frame, science not only contributed to a clearer definition of the collectively accepted issue of social organisation, but also stimulated the formulation of a solution in terms of rationally conceived rights which are mutually attributed and borne by individuals. It is crucial to remind ourselves again, however, that from the time of its institutionalisation, science had been the preserve of the state,[58] and that the rights frame extended far beyond the state. The emerging notion of society did not remain confined to the space marked out by science and the state, as Toulmin's (1992) concept of 'cosmopolis' suggests, but extended in particular to the opposed and excluded sections of the population. In so far as science also served as the vehicle for the diffusion of the notions of mastery and improvement which from the start had been contained in the physico-theological assumptions supporting it (Groh and Groh 1991, 17–24), it undoubtedly helped to boost the sense of confidence and certainty of the social actors. The formation of the identity and particularly the collective mobilisation of those opposed to and excluded by the state and the scientific institutions established under its wing, however, cannot be plausibly traced back to science. For this we have to turn to the rights frame instead.

Early Modern Collective Mobilisation: Holland and England[59]

The novel cultural model represented by the rights frame, together with the new cultural orientations made available by it, had just begun to become recognisable in the late sixteenth century when it was drawn upon by the collective mobilisation and collective action of the Dutch against Spanish absolutism. The modern cognitive structures provided by the rights frame were thus still intermingled with medieval concepts and orientations. It required another fifty or sixty years for the rights frame to become worked out and established to such a degree that it could allow a thoroughly modern identity formation and collective mobilisation. This was the case for the first time only in the English Revolution. The crucial turning points in the rights discourse in these two countries when the emphasis shifted from religion to politics, and more strongly so in England than in Holland, were 1587 and 1643 respectively. A dual-level analysis of the rights discourse in the early modern period along the lines proposed in Part I reveals astonishing historical parallels between the Dutch and English cases, but also sharp differences in their respective socio-political semantics. Richard Saage's (1981) work based on pamphlet research, supplemented with that of Christopher Hill (1969; 1988; 1992) and Quentin Skinner (1978, II), proved particularly helpful in conducting such a discourse analysis.

In both countries, we see a fourfold configuration of forces involved in the framing and communication of violence and the political survival of society. Understanding themselves as protectors of the socio-political order, the Estates in Holland and the Parliament in England confronted monarchical absolutism with an objection against its concerted forcible effort to centralise the exercise of power in both the political and religious domains. In their struggle, both opposition movements were joined by a significant Calvinist minority who focused on the repressive religious politics of the state and linked up with commercial interests. In both countries, this minority not only became the main ideological and organisational force of the struggle, but also played a decisive role in curtailing the power of the radical anarchistic left wing of the opposition – the Anabaptists in Holland and the Levellers and Diggers in England.

Table 7.2: Chronology of the Revolt of the Netherlands against Spanish absolutism

1565	Philip II of Spain issues edicts against heresy, alienates nobility, and gives rise to crisis in the Netherlands
1567	Duke of Alba, backed by 9,000 troops, institutes the 'Council of Troubles', and executes prominent dissenters, including Egmont and Horn
1568	Outbreak of the Revolt of the Netherlands
1572	The capture of Brill by the Dutch Sea Beggars, followed by other towns; the Estates of Holland nominate William of Orange as representative of the King instead of the Duke of Alba
1573	The Duke of Alba is recalled by Philip II after a series of defeats
1574	The view that the king is subordinate to the natural representatives of the people, the Estates, gains currency in the northern provinces
1576	The 'Spanish Fury', i.e., the sack of Antwerp; north and south agree in the Pacification of Ghent to cooperate in expelling Spain
1577	Calvinist and popular uprisings
1578	Alexander Farnese, governor of Holland, improves Spain's fortunes
1579	Abortive peace congress at Cologne
1580	Philip II proscribes William of Orange; William presents his *Apology* to the States General putting into practice the Huguenot theory of resistance advanced by Du Plessis-Mornay
1581	The States General issues the Edict of Abjuration, formally deposing Philip II as sovereign of the Netherlands and declaring independence
1584	Assassination of William of Orange
1585	English army lands in the Netherlands in support of the Dutch
1587	Francis Vranck formulates the doctrine of popular sovereignty
1607	Armistice between Spain and the Netherlands
1609	Truce of Antwerp, obliging Spain to recognise the United Provinces
1622	Resumption of the war between Spain and the United Provinces
1648	Treaty of Westphalia ends the Eighty Years War between the Netherlands and Spain by forcing the latter to recognise the independence of the former

The respective sources on which the central powers and the opposition forces drew were also similar in Holland and England. Both the Hapsburgs and the Tudors had recourse to the absolutist ideology developed especially in relation to the French monarchy. The opposition movements in their early phase both appealed to existing medieval agreements – the *Joyeuse Entrée* in the Netherlands and the *Magna Carta* in England. Initially, when they still sought to protect the existing structure of privileges against encroachment by the absolutist monarchy, both movements established the legality and legitimacy of their anti-absolutist campaigns by recourse to historical precedents. Rather than blaming the monarch, they located the cause of the objectionable royal politics in misguided advisers who alienated loyal subjects. That a drastic change took place in the criticism of the absolutist state, however, is clear from a development in the two opposition movements' framings of the issue and hence in the semantics and cognitive structures of the discourse. Rather than appealing to history and religion, both movements started to make use of an abstract, principled mode of argumentation in which the concepts of natural, inalienable or mutually attributable rights and popular sovereignty played a central role. These concepts indicate the emergence and consolidation of a master frame, the rights frame, which allowed the formulation and consideration of such questions as the abolition of the monarchy and the establishment of a republican or constitutional government.

Despite the many graphic parallels, however, there are pronounced differences between the revolutionary movements in the Revolt of the Netherlands and the English Civil War. They become visible when one looks at the particular frames each communicated in the rights discourse once it had entered its second phase. In Holland, this was in the late 1580s and in England in the mid-1640s. The difference between the movements reveals the refinement and consolidation of the secularisation leap from religion to politics that had taken place in the intervening half a century. The frames by means of which the opposition movements delimit the issue of the political survival of society and seek to present a solution to it have a bearing on the legitimation foundations of the public exercise of power. The differences between the movements can therefore be located in their understanding of politics and law as well as in the use they make of such concepts as sovereignty, people and resistance.

Although the rights frame induced widespread mobilisation, the Dutch movement operated with the distinction between officials or magistrates and private persons, the former conceived in terms of the traditional *pater familias*, which led them to regard politics as the preserve of office holders. In accordance with the estate society of the early modern Netherlands, the office holders occupied the pinnacle of the people's hierarchy and as such were the only legitimate political agents of the people. In England, by contrast, the public political exercise of power was distinguished from the natural domination of the family head as something artificial attained by a contract between people who are equal and free. Consequently, politics could more readily be seen as a matter of the participation of all the citizens. The emphasis thus shifted to the individual as bearer of inalienable subjective rights.

More broadly than politics, then, a pronounced difference also existed between the Dutch and English movements on the question of the people or the social form of life that required political organisation. Following the French

Table 7.3: Chronology of the English Revolution

1628 Parliament refuses to support Charles I

1629 Charles I dissolves Parliament, imprisons its leaders, and rules without parliament for eleven years, the so-called 'Eleven Years Tyranny'

1640 After dismissal of the Short Parliament, the Long Parliament resolves to render personal monarchical rule impossible

1642 Outbreak of Civil War

1643 Adoption of the doctrine of parliamentary sovereignty

1649 The regicide: execution of Charles I; the English Commonwealth becomes a republic under Oliver Cromwell

1659 Richard Cromwell resigns

1660 Restoration led by General Monk: Charles II (1660–1685); James II (1685–1688)

1688 Glorious Revolution: William of Orange lands at Torbay to accept the Crown and James II flees to France

1689 Bill of Rights, limiting royal power by recognising the right of the people to depose the monarch when necessary

Calvinist *Monarchomachi*,[60] the Dutch conceived of the people in a holistic manner as a structured community that takes the form of an estate society and is concretely visible in the hierarchy of officials and magistrates. Here the individualistic orientations that were stimulated by the rights frame remained subordinated to the estate structure and were able to assert themselves strongly only later under the quite different conditions in England. In the latter case, the people consisted of equal and free individuals who possessed natural rights and originally lived a life free from the limitations of political power. It was only through a contract, the original compact, an exercise of human will, that these individuals have on utilitarian grounds come to the rational agreement to transfer part of their rights in a highly artificial arrangement to a political power who remained answerable to them. The Dutch movement indeed also regarded political power as the outcome of a contractual agreement between a ruler and the people. But whereas they thought in terms of the biblical covenant or *pactum* which led back to God, and whereas they employed it to re-establish or modify existing relations of super- and subordination, their later English counterparts no longer found it necessary to speak of God in this political context, nor to allow themselves to be limited by the existing social and political order.

In their respective conceptions of legitimate public political power, the opposition movements both in the Netherlands and in England had recourse to the concept of popular sovereignty. After an initial period of wavering, the

Dutch Estates, on the basis of their being the highest representatives of the people, declared themselves in 1587 the seat of sovereignty. In England, the idea of rule by majority started to operate in parliament and the doctrine of parliamentary sovereignty was worked out by 1643, while the radical opposition succeeded in extending the latter to mean the sovereignty of the people. Although the Dutch adopted the radical Calvinist idea of identifying sovereignty with the constitution as a whole, it was left to the movement in England to take the further step of establishing a link between popular sovereignty and legislation. In the 1640s, Parliament first accepted with Bodin that sovereignty is indivisible and then explicitly extended its claim to absolute legislative power. This also changed the concept of law itself. Rather than being an application of the laws of God and of nature, as it had still been regarded by the Dutch Calvinists, positive law was now seen as the will of Parliament, the conventional outcome of an institution that depends on the agreement of the individual members of the politically organised social community.

In both the Netherlands and England, the opposition movements appealed to the right to resist the monarch in order to bring an end to the misuse of absolutist power. The difference between the two movements at this level reflects the particular reception of the rights frame by each. In Holland, only office holders could legitimately resist the tyrannical abuse of power by the Spanish Crown with a view to correcting a corrupted legal state of affairs. Comparable tradition-bound arguments in England were marginalised by a more general framing of resistance as a derivative from the natural and inalienable rights of equal and free individuals. Radicals in particular appreciated the possibility that ordinary citizens could take the initiative and that this could be done to bring about political and social change rather than merely mending the existing state of affairs. Resistance, like toleration, thus allowed social groups to campaign for a series of civil rights such as freedom of religion, of speech, the press and petition as well as for the constitutionalisation of power through elections at different levels and the separation of legislative, executive and judicial powers. It is this constitutionalism that John Locke systematised towards the end of the century in order to provide an intellectual basis for the arrangement put in place by the Glorious Revolution of 1688.

The Late Eighteenth Century

What made its tentative appearance in the Netherlands was explicitly formulated and pursued in the English Revolution; what was barely recognisable as something modern in the former case assumed its full profile in the latter: not only the individual but also the constitution of society through collective action mobilised to solve a societal problem. Common to these cases, as to the American War of Independence and the French Revolution following them in the next century, was the fact that in each one the mobilisation of the collective action constituting society had been brought about through the mediation of the rights frame. What this means can be made clear by teasing out some of the implications of this master frame. All of the above-mentioned instances started from the problem of violence in the sense of the infringement and breakdown of the normative expectations maintained on the basis of the established legal framework consisting of a mixture of feudal law, canon law, revived Roman law and agreements such as the *Joyeuse Entrée* and the *Magna Carta*. Working this problem up into the issue of the survival of society in its political environment, they concentrated on the question of how society as a contract, society as a legal institution, civil society, could be organised to guarantee the rightful and proper exercise of public political power and to secure the safety and welfare of the population at large. By pursuing this issue publicly, all the early modern cases of collective mobilisation took the form of normative conflicts (Luhmann 1991, 140–42). They involved conflicts over norms or rights, conflicts both against and for norms or rights. Among the latter were the rights claimed by the church and the absolutist monarch to wield power by deciding between right and wrong, the legal and illegal; the right claimed by the population to resist the usurpation or unjustifiable use of power; the right claimed by individuals to possess a range of freedoms or liberties; and the right claimed by the people to make the law of the land. Finally, the intertwined normative conflicts against and for these various rights were given direction and guided by normative projections that became collectively known as liberalism – a concern with a general right to equal liberties, basic rights of due process, fundamental or basic rights of freedom, and rights-based limitations on the exercise of public political power. The constitutionalist strand of liberalism, which proved to be of particular importance in all four cases, was spearheaded in the early modern period by the Calvinist minorities in France, Holland and England in particular, frequently in alliance with commercial interests (Randall 1962, 128–30; Skinner 1978, II, 339–48). Towards the end of the seventeenth century, however, it was also adopted in state practice under the title of *lex fundamentalis* or fundamental law (Luhmann 1991, 142).

America

Well before the outbreak of the American War of Independence in 1775,[61] the perception of violence in the sense of infringed normative expectations had been spreading like a bush-fire through the British Colonies in North America

Table 7.4: Chronology of the American War of Independence

1765	Stamp Act passed by the British Parliament
1770	Boston Massacre
1773	Boston Tea Party
1774	British blockade of the port of Boston; First Continental Congress, Philadelphia
1775	Battle of Lexington; Second Continental Congress, Philadelphia
1776	Publication of Thomas Paine's (1995) pamphlet *Common Sense*; Declaration of Independence
1778	France joins George Washington's forces in the war against Britain, followed by Spain and the Netherlands
1781	Battle of Yorktown, Virginia, forcing the surrender of Lord Cornwallis to Washington
1783	Peace Treaty of Versailles: independence of the 13 North American Colonies
1788	Agreement on the Constitution of the United States of America
1789	George Washington elected as first president

by way of debates in both Britain and Europe as well as the Colonies themselves touching either directly or indirectly on the asymmetrical relations between the British Crown and the colonists (Gay 1969, 555–68). Drawing on and complementing the ideas of British and European radicals and Enlightenment *philosophes*, the colonists produced a flood of publications – pamphlets, sermons, newspapers and books – registering, analysing and denouncing every aspect of what was regarded as the tyrannical colonial government. The ensuing conflicts took shape around the perceived unjustifiable imposition of taxation by the British parliament on the colonies and were irreversibly escalated through the intransigence and incompetence of George III[62] and such events as the Boston Massacre, the Boston Tea Party and the resolute resistance of the colonists.

Document 1

The Declaration of Independence, 4 July 1776 (excerpt)

The Unanimous Declaration of the Thirteen United States of America

When in the Course of human events, it becomes necessary for one people to dissolve the political bonds which have connected them with another, and to assume among the Powers of the earth, the separate and equal station to which the Laws of Nature and of Nature's God entitle them, a decent respect to the opinions of mankind requires that they should declare the causes which impel them to the separation.

We hold these truths to be self-evident, that all men are created equal, that they are endowed by their Creator with certain unalienable Rights, that among these are Life, Liberty, and the Pursuit of Happiness. That to secure these rights, Governments are instituted among Men, deriving their just powers from the consent of the governed, – That whenever any Form of Government becomes destructive of these ends, it is the Right of the People to alter or abolish it, and to institute a new government, laying its foundations on such principles and organising its powers in such form, as to them shall seem most likely to effect their Safety and Happiness. Prudence, indeed, will dictate that Governments long established should not be changed for light and transient causes; and accordingly all experience hath shown, that mankind are more disposed to suffer, while evils are sufferable, than to right themselves by abolishing the forms to which they are accustomed. But when a long train of abuses and usurpations, pursuing invariably the same Object evinces a design to reduce them under absolute Despotism, it is their right, it is their duty, to throw off such Government, and to provide new Guards for their future security. – Such has been the patient sufferance of these Colonies; and such is now the necessity which constrains them to alter their former Systems of Government. The history of the present King of Britain is a history of repeated injuries and usurpations, all having in direct object the establishment of an absolute Tyranny over these States...

We, therefore, the Representatives of the United States of America in General Congress, Assembled, appealing to the Supreme Judge of the world for the rectitude of our intentions, do, in the Name, and by the authority of the good People of these Colonies, solemnly publish and declare, That these United Colonies are, and of Right ought to be Free and Independent States; that they are Absolved from all Allegiance to the British Crown, and that all political connection between them and the State of Great Britain, is and ought to be totally dissolved; and that as Free and Independent States; they have full Power to levy War, conclude Peace, contract Alliances, establish Commerce, and to do all other Acts and Things which Independent States may of right do. And for the support of this Declaration, with a firm reliance on the Protection of Divine Providence, we mutually pledge to each other our Lives, our Fortunes, and our sacred Honor.

(Source: Bramsted and Melhuish 1978, 224–27)

From the Declaration of Independence of 1776 it appears as though the war was quite traditionalistically regarded as duty-bound resistance against a tyrannical ruler and justified by reference to the protection of the existing rights and sovereignty of the people.[63] Yet there is evidence of an awareness of something beyond this traditionalist stance. Hamilton, one of the authors of

The Federalist, knew what was at stake in these conflicts and that it required the modern means of mobilised collective action at a critical moment in the history of the human species:

> The subject speaks its own importance; comprehending in its consequences, nothing less than the existence of the UNION – the safety and welfare of the parts of which it is composed – the fate of an empire... It has been frequently remarked, that, it seems to have been reserved to the people of this country, to decide by their conduct and example, the important question, whether societies of men [sic!] are really capable or not, of establishing good government from reflection and choice, or whether they are forever destined to depend, for their political constitutions, on accident and force. If there be any truth in the remark, the crisis, at which we are arrived, may with propriety be regarded as the period when that decision is to be made; and a wrong election of the part we shall act, may, in this view, deserve to be considered as the general misfortune of mankind (Hamilton et al. 1948, 1).

His emphasis on the need to take the necessary steps in a moment of crisis to allow 'reflection and choice' to have their sway, instead of 'accident and force', leaves no doubt about the preferred pathway. The normative projections drawn from the rights frame and informing this endeavour found expression in the modern constitution of the United States of America with its Bill of Rights as well as in the federal system of government it founded.

France

The aim of the mobilisation of the French Enlightenment[64] movement had been to smash the infamous Catholic monarchical system brought to such terrible perfection by Louis XIV and his chief minister Colbert or, in the overstated melodramatic turn of phrase of the day, 'to throttle the last king in the bowels of the last Jesuit' (cited in Randall 1962, 851).[65] This aim was formed against the background of an absolutist Catholic monarchy which in the eighteenth century still engaged in increasingly unacceptable practices: waging wars generated by ludicrous intrigues and leading to the devastation of peasant housing and crushing taxation; burning representatives of religious minorities for doing their pastoral duties; torturing to death members of religious minorities falsely accused of sectarian family murder; opposing the leading philosophical and scientific ideas of the time and the enlightenment they promised; practising a ferocious penal style assuming theatrical proportions in public; cultivating luxury and magnificence at court at the expense of subjecting the population to extortionary and confiscatory measures enforced by mercenary troops, and so forth. The struggle in which the Enlightenment *philosophes* opposed the old order, *la lutte philosophique*, was complemented by various other forms of action.

The mobilisation and action of the early modern French movement bear out the fact that the Enlightenment by no means constituted a homogeneous group. Rousseau, who sought to salvage classical republicanism and to give it a form appropriate to the demands of his time, strongly opposed the more typical conviction of the *philosophes* that the state could be depended upon to bring about enlightenment and reform. There were also the struggles of the bourgeoisie in the economic field and in free associational institutions such as salons, clubs, reading circles and secret societies where they often met with aristocrats and where new abstract principles were being experimented with and shaped in an atmosphere of debate (Koselleck 1988, 86–97; Eder 1985, 152–229; Huysseune 1993). Then there were the attempts of reformist administrators within the absolutist state itself, such as Turgot and Necker as well as of their principal rivals, the Physiocrats, to decentralise the state by the creation of a hierarchical system of assemblies of property holders (Baker 1992, 194–98).[66] These various attempts were in turn directed against the struggles of the provincial *parlements* under the direction of their presidents and magistrates to establish a system of public political checking of arbitrary monarchical government (Shklar 1987, 79–81; Baker 1992, 194, 195). In the rights discourse in eighteenth-century France, therefore, a whole range of social actors can be identified who gave rise to three competing frames, namely enlightened absolutism or despotism represented by the reformist administrators, Physiocrats and many of the *philosophes* and the bourgeoisie for whom they spoke; a potentially democratic yet populist republicanism proposed by Rousseau and his followers; and finally constitutionalism, advanced by some *philosophes*, the provincial *parlements* and some of the bourgeoisie.

The eighteenth-century ideals of freedom, equality, solidarity, toleration, democracy, cosmopolitanism, and humanity were in some way or another associated with all of the above-mentioned actors. These ideals indeed gave expression to the ideology of the nascent bourgeoisie, as has been emphasised since Marx, yet far from having been the preserve of this group, they contained a surplus of meaning that went well beyond the interests of any particular group or social class. They were normative – i.e. moral and legal – projections made in accordance with the cultural cognitive structure of the discourse of the time, the rights frame, and as such they provided the cognitive basis for numerous campaigns carried by the collective action of different social actors and the founding of a whole range of new rights-based institutions. Besides the abolition of the *ancien régime* in France, North America and elsewhere,

Table 7.5: Chronology of the French Revolution

1787	Dissolution of the Assembly of Notables; *Parlement* of Paris calls for an Estates-General; exile of the *parlementaires*
1788	Judicial reform reducing the powers of *parlements* resisted by provincial *parlements*; the Estates-General convened for 1789 and Paris *parlement* insists on retention of its form of 1614; publication of Sieyès' *Essay on Privileges*; the King's Council in favour of doubling the Third Estate's representation
1789	
Jan	Publication of Sieyès' *What is the Third Estate?*
Apr	Réveillon riot in Paris
May	Opening of Estates-General; Third Estate demands common verification of the powers of the three orders
June	The Third Estate constitutes itself as the National Assembly; the clergy joins the Third Estate; the Tennis Court Oath; the king is compelled to allow the nobility and clergy to meet with the Third Estate; movement of troops towards Paris and Versailles
July	Taking of the Bastille; peasant revolts and the Great Fear in the provinces
Aug	Destruction of the feudal regime; Declaration of the Rights of Man and of the Citizen
Oct	Women of Paris march on Versailles
1790	Assembly rejects Catholicism as state religion; adoption of the Civil Constitution of the Clergy
1791	Louis XVI and Marie-Antoinette take to flight, are arrested and brought back to Paris; the king takes the oath on the constitution
1792	
June	The king vetoes legislation; the Tuileries stormed and the king suspended
Aug	The royal family is incarcerated
Sept	Royalty is abolished
Nov	Discovery of the royal family's papers in the Tuileries
Dec	Robespierre demands the death of the king; appearance of Louis XVI before the Convention on two occasions
1793	
Jan	The Convention approves the death of the king; execution of Louis XVI
Feb	Declaration of war on Britain and Holland
March	Declaration of war on Spain
Apr	First Committee of Public Safety
June	Fall of the Girondins
July	Renewal of the Committee of Public Safety; Robespierre enters the Committee
Sept	The Terror on the agenda of the Convention
Oct	Proclamation of revolutionary government; execution of Girondins
Nov	Further executions
Dec	Crushing of the Vendéens by the republican army
1799	Napoleon Bonaparte's coup d'état of Brumaire

(A comprehensive chronology from 1770 to 1880 is contained in Furet 1992, 538–65) numerous other campaigns were undertaken. Among them were the establishment of rights, including basic rights of due procedure and basic civil rights or liberties; the reform of the law, the legal system and penal style; toleration of religious minorities, intellectual dissenters and sexual deviants; the creation of a climate of opinion necessary for the minimisation of war and the advancement of peace; changing people's minds to prepare for the abolition of slavery and, more generally, the reduction of human misery; universal and humane education; and so forth. The 'Declaration of Independence' of 4 July 1776 and the so-called 'principles of 1789', the *Déclaration des droits de l'homme et du citoyen* of 26 August 1789, as well as the various constitutions following them, are significant yet only the most obvious institutional outcomes of these campaigns. They gave representation to conflicting and competing values and interests through the establishment of rights, allowed political participation by citizens, and limited the power of the state, thus solving the problem of violence and hence resolving the issue of the survival of society in the political environment. As in the preceding historical cases, however, a whole new institutional infrastructure was brought into being whose characteristic uniqueness can only be understood by reference to the rights discourse and its cultural cognitive structure, the rights frame. This new institutional complex is represented by the rights-based constitutional state.

Document 2

Declaration of the Rights of Man and of the Citizen, 26 August 1789

The representatives of the French people, constituted as the National Assembly, considering that ignorance, disregard, or contempt of the rights of man are the sole causes of public misfortunes and the corruption of governments, have resolved to set forth, in a solemn declaration, the natural, inalienable, and sacred rights of man, so that the constant presence of this declaration may ceaselessly remind all members of the social body of their rights and duties; so that the acts of the legislative power and those of the executive power may be the more respected, since it will be possible at each moment to compare them against the goal of every political institution; and so that the demands of the citizens, grounded henceforth on simple and incontestable principles, may always be directed to the maintenance of the constitution and to the welfare of all.

Consequently, the National Assembly recognises and declares, in the presence and under the auspices of the Supreme Being, the following rights of man and the citizen:

Article 1. Men are born and remain free and equal in rights. Social distinctions can be based only on public utility.

Article 2. The aim of every political association is the preservation of the natural and imprescriptible rights of man. These rights are liberty, property, security, and resistance to oppression.

Article 3. The source of all sovereignty resides essentially in the nation. No body, no individual can exercise authority that does not explicitly proceed from it.

Article 4. Liberty consists in being able to do anything that does not injure another, thus the only limits upon each man's exercise of his natural rights are those that guarantee enjoyment of these same rights to the other members of society.

Article 5. The law has the right to forbid only actions harmful to society. No action may be prevented that is not forbidden by law, and no one may be constrained to do what the law does not order.

Article 6. The law is the expression of the general will. All citizens have the right to participate personally, or through their representatives, in its formation. It must be the same for all, whether it protects or punishes. All citizens, being equal in its eyes, are equally admissible to all public dignities, positions, and employments, according to their ability, and on the basis of no other distinction than that of their virtues and talents.

Article 7. No man may be accused, arrested, or detained except in cases determined by the law and according to the forms it has prescribed. Those who solicit, expedite, execute, or effect the execution of arbitrary orders must be punished; but every citizen summoned or seized by virtue of the law must obey at once; he makes himself guilty by resistance.

Article 8. The law may lay down only those penalties that are strictly and evidently necessary, and no one may be punished except by virtue of a law established and promulgated prior to the offence, and legally applied.

Article 9. Every man is presumed innocent until he has been found guilty; if it is considered indispensable to arrest him, any severity not necessary to secure his person must be strictly repressed by law.

Article 10. No one must be disturbed because of his opinions, even in religious matters, provided their expression does not trouble the public order established by law.

Article 11. The free expression of thought and opinions is one of the most precious rights of man: thus every citizen may freely speak, write, and print, subject to accountability for abuse of this freedom in the cases determined by law.

Article 12. To guarantee the rights of man and the citizen requires a public force; this force is therefore instituted for the benefit of all, and not for the personal advantage of those to whom it is entrusted.

Article 13. A common tax is indispensable to maintain a public force and support the expenses of administration. It must be shared equally among all the citizens in proportion to their means.

Article 14. All citizens have the right to ascertain, personally or through their representatives, the necessity of the public tax, to consent to it freely, to know how it is spent, and to determine its amount, basis, mode of collection, and duration.

Article 15. Society has the right to demand that every public agent give an account of his administration.

Article 16. A society in which the guarantee of rights is not secured, or the separation of powers not clearly established, has no constitution.

Article 17. Property being an inviolable and sacred right, no one can be deprived of it, unless legally established public necessity obviously demands it, and upon condition of a just and prior indemnity.

(Source: Baker 1987, 237–39)

The Transformation of Violence into Legitimate Power

In the above, it was argued that the early modern rights discourse that grew up around the problem of violence, which had been made into the societal issue of the survival of society in its political environment, had a complex outcome. On the one hand, it led to the recognition of both positive and negative rights guaranteeing political participation or the shared practice of citizens as well as individual freedoms or liberties. On the other, it eventuated in the establishment of the new institutional infrastructure of the constitutional state. From an abstract theoretical point of view, this implies that the rights discourse was a central factor in a profound transformation in the mode of coordination of social action. Above and beyond modes of action coordination centred on the direct use of force that predominated in the earlier part of the early modern period, the discourse provided the means as well as a social space within which less costly and more humane modes of coordination could be developed and institutionalised. It allowed the articulation of credible cognitive content and the institutionalisation of cognitive structures forming part both of people's heads and of culture. What is particularly striking when one considers somewhat more concretely the process of the coming into being of rights, and the institutional complex of the constitutional state as a whole, is the transformation that violence underwent as a result of the solution brought to bear on it by means of collective action mobilised through the rights frame. Violence was transformed into legitimate power in the sense of power exercised within certain clearly circumscribed limits and largely acceptable to the people involved.

171

Figure 7.2: Historical process of the transformation of violence

Rights frame	Constitutionalisation of the state
1572–1640/60s	1648 Dutch Republic
emergence of the rights frame	1688 English mixed monarchy
identity formation	1776 Declaration of Independence
collective mobilisation	1788 United States of America
	1789 Declaration of Rights of Man
1	2
cognitive-symbolic	institutional
transformation	transformation
cognitive	normative
institutionalisation	institutionalisation

The process of transformation of violence can be observed at two distinct levels – what may be called the cultural cognitive-symbolic and the institutional level. These two dimensions can be accessed by reference to the rights frame and the rights-based institutional infrastructure of the constitutional state respectively. Whereas the establishment of the various sets of rights and constitutions as well as eventually the constitutional state involved institutionalisation in the traditional sociological sense of normative institutionalisation, the interesting phenomenon of what may be called cognitive institutionalisation (Eder 1996, 202) is brought to the fore by the establishment of the rights frame. In turn, this cognitive institutionalisation was crucial to the identity formation and collective mobilisation that followed in the wake of the rights frame.

To be able to analyse the change in the mode of action coordination in terms of the transformation of violence into legitimate power, however, we need a few more theoretical instruments. For this purpose, I propose to make explicit the concepts of logics of development of society and of power of which use was made in much of the foregoing argumentation.

Logics of Society

Behind the emergence of modern society, as implied in the account given in previous chapters, lie a number of different dynamic forces. On the one hand, they contributed decisively to the erosion and breakdown of the medieval feudal order and, on the other, brought modern society into being. They are at times mutually supportive, but at other times contradict one another. For present purposes, four of these forces, sometimes also called 'logics' (Heller 1982, 281–98; Arnason 1994, 208–09), can be identified.

The first logic is the centralisation of power and the means of violence and, hence, the formation of the state. This process started in the medieval period, but gained in impetus in the fifteenth and sixteenth centuries during the Renaissance period, and then culminated in the establishment of the absolutist state or, more generally, the *ancien régime* in seventeenth- and eighteenth-century Europe. French absolutism under Louis XIV, the so-called 'Sun King', which was brought down by the French Revolution in 1789 and transformed into a modern constitutional state, is the paradigmatic example of this development.

The second logic of development of society is made up of technology and science. On the one hand, the development of technology, hastened by the manufacture of weapons, especially the cannon, culminated in the industrial revolution of the late eighteenth and early nineteenth century and the consequent heavy industrialisation of society. On the other hand, the philosophical revolution and the resultant institutionalisation of early modern science in the seventeenth century led to the scientific revolution which took place first in chemistry in the eighteenth century, passed through biology in the nineteenth century and physics in the early twentieth, and today has molecular biology in its grip. The fusion of science and technology has furthermore provided the basis of the predominant chemical and electronic industries of the twentieth century. From the start, however, the state monopolised this logic of development, particularly in the early modern period.

The remaining two forces operative in modern society are both connected with civil society in the sense of free and equal individuals and groups who are able to make unconstrained use of various forms of interchange, such as communication and money. The third logic is what has in the wake of Karl Marx's famous main work of 1867 become commonly known as 'capitalism'. It entails the establishment of private property, the global extension of the market, and the increase of inequality. The fourth logic, finally, which is also intrinsic to and indeed most characteristic of civil society, is what has come to be called 'democracy'. It takes the form of the project to realise ever more fully and to enforce through legal means the rights and freedoms of individuals, and thus to create greater equality among citizens and to decentralise and to civilise or rationalise power.

At the outset of the present part, the phenomenon of violence was investigated in three significant contexts that arose in relation to the historically specific intertwining of these different logics. The first was the long-term process of the formation of the state, particularly the monopolisation of force as well as of culture and science by the state. In this case, the focus was on absolutist violence. The second was the equally protracted process of the development of capitalism, during the early modern period particularly in the crucible of mercantilism. In this context, we were interested in capitalist violence. The Reformation, the Counter-Reformation and the subsequent Wars of Religion provided the third historical context of early modern violence. Here religious violence occupied the centre of attention.

Social, Administrative and Communicative Power

To be able to go beyond early modern forms of violence by tracing the emergence of more abstract modes of action coordination, it is necessary to make explicit the indispensable concept of power of which use has been made thus far. While Foucault's contribution to the recognition of the role of power in discourse is indispensable, Habermas' (1996, 143, 147–50, 173–76) threefold concept of social, administrative and communicative power, introduced not only in response to criticisms of his earlier work but also to meet the challenge of Foucault and his followers, is of particular importance is the present context.

The threefold concept of power embraces, first, social power in the sense of the ability of an actor to pursue his or her interests in the context of social relations despite opposition or resistance. This is essentially the Weberian concept of power that covers socially resourceful and powerful actors who are able to pursue their own interests, but it is also an element of Foucault's conception. To this is added, secondly, administrative power in the sense of the ability of the state administration or executive and the judiciary to establish, organise and apply measures deemed necessary for the attainment of collective goals. This dimension, heightened to an extreme degree, is a prominent part of Foucault's account of power. Most characteristically, Habermas includes communicative power in the sense of the ability of the members of society as citizens to make use of their communicative freedoms or rights to generate power potentials, for instance to posit legitimate law and to establish and regenerate administrative power. This dimension represents the positive side of power that is not well developed in Foucault's work or, rather, is only developed to account for the overall negative sense of power, i.e. the guidance and control of communication and action. Above all, however, Habermas' conception brings reflexivity into play, which is utterly lacking in Foucault. On the other hand, the hidden power structures emphasised by Foucault retain their relevance. Despite the transformation of violence into legitimate power, one has to bear in mind the likelihood that hidden power structures continue to exist and retain a certain degree of efficacy.

Considering the conceptual elaboration of logics of development and power above, I propose to use the following theoretical scheme to analyse the transformation of violence in the context of the early modern rights discourse: it is assumed that there is a link between the major forms of violence borne by the logics of development, which were presented in Chapter 6, and the threefold concept of power. In order to make the transformation of violence into legitimate power intelligible, capitalist violence in its pure form is regarded as being related to social power, while absolutist violence is assumed to point toward administrative power. In the case of religious violence, an attempt will be made to grasp its transformation by means of the concept of communicative power.

From Religious Violence to Communicative Power

An analysis of the cognitive-symbolic transformation of violence that eventuated in the establishment of the rights frame will have to concentrate first on religious violence and communicative power. The transformation of religious violence took place at the crucial turning point in the early modern discourse. During the late sixteenth and the early seventeenth century, religious violence was transformed, at least tendentiously, into communicative power. This transformation was marked by the emergence of the rights frame. The communicative power at issue here is that of a pluralistic community characterised by sub-cultural tensions yet a non-violent and tolerant but not necessarily conflict-free political culture. It is only by means of this communicative power, based on the rights or communicative freedoms of the human beings and citizens, that the legal norms and the normatively grounded constitution were generated whereby two further transformations could be effected: the transformation of the violence or arbitrary power of the absolutist state into legitimate political (in the narrow sense) or administrative power, and the transformation of capitalist violence into more or less regulable social power.

From Absolutist Violence to Administrative Power

When the absolutist monarchy first claimed and exercised the right to monopolise the means of physical violence, the social reality of violence itself changed from something immediate and direct pervading everyday life into something that could be regulated organisationally and legally and controlled by means of decisions. Violence was taken up and centralised in an institution and identified with power, absolutist power, the power of the absolutist monarch and state. In a sense, violence was institutionally transformed. Violence could be accessed and employed only in certain regulated and controlled ways (Elias 1982, 235–40; Willke 1992, 219), for instance, through state and military decisions. Since the absolutist state through *raison d'État* retained arbitrary disposal over the law, however, the latter did not and, indeed, under these conditions could not operate as a source of justification that legitimated the exercise of publicly relevant power (Habermas 1996, 145). Arbitrary absolutist power could not count on being accepted by the populace at large. In proportion as it lacked legitimacy, absolutist power retained the character of violence. Power and violence were one.

It was in the face of this unity of absolutist state power and violence that the movements that had been mobilised under the auspices of the rights frame and eventually constitutionalised the absolutist state, such as those in Holland, England, the American Colonies and France, entered the scene. These movements did two things. First, they brought the rights frame generated through communicative power to bear on the monopolised violence of the absolutist state. This means that they related new feelings, emotions or meanings, a new way of thinking and a new way of behaving, all in accord with the new cultural model that emerged from the rights discourse, to the reality of absolutist state power and violence. Secondly, these movements subjected the absolutist state to constitutional and political rules of legitimation. Under this twofold impact, violence underwent a further drastic transformation. This is the transformation that is relevant in the present context. On this occasion, its meaning as well as its institutional form changed fundamentally. Violence was not only cognitively or symbolically transformed by means of the rights frame, but it was also institutionally transformed by the creation of a new institutional complex, the constitutional state.

In accordance with this twofold cognitive-symbolic and institutional transformation, violence was subjected to a process of communication. In the medium of communication, the exercise of power was through democratically posited law and legitimate politics linked to the agreement or acceptance of those affected by power (Habermas 1996, 146–50; Willke 1992, 222). In addition to having been centralised and subjected to regulated decision-making in the context of the absolutist state, then, violence was by symbolic and institutional means civilised (Elias 1982) or rationalised (Habermas 1973, 358–59; 1989a, 1996, 300; 1992b) and thus rendered communicatively regulable.

From Capitalist Violence to Social Power

On the basis of communicative power and administrative power, it became possible for the first time to transform capitalist violence into a form of social power that could be regulated. Initially, capitalism took the violent form of the primitive accumulation of capital, involving both the enclosure movement and external explorations, trade on mercantilist principles, and colonialism. In the wake of the constitutionalisation of the state and the establishment of rights and a legal order or rule of law, capitalist violence in its original form was curtailed. It now had to operate within the limits of the law. In so far as this was the case, it took the form of the exercise of social power that is more or less legitimate or acceptable to the populace.

The transformation of capitalist violence into social power did not exclude, of course, its persistent tendency towards the creation of inequality against which democratisation, on the basis of further spurts of constitutionalisation, constantly battles. The subsequent history of the nineteenth century, when the social problem and the justice discourse displaced the early modern problem of violence and the rights discourse, provides enough evidence of the continuation of these contrary trends – not to mention the need for monitoring capitalism raised by the current phenomenon of bio-colonialism (Strydom 1999c, 25).

Rights and the Constitutional State

These three instances of the transformation of violence into more or less legitimate forms of power found embodiment in the formal establishment of both positive and negative rights, the constitutionalisation of the state, and in the organisation of society around the constitutional state. The new institutional arrangement, supported by wide-ranging processes of communication among members of society and citizens of the state, was thus able, at least to a significant degree for the time being, to tame capitalist,[67] absolutist and religious violence. This it did by separating and balancing the three powers crucial to the organisation and integration of society: money, administrative power, and solidarity (Habermas 1996, 150). The central political institutions embodying administrative power were linked to communicative processes of opinion- and will-formation and of law making, while being shielded to a significant degree from the illegitimate and distorting interference of social power.

The different dimensions of the new institutional complex (Willke 1992, 222; Habermas 1989b, 26–27; 1996, 150), which had been brought into being by collective action in accordance with the rights frame in the early modern period and consequently took a slightly different form in the various countries involved, are clearly visible against the backdrop of the multi-level process of the transformation of violence. Above all, it needs to be noted that, in accordance with the transformation of different types of violence through communication, it can be conceived in general as an institutional complex involving constitutionalised legitimate power. This means that it is made up of three distinct dimensions. The first consists of rights, a constitution and law, while the second embraces a formal political decision-making system wielding administrative power, which extends into the courts, the police, the prisons, and the military. Finally, the former two dimensions are surrounded by a penumbra of private organisations wielding social power as well as by a diffuse public possessing the ability to organise itself into voluntary associations and movements wielding communicative power. While the core of this institutional complex is occupied by a political system, it is ultimately based on and regulated by a normatively grounded legal system.[68]

The institutional complex of the constitutional state, however, owes both its coming into being and its continued existence to collective actors belonging to civil society. These actors had been able to mobilise on the basis of identities formed through cultural cognitive structures mediated by the rights discourse, and they continue to make use of their communicative freedoms to posit legitimate law so as to regenerate administrative power and to keep social power at bay.

The Rights Discourse as Crisis Discourse

A final caveat must be appended to the above analysis of the rights discourse. The apparent emphasis in the foregoing on the opposition movements and the constitutionalism promoted by them should not be allowed to mislead one into over-emphasising the significance of social or protest movements in the construction of society. They must at all times be seen in relation to the other social actors with whom they share a master frame within a given communicative and discursive context. As regards the relations between these different social actors, the literature suggests that different emphases are possible, some of which are clearly unacceptable taken on their own. Of crucial importance in unravelling these relations is to make an allowance for things to go wrong, but also for the possibility that they could be corrected.

As early as 1959, Reinhart Koselleck (1973, 12; 1988, 16) forwarded the interpretation that the abuse of power in absolutism created the conditions under which the subjects of the king for the first time discovered themselves as citizens. This discovery represented a significant gain in that it opened the possibility of a moralised or constitutionalised state power, yet the peculiar historical form in which it occurred rendered the formation of modern society pathogenic. In *Discipline and Punish*, Foucault (1979, 16) gives this same historical phenomenon a theoretically profound twist to mean that an inner world or 'soul' filled with arbitrarily manipulable contents had been produced by external power techniques. However, since he thinks strictly in terms of sheer power and confrontation, since he excludes communicative action, reciprocity and mutual understanding in the form of values, norms, institutions[69] and even cultural cognitive structures, since his work lacks a reflexive dimension, he is unable to go beyond a general account of modern society as a power-saturated arrangement. This he could have done by for instance acknowledging the gains in liberty, legal security and civil and procedural rights made on the basis of the interaction between the absolutist state and its subject population, and by showing how the pathological features of modern society could be identified, challenged and changed. Something of this kind was approached by Barrington Moore (1987) with his demonstration that violence contributed to the development of a democratic society. What Foucault left undone, despite his submission that '[p]ower ... circulates' (Foucault 1980, 98), Giddens (1987a, 10–11, 201–02)[70] recently captured by means of an account in terms of what he calls, harking back to Hegel's master–slave dialectic, the 'dialectic of control'.

This dialectic refers to the fact that, as surveillance and control from above call forth counter-strategies and struggle from below, a context is established within which those at the top necessarily presume a minimum degree of confidence and active compliance on the part of those below them, with the result that the latter are able to carve out spheres of autonomy for themselves and thus to influence and put pressure on the authorities. At the core of this dialectic of control and contestation is a set of reciprocal relations – involving communication, mutual understanding and mutual recognition – which provides the anchorage for the development of rights and, hence, a constitutional basis for the state. While Foucault stresses the dimension of surveillance and control and regards resistance as the only response to it, both Moore and Giddens offer a more balanced account by conceiving of contestation from below as more than sheer resistance. But even then one still requires the addition of the crisis theoretical perspective focusing on the pathogenesis of modernity proposed by Koselleck – although one might be unwilling, as I am, to accept the precise terms in which he states it. To underpin this critical perspective, finally, it is necessary to incorporate Foucault's irreducible concept of hidden and systematically latent power structures. It is only when these different moments are located within a communication and discourse theoretical framework, as emphasised throughout, that an approach adequate to the object in question begins to emerge.

In the above, the argument was developed that the rights discourse produced a master frame that made possible the necessary certainty, cultural orientations, identity formation and collective action mobilisation to establish a new rights-based institutional complex having constitutionalised legitimate power at its core. What needs to be added to this, however, is that the rights discourse actually turned out to be a crisis discourse. Despite its momentous achievements, the passage from violence to constitutionalised legitimate power was not as safe and smooth as it appears from a formal point of view. While power was subjected to a process of communication that linked its exercise to the agreement or acceptance of those affected, while it was thus civilised or rationalised and rendered communicatively regulable, this endeavour did not prove entirely satisfactory. On the contrary, the tiller was set to hold modern society on a persistent pathogenic course. The sails were trimmed, yet the boat was heeling not only sharply but also too close to the rocky coastline.

In the course of the rights discourse, as we have seen, modern society came to understand itself as an arrangement that not only required collective action to secure its own survival but that itself constituted such collective action in order to solve the collective problems with which it was faced. In the early modern period, this took the form of collective action that was mobilised in terms of the rights frame and transformed violence via the issue of the survival of society in the political environment into constitutionalised legitimate power. This first step in the constitution of modern society was highly productive. It gave rise not only to a consequential master frame, the rights frame, but also to a corresponding new rights-based institutional infrastructure, which in principle allowed the continuous reciprocal interrelation of the state and its citizens. Yet it nevertheless failed in a significant sense. Instead of being fully mobilised, collective action was blocked by the hegemonic overwhelming and forcible disallowance or exclusion of a number of potential participants. The protests, dissenting voices, appeals, cries and groans of Jews, humanists, representatives of the 'New Science' and the 'New Learning', religious minorities, witches, Indians, Africans, San, Khoi, aborigines, slaves, Enlightenment *philosophes* and women, went unheeded. As a result, power in the process of its centralisation and concentration was not fully connected to communication. In crucial respects, power was left uncivilised or unrationalised, devoid of sufficient limiting normative considerations, indifferent to good and evil.

It is these gaps in the communicative constitution and regulation of power that give the rights discourse the character of a crisis discourse. At issue in it is a pathological feature of modern society, one that has proved to persist over a considerable time-span. It concerns not only the predominance of cynical power politics over principled politics, or the prevalence of what sociologists, following Max Weber (1976, 468–69),[71] call 'formal rationality' or have elaborated upon under the title of 'instrumental reason' (Horkheimer and Adorno 1972)[72] and 'functionalist reason' (Habermas 1987a, subtitle). At least equally, if not more, important is the minimisation of politics[73] in the sense of the exclusion or reduction of participation, which entails the exclusion or reduction of both a plurality of contrasting and even contradictory points of view and their interrelation and coordination through communicative conflict.[74]

CHAPTER 8

Contributions to Enlightenment Sociology

Parameters of the Discursive Construction of Enlightenment Sociology

It is within the compass of the field opened up by the rights discourse that sociology was originally defined and given an existence. This context was not something given or static but a dynamic and changing one in that it was structured by the role played by the discourse in the overcoming of insecurity by establishing certainty anew. Centred around the unfolding process of the collective identification, definition and solution of a major collective issue of early modern times, it embraced not only the unsettling experience and perception of the problem of violence but also the establishment of the rights-based and legally regulated institutional infrastructure of the constitutional state. In the course of the development of the rights discourse, the participating social actors were confronted with the question of political involvement or opposition and of accordingly framing and communicating the issue of the survival of society in its political environment. Included were not only framings and communications of an overtly social and political kind, to be sure, but also related yet more distanced and reflective social scientific ones.

Opting one way or the other, the different social agents entered into competition and conflict over the common stake, the correct or collectively acceptable public framing of the issue. This competitive conflict is visible and accessible in the form of a semantic struggle in practical discourse over such social and political concepts as 'sovereignty', 'state', 'people', 'contract' and 'rights'. Each party sought to encourage a particular use of these concepts and thus to obtain control over them for the purposes of forming people's opinions and mobilising and organising them. On the one hand, the monarchy, the state and its supporters promoted the ideology of absolutism. On the other, the movements that emerged from the different sections of the population advanced some version or another of the utopia of rights, the constitutionalisation of the state, collective decision-making and the public exercise of power. From among these sets of social actors focusing on enlightened despotism, constitutionalism and democracy as well as people who observed them, particularly via the print medium, there also emerged authors who assumed a more reflective relation towards historical events, responses to them and the ensuing communicative conflict and frame competition. They were thus able to reintroduce into the discourse in a more polished or developed form concepts initially abstracted from the discourse itself. The names of such men and movements as More, Hobbes, Shaftesbury, Vico, Montesquieu, Rousseau, the Encyclopaedists (e.g. Diderot), the Physiocrats (e.g. Quesnay), Hume, Smith, Ferguson and Millar could for example be mentioned here. It is from this very base that the moral or social sciences emerged, including history, economics, psychology, anthropology and sociology.

While public opinion generated through the print medium already at this early stage started to play a crucial role, this semantic struggle also involved the deeper process of the constitution and reconstitution of the cognitive order of the time. This set of fundamental classifications and meanings, in terms of which people in the early modern period experienced and perceived the outside world as well as their own inner responses, took the form of the rights frame. The rights frame, as the outcome of the early modern discourse, brought together in a coherent and consistent form the variety of social and political concepts, the socio-political semantics, of the practical discourse of the time employed in pamphlets, sermons, admonitions, books and learned treatises. This it did by giving them a common cognitive structure. In its most abstract form, this cognitive structure found formulation in a philosophically formulated moral theory of rights. Besides the general socio-political semantics and the specific moral theory of rights, however, there also appeared a social scientific semantics that contained a distinct sociological strand, a sociological semantics. By contrast with the concern with the state, government and economics characteristic of politics and political economy, it focused on the wider social context, including the people, the contract among the people that preceded the contract between people and monarch, the social relations presupposed and served by economic relations, and the laws of social organisation. At the centre of the sociological semantics constructed in the course of the rights discourse, therefore, was the society whose survival within the political environment was the collectively accepted issue at the time. The prime sociological question concerned the society that came into view when human beings started to assume responsibility for their own organisation rather than being dominated by church and state, the society that is subject to the rules and laws created by that very society.[1]

The protracted process in which the semantic field of sociology slowly acquired its own integrity and internal standard of argumentative and conceptual consistency can be at least partially traced through the semantic struggles constituting the early modern rights discourse. It can be followed back as far as the sixteenth century to Thomas More's (1989)[2] utopian defence of society in the sense of associational living – the first use of the word 'society' in this sense in the English language (Onions 1976, 842) – against the employment of force and violence as a taken-for-granted part of statecraft. As against the ancient and medieval identification of society with the state, he was thus the first to begin to separate society from the state and to consider the question of its own particular organisation. In the sixteenth and seventeenth centuries, absolutism in turn appropriated the concept of society as a battle cry and weapon in the semantic struggle against its humanist, religious and commercial opponents. The monarchs of Europe evolved their own society around their courts, courtly-aristocratic society, which was indicated by the French expression *la société polie* and the English 'Society' (Elias 1982, 5). The aim was to obliterate the notion of a society of the people by securing the identification of society with the state in the sense of political society. The conception of court society was the means for achieving this. The religious and commercial movements following upon humanism, such as the Huguenots, the Dutch resistance movement, the English movements, and the bourgeois-Enlightenment movement, all struggled in the name of the people, popular sovereignty, constitutionalism and rights against absolutism with a view to formally establishing rights and freeing society from and protecting it against the state and other consolidated powers. Thus they provided a starting point for different developments. On this basis, the Scottish moral philosophers (e.g. Ferguson 1966; Millar 1806) could in the eighteenth century break with the identification of civil society and political society, allowing Hegel (1967, 266)[3] later to formulate the distinction explicitly. It also enabled the bourgeois-Enlightenment movement to provide not only cognitive but also institutional underpinnings for society distinct from both the state and estate society through the fostering of qualitatively new associational relations in the context of salons, coffeehouses, reading circles and secret societies (Koselleck 1988; Habermas 1989; Eder 1985a; Huysseune 1993). It is thus the movements which promoted society against the state and political society that decisively set sociological semantics and hence the discursive construction of sociology in motion.

The fact that the discursive construction of sociology cannot be divorced from the competition and conflict of antagonistic social groupings, each having its own framing of the situation and its own strategy of communication, highlights the close relation between the semantics of sociology and developments in the more general and culturally more potent socio-political semantics of the time. Influenced and shaped by the significant historical events of the period entailing reformation, civil war and revolution, concepts such as 'violence', 'conflict', 'war', 'disorder', 'sovereignty', 'tyranny', 'people', 'resistance', 'toleration', 'order', 'contract', 'society', 'rights' and so forth, proved to be politically, socially and culturally leading ideas in the collective attempt to understand and come to grips with the central issue of early modern times. As such, they decisively stamped the socio-political semantics of the time and provided a basis also for the semantic field of sociology. Sociological semantics focused on the very same issues articulated by these socio-political concepts and analysed them in terms of their social and societal connotations and implications. In so far as a moral philosophical concept and theory of rights rendered the general socio-political semantics of the practical discourse of the time consistent and coherent, moreover, it also provided a normative guideline for sociological semantics.

Thus far, we have seen that the discursive construction of sociology in its original form involved the generation of a sociological semantics in relation to the socio-political semantics of violence and sovereignty of the time, on the one hand, and the moral theory of rights, on the other. We have also seen that this sociological semantics was generated by communication and framing activities that typically went in two distinct directions. First, there were those who articulated sociological semantics in more or less close proximity to the state and its ideology of absolutism, and secondly those who did so while identifying more or less closely with the movements which opposed etatist absolutism with the utopia of rights, constitutionalism and democracy.[4] This competitive framing can be taken to represent the first principle or criterion of the discursive construction of the semantics of sociology. In addition to this first principle, however, a second one can help to make the construction of sociological semantics still clearer. It relates to the social function of the rights discourse as a collective attempt to deal with societal uncertainty. It is the case that the rights discourse, like any societal practical discourse, makes available different historical contexts in so far as it unfolds in two distinct phases. Initially, social actors are subject to given conditions, but from a certain point on they learn how to act in relation to those conditions. Relevant here is the turning point that took place in the rights discourse in the late sixteenth and early seventeenth centuries, discussed earlier, which separated the phases of a disturbing loss of certainty and a concerted attempt to recover it. But more important than the stark distinction between uncertainty and certainty are the different ways, as suggested by the concept of learning,[5] in which social actors go about dealing with the problem of the breakdown and the build-up of certainty – in this case, the problem of violence transformed into the issue of the survival of society in the political environment. The manner in which social actors deal with uncertainty points toward their approach to knowledge or cognitive structures, but it shows most clearly in the identities they form for themselves and, especially, in the social institutions they regard as the solution to the problem facing them.

The significance of this principle is therefore manifold. In the case of the rights discourse, the first reaction to the loss of certainty was to recreate order. This was done by falling back on forces beyond society, such as God or the old hierarchical order, which had the effect of giving priority to the authorities. This allowed strategies aimed at marginalising and excluding violence as well as the acceptance and justification of certain forms of violence as necessary. In a second step, the experience and knowledge gained in the face of the use of force by the authorities stimulated the formation of movements that saw violence as having a social nature. Far from being given, violence admits of being transformed. As a consequence, the emphasis shifted from the conception of society as an order allowing necessary forms of violence to society as a field that can be formed and shaped by social action. The insight into this possibility constituted a new certainty that provided the basis for the envisaging and creation of a new set of institutions.

The parameters within which the discursive construction of sociology can be regarded as taking place should now be clear. They are represented by two principles, each of which opens up a space delimited by two extremes. The first principle is the framing and communication of violence – communicative framing for short – that varies between the more or less authoritarian ideology of the *status quo* and the more or less democratic utopia of popular sovereignty. The second principle is the mode of dealing with the problem at issue in society – uncertainty management for short – conditioned by the phase-bound unfolding of the rights discourse. It varies between the conception of society as an institutional order and society as a field shaped by an ongoing struggle, between an organised society and a self-organising society.

In what is to follow, the discursive construction of sociology in its original early modern form is reconstructed by reference to a selection of paradigmatic figures within the field opened by the rights discourse understood as structured by these two variable principles (see Figure 8.1). While a more or less detailed presentation is offered only of the contributions of Thomas More, Thomas Hobbes, Giambattista Vico, Montesquieu, Adam Ferguson and John Millar, the discourse analytical approach adopted requires that reference also be made

Figure 8.1: Early modern sociology in the context of the rights discourse*

	COMMUNICATIVE FRAMING	
	Authoritarian status quo ideology	Democratic utopia
UNCERTAINTY MANAGEMENT Organised society/order	Bodin Grotius **Hobbes** (1651) Petty	**More** (1516)
Self-organising society/conflict	**Vico** (1725) **Montesquieu** (1748) Hume **Ferguson** (1767) **Millar** (1771)	Rousseau

* Only the authors whose names are in bold are discussed in some detail; the remaining names are selectively entered for exemplary purposes of contrast and comparison.

at the same time to other relevant authors such as Machiavelli, Bodin, Grotius, Petty, Bossuet, Shaftesbury, Locke, Hume, Smith, Rousseau, Turgot, Quesnay, Condorcet, Kant and others. Although the chosen examples occurred in temporally and geographically disparate locations and thus differ more or less sharply from one another, there are many similarities and interconnections among them that can only be explained by the fact that the rights discourse, stretching from the sixteenth to the eighteenth century, served as their common context.

Within these parameters, it should furthermore be emphasised, the process of the discursive construction of sociology itself unfolds according to the twofold symbolic and power logic of the rights discourse. This is a dynamic process that is impossible to capture by means of a diagram. On the one hand, the validity of the arguments and positions advanced in the discourse exerts a symbolic or logical compulsion that confronts and changes or even dissolves the existing cultural or symbolic authority. On the other, the materiality and organisation of the discourse brings the power of existing relations and institutions into play. The discursive construction of sociology takes the form of the appropriation of sociological semantics by means of some historically specific combination of validity and power. Its abiding reference point is the cultural logical moment of discourse that provides the space within which a hegemonic arrangement can assert itself. At a certain point in time and space, a particular version of sociological semantics is empowered while a competing version is concomitantly disempowered, and so forth. Sociology thus finds its place in the ongoing dynamic process of the changing relation between validity and power which is structured by the predominant societal practical discourse according to its two contingently variable dimensions of communicative framing and uncertainty management.

Initial Constructive Contributions

In accordance with the phase-like development of the rights discourse in Europe, the initial contributions to the discursive construction of sociology in the early modern period were not made uniformly, but followed a protracted sequence through the different countries. These initial constructive steps depended, therefore, on a number of closely related factors: the socio-political challenge represented by the formation of the absolutist state and the pene-tration of capitalism into social life, which made for uncertainty; awareness of the issue of the actual conditions of the survival of society; the collective formulation of the question of how society should be organised to avoid the evils of the early modern European form of life, which made for a new certainty; and, finally, the mobilisation of collective political action to bring about the envisaged changes. The sequence that the original contributions to the construction of sociology followed started in England (More) and, presup-posing developments in France and the Netherlands, in a spiral-like manner passed through England (Hobbes), Italy (Vico) and France (the French Enligh-tenment, i.e. Montesquieu), only to return to Britain where it culminated in the Scottish Enlightenment (Ferguson and Millar). These contributions were related to one another, and to a varying degree were integrated into the emerging sociological semantics in the medium of public communication in the context of the major practical discourse of the time, the rights discourse. It is at this level that the construction or, rather, the discursive construction of sociology in its original form took place. Subsequently, of course, the discursive construction of sociology was taken up anew in France, particularly in the post-revolutionary period, but this time within a completely different context, namely the one provided by the justice discourse.

Thomas More

The response to the violence of absolutism and capitalism and, hence, the concern with the actual conditions of survival in the early modern period took both a political and a social form. This provided the basis for the new concept of the political introduced by Machiavelli (1975) and the new concept of the social formulated simultaneously by the utopian tradition of the Renaissance and Reformation (Windelband 1958, II, 425–31; Habermas 1974a, 50–56; Skinner 1978, I, 213–62; Manuel and Manuel 1979; Saage 1990, 15–17). Of first importance among the latter authors, who include also Campanella, Andreae, Bacon and Winstanley, is Thomas More (1480–1535) whose early unequivocal isolation of the social dimension in his *Utopia* (1989 [1516]) came to serve as the model for the succeeding development.

The starting point of More's *Utopia* (Book I, 15–21) was the violence associated with the absolutist state, from war to draconian justice, and the capitalist enclosures as well as the resultant misery of the mass of the people. The central question for him was how the social order could be organised in order to preclude this catalogue of evils (Book II). Although More took the ideal state Plato had projected in *The Republic* as his example in working out an answer, his humanistic version contained a characteristically modern twist. It is not only that he presented it in the form of contemporary travel reports rather than an essentialist analysis of justice. More importantly, he concentrated on society rather than the state, thus making a transition from the classical theory of government to social theory. In addition, he rejected the ingrained tendency to circumvent the evils, injustices and crises of the age by escaping into the past in favour of insisting that human beings are the authors of their own social institutions. The survival of early modern society within its political environment could be secured by organising the institutional reproduction of society appropriately. This mode of organisation shows all the hallmarks of the early modern rights frame.

Anticipating the agreement that would later emerge from the confessional conflicts and controversies of the sixteenth and seventeenth centuries about the need for the right of religious freedom, More (1989, 97) regards toleration as an essential principle of the social organisation of the perfect and happy island society of Utopia. As a jurist, he also made use of the principle of equality before the law (38, 85) as a guiding idea for the organisation of society. Characteristically, however, More goes much further. What is required for the correction of the perverted arrangement of the time is the elimination of class distinctions and above all the abolition of private property in which the former are rooted (38–40, 116–18). The place of private property is taken by the equality of claim or title for all members of society in respect of common property. The organisation of society on this foundation is the condition for the realisation of the ideal goods of society, the good life.

The image of a perfect and happy society on the island of Utopia, the projected utopian vision, which More contrasts with and opposes to the violence-ridden and war-torn society of early modern Europe, possesses a special quality that is not without importance for an understanding of a particular aspect of the construction of sociology. This image or vision represents a fiction in the sense not of just anything whatsoever that can be dreamed of or hoped for, but rather of the imagination of something real, something actually existing (Habermas 1974a, 58–59; Saage 1990, 14, 16–17, 18). It involves the sketching of the organisation of society so realistically that it can be imagined as something actually existing under specific conditions, despite the fact that it is known not to exist. This fictitious reality is in a critical manner opposed to the existing state of affairs. The conviction that society can be properly organised only on the basis of a certain range of rights is tested by means of presenting it in the form of a fiction deemed to be an example drawn from experience. To the extent that it is sufficiently credible, to the extent that it is conceivable as actually existing, the prescription it contains for the organisation of society can be indirectly verified by reference to past experience. Under specific historical conditions, it thus opposes a conceivable alternative to the existing state of affairs, its surplus content pointing critically beyond the latter.

In contradistinction to the later temporal utopias or euchronias of the late-Enlightenment, e.g. Mercier's *L'An 2440* or Condorcet's *Esquisse*, More's represents what Richard Saage (1990, 16)[6] has called a spatial utopia. This is not only because the utopian counter-world of an isolated island society is separated by a spatial distance from the present, but is in particular due to its nature as a thought experiment which is not yet seen in terms of its possible practical realisation through a revolutionary transformation of society as a whole. Rather than being its founder or creator, More's narrator only discovered the island society of Utopia, the perfect social organisation which he seeks to describe as closely as possible in order to facilitate the public's identification with it.

The peculiar character of More's model of society is attributable to the phase-bound location of his contribution to the construction of sociology within the framework of the rights discourse. The unfolding of the discourse traverses a trajectory from uncertainty to certainty in the course of which a cognitive frame becomes established which progressively makes possible both identity formation and collective action mobilisation. During the earlier part of the discourse, before the realisation dawns that society is a field which can be actively formed and shaped, social reality is not only understood in the more static terms of a given order, but is also approached in a more distanced yet not necessarily uncritical manner. This explains More's concern with an organised society or an order of social relations as well as his thought experiment in the form of a spatial utopia.

It is with this discourse theoretical insight into the construction of sociology in mind that it becomes possible to see a relation between the contribution of Thomas More and the role that fictitious realities played and can still play in sociology. Interesting in this context, but reserved for treatment elsewhere, is the role literature in fact played in the founding of classical sociology in the nineteenth century (see e.g. Lepenies 1988) as well as the contemporary conviction that fiction is of the utmost importance for coming to grips with social reality in the postmodern age (Rorty 1989; Knorr-Cetina 1994). Like More's spatial utopia, these latter two instances also belong to the earlier part of the respective societal discourses within the context of which they took place – the nineteenth- and twentieth-century justice discourse and the late twentieth-century responsibility discourse respectively.

Thomas Hobbes

Although a philosopher with a breadth of interest stretching from natural science to government, Thomas Hobbes (1588–1679) can be regarded as having contributed decisively to the construction of sociology midway through the rights discourse. This is due to his explicit attempt to account for the origin of society and to develop a novel and thoroughly modern model of society. Within the framework of the discourse, a considerable period of time separates Hobbes' *Leviathan* (first published in 1651) from More's *Utopia* – a period during which an immense intensification had taken place in the centralisation of state power, the confessional conflicts triggered by the Reformation, and the expansion of market-based capitalist economic activity. This is the very period in which the rights discourse started to undergo the momentous shift, discussed earlier, from religion to politics, from history to reason, from personal monarchical sovereignty to state or governmental sovereignty and, indeed, to popular sovereignty, from classical practical philosophy and humanism to the mechanistic worldview underlying science, and finally from profound socio-political uncertainty to the first groping attempts to deal with it in a more rational way. For all the differences that this change in the discourse introduced between More and Hobbes, the distance it covered, however big, was not yet sufficient to allow the latter to conceive of society other than in terms of being organised rather than self-organising, in terms of order rather than construction. Perhaps the most important difference imposed between them by the discursive turn can be clarified by reference to science or, more specifically, the mechanistic worldview. But then there is of course still the much more fundamental disagreement between the two which goes back to the respective ways of framing and communicating the problem of violence informing their contributions to the discursive construction of sociology.

Framing of Social Reality

Hobbes did not lack first-hand experience of the evils, injustices and crises of the age, nor was he oblivious to the debates accompanying them. On the contrary, in England he had the opportunity to observe not only the conflict between the large landholders and merchants, on the one hand, and the Crown, on the other, over natural resources such as metals and ores, but also the brutal destruction of the peasantry by landlords in the course of the long-drawn process of the enclosure of the commons (Merchant 1989, 212–13; Sommerville 1992, 5–27). The acute sense he displayed of these different theatres of operation as tragic battlegrounds was undoubtedly sharpened by his observation of religious and civil war in France as well as his personal embroilment in the English Civil War. As a frequent traveller, he found himself in France when Henry IV was assassinated and again when Richelieu's troops subdued La Rochelle (Koselleck 1988, 23). During the 1640s, Hobbes once more spent time in Paris, but on this occasion as an active member of a group of English royalist émigrés rather than as a student or academic. In 1640, he felt himself compelled to flee the country in the wake of the dissolution of the English Parliament as he feared reprisals against supporters of the monarchy (Randall 1962, 536; Merchant 1989, 206; Sommerville 1992, 18). In the midst of capitalist transformation, civil war and revolutionary turmoil, struck by the violence, anarchy, disorder and uncertainty of the historical situation, Hobbes pursued only one clear goal from his first political publication in 1628 to his late work *Behemoth* of 1682: to escape the permanent dangers of an uncontrolled political situation by making possible survival in peace and order. It is this experience-saturated grasp of the early modern issue of the survival of society in the political environment as a concrete social problem that led him to raise the sociological question of the origin of society and the persistence of social order. This he did in exemplary form in his masterpiece, the *Leviathan* (Hobbes 1973 [1651]).[7]

It is in the way that he frames and communicates the problem of violence or the issue of societal survival that Hobbes differs most sharply from the humanistic More. Intellectually, to begin with, social order for him, in contrast to his predecessor who fictively imagined it, represents a concrete empirical problem that is rooted in experience and is thus available in knowledge obtained through the senses. It is empirically directly observable in material existence and it is objectifiable by means of the new scientific worldview, i.e. the atomistic mechanistic worldview which was developed by Galileo, Bacon, Descartes, Mersenne and Gassendi, all men with whom Hobbes had some kind of contact during his lifetime. This cognitive framing enabled Hobbes to be the first one to construct a 'social physics' (Randall 1962, 940), 'physics of sociation' or 'mechanics of the societal state' (Habermas 1974a, 72, 71).[8]

Normatively, in the second place, Hobbes regards the issue of societal survival, by contrast with More, in a morally neutral or, rather, naturalistic way. Human beings, who are characterised by natural fears, and desires, possess no moral qualities such as for instance rights and are not capable of moral responsibility. Consequently, their motions in social space need to be regulated and controlled through socialisation and the rules, norms or institutions constituting the social order. The dilemma posed by the problem of having to derive a normative or moral order from natural fears and desires which could in turn satisfy the latter was an insurmountable one Hobbes could circumvent only by studiously and laboriously suppressing it.

Finally, his aesthetic or conative framing of violence and societal survival, which concerns the qualities or meanings inherent in human expressive relations, likewise contrasts sharply with that of his predecessor. Rather than having a positive and optimistic image of human beings, he borrowed a negative anthropology from Machiavelli and Calvinism, emphasising human nature as evil and corrupt in a depraved world and as depending on a higher power for salvation. Human nature, like nature more generally, is not something that generates autonomy but rather calls for domination. Taken together, the above three framings constituted and were reproduced through a symbolic form of communication or ideology of a scientistic, authoritarian and etatist kind that represented the diametrical opposite of More's more egalitarian, popular and democratic orientation. Hobbes' contribution to the discursive construction of sociology rests entirely on this particular framing and communication of violence and social order.

Model of Society

Hobbes' sociology consists of his mechanics of society. For him, society was a central mechanism in the solution of the problem of violence, anarchy, chaos, disorder and uncertainty so characteristic of the age – but society conceived in a special way. In the 1640s, the mechanical philosophy of nature, which arose from the contributions of Galileo, Bacon, Descartes, Mersenne, Gassendi and others and received encouragement from the state in its drive to monopolise knowledge, promised to restore the order and certainty that had been lost to cosmology, religion and socio-political life as a result of the breakdown of feudalism and the metaphysical-religious worldview. Hobbes made his contribution to the construction of sociology, oriented toward social order, in the terms of this new worldview, also referred to as science. His starting point in accounting for society is the state of nature, the raw material of which society consists.

Assuming that human beings are by nature given to competition, domination and glory and, hence, are fearful, unfriendly, hostile and violent, he regards the state of nature as a pre-social, purely political condition in which every individual fears death and consequently engages in a life-and-death struggle to secure self-preservation (Hobbes 1973, 63–66). The sequence of violent conflict situations that ensues makes of the state of nature one of anarchy, chaos, disorder and uncertainty. In this context, the predominant early modern issue of the survival of society in the political environment presents itself graphically to Hobbes. Reason, or the interest of all individuals in peace and order, dictates that the condition of disorder and uncertainty represented by the state of nature should be brought to a close. This can be effected only by the introduction of society in the sense of a state of social order and peace.

In Hobbes' view, however, not just any society will do under the conditions of early modern times. Neither the hierarchical estate society of feudalism, nor the communal society based on common property, such as for instance envisaged by More, was suited to bring order and peace to the individualistic, pluralistic, market-based relations of seventeenth-century Europe. Far from being unequal, individuals were by nature equal, and far from sharing everything, they by necessity engaged in relentless competition and conflict. Instead of the hierarchical and communal models, therefore, he proposes the mechanical model of society. Analogous to a machine, society is objectified and inspected from the point of view of the causal lawfulness according to which it reproduced itself or the general conditions in terms of which it functioned. Thus, taking into account the constitution and characteristics of human nature, this model specifies that set of rules or institutional arrangements which is necessary to constrain or compel human beings to behave and to react to each other in such a way that social order results (Hobbes 1973, 66–74, 87–89). The rules or institutions of social life making possible social order are necessitated by the natural compulsion of the fear of violent death and represent a social compulsion taking the form of a legal order backed by coercive sanctions. In order to circumvent the standing dangers of a runaway and uncontrolled political environment, individuals by natural compulsion seek the security and peace of a social order that they set up by means of entering into a social contract uniting them into a community of interests. Through the creation of order and peace, the social contract is aimed at securing the interests of individuals, to advance the general welfare and to make possible a comfortable and happy life. It consists of laws and norms that are formal and general so as to guarantee the formal freedom, equality and duties of the individual members. They allow and regulate property, create free areas for the pursuit of private interests, make the actions of others predictable, secure social expectations and make social intercourse possible.

If one considers Hobbes' (1973, 66, 110–17) conception of society purely in terms of its content, namely as a legally based social order securing individual interests, social intercourse and general welfare, then it would seem as though he anticipates what would later be considered a liberal society guaranteed by a constitutional state.[9] Yet in terms of his mechanics of society he goes much further. It is only when he indicates how the survival of society could be secured within the political environment, that is, only when he introduces a contract of sovereignty, government or subjugation over and above the social contract, that the thrust of his mechanical model of society becomes completely apparent. It is tantamount to subordinating his liberal society to an absolutist monarch (Hobbes 1973, 90–96, 109). For the purposes of the creation of social order, he was convinced, the social contract in and by itself is necessary but not sufficient. Society is the key component of the solution to the state of nature, but if left to its own devices it would slide back into the state of nature and be devoured by conflict and violence. To function adequately, the social contract needs backing, its validity requires to be enforced. From this necessity results the contract of government in terms of which all individuals hand over their rights, authority and power to a single authority with a monopoly of violence or force: the unlimited and uncon-ditional or absolute authority of the state, which is identical with the will of the monarch. In accordance with Hobbes' mechanical model, the absolute sovereign is the form of society, the sanction or external embodiment of the social contract, and as such it is analogous to a mechanic or technician operating the machine from the outside (Merchant 1989, 210).

To this mechanistic understanding of society and of its social and political reproduction, it should be noted, Hobbes adds a characteristic claim. It is central to his solution to the issue of the survival of society in the political environment. It concerns the fact that the knowledge made available by his new scientific approach is of such a nature that it can be used to intervene in society with a view to bringing about social and political order (Habermas 1974a, 71–72). Once exact knowledge has been gained of the mechanics of society, it can be used by the mechanics or technicians of the state to bring about a desired state of affairs. It is a technical kind of knowledge that can be applied to create social and political order, for instance, by eliminating what haunted Hobbes all his life, namely civil war.

Giambattista Vico

During the earlier part of the second phase of the rights discourse, the construction of sociology received an impetus in a dialectical direction from the lively opposition generated by the doctrine of natural law and social contract in general and in particular Hobbes' egoistic assumptions, negative anthropology and etatist political orientation. The period involved here roughly spans the years between 1670 and 1730. Most prominent were English moral philosophers such as Richard Cumberland (1632–1718) and Anthony Ashley Cooper, Earl of Shaftesbury (1671–1713), who fought an indefatigable battle against Hobbes' 'selfish system'. They emphasised the essentially social nature of human beings as well as the fact that the social bond holding the human world together is founded not on contracts alone but also on 'natural sympathy' or social affections (Shaftesbury 1900). The dialectical interchange was further intensified by the intervention of the London-based Dutch physician, Bernard de Mandeville (1670–1733), who in his *The Fable of the Bees; or Private Vices Public Benefits* (1995 [1714]), which contained a section entitled 'A Search into the Nature of Society', revived the 'selfish system' of Hobbes against the moralists' optimistic view of the social nature of human beings. He argued that society as a system of interdependence not only rests on the struggle of self-seeking individuals pursuing their own interests, but also relates their private vices in such a way that they unintentionally serve the public good (Windelband 1958, II, 524; Randall 1962, 754–61). Many years ago, Werner Sombart (1923) suggested that we search among these English moral philosophers for the founders of sociology. The most significant outcome of this development beyond Hobbes is to be found, however, not in England but in Italy – in Vico's (1970) *New Science* which was originally published in 1725.[10] Critically engaging with the natural law and contract theoretical traditions, political and moral philosophy, and with the scientific developments of the time, this work represents the first and indeed a very impressive attempt to construct a comprehensive historically informed and theoretically based science of human society, or what would later be called sociology.

Framing of Social Reality

Already in his early writings, Giambattista Vico (1668–1744) polemicised strongly against the mechanistic worldview, particularly as represented by Descartes, from the point of view of the humanistic tradition of rhetoric operating with the classical concept of prudence. Sharply distinguishing the human world from external nature and natural processes, he rejected the extension of the deductive method to the disciplines dealing with the human world and insisted that the truth produced by science is not sufficient to provide the certainty humans require for their conduct. This could be done only by maintaining the relation with the classical tradition through the retention of humanistic rhetoric. It was only some fifteen or sixteen years later, however, that he succeeded in mediating between the classical and the modern methods and reconciling them to his own satisfaction, thus providing the basis for his *New Science*. This achievement involved a number of strands reflecting a set of complicated and nuanced relations to his different predecessors.

An enduring core element of Vico's *New Science*, which shows the direct connection of his work to the rights discourse, is the alternative or new system of natural law he opposed to the seventeenth-century natural law theorists. Rather than Grotius' strictly rational deductive system of rights which only drew the logical consequences of the principle of society; rather than Hobbes' doctrine of rights as emanating exclusively from the absolute monarch which can be accounted for in terms of a demonstrable mechanical science of society and politics; and rather than the combination of their respective notions of absolute rights and eternally just laws in Pufendorf, Vico put forward the theory of a historically developing set of institutions in relation to which rights and laws vary. Society itself needs to be taken into account, and this must be done not from a mechanistic but from a historical point of view. It is not sufficient to regard society as a rational contract since it needs to be placed within the context of the historical process of its development. Vico's system of natural law is thus not that of the philosophers but rather that of the people, of different societal groupings.

This does not mean, however, that Vico turned completely against the nascent modern science on which Grotius, Hobbes and Pufendorf drew. On the contrary, he considered his own new science as a development that belongs to the *Novus orbis scientiarum* or new world of sciences envisaged by Francis Bacon at the outset of the seventeenth century. More specifically, he stressed the importance of knowledge by reference to causes. It is at this juncture that Vico (1970, paragraphs 331, 349) developed his famous version of the theory of knowledge according to which human beings are able to obtain true knowledge only of what they make themselves. For him, it is not just a matter of human beings being able to obtain knowledge of the human world of institutions because they make it themselves, but more profoundly still that they are able to understand themselves in that they are able to understand their own past and that of others, to imaginatively reconstruct their actions, works, achievements, failures, suffering, hopes and fears, their customs, laws, symbols, words and ideas. Such a reconstruction, which since the nineteenth century has been called 'hermeneutic understanding',[11] is neither a description nor a collection of facts but rather the capturing of a possible world – which is something different again than More's projection of a utopia. In fact, the most basic and most characteristic insight of Vico's masterpiece is that it is this very ability that allows human beings in the first place to create, communicate, to imagine goals, form societies and become fully human.

As a reconciliation of the ancient or classical and the modern methods, Vico's new science possesses two distinct dimensions. On the one hand, it is a *scienza* in the sense of a science of the human world that delivers knowledge possessing the quality of truth. On the other hand, it is a *coscienza*, i.e. consciousness or conscience, in the sense of the historical and hermeneutical understanding of the human world that provides human beings with certainty. The complementarity of truth and certainty is a matter of crucial importance to him (Vico 1970, paragraphs 137–42).[12] The knowledge of philosophers and the representatives of the modern method, however precise, remains abstract until such time as it enters the consciousness and convictions of people who are prepared to act upon it in a concrete situation. Human beings never act on the basis of the truth alone, but always relate it to what they regard as certain. Human choice and human action, which are by nature uncertain, can be rendered certain only by the morality of the people involved, their *sensus communis* or common sense, their judgement under historically specific, concrete circumstances. Uncertainty and the relative nature of common sense are related to the fact that, while human beings are social by nature, their sociality assumes its guise only within a changing complex of institutions and their humanity only develops in the course of time. While Vico did bring out the element of communication in the case of the modern period, he for the most part presented common sense as being devoid of reflection and hence as a matter excluding deliberation and agreement. In this he was strengthened by his orthodox Catholicism which he avowedly retained, despite the fact that he was able to break with the scriptural conventions still confining most of his predecessors and thus to advance a secular interpretation of the historical development of society. The comprehensive historical and systematic study of human society proposed by Vico was shaped by this orientation of his with its novel combination of intellectual, moral and conative framing devices.

Model of Society

Vico's contribution to the construction of sociology was made within the context of the rights discourse in a location less afflicted by the religious civil wars and conflicts than war-torn and conflict-ridden north-western Europe and France and thus also less agitated by collective mobilisation. Indeed, at the time of the publication of his major works, differences had already been settled and institutional arrangements established for a considerable period in Holland, Germany and England, the homelands of the major philosophers and theorists he admired and argued with in his writings. While he was thus able to assume a more distanced and dispassionate position than for instance his predecessor Hobbes, he nevertheless displayed an acute awareness of the problem of violence of the age and took on the issue at stake in the early modern discourse, the issue of the survival of society in the political enviro-nment, in a quite deliberate way. Simultaneously, the fact that his contribution to the construction of sociology was located in the second phase of the rights discourse allowed him to appreciate that society is not a given order but rather a field shaped by an ongoing process of conflict and struggle.

Like Hobbes, Vico (1970, paragraph 1004) starts from what he too calls 'the state of nature' representing the chaotic, bestial, promiscuous past of humanity characterised by savagery, cruelty and violence. But in criticism of the ahistorical and rationalistic conception of his predecessors, he insists that it is neither a matter of a simple distinction between the state of nature and order, nor one of rational human beings being present already at the outset. Far from a momentary transition, the development from the bestial wilderness to the world of nations or the order of the civil world required a protracted process that passed through three stages. Upon the initial foundation of humanity by the creation of the institution of religion complemented by marriage and burial in the age of gods, during which people believed they lived under divine government, followed the age of heroes and finally the age of human beings (Vico 1970, paragraph 31). While the second stage was charac-terised by the domination of the aristocracy by sheer superiority of force of arms, the third coincided with completely unfolded humanity, 'rational humanity' displaying 'fully developed human reason' (Vico 1970, paragraphs 973, 326). Examples of this stage are to be found not only in seventeenth- and eighteenth-century Europe, but likewise in the Roman Republic. In contradiction to rationalism which assumed that fully human beings created the institutions of society, Vico argued that institution building during the first stage and even the second was undertaken by beings who were still beasts or, at least, not yet fully human. Rather than being given at the outset, rather than being a presupposition, humanity is an effect, a product or a consequence of institution building. By building institutions and making the human world in a long-drawn-out process, human beings at the same time made themselves, shaping both their bodies and minds (Vico 1970, paragraphs 520, 692).

Given his processual rather than dualistic (i.e. state of nature/order) conception, it is clear that Vico assumes a rather differentiated perspective on violence. The historical process is at one and the same time one of reason and of utility and force. The savagery and cruelty of the bestial condition is not only carried over into the first stage, but the second heroic stage is in particular marked by violence, namely aristocratic violence. In the unfolding of the third stage, too, violence is strongly in evidence. According to Vico's interpretation, the popular commonwealths that follow the overthrow of the aristocracy are typically rendered unstable by the general pursuit of private interests backed by force, and thus characterised by factions, seditions, civil war, foreign wars and consequently the threat of total disorder and ruin. It is this danger that brings the monarchical form into being, as had been the case earlier with Augustus in Rome as well as with the monarchies of seventeenth- and eighteenth-century Europe. In fact, Vico (1970, paragraph 1008; see also 927) sees clearly that the formation of the monarchy centrally involves the monopolisation of all violence and force: 'to preserve the latter [i.e. the nation or society] from destruction a single man must arise...and take all public concerns by force of arms into his own hands, leaving his subjects free to look after their private affairs and after just so much public business, and of just such kinds, as the monarch may entrust to them'. Vico's theory of the stage-bound historical development of society, it should be borne in mind, is a theory of course and recourse in the sense of a cyclical rather than a progressive theory. In the course of time, society not only develops through three stages but, after their completion, re-traverses the same stages in the same order – needless to say, with the difference that history makes. For example, Roman history passed through a full cycle that is being repeated after the fall of the Empire. The Dark Ages correspond to the age of gods and the Middle Ages to the age of heroes, with the Renaissance inaugurating the latest historical manifestation of the age of humans. Now, this cyclical conception implies that the monopolisation of violence and force is not permanent. In fact, it is certain that it will not last. This framing of violence extends to the issue of societal survival that structures his contribution to the construction of sociology from the inside.

In keeping with his theory of development, Vico understands the question of the survival of early modern society in its particular political environment against a historical background. Throughout the different stages, he focuses (1970, paragraphs 246–47, 916–18, 925–27) on the basic relation between society and politics on the assumption that government must conform to the nature of those governed, or to the morality of the people. During the first stage, when people were fierce and cruel, restrained only by a terrible religion, a theocratic government ruled according to what was believed to be the commands of the gods. During the second stage, when the nobility arose from established families and dominated the rest of the population, a government of the most powerful, an aristocratic type of government, prevailed. It was only with the appearance of fully developed human beings, who are intelligent, modest, benign and reasonable and who recognise the restraint of conscience, reason and duty, that human government based on natural equality, equality before the law and at times also freedom, becomes possible. While both the free cities and the monarchies of early modern Europe fall into this category, Vico regards the latter as logically following upon the former and thus evaluates monarchy as the most appropriate and indeed the best form of human government (Vico 1970, paragraphs 1008, 1083, 1092). Its perfect form monarchy reaches in enlightened absolutism. This evaluation encapsulates his framing of the issue of societal survival in the political context of early modern Europe.

Early modern society, torn apart by internal conflicts and power struggles, required for its constitution a universalistic legal order beyond private interests that is best represented by the monarchical form of government which itself presupposes popular sovereignty. The legal order, which reflects popular sovereignty, involves equality in civil rights in respect of the common people and the nobility, which is realised in particular in equality before the law. Equality in principle is complemented by arrangements aimed at the moderation of the power of the nobility and the administrative advancement of the collective interests of the population. Under these conditions, legislation becomes the central instrument for transforming the human vices of violence, avarice and ambition into military, merchant and government institutions. Thus it provides the basis of the strength, wealth and wisdom of a commonwealth and creates the possibility for civil happiness. In a flash of genius, Vico showed that the transformation of violence into legally based societal power securing the survival of early modern society involved a symbolic process. Due to the development of language, involving centrally the gaining of sovereignty over it by the free people, the meanings of the law could be modified in such a way that it was no longer the preserve of the nobility but was binding for everybody (Vico 1970, paragraphs 32, 936). This clear treatment of societal survival notwithstanding, Vico was and remained convinced that no sociopolitical arrangement can endure, not even what he regarded as the perfect monarchy based on popular sovereignty that increasingly became a reality in seventeenth- and eighteenth-century Europe. Despite his historical orientation, therefore, there is no temporal utopia or euchronia attached to his solution to the problem of the survival of society, as would be the case in the late Enlightenment.[13]

The concept or model of society which Vico operated in his *New Science* is a highly differentiated and nuanced one. Being built into a historical theory, as we have seen, it is obvious that society is not and indeed cannot be conceived in terms of order. Uppermost for him is change. Accordingly, society is best conceived as a historically specific complex or ensemble of institutions and relations that is subject to change. Generally speaking, the process of change, which passes through three repeating stages, has two dimensions. On the level of content, the process is driven by historically specific class conflicts and power struggles through which recondite wisdom and common wisdom are combined. Descriptions of the details of the process abound in Vico's work. On the level of form, the process is structured in such a way that it goes in a certain direction, exhibited by the trajectory from the divine through the heroic to the human, and back again to the beginning. To capture this latter dimension, Vico propounds a theory of providence, what he refers to as a 'rational civil theology of divine providence' (Vico 1970, paragraph 385), which accounts for the fact that human beings, although pursuing their own particular goals, unconsciously contribute in uniform ways to collective goals.

Like his theory of social change, Vico's conception of the complex or ensemble of social institutions and relations that is subject to and undergoes change is of much sociological significance. On the horizontal axis of historical development, this complex or ensemble repeats itself in a different form in each of the three succeeding stages. On the vertical axis of its composition, as it were, Vico (1970, Book Four) regards it as being made up of some ten different dimensions. At the core of the complex or ensemble is a civil order consisting of a social and a political component. On the one hand, there is a range of historically specific institutions, initially religion, marriage and burial, to which are subsequently added others, such as trade and commerce in the modern period. On the other hand, it is complemented by a corresponding form of government, whether theocratic, aristocratic or human. Such a civil order is possible only in conjunction with a corresponding stage of development of human nature, whether poetic, heroic or human, and the custom as well as the natural law or right appropriate to it. This whole plexus is shot through with communication carried on through the medium of a historically specific form of language consisting of its own particular characters, namely hieroglyphics, abstract universals or the words of the ordinary everyday modern languages. The mode of communication made possible by each of these linguistic substrates and their institutional underpinnings is decisive for the way in which the civil order is regulated and justified. Here Vico distinguishes historically specific types of law or jurisprudence and related types of judgement which rest on corresponding forms of authority. The latter stretch from divine authority, which is never called to account, through heroic authority, based on solemn formulae, to human authority predicated on trust. As regards the justification or the giving of reasons for these different complexes of jurisprudence, judgement and authority, recourse is had to divine reason, reason of state and natural reason respectively. The first involves appeals to revelation, prophecies or oracles, and the second appeals to the knowledge of discerning experts. By contrast, natural reason, which is typical of the 'naturally open, generous, and magnanimous...commonwealths' of modern times, is the reason of the people who have become masters of ordinary everyday language and are therefore able not only to write and enact laws in accordance with its meanings, but also 'to make public what had been secret' and thus to render 'the powerful and the weak equal before the law' (Vico 1970, paragraph 953).

Over and above these various analytical dimensions of society, Vico also introduced a synthetic conception, a conception of the whole, which is of the utmost importance from the point of view of his construction of sociology. In keeping with his twofold emphasis on history and society, on a theory of history and a theory of society that leaves room for its interpretative understanding, two conceptions of synthetic unity are discernible in his work. The first, what he calls the 'sects of time' (Vico 1970, paragraphs 975–79) corresponding to the three stages of historical development, concerns the spirit of the age in the sense of the historical and cultural unity of society which gives it its particular quality or style. Historically, 'religious times' were succeeded by 'punctilious times' which in the modern period were in turn displaced by 'civil times'. Here we witness Vico's concept of society as a whole, a historically specific and hermeneutically interpretable whole. The second synthetic notion is the general unity of the historical process embracing the whole of the world of nations. Vico (1970, paragraph 915) referred to it as 'the unity of spirit'. Although still presented in terms of a providential divinity, he explicitly understood by it the regulation or governing of human action and the historical process by rules that are hidden from human beings (Vico 1970, paragraphs 342, 344, 1108). While human beings pursue narrow ends, the process generated by their actions unfolds in such a way that it turns out that, on the whole, they are actually making a contribution to wider ends. Randall (1962, 960) speaks here of Vico's 'controlling idea of an "evolution" of social institutions'.[14]

The most astonishing feature of Vico's contribution to the construction of sociology is that he conceived of history as the genetic process of the generation and change of society that is structured by knowledge and, hence, is also accessible via knowledge. Like the process, human institutions are structured by 'a mental language common to all nations, which uniformly grasps the substance of things feasible in human social life' (Vico 1970, paragraph 161; see also 347). To trace this process and to comprehend these institutions, therefore, it is necessary to follow the unfolding of these cognitive structures and to analyse them closely. This is done, as Berlin (1979a, 113) makes clear, by tracing knowledge as a social process through 'the evolution of symbols – words, gestures, pictures, and their altering patterns, functions, structures and uses'. Vico's new science, his sociology with its historical, hermeneutic, genetic, cognitive and structural dimensions, proceeds by studying not only the process through which human beings make their society and themselves and the outcome of that process, namely social institutions and the human world of nations. At the same time, it also concentrates on the cognitive structures and symbols that give form to the process and its varied contents.

Enlightenment Constructions
The French Enlightenment: Montesquieu

Although Vico's work was apparently hardly known in the eighteenth century, exerting its immense influence only in the nineteenth, he somehow did enter the Enlightenment in a number of respects. The best known among them is his theory of knowledge according to which human beings make their own history, which entailed a shift from a teleological to a genetic view of history and opened the way for a critical perspective on the depraved society of the present (Jauss 1990a, 27–28).[15] The first intimations of one of the most characteristic synthetic ideas of the Enlightenment, i.e. that human history is the natural development of human nature, were also to be found in Vico (Windelband 1958, II, 526). Perhaps most interesting, however, is his highlighting of the cultural creative power of the imagination, which provided the first modern justification of myths of a new beginning (Jauss 1990a, 27, 52–59). Up until after the French Revolution, when its place was taken by the myth of progress, the French Enlightenment had been dominated by the myth of the new beginning of history or of the founding of a society of freedom and equality. Vico's idea of a new science in the general sense of a science of the human world also proved to be a typical eighteenth-century Enlightenment idea, what at the time was referred to as 'the science of human nature' or 'the science of man',[16] which contained not only elements of history, politics, anthropology, psychology and economics, but also a particularly strong strain of sociology. A comparison of Vico and Montesquieu, the French *philosophe* who had made the most important contribution to the construction of Enlightenment sociology, reveals so many similarities that it comes as a surprise to see Montesquieu's claim to originality being supported by the scholarly opinion that he had not read the *Scienza Nuova* (Berlin 1979a, 134).[17] Apart from the above-mentioned generalities, of which he certainly did not share the myth of a new beginning, the similarities concern some of the most characteristic details of Montesquieu's famous book of 1748, *The Spirit of the Laws* (1989).[18] Be that as it may, from the analytical point of view adopted here, it is significant that Montesquieu more or less shares with Vico not only his communicative framing of the problem of violence and the issue of the political survival of society, but also his model of society.

In his instructive interpretation, Raymond Aron (1979, 61–62) writes that Montesquieu is usually regarded as a precursor of sociology rather than as a sociologist due not merely to the fact that the word 'sociology' was still lacking, but especially because he showed no interest in modern society, i.e. modern society understood as being defined by industrialism or capitalism. Aron himself nevertheless claims that he was 'the first of the sociologists' since he regards Montesquieu as having transformed classical political philosophy into sociology. Not only did he operate with a 'total conception of society', but he also attempted to develop a sociological explanation of all aspects of collectivities. It is possible, to be sure, to be still more decisive in claiming Montesquieu for sociology. As soon as one recognises that modernity, far from being exhausted by industrialism or capitalism, already began in the sixteenth century with the rights discourse, then it becomes clear that this first-generation *philosophe* was directly concerned with modern society. The serious attention he gave to questions of political regime and liberty in conjunction with his comprehensive theory of society does not indicate that he remained caught up in the snares of classical philosophy or classical theory of politics, but rather locates his work squarely within the context of the early modern rights discourse. In *The Spirit of the Laws*, moreover, Montesquieu advanced the idea of the science of society later called sociology by reference to the early modern issue of the survival of society in its political environment.

Framing of Social Reality

Charles-Louis de Secondat, baron de la Brède et de Montesquieu (1689–1755) was a member of an old Protestant family that was not merely compelled by the experience of the Wars of Religion to revert to Catholicism, but also came to place a high premium on tolerance. The family was an aristocratic one, belonging to the *noblesse de la robe* and owning the office of presidency of the *parlement* of Bordeaux, which was inherited by Montesquieu in 1716. It witnessed the consolidation of absolutism under the Sun King and the concurrent royal competition with and onslaught against the aristocracy. During Montesquieu's own lifetime, the Regency of Philip of Orléans and the reign of Louis XV, the social and political structure erected by Louis XIV was in the process of breaking up, not only creating uncertainty but also exacerbating certain features of absolutism. It was this background that allowed him to appreciate the early modern problem of violence and to develop a critique of institutions supporting it.

The Church, particularly the Inquisition, was subjected to a penetrating analysis that received much applause from his readers, but his critical attention was more specifically focused on the absolutist monarchy and state of his time. While the first half of the eighteenth century saw the *philosophes* preoccupied with religion, literature and art, Montesquieu already engaged in critique that exhibited a political intent. This is borne out by his first work entitled *Lettres persanes* (Montesquieu 1949 [1721]) in which he gives a portrayal of France through Persian eyes. He absolutely detested the intolerance, violence and inhumanity of the age, particularly as embodied by absolutism – the politics of fear associated with it, the police brutality propping it up, the inhuman punishment of convicts, the inequitable tax system, the animalistic treatment of subjects, the depoliticisation of the subject population, its bellicosity, and so forth. In a humanitarian vein finding such a wide resonance that it made him the most popular author in the eighteenth century, he campaigned for practical reforms aimed at religious tolerance, the abolition of the slave trade, the humanisation of criminal justice, distributional justice and peace. More fundamentally still, however, he directly addressed the issue of the survival of early modern society in its political environment.

How could the violence that threatens the continued existence of society be channelled or transformed so as to secure the survival of society? How could the volatile political environment be structured and regulated to assure the existence of social life? During the earlier phase of the rights discourse, particularly in the wake of the Wars of Religion, the political situation as a whole seemed completely uncontrolled and even uncontrollable, with the result that the threat of violent death generated a pervasive fear of anarchy. In the first half of the eighteenth century, however, conditions had undergone an appreciable change. Montesquieu entertained a different fear. At this stage, the all-pervasive dangers of a completely uncontrolled political situation had been brought under control and subjected to regulation. Not only in France, but particularly there, absolutism was the solution to this problem. This solution generated its own problems, however. They formed the core of Montesquieu's experience and perception of the issue of societal survival. Rather than anarchy, he feared despotism in the sense of arbitrary rule or government without laws. While he had the wider political environment in view, his major reference point was the arbitrary rule of Louis XV and his mistress, Madame de Pompadour, together with the clerics and financiers dependent on them. In addressing the issue of the political survival of society, Montesquieu embedded himself in the theory of rights and sovereignty being developed in the rights discourse and designed a sociology with a strong political and legal but also a historical dimension.

Montesquieu's framing of the early modern societal issue was cognitively or intellectually first of all shaped by the education that he had received in the Oratorian tradition. Important to him, therefore, was Descartes and particularly Malebranche who had transferred the former's rationalism from the physical world to the mental world (Windelband 1958, II, 407). This broad Cartesianism predisposed Montesquieu to frame society with reference to the natural law tradition in terms of both the laws of human reason and natural or civil jurisprudence. Accordingly, it was assumed not only that human society is dependent on a uniform human nature, but also that rational analysis of human relations established a standard or criterion of the goal towards which societies ought to tend (Aron 1979, 53–57).[19] It was on this latter basis that Montesquieu developed, although on the whole sympathetic, patient and cautious, a morally motivated critique of human institutions taking the form of an exposure of illusions and delusions. Secondly, Montesquieu was under the influence of Locke, the philosopher who had pushed to the foreground the theory of knowledge known as empiricism and later called positivism (Kolakowski 1972, 41–42) according to which observation, sensation or experience is the sole source of knowledge of the external world. This more empirical epistemology predisposed him to attempt to make sense of the diversity of actual societal structures as they appeared in history and the early modern world by arriving at an intelligible order through observation, causal analysis and classification into a small number of types. As regards observation, he drew on such sources of data on actual societies and their structures as historical documents, the growing travel literature of the early modern period, and his own sojourns in countries as far apart as Italy, England and Hungary. As regards analysis, he considered societies as being shaped by two major categories of force: physical or material causes, such as the geographical milieu, including climate, soil and population size; and moral or socio-cultural causes, such as religion, property, communication between societies, trade, revolutions in trade, and currency.

As regards classification, he employed a typological method to organise the diversity of societies into a small number of social types. Proceeding in what may be described as a theoretically informed, historical-hermeneutical manner, the focus was on 'the general spirit of a nation' or 'the spirit of the laws' (Montesquieu 1989, 310) of each society in the sense of the overall configuration constituted by human nature, material and socio-cultural conditions, and the laws, manners and customs peculiar to each. In this way, Montesquieu steered a highly innovative course between the all too abstract theoretical approach of rationalism and the all too concretistic factual approach of empiricism, and thus gave effect to the differentiated epistemology characteristic of the Enlightenment (compare Aron 1979; Seidman 1983, 25–27).

Montesquieu's normative or moral framing of society is apparent from his classification of societies. While he sought to typologise each society as a whole, politics was assigned a central position in this sociological endeavour of his. In keeping with the core issue at stake in the rights discourse, he assumed that whereas the form of government or political regime depended on social foundations, the form taken by society as a whole is decisively shaped by the way in which power is politically exercised. To arrive at an overall grasp of different societies, to determine 'the spirit of the laws' characterising each, it was necessary therefore to distinguish different forms of government. Such an exercise was not devoid of normative implications, however. In terms of the rights frame, Montesquieu therefore did not only distinguish among forms of government by reference to the number of individuals possessing rights or sovereign power, namely the republic, monarchy and despotism (Montesquieu 1989, 10). By introducing the further criterion of moderate and non-moderate government (Montesquieu 1989, 29–30), he simultaneously also contrasted forms of government that were respectively least suited and best suited to solve the problem of the survival of society under modern conditions. At the one extreme, the despotism towards which the absolutist monarchies of the age were tending, the absolute form of political evil threatening the survival of society, needed to be avoided at all costs. Although in principle libertarian, democracy at the other extreme historically showed a tendency to absolutise the sovereignty of the people and thus to become illiberal and to breed the despotism of a single, powerful, popular ruler. The form of government that was best suited to foreclose the emergence of both types of despotism was, in his view, monarchy based on a distinction of social classes and a separation of powers, thus allowing the continuous balancing of powers to secure the conditions of liberty and moderate government.

Finally, the aesthetic or conative framing device Montesquieu employed to structure his contribution to the construction of sociology in relation to the early modern issue of the political survival of society casts more light on his overall position. What meaning does he ascribe to human expressive relations and society so as to be able to conceive of sociology in an Enlightenment vein[20] as a combination of theory and reliable information that could help to cure people of their prejudices and to enlighten them and thus to secure the survival of society? In his criticism of Hobbes, Montesquieu (1989, 6) argued that the state of nature, far from being a condition of universal war that called forth political absolutism to bring about order, peace and security, witnessed people who were neither organised nor strong enough to attack others and even less entertained the essentially social desire to subjugate or destroy rivals. Warfare was possible only once societies had come into being and had given rise to inequalities. Human beings are not naturally bellicose but rather social by nature. The rivalries and wars that infuse their relations with tensions and throw them into disarray are all social phenomena and therefore can be intrinsically linked to the very nature of society.

It is this framing of social expressive relations that not only led Montesquieu to relinquish the ideology of order advanced by Hobbes, but also prevented him from following the utopian road of some of his late-Enlightenment successors such as Condorcet (1955) and Kant (1963), who projected the possibility of absolute or perpetual peace. The differences, inequalities and conflicts endemic in social life cannot be eliminated but call for regulation and moderation. This is Montesquieu's (1989, 17–19) most characteristic position.[21] Serious conflict must be transformed into normal social conflict, contestation and competition. This is best done by admitting all the different social forces to society, guaranteeing a minimum of liberty for all individuals constituting these forces, and institutionalising their normal operation in society. The most appropriate political-legal solution for human society is a constitution that makes possible a balance of powers, a mosaic of countervailing powers that sees to it that no power is unlimited (Montesquieu 1989, 154–86). While rational analysis dictates that this is the ideal solution, Montesquieu was fully aware that there is no such thing as a single universal solution. Any solution has to be in accord with the general spirit of the society to which it applies. The English constitution, or at least in his interpretation (Montesquieu 1989, 156–66),[22] provided him with a model of the separation and the balance of powers, yet he saw clearly that it could not be transferred lock, stock and barrel to France, for instance, which required its own appropriate solution. This would take the form of a constitutional monarchy with the retention of a significant role for the nobility in government to guarantee a balance of powers and thus a moderation of power.

Montesquieu's overall framing of the early modern problem and issue complex of violence and societal survival brings together a rational-empirical framing of factual reality with a morally motivated critical approach to human institutions and an image of society as being fraught with conflict and in need of being moderated. He thus represented an idea-guided focus on concrete reality with an emphasis on liberty within a constraining context. The combination of these framing devices allowed him to construct and communicate a position in the rights discourse that linked up with the general eighteenth-century ideological current known as liberalism.[23] Liberalism as a broad current, which received its name only in the nineteenth century, yet then designating a sharply reduced variant,[24] is a derivative of the rights frame that became established for the first time in the late sixteenth and early seventeenth century, which itself in turn is an instantiation of the characteristically modern liberal-egalitarian-discursive cognitive order. Nevertheless, Montesquieu can be regarded as one of the people who laid the foundations of this current. Within its context, he represented one particular strand or variant among a number of competing ones. Montesquieu was an aristocrat who inveighed against the absolutist monarchy by means of rights-based legal-constitutionalist ideas. This accounts for the varied impact of his communicative contribution to the rights discourse. On the one hand, his critique of absolutism and the enlightened despotism of the various defenders of the absolutist state served the more general bourgeois-Enlightenment cause but, on the other, clashed with the frame of classical republicanism. Rather than the liberty of the citizens as against the state and the moderation of power through the counterweight of their rights asserted in intermediate bodies and associations, a radical democrat such as Jean-Jacques Rousseau (1966) stressed the inalienable and undivided sovereignty of the people which finds direct expression in the *volonté générale*, the general will. Montesquieu's twofold etatist and republican attack does not imply, however, that his framing can simply be identified with liberalism in the later sense of a celebration of strategic action oriented towards the acquisition and maintenance of positions of power. Such an interpretation is inspired by an understanding of liberalism that stems from Locke, Smith and Marx, which stresses civil society as a private, pre-political economic domain rather than as a public, politically relevant domain, as did Montesquieu.[25] Moreover, his central concern with law, the constitution and relations of equity or rights, inspired by his contact with the natural law tradition,[26] makes such an interpretation impossible.

Model of Society

Montesquieu's contribution to the construction of sociology on the basis of his particular framing and communication of violence and societal survival centred on a model of society that is properly intelligible only by reference to his location in the second phase of the rights discourse. By the time of the publication of *De l'Esprit des Lois* in 1748, the trajectory traversed by the discourse had already passed from uncertainty to certainty, with the result that the rights frame, which was by now well established, made possible both identity formation and collective action mobilisation in relation to the solution of early modern society's most pressing societal problem. By contrast with the earlier part of the discourse, when society was still seen as a given order, he shared Vico's realisation, yet now more acutely and more directed toward the present than the author of the *Scienza Nuova*, that society is a field that is actively formed and shaped by an ongoing process of conflict and struggle. While this is the most characteristic feature of Montesquieu's model of society, various other dimensions need to be clarified to render it fully comprehensible.

What distinguishes Montesquieu as a sociologist, to begin with, is his emphatic concept of society, what Aron (1979, 62) calls his 'total conception of society' or his conception of society as a whole.[27] The crucial Book XIX of *The Spirit of the Laws* is devoted to this conception of his to which he himself refers as the 'general spirit of a nation' (*l'esprit général d'une nation*) (Montesquieu 1989, 308–33, here 310; 1951, 556). Society emerges on the basis of a common or uniform human nature and consists of moral, legal and political components that assume a different form or configuration depending on the material and socio-cultural factors or conditions that shape the whole. On the one hand, the components of which society consists are shaped by physical or material conditions such as the geographical milieu, particularly the climate and the soil, and the size of the population. On the other, they are subject to socio-cultural factors such as religion and the organisation of labour and trade. The societal components shaped by these two sets of conditions are first of all of a moral nature. There are customs in the sense of external modes of conduct and manners in the sense of internalised rules of conduct and principles. Society is secondly made up of law which itself embraces various kinds of legal norms. They stretch from civil law through criminal law to public law and even the law of nations or international law. Finally, society consists of a government or political regime, based on customs and manners and, in moderate cases, regulated by law, which determines the way in which public power is exercised. The concept of society refers to the configuration that emerges from these various components and conditions, and as such it encapsulates the particular quality of a given territorially based and historically specific group of people. In this sense, one can distinguish between, for instance, the general spirit of England and of France, or of China and of Japan. While exhibiting astonishingly comprehensive comparative knowledge, Montesquieu also operates with unifying concepts. He speaks of 'mankind' (*les hommes*) and of 'a general spirit' (*l'esprit général*) embracing them (Montesquieu 1989, 310; 1951, 558), which points toward society in a more general sense than any one of the numerous specific cases to which he refers.[28] The implied notion of a society of humankind would later become a cherished concept of his Enlightenment followers and successors. Already in his case, therefore, the possibility was opened for sociology to assume the form of a science of universal or global processes rather than being confined to particular national societies or nation-states.[29]

Perhaps the most central feature of society as conceived by Montesquieu, however, was social conflict (Aron 1979, 28, 33, 60; Berlin 1979a, 158). This is clearly borne out by his analysis of the English constitution (Montesquieu 1989, 156–66) as well as historical cases, such as the relationship between the plebeians and patricians in Rome (Montesquieu 1951, 111–16; 1989, 172–77). What interested him in the first place was the heterogeneous composition of society, the fact that it consists of different groupings or social classes that are distinct from one another due to their own particular social and cultural traits. The ideals that people entertain and the ends or goals they pursue, even within the same society, are many and varied and hence often incompatible. Secondly, he emphasised the rivalry, competition and conflict that necessarily ensued between or among the different groupings or classes. For him, this social conflict was of the utmost significance in that it was the medium in which a balance of the different social powers was maintained. Were it not for such a balance, power would not be moderated, nor the liberty or the subjective freedom of the members of society be secured. If the different groupings or classes are to be free to live their own socio-cultural forms of life, if its members are to be free to pursue their own chosen ends or goals, then society can only and must take the form of a state of agitation, an unstable equilibrium. Society as a configuration of materially and socio-culturally shaped customs, manners, laws and government can be socially integrated and legitimated only if social conflict is allowed to play its part. The fact that Montesquieu adopted a model of society that recognises both heterogeneity and conflict as being essential to social integration and legitimation explains why he rejected out of hand Hobbes' proposal (Montesquieu 1989, 6) and why his work contrasts so sharply with Rousseau's (Montesquieu 1989, 22–24). Whereas Hobbes (1973) proposed that the absolutist state bring about peace and order by the imposition of a single system of norms, Rousseau (1966) returned from socially determined inequalities and conflict to the natural equality of the state of nature and accordingly insisted on the absolute sovereignty of the people. For Montesquieu, social integration and legitimation are not a matter of a moral consensus, a commitment of all the members of society to the same values and norms, irrespective of whether it is imposed from the top by the state or grows up from below out of the majority of the people.

To the exposition of his emphatic concept of society Montesquieu linked a conception of history that would later be given a pointed interpretation he would not have been willing to endorse. In every society, according to him (Montesquieu 1989, 310), a particular material or socio-cultural cause or factor tends to predominate, whether geographical and climatological milieu, customs, morals, law, or maxims of government. The sociologically significant point is, however, that historical evidence shows that in the course of time socio-cultural conditions gradually come to take precedence over material conditions. This means that whereas in archaic societies nature and climate predominate almost exclusively, later on in history socio-cultural conditions become more significant and tend to prevail. It is crucial to note that, unlike his Scottish followers, Montesquieu did not interpret this natural history of society in terms of a possible improvement in the human condition, nor in the terms of later French and German authors, such as Condorcet and Kant, or even later sociologists like Comte or Marx, who formulated and embraced a theory of progress and a philosophy of history. Since nature commonly moves slowly, the change he detected here in the historically variable asymmetry between material and socio-cultural conditions in his eyes takes place only very gradually.[30] Nor did he draw the conclusion that a later society shaped by socio-cultural conditions is necessarily superior to an earlier one subject to material conditions. What was appropriate to one society under certain circumstances was not necessarily equally appropriate to another under different circumstances. Moreover, while there was evidence of moderate political regimes far back in the past, the evil of despotism threatened to become a reality in a historically late, socio-culturally determined society such as the France of Louis XV. At the same time, he was also acutely aware of what may be called the dialectic of progress or the dialectic of enlightenment: 'In a time of ignorance, one has no doubts even while doing the greatest evils; in an enlightened age, one trembles even while doing the greatest goods. One feels the old abuses and sees their correction, but one also sees the abuses of the correction itself' (Montesquieu 1989, xliv).

The position taken by Montesquieu can be accounted for by the particular significance he ascribed to history and politics respectively in his constructive contribution to sociology. Although history[31] was important to him as a source of information or data, he did not see it as the vehicle of the unfolding or development of society along a linear path leading to the fulfilment of some telos, the meaning of history. In other words, he did not construct sociology on the basis of a philosophy of history. Instead, he regarded politics as the means through which society changes or develops and is integrated. Social change or development in the medium of politics or conflict is quite different, however, in that it goes in spurts and in different directions, sometimes advancing and at other times suffering a setback. The fact that Montesquieu located politics rather than history at the heart of society, the fact that he adopted an apparently immanent societal view, may be one of the main reasons why he is so often regarded as an empiricist or positivist.[32] In contradistinction to this interpretation, however, it should be pointed out that he did retain a reference to a transcendent goal (Montesquieu 1989, 7–8),[33] yet one that is immanently grounded. In Book I of *The Spirit of the Laws*, this immanently grounded transcendent reference point is articulated in the language of rights through an analysis of the relation of natural law, on the one hand, and positive law, on the other. Here he firmly held that differences, inequalities and conflict must be moderated not only within society but also between nations. In periods of calm, adversaries should do one another all the good they can, and in periods of agitation, such as conflict and war, as little injury as possible. This goal, which is directly drawn from politics by means of rational rather than empirical analysis, is what we should regard as the one towards which all societies ought to tend.

Both the central position that Montesquieu ascribed to politics, and his reference to an immanently grounded goal making possible a rational and critical analysis, can clearly be led back to the structuring effect that the macro-frame generated by the rights discourse exerted on his construction of sociology.

The Scottish Enlightenment: Adam Ferguson and John Millar

A characteristic concern of the Scottish Enlightenment[34] of the third quarter of the eighteenth century was a type of investigation for which they did not yet have an appropriate name. Dugald Stewart therefore provisionally called it 'theoretical or conjectural history' or 'the natural or theoretical history of society' (cited in Lehmann 1930, 231). A whole series of famous titles gave expression to this concern.[35] Having been conceived under the impact of the author they regarded as the Bacon of their science, Montesquieu, it took the form not of a philosophy of history, as Szacki (1979, 78) recently mistakenly still claimed, but rather of historical sociology in the sense of a theoretical understanding of historical processes.[36] For the Scottish Enlightenment, the natural history of society referred to the processes by which society is produced, as Dugald Stewart stated explicitly (cited in Lehmann, 1930, 231), and thus concerned something more permanent and theoretically significant than the transitory features of the hour or even the epoch.[37] Of all the Scottish authors, Adam Ferguson (1723–1816) and John Millar (1735–1801) pursued the construction of this variety of Enlightenment sociology most consistently and systematically. In so doing, Millar (cited in Lehmann 1960, 135) conceived of himself as a 'philosophical historian' – i.e. his anticipation of the concept of sociologist – in the sense of a social scientifically oriented theorist who seeks to provide an explanation for the facts made available by the historian.[38] Aside from the French connection, which was itself mediated through the Continental tradition of natural law or natural or civil jurisprudence (Forbes 1975; Skinner 1978; Stein 1980; Pocock 1985b), their version of sociology on the one hand also rested on the indigenous British traditions of both empirical science, as represented by Bacon, Newton and Hume, and moral philosophy and civil jurisprudence, as put forward by Cumberland, Shaftesbury, Carmichael, Hutcheson, Berkeley, Hume and Smith. On the other, it was developed within the context of two broad and interrelated areas of practical concern in which the Scottish authors cultivated a special interest in the period stretching from the Union of the Parliaments in 1707 through the French Revolution to the parliamentary reform finally effected in 1832. They were first the problem of law and secondly the problem of politics, government and public policy, including political economy (Lehmann 1960, 96–108; Pocock 1975, 493–504; Hont and Ignatieff 1985). It is their intense concern with these legal and political questions, in addition to the overriding significance that the tradition of natural law or civil jurisprudence possessed for the Scots,[39] that points toward the fact that the construction of sociology in the vibrant intellectual atmosphere of eighteenth-century Scotland was likewise given structure by the early modern rights discourse. The contributions of Ferguson and Millar, like that of Montesquieu, demonstrate that the appearance of sociology is not attributable solely to secularisation or the emergence of science and its extension to the human domain, nor even to this plus transformative economic forces and developments, but in particular also to the opposition of society to the absolutist state or more generally the *ancien régime*.[40] Within the framework of the Europe-wide rights discourse, concerned with questions of rights, sovereignty and the relation between society and state or the survival of society in its political environment,[41] new developments took place that called forth a novel theoretical construction of reality. Ferguson and Millar articulated the latter more consistently and systematically than any of their predecessors.

Discourse of Modernity and the Construction of Sociology

Framing of Social Reality

Ferguson and Millar made their respective contributions to the construction of sociology towards the end of the rights discourse. At this stage, the establishment of a macro-frame had long ago already substituted a high degree of certainty for the uncertainty caused by the breakdown of feudalism and the religious-metaphysical worldview. Relative clarity had been achieved, at least in England if not yet in Scotland, over questions concerning sovereignty and rights. Constitutional arrangements had been put in place in the wake of the Glorious Revolution and subsequent developments confirmed the importance of Parliament and led to the recognition of ministerial responsibility. The Act of Union with Scotland had been passed more than half a century earlier in the year 1707 and, although not polarising the Scottish people inordinately, did give rise to strife which coloured the context in which the Scottish authors made their contributions to the Enlightenment. A number of additional factors further conspired to raise the political temperature in the second half of the eighteenth century during which the two Scots made their contributions. Internally, George III's (1760–1820) extension of the royal prerogative and incompetent rule bred political strife. It led not only to the revolt of the American Colonies and the Irish revolt against mercantile regulations, but also to the second big wave of agitation by the radical movement dedicated to parliamentary reform, thus blighting the first half of his reign. Externally, conditions across the Channel led to the French Revolution, the radical phase of which caused a reaction in England that put an end to all hope of political and social reform – until after the Battle of Waterloo. It was in this context, shaped by the longstanding struggle between landowners-cum-merchants and absolutism, between Parliament and Crown, or between Whigs and Tories, and in Scotland between Presbyterian, Whig, aristocratic groups and Episcopal, Jacobite, provincial groups, that Ferguson and Millar encountered a number of more specific problems.

In the wake of the Union, the far-reaching transformations of a broadly economic nature that had taken hold of England already in the previous century started to make themselves felt also in Scotland. Although this was before the dawn of industrialism, with commerce still being dominant, the authors of the second half of the eighteenth century were keenly aware not only of changes in production, the increasing division of labour and the growth in wealth, but also of the consequences of these developments. For them, the economic problems were at one and the same time social, legal and political problems. Among their consequences were challenges to the agrarian way of life, a growing distance between Highland culture and the urban commercial

216

centres, legal problems of adjustment to a changing agricultural, commercial and eventually industrial situation, the need to tone down the harshness of Scottish law, the necessity of constitutional refinements, and questions of political direction and government. While representatives of the Scottish Enlightenment such as Ferguson and Millar focused on these various problems with a new realism rather than engaging in purely formal analyses, they did not lose sight of the larger questions of rights, requiring legal changes and a new foundation for law in history and in moral philosophy, and constitutional arrangements. As in the case of Montesquieu, politics was central to the respective constructions of sociology advanced by Ferguson and Millar. Ferguson, although a Jacobite who was unwilling to pose as a consistent radical reformer, did insist that knowledge is linked to power, and that the latter therefore requires to be exercised in a manner that enjoys legitimacy. He thus assisted his younger contemporary Millar, regarded by Lehmann as the leading apostle of liberalism[42] in Scotland at the time, to provide grist to the mill of the reform movement of the late eighteenth century. On the basis of a general right to freedom, the central issue for both was how to guarantee the safety of citizens and the security of their property, i.e. how to secure the survival of civil society, by a constitutionally regulated system of government without repression and encroachment on liberties spelling the end of the active or participatory virtues and eventually the public political spirit itself. This particular orientation of theirs had been prepared by Francis Hutcheson (1995b), the so-called 'father of the Scottish Enlightenment' (Campbell 1982), who wrote against the background of the Grotian and Pufendorfian tradition of natural law and rights (Haakonssen 1990, 76–77, 82).

In their framing of the issue of the survival of society in its political environment as it presented itself in the last third of the eighteenth century, the men of the Scottish Enlightenment cognitively or intellectually quite consciously adopted a scientific orientation. Considering the Enlightenment 'science of man', this was not untypically a broadly social scientific orientation embracing various strands that were not particularly clearly distinguished from one another. The disciplinary division of labour in the social sciences became established, of course, only in the wake of the protracted nineteenth-century academic revolution started in Germany which took hold first of history, then economics, followed by anthropology and sociology and finally psychology (Collins 1994, 25–46). Characteristic of the Enlightenment, particularly of its Scottish instantiation, however, was a shift within this general social scientific orientation specifically towards the sociologically relevant dimension of social reality (Lehmann 1960, 112; Gay 1969, 319, 323; Eriksson 1993).[43] With authors such as Bacon, Descartes, Newton, and Hume in the background, social reality was approached as empirically accessible, yet not without being guided by a theoretical frame of reference. Although a mechanistic residue shows in both Ferguson and Millar, predecessors such as Shaftesbury, Hutcheson and Montesquieu led them to regard social reality as a specifically human social reality. Data were obtained through historical sources, ethnological materials and the observation of contemporary tendencies, developments and problems in the economic, legal, political and cultural fields, while their exposure to historical and anthropological information encouraged the development of a strongly comparative point of view.[44]

The fact that Ferguson and Millar drew more or less heavily on the tradition of British empiricism did not prevent them from employing moral framing devices that were far from morally neutral. On the contrary, both the tradition of moral philosophy from Shaftesbury (1900) through Carmichael and Hutcheson (1995b) to the Scottish school,[45] and the fact that society took on shape in a struggle against absolutism, impressed on them the significance of the moral dimension of social reality and its connection with the legal and particularly the political dimension. They nevertheless exhibited the ability to build this moral commitment into their analyses with a certain detachment. Ferguson, a major concern of whom lay in the field of ethics, was convinced that a scientific approach to social reality was necessary in order to understand moral conduct (MacRae 1969, 28–29). Not only do human beings possess a propensity to seek perfection through the use of their faculties, but their best conceptions, movements of heart and social nature suggest a standard by means of which human action, the state of society and the norms of government can be judged. Similarly, Millar assumed that human beings have both a disposition and capacity for improving their condition. It manifests itself clearly in the historical trajectory from a concern with material wants through a cultivation of a moral sense to the establishment of institutions and government. More important to him, however, is that it can be seen also in the historical trend towards the diffusion of liberty to an increasing number of people over an increasingly wide area and its political implementation in a government capable of distributing rights and thus securing justice. It was their incorporation of a normative standard by way of comparable moral framing devices in conjunction with a social scientific orientation that allowed Ferguson and Millar to develop a critical approach to existing practices and social institutions. On the one hand, this form of critique was kept immanent within historical limits so as not to become abstract (Habermas 1969b, 215–30; 1971, 38), and, on the other, it was less a matter of advancing a moralistic condemnation than one of exposing the illusions inadvertently entertained by the various social actors. The critique Ferguson and Millar developed of hyper-rationalism and their unwillingness to accept the ideas of a homo-geneous society and of necessary and inevitable advancement furthermore indicate that they turned a self-critical eye towards the potential illusions lurking in their own mode of framing social reality.

The way in which Ferguson and Millar aesthetically or conatively framed violence and the political survival of society and were thus able to ascribe meaning to human action and to the relation between human beings and their world goes back to the tradition of Shaftesbury, Carmichael and Hutcheson. In accordance with this tradition, they rejected Hobbes' egoistic and selfish image of human beings in favour of regarding them as altruistic and social from the outset – which does not exclude, to be sure, the possibility of dissension and conflict. Most basically, they were informed by Shaftesbury's (1900)[46] conceptions of perfection and enthusiasm: the harmony, beauty and perfection of the universe awakens enthusiasm in human beings for all that is true, good and beautiful and thus directs them toward universal values. If Shaftesbury remained attached to a certain individualistic understanding, however, Carmichael's (Moore and Silverthorne 1985) and Hutcheson's (1995a; 1995b) turn from this prepared the ground for Ferguson and Millar to go strongly in a social direction. For them, human beings are capable of learning, of gaining insight into the social, of resolving to be free and respecting the rights of others, and of establishing and recognising certain rules governing their own actions and those of others. It is in terms of this framing that the individual in Ferguson's and Millar's contributions to the rights discourse and the construc-tion of sociology appears as active and participatory, and that the relation between human beings and their political environment gives evidence of a move-ment towards improvement, albeit by way of interruption and discontinuity.

By employing the intellectual, moral and motivational framing devices in the way suggested by the above analysis, Ferguson and Millar were able to construct and give symbolic form to a frame by means of which they communicated a distinct identity in the rights discourse. As in the case of their French predecessor, it was a constitutionalist identity forming part of the broader ideological current that became known as liberalism after the *Liberales* in the Spanish Cortes of 1820 (Bramsted and Melhuish 1978, 3).[47] Montes-quieu's defence of the British constitution, or at least his interpretation of it, encouraged them in their inclination, formulated by David Hume when he said that 'liberty is the perfection of civil society' (cited in Lehmann 1960, 105), to link up with Locke[48] and the constitutional arrangements achieved in the wake of the Glorious Revolution. Their liberalism thus gives evidence of an appropriation of ideas deriving from both Locke and Montesquieu. Ferguson argued emphatically in favour of the spirit of liberty and a constitution that guarantees not only liberty or freedom but also active participation and even agitation and conflict. For a salutary and just result is forthcoming only when different active powers, which singly might be partial and wrong, are brought into a balance and allowed to mutually correct one another. In his mature years, Millar was the leading spokesman of liberalism in Scotland that concerned itself both with a general right to freedom and classical liberal rights. He emphasised law as the institutional basis of liberty and valued the British constitution as a nodal point in the growth and diffusion of liberty. This was complemented by a future-oriented desire for human improvement, supported by a scientific temper, an analytical frame of mind and a readiness to critically assess existing practices and institutions. The adoption of this broad liberal, humanitarian, constitutionalist identity and moral theory of rights accounts for the oppositional position Ferguson and Millar consistently took in the rights discourse against Hobbesian absolutism, against Rousseau's radical democratic republican majoritarianism and civic moralism, and against the extension of the royal prerogative, resistance to parliamentary reform, the remnants of serfdom, and slavery.[49]

Model of Society

Considering the connection between the general socio-political semantics of the practical discourse of the time and the sociological semantics emerging from it, the quite similar way in which Ferguson and Millar symbolically packaged and framed the issue of the survival of early modern society in its political environment shaped their respective contributions to the construction of sociology. Within a broad liberal, humanitarian and constitutional frame, they adopted a theoretically informed, empirically oriented approach towards social reality, what they called 'civil society'. They understood civil society in terms of its idea, namely liberty, and critically analysed it by reference to its historical development and concrete structural and institutional features. The character that their construction of sociology took, specifically their model of society, was decisively structured by their relation to the phase structure of the rights discourse. Louis Schneider (1972) discovers an unresolved tension in Millar's sociology between his emphasis on a low level of rationality in history and a high level of *laissez faire* in the organisation of society, on the one hand, and his critical analysis of certain institutions and his support for the American War of Independence and French Revolution, on the other. Habermas (1969a, 218–19; 1971, 38–39; 1974a, 77–78) interprets the sociology of the Scots more acutely as exhibiting both conservative and critical intentions. This stereoscopic orientation was due to the fact that they at one and the same time assumed that society developed naturally yet demanded the critical investigation of institutions and authorities. I take this tension or, rather, duality as indicative of two things: the analytical or theoretical position taken by Ferguson and Millar, as well as the place the two – not without some differences between them – occupied within the context of the rights discourse, and the corresponding mode of dealing with uncertainty adopted by them. First, Ferguson and Millar understood society or, rather, civil society, on the one hand in terms of the tradition of Locke and Smith with its emphasis on the pre-political economic dimension as a self-regulating complex, and on the other in terms of the Montesquieuian tradition with its emphasis on the political dimension of differences, inequalities, conflicts and power balances in terms of collective self-organisation.[50] Secondly, from their vantage point late in the second phase of the discourse, indeed quite close to its end, Ferguson and Millar not merely experienced the overcoming of uncertainty by the unequivocal establishment of the rights frame, but also witnessed the formation of the new broad liberal identity and the mobilisation of collective action. Considering the situation in Scotland at the time, it could be added that they enjoyed some of the fruits of these achievements. With the period of religious and political strife coming to an end, with the English Civil War, the Glorious Revolution and the Union behind them, they were admirers of the British constitution as the largely unintended outcome of a protracted process of conflict. On the other hand, they were convinced, Millar to a higher degree than his older contemporary, that liberty had not yet been achieved to the degree that was possible at the time. Various features of their own time strengthened them in this conviction. They included the endangering of liberty by royal tyranny and pretensions to absolute power, the lingering on of serfdom, the perpetuation of slavery, and absolutism on the Continent. Both an achievement such as the British constitution and the possibility of realising humanitarian ideas and extending liberty and participation had a formative impact on the model of society that Ferguson and Millar adopted. Within such a context, neither the development nor the application of a static conception of society would have made any sense. Rather than an organised society, therefore, they worked with a model of a dynamic, conflict-ridden, self-regulating and self-organising society. In their time, people had become aware of a core of such self-regulation and self-organisation. Under the conditions of what they referred to as 'civilisation' or 'civil society', the issue of the survival of society in its political environment presented itself to them in a particular form. It demanded a concerted effort to attain a level of organisation and integration that is in keeping with a justifiable political monopolisation of force, yet an effort that retains past achievements in so far as they contribute to the direction and regulation of new arrangements.

Acknowledging social reality as gradually delineated in early modern socio-political semantics, both Ferguson and Millar were in command of an explicit and highly differentiated concept of society reflecting the process of secularisation, economic transformation and religious and political strife. Conceptually, it was developed in opposition to the contractarian fiction of a state of nature, whether Hobbes' war of all against all or Rousseau's ideal state from which civilisation has departed, yet both authors retained a concern with the question of human nature.[51] Once they had established that society rested on certain philosophical-anthropological and historical-anthropological foundations,[52] they shifted the emphasis in a sociologically significant manner to the historicity of society. Following Shaftesbury and Montesquieu, they recognised the inalienably social nature of human beings and the fact that society presupposes certain innate human traits. More characteristically, they stressed that human beings are capable of learning. The development of their latent capacities, however, depended on the social structure into which they were integrated. Of fundamental importance, in their view, are social relations mediated by language and symbolic communication and their cultural effects, such as habit, custom, cultural tradition, rules, cultural values and the distinction of right and wrong. Through conflict and the improvement of techniques and technology, there arise from this base not only political structures and institutions such as the state, but also economic structures and institutions. The socio-cultural framework together with these various structures lend society a particular character that both creates possibilities and sets limits to the realisation of latent human capacities. This concept of society did not entail, as later in the case of Auguste Comte for instance, the reduction or obliteration of the individual. Ferguson and Millar both regarded the individual *qua* active agent and bearer of rights as being of the utmost importance. On the other hand, instead of allowing this to mislead them into the atomistic individualism of the second-generation representatives of the French Enlightenment, they developed a genuinely sociological concept of society.

Rather than a stable order, the Scots conceived of society as a living web of active, both cooperative and conflictual, social relations. Where stability prevails, social disintegration and decline can be expected to set in. Through the creation of new ways of doing things and new forms of regulation and control, by contrast, society continually breeds new conditions for its own existence. It is something dynamic that is constantly subject to change, to a dialectics of growth and transformation (Lehmann 1930, 57–65; 1960, 134–35). If it is the task of the historian to follow and record such change, Ferguson and Millar felt with Montesquieu that it was left to the sociologist, alias 'theoretical historian', to render it conceptually intelligible and thus to provide the educator and politician with a basis for the determination of the desired direction of development. The most distinctive assumption from which the two Scottish authors proceeded in the case of their dynamic conception of society is the principle of the active nature of human beings. Whereas Ferguson (Lehmann 1930, 114) stressed the principle of human striving toward perfection, Millar (1806, 3; Lehmann 1960, 129; Habermas 1969b, 217; 1971, 36) emphasised humanity's disposition and capacity for improving its conditions. Due to the fact that the natural, biological or anthropological endowment of human beings, which varies only within a very narrow range, and the available means for unfolding it are both comparable across the whole species all over the globe, they regarded the change that was generated from this motivational foundation as being neither arbitrary nor random and even less accidental. Even under distinct historical conditions, the activation of this endowment and the development and realisation of latent human capacities are manifested in a remarkably uniform phasing of social change. By contrast with Montesquieu, who only obliquely suggested a gradual reversal in the predominance of physical and socio-cultural factors in the course of history, Ferguson and Millar put forward a bolder theory of development, or what some commentators in the light of nineteenth-century developments would later too strongly interpret as an evolutionary theory.[53]

Basing themselves on historical data and focusing on socio-historical reality in the concreteness of a particular place and time, Ferguson and Millar took in the historical process more or less in its entirety. The aim was to render this natural history intelligible by grasping it theoretically or sociologically. This entailed three steps: identifying the origins of socio-cultural, legal, political and economic institutions; tracing their gradual development up to the present according to a number of more or less clearly identifiable steps, without passing over discontinuities and regressions; and, finally, explaining the social change involved by means of factors or forces inherent in the process itself. Building upon human action, such dynamic factors or forces driving the development of society included technology, economic and political organisation, cultural symbols, moral standards, communication and the extension of both the means and opportunities for communication. Of particular importance to Ferguson and Millar, however, was social conflict. Unlike Adam Smith, whose interest in the economic phenomena of markets and exchange led him to operate with stages conceived of in terms of the means of subsistence, Ferguson and Millar cultivated a broader sociological concern focusing on types of social structure and indeed societies (MacRae 1969, 33).[54] While the economic dimension was crucial to them, it was in principle regarded in relation to the legal, political and cultural dimensions.

According to Ferguson, society develops from the savage state through the barbarous state to civil society or the polished state (Ferguson 1966, 98, 58).[55] Economically, the first rests on fishing, hunting and collecting (Ferguson 1966, 82), the second on herdsmanship and agriculture (Ferguson 1966, 97), and the third on increasingly complex commercial and manufacturing activities (Ferguson 1966, 180–203). Property institutions, social classes and political institutions make their appearance in the context of barbarism. On the whole, society develops from a so-called 'rude' to a 'polished' state. This involves a change from uniformity to differences, from a military to an economic emphasis, from unregulated wars to those – when they do occur – subject to law and tempered by humanity, from cruelty and inhumanity to mercy and humanity, from perpetual violence and destructive conflicts to constructive conflicts, and from political domination to free states characterised by citizens enjoying a high degree of liberty and a legitimate government.

Although Millar exhibits a much stronger concern with technology and economic forces than his older contemporary, even up to the point of appearing to adopt a techno-economic determinism (e.g. Lehmann 1952, 41; Therborn 1977, 160), he likewise gives much greater emphasis to legal, political and moral matters. Economically, he identifies a hunting and collecting stage (Millar 1806, 61), followed by a pastoral and nomadic stage (57–60) and then an agricultural stage (67) which overlaps with the latest commercial or industrial economy (87–88).[56] That he locates this dimension in a wider context, however, is apparent from his view that, whereas in the earlier stages humans are occupied predominantly by subsistence and the satisfaction of material wants, they increasingly concern themselves with the cultivation of human qualities, the establishment of social, economic and legal institutions, such as property, and the development of law and legitimate political institutions (Lehmann 1930, 221–23; 1960, 129). Indeed, the very subject of *The Origin of the Distinction of Ranks* bears this out. Significant from the point of view of the relation between his construction of sociology – here his developmental theory – and the rights frame is his inexhaustible interest in the gradual appearance in the course of the development of society of relations of dominance and subservience, the social conflict attending these relations, the need for human beings to collectively determine the conditions of their own existence, the acquisition of rights by individuals, the support of such rights by the establishment of legitimate political institutions, and what he refers to as the 'diffusion of liberty through a multitude of people, spread over a wide extent of territory'(cited in Lehmann 1960, 127). Millar (1806, 4) thus detects a natural progress in the development of society that on the whole presents itself as a move from rude to civilised manners and internally involves a gradual displacement of ignorance by knowledge, with the different stages being given form by particular customs and laws. As is borne out by his analysis of the British politics of his time, particularly the tug of war between the Tories and Whigs, Millar (Lehmann 1960, 125; Habermas 1969b, 217–18; 1971, 37–38) was convinced that his theoretical history or sociology stood on the side of the advancement of knowledge. Rather than assisting the privileged classes in maintaining the *status quo* by securing tradition and emphasising sentiment, symbolism and prestige factors, he aligned his own work, which embraced a scientific temper and analytical frame of mind, with a desire for human improvement and the acquisition of liberty by all classes.

In conceptualising and analysing the socio-historical process, both Ferguson and Millar had recourse to the word 'progress', the more general use of which in the eighteenth century had its roots in a sense of a movement from worse to better that derived from experiences of improvement in fields as diverse as agriculture, reading and science (Onions 1976; Williams 1979). Ferguson's conception of change and gradual development was based on his 'principle of progression' (Lehmann 1930, 58),[57] and Millar (1806, 4) regarded the history of society as exhibiting 'a natural progress'.[58] For both, progress was associated with such ideas as history, improvement and civilisation that started to acquire new meanings in the eighteenth century. Fixing on these various signs, one is strongly inclined to interpret the meaning of our authors in the light of late eighteenth- and nineteenth-century developments or, at least, to identify it with what is regarded as the general spirit and particularly the universalist orientation of the Enlightenment. What can hardly be over-stated, however, is that such an interpretation not only does violence to the Scottish theoretical historians, but is at the same time also utterly misleading as far as understanding sociology in a context-sensitive way is concerned.

It is indisputably the case that Ferguson and Millar shared certain characteristic eighteenth-century – and that would mean to say, modern – senses of the concepts mentioned above.[59] By 'progress' they no longer understood simply a procession or journey, but already a developing series of events entailing a movement from worse to better exhibiting a discoverable sequence or pattern. This sense was supported and strengthened by other associated words. 'History', for instance, was taken to refer to a connected and continuous process, and through the additional connotation of human self-development, first introduced by Vico, it was freed from an exclusive association with the past and related to the present as well as to the future. The word 'improvement' was for them no longer confined to enclosures, the development of agrarian capitalism and economic operations aimed at profit, but had acquired the wider meaning of 'making something better'. Similarly, they understood by 'civilisation' not only the historical process whereby human beings distance themselves from their savage origins and barbaric past, but also the polished state or condition of refinement achieved by it.

Here something of the greatest moment should be stressed, however. Although Ferguson and Millar made use of these concepts and shared the new senses they started to acquire in the eighteenth century, these two authors did not and indeed were not able to go all the way toward the abstraction of the processes designated by the concepts.[60] Neither the concept of history nor the concept of progress used by them had yet acquired its characteristic and controversial high-modern sense. Whereas Ferguson and Millar operated within the context of the rights discourse, these concepts came into their own for the first time only within the completely different context of the justice discourse. Both Ferguson and Millar produced their seminal works prior to the occurrence not only of the French Revolution, which repelled both due to the fact that it had overthrown too much, but also the establishment of industrial capitalism. Yet it was only as a result of the course taken by the French Revolution after its first phase and the consequences of the Industrial Revolution that the concepts of history and progress were given their abstract high-modern meanings. The full development of the modern ideas of history and progress had to await the political and industrial transformations of the late eighteenth and nineteenth centuries as well as the intellectual systems of the late Enlightenment, idealism, and socialism, particularly Marxism.[61]

While they were indeed representatives of the Enlightenment, broadly speaking, Ferguson and Millar belonged to an earlier generation than Condorcet (1955) who, as disciple and biographer of Turgot, together with Kant (1957; 1963) most paradigmatically gave expression to the late-Enlightenment philosophy of history and belief in universal progress. It was Turgot (1995) who in 1750, strangely enough in a religious context, first put forward the modern idea of progress, but it had to await Condorcet's biography of Turgot and other writings to receive wide currency (Manuel and Manuel 1979, 455).[62] The full articulation of this and other associated concepts presupposed the occurrence of the French Revolution and, in particular, the radical turn of the Revolution and the disillusioning experience of the middle strata as a result of the fall of the Girondins (Mannheim 1972, 200–01).[63] Condorcet, a Girondin who had fallen from grace and eventually paid the price of his life, translated it into the concept of progress, which embraced a number of necessary transitional stages moving in a unilinear direction towards a state of perfection. It should furthermore be borne in mind that Turgot, Condorcet and Kant were exceptions even in the late eighteenth century when hardly anyone had yet been willing to embrace a thoroughgoing progressivist position (Manuel and

Manuel 1979, 453–60). Ferguson and Millar are much closer to the pre-revolutionary Encyclopaedists, including all the major *philosophes*, who did not yet dispose over a concept of universal history and progress transposed into a temporal utopia projected into the future, but combined a deep-seated feeling of the inevitability of decline and decay in all things, including societies, with the conviction that the pursuit of public good or happiness was worthwhile. Not unlike Vico earlier in the century or even his own Scottish mentor Hume, Ferguson in fact held a cyclical view of history according to which the onset of 'decadence' in the progress of societies and their consequent 'return to weakness and obscurity...[is]...necessary and inevitable' (Lehmann 1930, 148).[64] Millar, on the other hand, rejected the conviction that civilisation contained the seeds of its own destruction, yet he did so in favour not of a utopian idea of progress but of a more historically grounded and politically informed liberal constitutionalist approach which allowed for contingency and openness. It is a question of how a society deals with external political and economic exigencies and with historically ineliminable internal status and class distinctions.

Although neither Ferguson nor Millar offered a formal or general sociological account of institutions, social organisation, social structure and types of societies, their respective writings are replete with evidence that both of them had given much thought to the complex of relations and structures that undergo change in the course of the natural history of society. The interrelation and interdependence they saw among the cultural, social, legal, economic and political dimensions of society, particularly clearly and sharply in the case of Millar, allowed them to focus on society as a configuration of symbolic structures, institutions, social structures, relations and functions which changed in respect of both its historical quality and its level of complexity. The fact that such configurations represented historically specific instantiations within the context of the natural history of society, however, prevented them not only from adopting a strictly typological approach, as Montesquieu still tended to do, but also from introducing a purely functionalist one.

Both Ferguson and Millar were acutely aware of the constitutive significance that language, communication, the power of expression, the interpretation of meaning and, by extension, custom and tradition have for society.[65] From here their comparable analyses went in various directions. As regards social institutions, both concentrated on the analysis of sexual relations, the family, marriage and kinship and their expansion into associational relations.[66] The ramifications of the constitutive dimension were on the other hand pursued in the analysis of socio-cultural institutions such as science and knowledge, morality and law, religion, and literature and art.[67] Whereas the analysis of the family gave Millar in particular the opportunity to study the increase in the freedom and independence gained by family members in the course of the transformation of the core social institutions, both authors emphasised the significance of law as well as mutual trust for the securing of rights and the realisation and expansion of liberty (Ferguson 1966, 154–67, 261–72; Millar 1806, 230–42). Knowledge, to which accrued much social importance, served them as the surest index of the advancement of the human mind. Not only did it entail the increase of power over natural processes and their effects, but it also came to pervade every dimension of civil society.

Besides the constitutive social and socio-cultural components, Ferguson and Millar were in particular interested in the economic and political dimensions of society, the former the more basic of the two and the latter the more important. It is the relation that these two dimensions came to assume to the core social and socio-cultural dimension in the early modern period that determined the central societal problem of the time: the survival of society in its political environment.

By contrast with Smith, neither Ferguson nor Millar was an economist, yet both appreciated the significance of the economic dimension and understood economic theory. In fact, Millar made a distinctive contribution to economic theory by emphasising the role of capital in the creation of profit (Lehmann 1960, 128). In their view, economic factors structured society in such a way that it was a field or scene of contestation in which the participants contended for power, privilege and equality. These factors asserted themselves particularly strongly since the Neolithic revolution had led to the establishment of the institution of property, in this case property in land. This institution with its economic, social and moral aspects in particular commanded the attention of the two Scottish authors (Ferguson 1966, 74–107; Millar 1806, 67, 71).[68] Not only did landed property provide the basis for an increase in the influence and power of particular families and, hence, the emergence of permanent inequalities, but simultaneously it also stimulated military developments as well as the emergence of political institutions which were often completely dominated by these very families. In medieval and early modern Europe, this coincidence of interests had been reflected in the domination of the overlapping feudal, military and ecclesiastical hierarchies. In the early modern context, however, various developments, including science, commerce, and liberty, had partially eroded and partially replaced this arrangement. Both Ferguson and Millar saw technical and commercial development in particular as having come to play a significant role. While they assumed that varying natural abilities made inequality inevitable and that the unequal distribution of property, although partially cutting across the former, complicated and exacerbated inequalities, they regarded economic factors as having been responsible for the division of labour that had such a marked effect on the social structure of early modern society. Ferguson (1966, 184–88)[69] discovered this impact in the difference between 'liberal' and 'mechanical' occupations and corresponding differences between personality types and sub-cultures. Over and above this, Millar (1806, 220–42) appreciated that the impact of the division of labour reached beyond the production process into the very structure of society itself, from its rank or status and class structure to the rural–urban divide. Both authors were sensitive, moreover, to the potentially deleterious effects of the division of labour for the integrity of the personality and the integration of society.

As in the case of Montesquieu, Ferguson and Millar attributed special importance to politics in their conceptualisation of society. Through their relation to the institution of property, the political institutions articulated closely with the economic dimension. Ferguson (1966, 24, 146–54) saw the state as the outcome of conflicting interests centred on the ownership or lack of property. For Millar (1806, 195–229),[70] who regarded social relations as being power relations, property determined the distribution of power, while the latter in turn provided the basis for the state and shaped the form taken by the government. The state was an organ of power, and government was legally or constitutionally based authority that allowed the regulation and control of the exercise of power in formal and institutionalised contexts. Crucial for Ferguson and Millar (Ferguson 1966, 154–67; Millar 1806, 230–42), however, is that such power and authority simultaneously implied a mutual regard of rights and hence liberty in a fundamental sense – something that had become acute by their own time. This did not prevent them from being convinced that relations of dominance and subjection were virtually always present and hardly eliminable. However, such relations admitted of moderation or amelioration. On the one hand, society and its institutional forms develop through more or less unconscious adaptive changes, but on the other there is historically increasing room for planning and conscious modification (Lehmann 1930, 154–55; 1960, 136) that could lead to improvement, although the possibility of deterioration is never excluded. The question of rights, particularly of liberty, repeated itself in the context of ineliminable differences and the resultant phenomenon of structured social inequality. Just as Ferguson stressed the possibility of the achievement of a more complete existence, so Millar regarded the pursuit of the goal of a more equitable and a more just society as worthwhile, yet only to the extent that the reality of existing distinctions and inequalities is reckoned with. These distinctions and inequalities are what make of society the scene of contention it is, 'the very scene in which parties contend for power, for privilege, or equality' (Ferguson cited in Lehmann 1930, 144). Accordingly, Ferguson the moderate liberal and Millar the more strident reformer[71] took the task of the state and government of their own time most appropriately as being the prevention of the disappearance of society by looking after its defence, maintaining the peace, securing the rights of individuals, protecting the pursuit of different interests, and seeing to the administration of justice and general welfare.[72] Political institutions as social institutions always reflect the general state or the type of society in question, but where communication has penetrated society, government and opinion, on which the former rests, have to be brought into accord (e.g. Millar 1806, 236). While this could be achieved in different ways, for instance by establishing a balance between the two or by state domination over opinion, Millar in particular insists that the justification of government and the criterion for the evaluation of public policy is the general welfare of the whole society.[73] For both Ferguson and Millar, however, the most immediate indication of whether relations have assumed their proper form is to be found in the degree of the distribution of rights and, hence, active participation and public spirit.[74]

Armed with the modern concept of society, Ferguson (1966) and Millar (1806) not only identified historically specific societies, such as early Anglo-Saxon society, feudal society, the Roman empire and Western European commercial societies, but also theoretically important principles relating to both the organisation and the increase in the complexity of societies.[75] In very early society based on kinship, mother-right and gynaecocracy or mother headship was later replaced by father-right and headship. Once the institution of property became established, kinship made way for the hierarchical organisation of relations under dominant landholding families. This had still been the case in early modern society in which, according to Millar (1806, 14–108),[76] the feudal, military and ecclesiastical hierarchies coincided. In commercial societies, to which correspond the early modern territorially based, monarchical state, the major principle is that of association and selection based on contracts and trust according to which distinct and indeed unequal occupational and professional groupings, each with its own class spirit or morale, come to stand in competitive and even conflictual relation to one another. Millar (1806)[77] in particular developed a wide-ranging analysis of the division of society into social classes, covering, as well as earlier historical examples, the sharply drawn fourfold division of feudalism and the more flexible threefold class structure of early modern commercial societies, which he saw as tending towards collapsing into a two-class system consisting of owners and wage-earners or labourers. Although such class division emerged and underwent change in the course of the natural history of society, he nevertheless held to the view, unlike later authors such as Karl Marx, that the complete disappearance of social distinctions and divisions cannot be envisaged. On the other hand, their political moderation or mitigation was not only possible but desirable. From Montesquieu they borrowed the view, which was developed by Ferguson in particular,[78] that the political form of society correlated with the size and degree of complexity characterising it. In small and undifferentiated societies with a high degree of solidarity and natural inequalities, a democratic type of government was more likely. In the case of the opposite extreme, such as empire-states engaging in imperial aggrandisement and territorial expansion, society tends to disappear under the weight of despotism. Large and complex societies, such as early modern commercial and manufacturing societies, organised as bureaucratic states and characterised by distinctions and rivalries between specialised interests and activities, make democracy difficult to achieve. The place of the latter tends to be taken by representative government or even monarchy.

Although Ferguson and Millar were preponderantly interested in the early modern European societies of their time, which not much earlier had become organised politically as territorially based states, their writings give evidence that they did entertain a synthetic or global concept of society. Whether they thought of it in terms of either its international extension or of humanity, communication occupied a central position in their minds (Ferguson 1966, 167–79; Millar 1806, 295–96).[79] Whereas the development of the means of communication and the increase in the opportunities for communication represent the conditions of civilisational advance, communications of various kinds establish relations between different societies and unite the endeavours of humankind into a common purpose. Trade and exchange, depending on the expansion of the market, can be regarded as one such form of communication. But of particular significance for them is the communication of culture. Emphasis is given to scientific knowledge or more generally intelligence, yet the role of works of literature and art is also clearly recognised. More important even than intellectual culture, however, is what had been centrally at stake in their own time, namely the communication of normative culture. This included the diffusion of legal and constitutional concepts and the extension of liberty to larger and larger sections of the world population – at the time, for instance, to the American Colonies and France. Ferguson and Millar thus complemented their more specific concept of society with a nuanced global concept.

In their contributions to the construction of sociology, to summarise, Ferguson and Millar adopted a multifaceted approach. As regards the dynamic forces or logics of societal change, transformation and development, they took into account the process of the formation of the state, the development of technology and science, and within civil society both capitalism and democracy. That democracy in the sense of civil society based on rights and law and organised politically was of special importance to them is apparent from the manner in which they embedded their theory and analysis of civil society. It was buttressed, on the one hand, by a historical interest in moral, legal and political philosophy and, on the other, by an intense concern with theories of law and rights of their day. Ferguson and Millar not only exposed the normative presuppositions of civil society, but they also explored the possibilities of its political organisation and indicated their own democratic aspirations.[80]

CHAPTER 9

Discursive Construction of Enlightenment Sociology

Public Communicative Construction

In the previous chapter, an analysis was conducted of a selection of authors who contributed more or less directly and significantly to the construction of sociology within the context of the rights discourse – More, Hobbes, Vico, Montesquieu, Ferguson and Millar. Their achievements can be seen in the respective constructive contributions they made to the semantics of sociology in relation to the practical discourse and hence more general socio-political semantics of the early modern period. The latter, which took form in dependence on such events as the Reformation, the Dutch Revolt, the English Civil War, the American War of Independence and the French Revolution, was rooted in the experience of violence, focused on the issue of the survival of early modern society in its political environment, and expressed in the language of rights. The analysis for the most part concentrated on the micro-level of the framing elements or devices employed by each of the authors in their respective constructions of sociology. A step was also taken towards the meso-level to determine the frame within which each symbolically packaged his propositions, commitments and motivations with a view to communicating a clear identity and thus distinguishing himself from others. Within this scaffolding of framing devices and frames, an attempt was then made in each case to highlight the emerging sociological semantics.

At this stage, finally, it is necessary to bring the analysis to a close by shifting to the macro-level to render explicit and draw conclusions about the construction of sociology as such within the master frame made available by the early modern rights discourse. The need to undertake such macro-analysis is given with the fact that early modern sociology cannot be identified with the particular constructive contributions of the authors considered. The construction of sociology in the proper sense of the word takes place only in the differentiated relations established around sociology in the context of the rights discourse and, therefore, does not admit of being reduced to the originality or ingenuity of the different authors. Rather than looking for the coherence and consistency of sociological semantics in the individual authors, the rights discourse as punctuated by sociology must be investigated in order to determine how sociology was constructed in public communication. The source of the authority of sociology is not to be found in the subject but in the discourse. At the centre of attention here, therefore, is the manner in which sociology is constructed at the macro-level through the combination and elevation of the micro-level framing devices and the meso-level frames of the different authors in the medium of communication and discourse ultimately structured by the rights frame. Of importance, too, is the third point of view represented by observers, evaluators and commentators in the process of public communicative or discursive construction.

As regards the structuration of this process, the twofold symbolic and power logic of discourse, which is articulated in a dynamic process in the course of the discourse, is of much significance here. In so far as validity is not treated in isolation but located in a discursive context, it has to be seen in relation to power. While the validity of the arguments advanced in the discourse exerts a symbolic or logical compulsion that confronts and changes or even dissolves the existing cultural or symbolic authority, the materiality and organisation of the discourse brings the power of existing institutions into play. Sociology is constructed in that certain micro-level framing devices and meso-level frames constituting sociological semantics are appropriated while some are assimilated, others subordinated and still others excluded in accordance with a historically specific combination of validity and power. This configuration is shaped by the competition, conflict and struggle over the more general sociopolitical semantics of the time. The particular combination or configuration assumed at a given point in time is indicated by the collective identity prevailing and the collective mobilisation taking place in relation to it as well as the contrasting dynamics of suppression and exclusion accompanying it. Sociology, it could therefore be said, finds its place in the ongoing dynamic process of the changing relation between validity and power which is structured by the rights discourse according to its two contingently variable dimensions of communicative framing and uncertainty management.

More in the Sixteenth-Century Discourse

Sociology started to emerge tentatively for the first time when the reality of society came to awareness against the background of the loss of authority of the religious-metaphysical worldview, the claim to sovereignty and centralisation of power by the absolutist monarchy, and the intrusion of mercantilist-capitalist economic activities into traditional forms of life. This realisation was facilitated by the rights discourse and structured by the rights frame. Starting from the problem of violence, the discourse developed with the building of the issue of the survival of early modern society in its political environment. This issue concerned first the integrity of society as such, and secondly the legitimacy of the exercise of public power. Thomas More was one of the first, if not the first, to articulate the new awareness of society, which he quite consciously shared with his friends, the northern humanists such as Erasmus, Busleyden, Giles, von Hutten, Desmarais, Le Sauvage, Budé, Tunstal and Warham.[1] It was actually Erasmus who had given him the basic idea and encouraged him to put it in book form. This he did in *Utopia* in terms of the central issue of the rights discourse as framed in its early phase. Starting from the prevailing violence of the age and bearing in mind both the problems of social integration and the justification of the exercise of public power, he developed a sketch of a tolerant, free and non-repressive society that is subjected to laws made by itself. This argument formed part of the more general humanist contribution to the debates about violence, war, the conduct of European princes and so forth that constituted the rights discourse. More's friends were crucial in helping him to insert *Utopia* into the rights discourse, and through their evaluation of the work lent it a validity and symbolic authority that launched it on a long, if chequered, career far beyond the context delineated by the rights discourse. Referring to the work, the leading French humanist, Guillaume Budé, for instance wrote that 'our age and succeeding ages will hold his account as a nursery of correct and useful institutions' (cited by Manuel and Manuel 1979, 132).

The Reformation that erupted shortly after the publication of More's *Utopia* not only opened up a schism in the Church but also turned the whole intellectual world upside down. Faced with this new constellation of power and validity, More was compelled to make clear where he stood in the rights discourse. *Utopia* represented a novel form of rhetoric that combined earnestness with playfulness and mockery in seeking to be didactic through entertainment. Central to it was a conception of society that was only imagined as being real and therefore was not and, indeed, could not have been regarded by either More and his friends or his readers as a programme of action for the transformation of the *status quo*.[2] In the wake of the 'pestylent errours' and 'stynckyng heresyes' of world-historical proportions introduced by Luther, however, the *Utopia* was shorn of its humour, wit and satire, and its fictitious reality was in the deadly earnest of the Reformers and revolutionaries taken as a real alternative. The appeal of Thomas Müntzer, the Anabaptists, and other Protestant leaders in the Peasant Wars to various aspects of *Utopia* revolted and alarmed More to such an extent that he distanced himself not simply from the unintended consequences of his work but from the book itself. Against the will of its author, the utopian vision projected in the book was taken up in the rights discourse and communicated far beyond the humanist circle in which it originated. Revealing a novel and compelling reality, it reconstituted the historically specific semantic world of the rights discourse. Through the validity or credibility attaching to it, the conception of society contained in *Utopia* lent symbolic authority to the argumentative logic of the discourse. It is as such that it allowed the people to claim to have morality on their side, thus empowering them to form an identity, mobilise collectively and make advances on the rights and popular sovereignty front at the expense of monarchical sovereignty. 'The people' here refers not only to Protestants but, since the late sixteenth century, also to Catholics, while commercial interests – as in the case of More – had from early on been included. The Wars of Religion in France as well as the Dutch Revolt and the English Civil War are sources of relevant examples. It is this same novel reality in respect of which compelling arguments could be advanced in real life, designated by the concept of society, that marks the beginnings of the semantics of sociology. Although drawing on More's contribution, it depended above all on the constructive effect generated in public communication.

Hobbes in the Seventeenth-Century Discourse

As attested by the unfolding of the rights discourse, however, the concept of society did not remain the preserve of the people. Just like validity or symbolic authority, power flows in a circuit and thus periodically undergoes dynamic shifts. From the aristocracy, monarchy or state it shifts to the people and back again, and so forth. To the extent that this occurs, not only does the semantics of the broader practical discourse undergo a transformation but the prospects of sociological semantics also change. Under the conditions of absolutism, the aristocracy, the monarchy and the state obtained control over the concept of society, as reflected in the remarkably similar development of the English *high society*, the French *haute société*, and the German *die gute Gesellschaft*.[3] This appropriation of the concept of society occurred in the course of the unfolding of the first phase of the rights discourse and, indeed, to the detriment of the control of the people over the concept – but only temporally as the distribution proved quite unstable. To the extent that power and symbolic authority were on the side of the aristocracy, monarchy and the state, the rights frame opened up the structural opportunity for sociology to be constructed at the macro-level in a manner that brought it much closer to the requirements of the *status quo*. Hobbes' constructive contribution to sociology provided a starting point for a response to this opportunity structure created in the course of the rights discourse.

Hobbes was directly involved in a variety of the debates that constituted the rights discourse.[4] During his student days at Oxford, he was sensitised by the controversies over the relation between the papacy and secular powers, including both Pope Paul V's Interdict against Venice and his condemnation of the English oath of allegiance. Subsequently, he continued to make widely discussed contributions to both the debates about the nature and limitations of royal power and those about church government that raged before, during and after the Civil War. Particularly important to him was the need to refute the common Puritan and Jesuit position in favour of limited monarchy and legitimate resistance. At the same time as being involved in public debates and controversies, however, he also sought to make a contribution to philosophy and science. Indeed, these two sides of his work were interdependent and closely interwoven.

At the core of Hobbes' concerns was the dominant issue of the time, the survival of society in its political environment, which he clearly grasped in its twofold nature as a problem both of social integration and of legitimation. His first publication, a translation of Thucydides' history of the Peloponnesian war, was intentionally addressed to his fellow subjects. Not only did he wish to expose what he believed to be the folly of democracy, but he also and especially wanted to warn them against the devastating consequences that civil war invariably has for the integrity of society. The context was the conflict between Crown and Parliament, which intensified in the 1620s and culminated in the outbreak of the Civil War in 1642 – a widely fluctuating conflict that saw the victory of Parliament and the execution of the king, the Restoration, and ten years after Hobbes' death finally the Glorious Revolution. Hobbes, an unwavering royalist, consistently defended the view that the integrity of society can be secured only by a political arrangement according to which an absolute sovereign governs by means of complete and unquestioned disposal over power. This position was in competition and conflict not only with the constitutionalism of the Parliamentary forces, which later culminated in Locke's justification of the Glorious Revolution, but also with the utopian democratic visions in the tradition of More, which were represented by the radical Levellers, Diggers, Ranters and Fifth Monarchy Men in the Civil War period, only to be ruthlessly suppressed by Cromwell. It was in this competition, conflict and suppression that Hobbes' absolutist ideology gained a profile and a staying power. Although Hobbes was never elected to the Royal Society due to the reputation for heresy and atheism he earned himself through the religious indifferentism of his absolutist solution, his position was nevertheless enhanced by the recognition he received from influential figures such as Sir Kenelm Digby, Sir Robert Filmer and William Petty, the relations he maintained with important philosophers such as Mersenne and Descartes, and his connections with the aristocracy and the king himself.

Crucial from the point of view of the macro-level construction of sociology, however, was the reception afforded Hobbes by the strong opposition to his absolutist and individualist 'selfish system'. Hobbes (1973, 89) had set the scene by expressing a widely held view of his time as his most characteristic argument in Chapter 17 of *Leviathan*: naturally fearful, hostile and warlike individuals concerned with their own self-preservation bring an end to the state of nature by creating society through entering into a covenant, but since the relations thus established are artificial a common power in the form of an absolutist monarch is required to enforce the agreement. This formulation of the problem had the effect not only of making a distinction between society and government or state, but also of drawing attention specifically to society. The latter indeed assisted Hobbes' friend and admirer, William Petty (1719; see also Bonss 1982, 63–64), to develop a social natural science in his *The Political Anatomy of Ireland*, written in 1672 and published in 1691. But it was the Hobbesian opposition, particularly the English moral philosophers of whom Shaftesbury (1900) was the most outstanding figure, who fixed on society. For them, society was neither a warlike nor an artificial condition. Rather, human beings are originally endowed with altruistic inclinations, while the completion of the entire human being is possible only in relation to others, the social whole. The significance of this development against and beyond Hobbes' intentions is that the concept of society was thus lifted out of the debates in which Hobbes had still been caught up and was inserted in a more generalised form into the rights discourse. Contact points and continuities were thus made available for the construction of sociology. From Hobbes' concept of society and his three forms of sovereignty-based government, aristocracy, democracy and monarchy, a line runs via these mediating figures to a whole series of sociologically crucial men and movements. Among them are Vico, the French Enlightenment, especially Montesquieu, and the Scottish Enlightenment. From these sources stemmed the framing devices and frames out of which Enlightenment sociology as a science of freedom or, more generally, rights was constructed in the eighteenth century.

The Eighteenth-Century Discourse

Vico

On all accounts,[5] Vico was an isolated figure in the eighteenth-century discourse whose *Scienza Nuova* became influential, indeed to an extraordinary degree, only in the nineteenth century as a result of Jules Michelet's publication in 1827 of selections from his works.[6] Besides the school of so-called 'Vichiani' he had founded in Naples and a group of followers in Venice, his work received relatively little attention in his own day, and of those who actually read him not many apparently understood his real originality. This does not mean, however, that his framings did not enter into the construction of Enlightenment sociology. On the contrary, they did and were reproduced in the process, even if not in their complete form. Considering the extent of the remarkable similarities between Vico and Montesquieu, French Enlightenment sociology, like the Scottish equivalent through him, was by no means so unprecedented as is often portrayed. Irrespective of whether Montesquieu had actually met Vico and read his work or not, there can be no doubt about the fact that he was well aware of the existence of Vico and his writings and participated in discussions of the Italian's ideas (see Bierstedt 1978, 24, contradicting Berlin 1979a, 134).

Precisely how his ideas entered subsequent eighteenth-century developments, however, remains unclear. This is borne out by the contradictory positions taken by experts such as Berlin and Bierstedt. The necessary information for a reconstruction of the construction of sociology in eighteenth-century public communication relative to Vico's contribution is therefore still lacking. What is certain, however, is that at this stage a more or less dense network had been in place all over Europe along which communications flowed quite readily.[7]

Montesquieu

By the time that Montesquieu wrote his *De l'Esprit des Lois*, i.e., well after the establishment of limited constitutional monarchy in England, the rights discourse had been so far advanced that various central assumptions and concepts had become consolidated. The rights frame allowed him to operate with a clear distinction between society and state, or what he himself (Montesquieu 1989, Book XIX, 310 and Book II, 10) referred to as 'the general spirit of a nation' (*l'esprit général d'une nation*) and 'government' (*gouvernement*). As suggested by the form in which he cast the former, the concept of society was for him no longer just a weapon in a political struggle, but had migrated from the general socio-political semantics of the societal practical discourse to sociological semantics. Taking it seriously in this consolidated form, he was able in a decisive manner to place politics at the heart of society and to analyse the different forms of government within the context of social relations and social organisation. At the same time, the master frame emerging from the rights discourse led him, in conjunction with his cultural and social structural position, to envisage a particular relation between society and state as the most appropriate one under modern conditions. This took the form, despite his tendency to stress monarchy, of a broad liberal constitutionalism to which he had been predisposed by his family background. On the one hand, this idea reached him through discussions engendered in France by the Huguenot refugees who had settled in London towards the end of the previous century. During his sojourn in England between 1729 and 1731, on the other hand, he was supported in taking this position and became fully convinced that the political freedom and rule of law achieved there to a significant degree were practical possibilities open in one way or another to all of modern Europe.

De l'Esprit des Lois, like most of his other writings, is replete with indications that it had been developed in relation to the debates which generated the rights discourse.[8] They stretched from the debate about the reform of criminal law and the ending of torture and brutal public executions, of which he had first-hand experience as a jurist, through the debates about religious intolerance, the war policies of the French monarchy, the pursuit of universal monarchy by Spain and imperialism and imperialist aggrandisement, to the very important debate about the nature and limits of monarchical power. In these debates, Montesquieu addressed the issue of the survival of society in its political environment in such a way as to make an impact on the power holders and public opinion. Particularly important to him, not unrelated to his aristocratic background and sympathy with the *Fronde* opposition to monarchical absolutism, was the potential role of the provincial *parlements* in moderating the public exercise of power through the introduction of checks and balances. Aside from trying to influence the government on questions of public finance, for instance, he analysed the causes of the collapse of states and empires, and in numerous writings communicated warnings about the dangers and futility of imperial wars of conquest as well as of the supreme political evil, despotic government.

While engaging in these public debates, however, Montesquieu at the same time sought to develop a science of human beings as social beings, a science of society, what later would be called sociology. Through his many scientific friends and connections, he learned as much as possible from developments in the sciences, especially medicine, but then transferred the relevant insights to his favoured area, the social field. His writings are therefore a virtually inexhaustible source of the relation made possible by the rights discourse at this stage between the more general socio-political semantics in terms of which historical events, social conditions and political questions were publicly discussed and the emerging sociological semantics. To appreciate the construction of sociology, one has to make a sharp distinction between the two levels of semantics and focus on the emergence of sociological semantics from the semantics of the broader practical discourse.

The construction of sociology in the context of the rights discourse during the Enlightenment period centrally involved the incorporation of Montesquieu's specific contribution into a wider framework through an intricate network of communication activated by supporters, adversaries and commentators. On the one extreme, Montesquieu found many supporters among the representatives of the Enlightenment, in France and especially in Scotland, despite the fact that many of them also developed various critical points in relation to *De l'Esprit des Lois*. Voltaire, his fellow first-generation *philosophe*, regarded him as having reminded people that they are free and that in most of the world humankind had lost its rights. Rousseau owed much to his predecessor in his writings, particularly in *The Social Contract* where Montesquieu's name is often mentioned. Jaucourt, general writer of the *Encyclopédie*, incorporated many of Montesquieu's ideas into this influential Enlightenment publication. D'Alembert, one of the principal editors of the *Encyclopédie* and friend of Montesquieu, spoke of the latter as 'a Newton in his science'. His admirers in Scotland, where he had his greatest following, undoubtedly shared this evaluation. Ferguson, whom English-speaking authors (e.g. MacRae 1969) often regard as the founder of sociology, freely admitted that not only his own point of view but much of his information depended directly on Montesquieu. At the other extreme, clerical critics of Montesquieu's writings vehemently defended the theological philosophy of history put forward by Bossuet, Louis XIV's court theologian, against his apparent frontal attack on the Catholic church and the church-backed absolutist monarchy. What they in effect highlighted against their own intentions, however, was precisely Montesquieu's more plausible alternative account which excluded divine purposes in favour of leaving room for human causes only – albeit partially conditioned ones – in politics and the development of society. More important than the clerical critics, however, were a number of other actors who in some sense or another opposed Montesquieu's liberal, humanitarian constitutionalism, also as restated by Jean-Louis Delolme in his *Constitution de l'Angleterre* (see Baker 1992, 194), in favour of the absolutist state or, at least, enlightened absolutism. Among them were the reformist administrators of the state, such as Turgot and Necker, the Physiocrats, and finally most of the Enlightenment *philosophes*. While both the administrators and Physiocrats were against the provincial *parlements* defended by Montesquieu in the name of a politics of checks and balances in favour of a new system of decentralised assemblies orchestrated by the state, the *philosophes* found him not sufficiently sympathetic and enthusiastic about vigorous reform from the top. Finally Rousseau, founder of the republican democratic tradition shaped into a revolutionary force by Robespierre, differed very sharply from Montesquieu in so far as he stressed equality rather than freedom, and undivided popular sovereignty rather than the separation of powers. It was through the criss-cross of the various lines of communication activated by such supporters, adversaries and commentators as these that took place largely in the public domain that Montesquieu's contribution was taken up in the process of the discursive construction of Enlightenment sociology. Certain concepts, framing devices and framings contained in Montesquieu's writings and discursive contributions were publicly constructed within the broader context of the rights discourse as belonging together and as forming part of a new social scientific or sociological way of relating to and making sense of reality.

The Enlightenment sociology that was thus constructed in relation to Montesquieu contrasted not only with the sociology contained in Hobbes, but also with the sociology suggested in the works of many of Hobbes' opponents. Rather than being atomistic, it emphasised culturally and socially different groupings or classes; rather than being empiricist, it contained a rationalist component and entertained a conception of society as a whole; rather than being utilitarian, it made reference to goals towards which societies ought to tend. Nor did this Enlightenment sociology conform either to Hobbes' Erastian position or to Rousseau's republican majoritarianism. Rather than assuming that it is for the sovereign to determine what is right and wrong, irrespective of whether the absolutist monarch or the *volonté générale*, it focused on the conflictual process in the medium of which collectively binding decisions and arrangements are arrived at. Nor, finally, did it share the assumption of the traditional empiricist sociology based on Baconian anthropological assumptions, such as for example Petty's 'political arithmetic', according to which society is a natural condition that is generally shared by humankind. As suggested by the analysis of society with reference to its political form, first uncritically in Vico and then liberal-critically in Montesquieu, strengthened by Rousseau's democratically informed critical position, sociology was increasingly consciously constructed as being concerned with society as itself a constructed reality to which appertains the quality of legitimacy.

Ferguson and Millar

The contributions of Ferguson and Millar and the emergence of 'theoretical history' in the Scottish Enlightenment bear out these various trends in the construction of sociology in the context of the rights discourse. This is not merely attributable to the fact that they drew heavily on Montesquieu, but can be accounted for in particular by reference to the rights frame. In the second half of the eighteenth century when Ferguson and Millar produced their major works, the macro-cognitive structure of the early modern rights discourse had been so well established that it provided guidance for the formation of micro-level framing devices, symbolic packages and meso-level frames, and structured the process of their combination and elevation to the macro-level in the medium of communication and discourse. The great success with which Scotland adopted and creatively continued core European Enlightenment ideas, gained international recognition as a leading centre of learning, and provided the central ideas of both the American constitution and the parliamentary reform in Britain, serves as an indication of just how secure and stable the rights frame had been at that stage and what impact it had on both identity formation and the mobilisation of collective action.

The degree to which both the framing devices and the frame employed by Ferguson and Millar were felt to possess a compelling force, the degree to which their arguments were seen to be valid, can be led back to the symbolic logic of the rights discourse as represented by the rights frame. The issue of the survival of society in its political environment could be plausibly framed in moral terms by incorporating a normative standard emphasising the diffusion of liberty. Intellectually, a scientific framing device of a social kind was seen as the most appropriate to make sense of a reality made up of individual and collective moral conduct conditioned by cultural, legal, economic and political factors. Conatively, the image of human beings as active, communicative and participating agents integrated smoothly with the intellectual and moral framing devices through the symbolic logic provided by the rights frame. In this very medium, Ferguson and Millar were led to symbolically package their micro-framings of social reality and communicate a clearly profiled identity in terms of liberal, humanitarian, constitutional ideas.

The power logic deriving from the material basis and organisation of the rights discourse that affected the force of the arguments put forward by Ferguson and Millar was embodied by the Hanoverian state under George III. The union with England and the consequent penetration of the British state into Scotland gave rise to political strife and even Jacobite armed conflict. Through extensive patronage and institutional development, however, the state was able to interrelate and mediate the different interests, thus avoiding excessive polarisation and helping to provide conditions for a remarkable cultural efflorescence. In some way or another, the leading representatives of the Scottish Enlightenment themselves were dependent on state patronage and, being acutely aware of the tensions and conflicts running through the social and political situation, sought to channel them in a constructive direction. Society appeared to them as an arena of contestation in which a contingent yet salutary and just result is pursued through active participation and conflictual relations. Although putting forward liberal, humanitarian and constitutional ideas and against that background developing a critical analysis of existing institutions, in these circumstances neither Ferguson nor Millar espoused a radical or revolutionary position. Even externally, as in the case of the American War of Independence, Ferguson moderately defended the British position and acted as secretary of a conciliation commission to Philadelphia. Millar, on the other hand, did support the American colonists in their cause. In the case of the French Revolution, he initially entertained high hopes for its success, but felt himself compelled by the dramatic turn of events in the early 1790s to adopt a negative evaluation. Although tempering his arguments, Millar's commitment to parliamentary reform, the abolition of serfdom and slavery, the prevention of wars fuelled by princely ambition and avarice, and the reduction of human misery remained intact. The reservations exhibited by Ferguson and Millar, despite the adoption of a liberal con- stitutionalist identity involving a reference to natural law, can be interpreted as pointing towards the fact that they were participants in a dominant or hegemonic discourse. This discourse both subordinated or suppressed discursive contri- butions made by people lower down the social ladder and excluded women.

The above sketch of the configuration of validity and power in their time already sheds some light on the various debates reproducing the rights dis- course in eighteenth-century Scotland in which Ferguson and Millar took part.[9] The most pervasive debate was the one concerning the relation between the more British-oriented Presbyterian, Whig, aristocratic section of the popu- lation and the more locally rooted Episcopal (i.e., Roman Catholic), Jacobite, provincial groupings. It included questions concerning absolute power, the royal prerogative and royal tyranny, and extended to embrace the American War of Independence, the French Revolution and parliamentary reform. This debate was couched in the general socio-political semantics of the time, but at the same time also threw up philosophical and social scientific terms. It is here, with the renewal of the natural law tradition, that the battle-lines of this debate proved to be much more complicated from the point of view of the intellectuals. In contradistinction to Hume and Smith who put forward a deterministic philosophy and a harmonious social theory, Ferguson and Millar, notwithstanding the differences between the two in so far as they respectively approached Jacobite and liberal Whig positions, were more concerned to assert active and free participation, public discussion and opinion, and to acknowledge the significance of political conflict in human affairs, while nevertheless appealing to rights and relations of equity. Controversies about legal reform, serfdom, slavery, human misery, European absolutism and eventually also the French Revolution dovetailed closely with the more general Scottish debate. Their systematic exploration of the phenomenon of social reality, while stimulated by the British and French traditions represented for instance by Shaftesbury and Montesquieu respectively, took place in and through these debates which both helped to sustain and bring home the structuring effect of the rights frame. As forums of these various debates served the universities and the numerous clubs, academies, literary societies and eventually more formal organisations, supported by a rapidly expanding printing industry, which carried the institutionalisation of the Scottish Enlightenment.

The sociological contributions that Ferguson and Millar had made in the context of the rights discourse did not remain confined to their works and their own circles in the universities and Enlightenment societies, but were taken up into the larger process of the construction of sociology which unfolded in public communication and discourse. This was all the more the case since their teaching and writings belonged to a larger historical movement which was much noted both at home and abroad. The thematisation of their contributions in the public sphere assumed a number of different forms. Their concepts, framing devices and the liberal-humanitarian-constitutionalist frame through which they had been packaged, their sociological semantics and the self-image they communicated, were not only positively taken up, commented on, appropriated and perpetuated and thus inserted in a more general form into public communication and discourse. At the same time, they were also criticised and countered by adversaries who sought to advance different concepts and framings – e.g. absolutist, commercial-liberal and republican – or even a different semantics altogether – e.g. the semantics of the nascent competing disciplines of history or economics. In addition, there were also those participants in the rights discourse who merely observed Ferguson and Millar and who assisted in generalising their contributions to the public sphere by registering or evaluating their existence. Ferguson and Millar had made their signal contributions, but the process of the construction of Enlightenment sociology was driven and immensely broadened out by the participation of social actors in public communication and discourse who supported, developed, opposed or observed their communicative and discursive involvement.

Enlightenment sociology, taking the form of a specific semantics that derived from and concentrated the general socio-political semantics of the time, thus made its appearance as a public construction at the macro-level consisting of micro- and meso-level framings communicated by particular social actors yet making sense only within the historically specific discourse of early modern society, the rights discourse.

Besides the huge impact he had in Scotland, Ferguson proved able to communicate his concern with the new phenomenon of social reality as well as his particular framings of it in a very effective manner abroad. As the medium of this served in particular his most important book, *An Essay on the History of Civil Society*. At home, the most distinguished eighteenth-century British philosopher, David Hume, discerned 'an elegant and singular genius' in the 'admirable book' (cited in Lehmann 1930, 238), while such celebrated authors as Smith, Kames, Robertson and Stewart respectively regarded him as a rival, treated him as a worthy object of criticism, quoted him freely in historical writings, and admired and expounded his work. Corresponding to Hume's evaluation, highly distinguished contemporaries of his such as d'Holbach in France and Herder in Germany were most impressed by the work. Translations into various languages facilitated the incorporation of the work into the Europe-wide discourse of the time and the attainment of the semantics of Enlightenment sociology, as deriving from Shaftesbury and Montesquieu and given form by Ferguson, to a widely recognised existence. A personal interview with Voltaire and election to membership of the Berlin Academy of Science during a visit to Germany underscored and strengthened this assimilation of Ferguson's contribution to the construction of sociology in the public domain.[10]

Both Millar's teaching and writings met with much acclaim during his lifetime, and echoes of his fame as one of the 'illustrious men' of eighteenth-century Scotland could still be heard as late as 1837 and even 1860. From among his compatriots, it was in particular Millar's younger contemporary Dugald Stewart who encapsulated the thrust and identity of Enlightenment sociology when he referred to the line of development from Montesquieu to Millar as 'the natural or *theoretical history* of society' which involved tracing 'the process by which [society] *has been produced*' (cited in Lehmann 1960, 107; 1930, 231).[11] Either in the original or in translation, such works as *The Origin of the Distinction of Ranks* and *A Historical View of the English Government* made their way also into America, France, Germany and other European countries. His characteristic sociological approach, which found expression in his fondness for theoretical interpretations of history and broad generalisations, proved very influential and was taken up into the discourse of the time – even as far away as Germany where the well-known author Christian Garve indefatigably promoted the sociological ideas of the French and Scottish Enlightenment. On the other hand, this very approach, and hence in effect the process of the construction of sociology, also attracted the attention of a whole range of adversaries and detractors, from historians, who regarded it as too theoretical, through representatives of religious conservatism whose orthodoxy was scandalised by Millar's liberalism, to politicians and educators who saw his 'jacobinical and scurrilous' work as a threat to the established order (cited in Lehmann 1960, 148). His more specific framings of social reality as well as his liberalism were carried forward and generalised by a whole series of authors who contributed to the *Edinburgh Review*, the most influential literary and political journal in Great Britain at the time. This journal, in turn, had a pronounced impact on some of the most important opponents of Tory repression in the 1790s and proponents of parliamentary reform and, through them, on the reform movement, which eventually succeeded in 1832.[12] Earlier, through Scottish-born John Wilson, professor of law at Philadelphia and one of the principal founding fathers and framers of the American Constitution, and through the famous James Madison, fourth president of the United States, Millar's theoretical history or sociology had assisted in the formulation of a solution to the issue of the survival of society in its political environment as it presented itself across the Atlantic.[13]

Enlightenment Sociology

The Integrity of the Early Modern Rights Discourse

A standard question in the literature on the Scottish Enlightenment concerns the reasons for the apparent discontinuity of the sociological contributions of Ferguson and Millar. This is clearly a problem with a direct bearing on the construction of sociology, yet there is little evidence that it is so understood. Lehmann (1930, 240–42; 1960, 145–49, 159–60) talks of Ferguson's 'eclipse' and Millar's 'going out of sight', and MacRae (1969, 34–35)[14] asks why sociology developed from the work of Comte, who led it in the wrong direction, rather than directly out of the exemplary theoretical and analytical contributions of the two Scottish authors. Lehmann and MacRae each draw up a more or less extended list of factors or historical events that could account for the oblivion into which Ferguson and Millar fell. Included are, for instance, religious and political opposition to the ideas of Ferguson and Millar in Great Britain, the Europe-wide conservative reaction against the Enlightenment and the French Revolution, the disillusioning political experience of the years between the French Revolution and the culmination of the defeat of Napoleon in the Concert of Europe and the Holy Alliance, and the emergence of

Romanticism, nationalism and speculative idealism. Over and above these factors, however, none of the authors attempts to provide an explanation of the phenomenon.

To approach an explanation, it should be recognised, on the one hand, that the eclipse Lehmann and MacRae have in mind is of course only a relative one, one largely confined to Britain.[15] For as Lehmann himself is aware, in the German tradition the authors of the Scottish Enlightenment had been known throughout the nineteenth century and, indeed, also the twentieth,[16] while in France both Saint-Simon and Comte drew directly on Ferguson and Millar. On the other hand, it should be appreciated that the shift from the eighteenth to the nineteenth century, from the age of political liberalism to conservatism and economic liberalism, despite various continuities, represents a radical change or discontinuity with its own particular character which did not remain without consequences for sociology. Peter Gay (1969, 323), historian of the Enlightenment, is one of the few who appreciates this when he writes that '[w]hatever may have become of sociology in the nineteenth century, when the discipline got its name and took a distinctly conservative and nostalgic turn, in the Enlightenment, when it was invented, it was a science designed to advance freedom and humanity'. The peculiar character of this discontinuity assumes a still sharper profile from a cognitivistic communications and discourse theor-etical point of view. A brief indication of what this amounts to is in order here.

The late eighteenth- and nineteenth-century phenomena listed by Lehmann and MacRae as contrasting with the situation of the Scottish Enlightenment possess a certain significance which becomes clearer when one adds to them others besides, such as the industrial revolution, the scientific revolution, the conservative-liberal theory of progress and socialism. The significance of all these events and intellectual or ideological currents rests on the fact that they constitute a new set of societal problems and, correspondingly, a new societal discourse which are distinct from the early modern societal problem and discourse. The discontinuity in question here separates the problem of poverty, the social question and the justice discourse of the nineteenth and twentieth centuries from the preceding rights discourse which grew up around the problem of violence and entailed the posing of the political or constitutional question. The boundary line between them is marked by the essential completion – at least of the first cycle – of the process of the enunciation of the doctrine of rights, the formulation of constitutions and the constitutionalisation of the state in the late eighteenth century. The end of the American War of Independence and the closure of the first phase of the French Revolution are the most important historical milestones here.

It is of course the case that sociologists have always been aware of the difference between the early modern period and the modern period which they see as having begun with the French Revolution and the industrial revolution (e.g. Parsons 1977b, 291; Giddens 1984, 5–11). Both more conventionally oriented authors, such as for instance Szacki (1979, 89–90),[17] and Marxist oriented authors, such as for instance Therborn (1977, 156–63), recognise an epochal discontinuity. For Therborn, Ferguson and Millar belong as much 'to the close of an epoch' as for Szacki sociology belongs 'in another epoch'. The crucial point is, however, that both approaches reduce the early modern period in their own particular ways to the prototypical preparation or the prehistory of sociology. On the basis of some form of limited epistemology and method-ology, most often ontological or realist rather than constructivist, a distorted interpretation is created by reading later developments backwards into the past. In its central thrust, this typically takes the form of a distinction between philosophical or proto-scientific and truly scientific concerns. Therborn regards the early modern epoch as a philosophical rather than a sociological one, and criticises Ferguson and Millar for cultivating moral concerns rather than appreciating the class struggle. Szacki sees the modern period as one eschewing the pursuit of ideals, emphasising history, exchanging an interest in political systems for social and national bonds, and taking up the challenge of the advances in the natural sciences. These, to be sure, amount to superficial interpretations. The early modern period is not grasped in its integrity, as is the case when it is theoretically regarded as a communicative and discursive phenomenon and methodologically accessed through discourse. The nineteenth-century concern with the survival of society in its social environment indeed intensified the reflexive dimension so as to bring the identity of sociology particularly sharply into focus, but this does not imply that the earlier concern with societal survival in its political environment had no bearing on sociology. On the contrary, sociology cannot be properly grasped unless its construction in the context of the rights discourse is taken seriously. It is only when one adopts a more adequate interpretation of history that one is led to the discovery of Enlightenment sociology.[18]

The Enlightenment Reinterpreted

There is also a complementary error that has become particularly common-place in the past decade or so but of course has a much longer history. It consists of the assimilation of part of the early modern period to the modern period in a manner that falsifies the historically specific concerns and semantics of the former. In its most prevalent but unreflected form, it is present wherever the early modern period is ignored in favour of letting sociology start with Comte.[19] In its most acute form, it is to be found in Habermas' conception of the project of modernity and the corresponding understanding of sociology as a critical-emancipatory discipline resting on foundations going back to the eighteenth-century liberal public sphere and laid by Kant, Hegel and Marx. During the last decade or so, Habermas' position has been reversed by the post-structuralists and postmodernists,[20] with the result that the Enlightenment is blamed for all the ills of late twentieth-century society. The progressive orientation of the Enlightenment, which informs also the human and social sciences, is either regarded as actually forming part of a new all-encompassing disciplinary order specialised in social control or as having contributed through its consequences in the intellectual and practical spheres to the widespread late twentieth-century disillusionment with and rejection of modernity.

The interesting point is that this new interpretation of the Enlightenment is at best only a complementary repetition of the same erroneous interpretation we find in Habermas or in the unreflective presuppositions of perhaps the majority of sociologists. Common to them all is that the concept of progress and the philosophy of history, which stem from the late Enlightenment, idealism, socialism and liberalism, are projected backward into the pre-revolutionary Enlightenment which had been more concerned with legal and political or constitutional questions and the development of society in the medium of conflict and contestation than with history and its meaning. The only difference among them is that what many sociologists naively accept, Habermas consciously adopts in a positive sense and his contemporary opponents equally consciously reject as something negative. Paradigmatic, albeit quite different, examples of the focus on politics in relation to society and on conflict and contestation are provided by the writings of Montesquieu, Ferguson and Millar, and before them, Hobbes and Vico. Even when history gains increasing importance, as in the case of Vico and the two Scottish authors, it is not the primary medium of the unfolding of society and even less is it a vehicle following a linear path aimed at the realisation of some telos. Rather, the unfolding of society takes place in the medium of conflict and is characterised by advances, setbacks and even radical reversals with potentially devastating consequences for society and civilisation. Like Vico before him, Ferguson entertained a cyclical or at least quasi-cyclical view, while Millar, although rejecting the compulsive style of framing implied by cyclical thinking, stressed, like Montesquieu, the contingency, openness and vulnerability of a historical process which is nevertheless not completely devoid of some direction.

The error of the interpretative tendency in question here is twofold. On the one hand, it ultimately involves an uncritical reception of the frame of the dominant social actor of eighteenth-century France, what has been called 'the rationalist [frame] of the social' (Baker 1992, 202)[21] represented by absolutism and its supporters such as state administrators and the Physiocrats. Both the philosophy of history and the concept of progress had been represented in the first instance by the church in the person of Louis XIV's court historian, Bishop Bossuet, and were given a new lease of life by Anne Robert Turgot, Baron de l'Aulne (1995), the great administrative reformer who sought to save the absolutist state from the crisis staring it in the face, and then definitively by Turgot's biographer, the Marquis de Condorcet, an official of the absolutist state (Manuel and Manuel 1979, 453–518). With the addition of Pietism as a second source (Mannheim 1972, 201), the philosophy of history and the concept of progress were carried forward by idealism and socialism as well as nineteenth-century liberalism. It is on this foundation that both Habermas (e.g. 1973, 357–59; 1989a)[22] and his contemporary opponents stand.

On the other hand, this interpretative direction operates with a concept of the Enlightenment[23] that is as untenable as it is undifferentiated. In the first instance, as suggested, there is the failure to grasp the phase-structure of the development of the Enlightenment or, more precisely, its phase-structure in relation to the discontinuity between the rights discourse and the justice discourse.[24] Due to the tendency to read the Enlightenment from the vantage point of nineteenth-century concerns and thus to assimilate the rights discourse to the justice discourse, the crucial distinction between the more politically oriented Enlightenment and the more historically and progress-oriented late Enlightenment is overlooked. Secondly, no distinction is made among the culturally and institutionally different collective actors[25] who communicated distinct cognitive frames in the rights discourse during the Enlightenment period. In the case of France (Furet 1981; Baker 1992), a distinction has to be made among at least four major groupings. They included the administrative reformers and the Physiocrats, who were positively disposed towards absolutism; secondly, the Encyclopaedists, most of whom were against the absolutist state yet saw its turn towards enlightened despotism as a potential vehicle for meaningful reform; thirdly, liberal constitutionalists like Montes-quieu, who appreciated cultural and social differences and sought a division and balance of powers; and, finally, the popular republican democrats such as Rousseau. In the case of Scotland (Kettler 1965, 29; Wuthnow 1989, 251–64), a corresponding differentiation is necessary. Here a line can be drawn between, on the one hand, Hume and Smith who took a more positive and harmonious view of the role of the Hanoverian state in Scotland, and Ferguson and Millar, on the other, who, despite their respective Jacobite and liberal Whig orientations, insisted on active and free participation and the public spirit as well as on the role of differences, conflict and contestation in social life – without losing sight of the natural law or civil jurisprudential emphasis on rights and relations of equity.

As long as the dominant rationalistic frame of the eighteenth century is uncritically accepted, and as long as a differentiated interpretation of the Enlightenment is lacking, it is impossible not only to grasp early modern society in its integrity but also to discern the golden strand of Enlightenment sociology running through yet intertwined with other intellectual and especially social scientific concerns of the time. By contrast, the cognitivist communication and discourse theoretical approach presented here in the form of an analysis of the discursive construction of sociology allowed us both to gain access to early modern society via the problem of violence and the rights discourse, and to identify Enlightenment sociology as the well-defined endeavour to clarify society in so far as its survival presents itself as an issue that can be resolved only if its turbulent and volatile political environment, on which a number of political, economic and socio-cultural forces converge, is stabilised to a sufficient degree.

Rationalistic, Contestatory and Communitarian Frames of the Social

Sociology in its original form of Enlightenment sociology emerged with society in opposition to the absolutist state, concerned less with history than with politics in the sense of irreducible differences, plural relations, limitations on state power, active participation, public opinion, conflict and contestation. The problem of society was originally perceived and articulated in relation to the problem of politics. It was directly related to such ideas as liberty, humanitarianism, constitutionalism and, most characteristically, a politics of contestation and compromise. The latter accounts for the strong opposition registered by Montesquieu as well as Ferguson and Millar against both the pronounced rationalism and the majoritarian or communitarian republicanism of their time. It would of course be tantamount to an unjustifiable idealisation to overlook the fact that the insistence of these men on differences, social inequality, conflict and contestation was somehow related to a defensive attitude toward their own privileged positions. There is no doubt about the fact that Montesquieu desired to see the continuation of a society in which the aristocracy plays a meaningful role. Likewise, Ferguson and Millar inadvertently participated in or looked on in connivance at the not untypical eighteenth-century screening out of both the culturally and politically mobilised lower social strata and women from the hegemonic and exclusionary rights discourse. Nevertheless, they did not celebrate conflict and contestation in the sense that

Habermas (1994, 3; 1989a, 132; 1992b, 447) critically ascribes to the liberal understanding of the political process, namely as purely a matter of 'the competition of strategically acting collectivities trying to maintain or acquire positions of power'.[26] As has become apparent in an earlier exposition, Montesquieu as well as Ferguson and Millar anticipated that the process of conflict and contestation would yield a rational outcome. Montesquieu retained a reference to a rationally derived goal toward which all societies ought to tend. Ferguson and Millar in turn were convinced that only a process that retains a reference to liberty and relations of equity and allows the balancing and mutual correction of partial powers could lead to a salutary and just result. All three of these Enlightenment figures thus committed themselves to a comparable version of a normative political position deriving from a modernised version of natural law. It is this relation that allowed them to develop a diagnosis of the current situation and motivated them to take part in some aspect or another of the campaign for the institutionalisation of the necessary legal and political conditions for securing the survival and the adequate self-regulation and self-organisation of society.

What is remarkable from the point of view of the discursive construction of Enlightenment sociology is that Montesquieu, Ferguson and Millar did not confine themselves like moral or political philosophers to the normative political theory they adopted. At the same time, they took a step back so as to assume a more distanced or detached position in relation to the larger context of society. For them, society was the structured setting within which all social actors or collectivities and all those holding normative political positions, including them-selves, are located. Rather than just taking a moral or political philosophical view, rather than just engaging in moralisation in the sense of propagating their own normative commitments, they approached social reality from a socio-logical perspective. Rather than choosing one particular position from among the range of available ones and putting it forward as the only justifiable one, they located them all within a common all-encompassing context – thus relativising all, including their own, while maintaining the indirect reference of their normative (i.e. liberal, humanitarian, constitutional) political theory. Society embraces indelible cultural and social differences as well as social inequalities that might not admit of elimination yet do not exclude trans-formation. These differences and inequalities constitute it as a scene of active participation in the public spirit, a structured setting of conflict, contestation and compromise as well as of cooperation, agreement and decision-making. Enlightenment sociology was constructed in relation to the contributions of Montesquieu and Ferguson and Millar as being concerned with the conflictual or contestatory nature of the constitution of society and its self-organisation

253

through participatory politics. As such, it was predominantly articulated in terms of a conflictual or contestatory frame of the social which contrasted sharply with, but also fed on, both the 'rationalist [frame] of the social' and the majoritarian or communitarian '[frame] of classical republicanism' (Baker 1992, 202).[27]

Like these latter two frames, Enlightenment sociology was rendered possible and took form through the cognitive structures represented by Enlightenment universalism. The latter consisted of a universal frame, what we have called the rights frame, which was derived from the modern cognitive order stressing social relations: the association of free and equal human beings who, basing themselves on the assumption that the principles of social action can be universalised and that all the participants in the social situation can agree – or at least rationally disagree – about those principles, coordinate and regulate their own activities through discursive procedures. Far from being concerned with the philosophy of history and progress, Enlightenment sociology under the title of 'theoretical' or 'conjectural history' focused on society, its survival and self-organisation, within its political environment, with the latter in turn being conceived as involving the appropriate arrangement of sovereignty beyond the absolutist state through the distribution of rights by means of the law and their mediation by public contestation and discussion. The philosophy of history and the theory of progress came to displace this eighteenth-century understanding of society only in the next century when a new epoch focused on the problem of poverty and articulated by the social question was opened up in the medium of the justice discourse. Only at that stage, when the market-based capitalist economy, the industrial revolution and the scientific revolution started to take effect, was the core insight displaced on which Enlightenment sociology was originally based. This is the very insight that so many – e.g. Habermas (1994; 1996), Touraine (1995), Unger (1987a), Dryzek (1990), Benhabib (1989; 1992), Calhoun (1993), Swan (1993), Honneth (1995) and many others[28] – are today seeking to recover by turning away from the philosophy of history and the concomitant monolithic notion of civil society and public sphere towards the recognition of deep-seated differences, public access problems, and a participatory, deliberative and contestatory politics.[29]

Diagrammatically, the discursive construction of Enlightenment sociology can be represented as in Figure 9.1. The process of construction took place in the medium of the early modern societal practical discourse in a discursive space delineated by the parameters of communicative framing and uncertainty management. The process was cognitively structured by the rights frame. Starting from the contributions of Montesquieu, Ferguson and Millar, it was constructed and its semantics developed in terms of a pluralist contestatory

Figure 9.1: Discursive construction of Enlightenment sociology

	COMMUNICATIVE FRAMING	
	Authoritarian status quo ideology	Democratic utopia

UNCERTAINTY MANAGEMENT		
Organised society/order	Etatist rationalistic frame of the social	
Self-organising society/conflict	**Pluralist contestatory frame of the social**	
		Popular communitarian frame of the social

frame of the social. The latter was more or less sharply distinguished from two competing frames of the time which helped to define and thus to give it a clearly identifiable profile. The first was the etatist rationalistic frame of the social that was represented by those who identified with the state or supported enlightened despotism, such as the enlightened administrative reformers, the Physiocrats and many a *philosophe*. The second was the popular communitarian or collectivist frame of the social put forward and defended by those who gave priority to undivided popular sovereignty, such as the republican tradition forwarded by Rousseau. The differences among these three frames are particularly visible from the way in which they respectively conceive of the institutional conditions necessary to secure the survival of society as well as from their images of society.[30]

According to the rationalistic frame, at the one extreme, society is a complex of distinct, competing private values and interests that are protected by the state and organised through processes of opinion- and will-formation under the guardianship of the state. At the other extreme, the communitarian frame portrays society as an ethical community that is self-consciously institutionalised in the form of the state. Avoiding both extremes, the pluralist contestatory frame involves a concept of society as consisting of a plurality of culturally and socially distinct and even unequal groupings with their own particular values and interests that stand in publicly relevant conflict and contestation, and as developing through such conflict and contestation. The

255

survival of this contestatory society does not depend on being centred on the state or being organised in any of the two previous senses of either being guarded by the state or itself becoming the state. Given that society consists of a whole range of different and unequal forms of life that remain formally unorganised, its survival is instead assured by allowing plural freedoms to assert themselves and to act to resist encroachments and gain liberty. This is done through the limitation of state power by fundamental human rights, the admission and representation of all culturally and socially distinct or unequal groupings, and the full participation of all those involved. Institutionally, this requires constitutional and legal arrangements that make possible democratic procedures. For it is only such procedures that can regulate the process of contestation and deliberation in a way that ensures that the outcome possesses legitimacy.

There is something particularly remarkable about the differences among these three competing frames that emerges from this stylisation. It resides in the fact that it is only the pluralist contestatory frame of the social that is accompanied by a stereoscopic perspective. Rather than somehow collapsing the distinction between state and society, as is the tendency in the case of the two remaining frames, it keeps in view both the process of the construction of society and the problem of the legitimacy pertaining to its self-organisation. It is in this sense that Enlightenment sociology should be understood. It was constructed as the science of freedom, as Peter Gay (1969, 323) calls it, in that, while joining the campaign for the institutionalisation of the legal and political conditions necessary for securing the survival of society, it took a detached approach according to which the political system was appreciated as but one component of a more encompassing complex yet dynamic society, which itself resists the purely normative orientation of the political, legal and constitutional perspective.

CHAPTER 10

Crisis and Critique: The Relation between Social and Political Theory

In the foregoing, it was argued that the rights discourse actually can and indeed should be regarded as a crisis discourse. It was not merely devoted to the collective consideration of the typically modern problem of the creation of society and of the mutual compatibility, reconciliation and consolidation of the different dimensions of society, as one would have expected given that it is an instance of the discourse of modernity. Instead it turned out to be a discourse about a problem that not only assumed crisis proportions but also called forth a solution that perpetuated the crisis. The birth of modern society in early modern times took place in and through a societal crisis that, rather than having been resolved, placed a stumbling block in the way of the development of society. Its persistent effects throughout the course of modern society suggest that this impediment is a stubborn one with which we still have to reckon. The question is what the precise nature of this crisis is.

Starting from phenomena of the twentieth century such as, for example, National Socialism, the Holocaust, the Cold War and the persistence of imperialism, various authors have proposed diagnoses of the pathogenesis of modern society. Among them are Reinhart Koselleck, Jürgen Habermas and Klaus Eder, all of whom assume that the pathogenesis and persistent crisis of modern society can be led back to the early modern period. The interesting point is that the discursive construction of Enlightenment sociology sheds light on the nature of this crisis. This is due to the fact that it represented from the start a critique of modern society. Crisis is always accompanied by critique, and by considering the critique, therefore, one is able to learn and become clearer about the nature of the corresponding crisis. Let us review the diagnoses of these authors against the foil of the critique of early modern society by Enlightenment sociology.

Critique and Crisis: Reinhardt Koselleck

In his famous book *Kritik und Krise* (1973) which recently became available in English (1988), Reinhart Koselleck establishes a systematic relation between critique and crisis – yet in such a manner as to give his own particular slant to it.

The absolutist state, according to Koselleck (1988, 15–50), was the temporally conditioned outcome of the Wars of Religion, which arose to fill the void left by the disintegrating cultural and political synthesis of Catholicism. It took the form of a formal structure entailing a monopoly of force and knowledge and, hence, the privatisation of its subjects. Politics, the preserve of the state, was separated from morality, the domain in which the subjects found a refuge. The Enlightenment (Koselleck 1988, 53–97) was an articulation of this latter domain, developing the universalistic morality excluded by the state and critically playing it out against the state as soon as the critique of its legitimation foundation, religion, had been completed.

Enlightenment critique, in Koselleck's (1988, 98–123) view, always understood itself as moral and thus as non-political. This was the case even with its critique of the state. Socially, it was embodied in the equally non-political institutions of the salon, the reading circle, the club and the secret society. Although deeply political, the later generations of *philosophes* remained convinced of the moral nature of their critique. The bourgeoisie, languishing in a non-political role, took refuge in utopia. At this point, Koselleck (1988, 122, 127–82) characteristically claims, critique became hypocritical, turning into an instrument by means of which the *philosophes* deluded themselves about the nature of their own activity. The bourgeoisie came to see the historical trajectory of the disintegration of absolutism in the wake of critique as an innocent process, the outcome of which had already been predetermined by morality. Believing that their critical moralisation of the relations among the subjects of the state would engender a moral solution to the absolutist state, adopting the utopia of the enlightened society that would come into being through moral critique, they failed to appreciate that their critique of the state was political and in fact involved the mobilisation of power and violence directed in a threatening and potentially destructive way against the state. The impending historical decision, the coming revolutionary overthrow of the *ancien régime*, was anticipated as a moral court rather than as a political event taking the form of a civil war involving the exercise of power and the use of naked violence. Consequently, the French Revolution, when it did occur, contained a significant element of surprise for both the *philosophes* and the bourgeoisie.

The Enlightenment covered over and made this self-delusion unrecognisable to itself by the adoption of the philosophy of history. Instead of envisaging the crisis of the coming revolution, it told the story of a new beginning, of progress and a perfect solution. In the period of the Enlightenment, therefore, when – according to Koselleck's (1988, 183–86) most central thesis – critique in the form of indirect political force created the crisis of state-centred society, modernity began with utopia as the answer to absolutism. Through critique in the form of moralisation and through utopianism projecting the enlightened society, the Enlightenment not merely excluded politics but – and this is Koselleck's (1988, 185) most instructive conclusion – turned its back on the necessity and unavoidability of politics in social life and the openness of all future decisions and events.

Critique and Crisis? Klaus Eder

Klaus Eder has endorsed both Koselleck's central thesis and his thought-provoking conclusion in his recently published *The New Politics of Class*.

On the one hand, Eder (1993a, 192) is convinced that '[t]he origins of the crisis of modern society have been well analysed by Koselleck'. Proceeding from the assumption that the typical experience of early modern society stemmed from its having been born in and through a societal crisis, he accepts that the crisis of absolutist society had been engendered by Enlightenment critique. This critique, which brought modern society into being, moreover had recourse to the philosophy of history, which led to the projection of a problematic solution. Instead of recognising the inherently political nature of society, a harmonious or consensual and conflict-free enlightenment society was envisaged. This explains, on the other hand, the central assumption of Eder's account of the crisis of modern society, which is also in accord with Koselleck's interpretation. Modern society finds itself in an endemic crisis in that it suffers from a lack of politics or, as he says, 'there is not enough politics' (Eder 1993a, 194)[1] in modern society.

Considering Koselleck's basic assumptions, which are clear from his book and further highlighted both by Habermas (1973, 355–59) in his early critical review of *Kritik und Krise* and by Victor Gourevitch (1988) in his foreword to the English edition of the latter, it is most surprising that Eder is apparently willing to accompany him so far down the same road. Koselleck's intention with his critical history of critique, from the humanistic criticism of the Bible via the Huguenot *émigrés* and Pierre Bayle to the Enlightenment, is to establish a link between critique and crisis in such a way that he is able to discredit the critical theory of society or critical sociology. Although Eder (e.g. 1988; 1993a, 42–62) no longer accepts Habermas' defence of the philosophy of history, something the latter himself (Habermas 1974a, 13; 1984, 145–55; 1992b, 442)[2] has

259

undertaken to abandon, it is obvious that, despite the position reported above, he could not possibly accept Koselleck's postulated relationship. For Eder, crisis and critique belong together, yet only in the sense that the diagnosis of a crisis implies the critique of that state of affairs with a view to overcoming it and thereby regaining autonomy and sovereignty. Instead of blaming critique for producing the crisis of modern society, as does Koselleck, he thus carries forward the opposing critical theoretical or critical sociological conviction that the resolution of the crisis of modern society calls for critique.

Comparable considerations apply to the question of politics. The account given in *Kritik und Krise* suggests that Koselleck tends towards the acceptance of Hobbes' position on politics. According to Gourevitch (1988, ix), Koselleck is less interested in salvaging any particular Hobbesian doctrine than in restoring Hobbes' characteristic insight that 'there is no escaping the constraints of political life, and that it is not possible to reduce some measure of contingency, conflict and compulsion to the status of differences of opinion or to resolve them by discussion and peaceful competition'. Here one must bear in mind that Koselleck is one of the most prominent followers of Carl Schmitt (1970), the leading political theorist of the Third Reich.[3] The latter insisted not only on the strong authoritarian state, but also that the political element as the essential core of the will of the ruler is inaccessible to rational reflection or questioning (Habermas 1973, 357; Saage 1990, 93–109). Koselleck's thesis that the crisis of modern society can be led back to the depoliticising effect of Enlightenment critique thus means that he wants to see critique eliminated and politics given back to the state.

Although it seems at first sight as though Eder assumes the same position as Koselleck on the lack of politics in modern society, it cannot be more than merely a formal correspondence. For, although accepting the thesis of the dearth of politics, he could not possibly be in agreement with Koselleck. Whereas Koselleck wants to restore politics to the strong state, Eder (1993a, 185–96)[4] wishes to see the restoration of a culture of contradictions and the unblocking of class politics, so that society can develop, as it is supposed to, through the conflictual communicative mediation of contradictory interpretations.

Crisis and Critique: Jürgen Habermas

In his review of *Kritik und Krise*, Habermas (1973, 357–58) in his characteristically acute way pointed out the error marring Koselleck's attempt to explain the early modern crisis and, hence, the pathogenesis of modern society.

According to Habermas, Koselleck approached the matter from the one-sided point of view of the dialectics of politics and morality. Rather than appreciating that morality was coextensive with the social, which in turn found expression in public opinion, he reduced it to private convictions. Koselleck, in Habermas' view, was motivated to pursue this reductionist step to its end due to the fact that from the outset he regarded the process of public discussion, through which public opinion was generated, as an instance of civil war which could be avoided only to the extent that the state had the monopoly of politics. This allowed him then to argue that Enlightenment critique engendered the crisis of state-centred society by depoliticising the state through its moralisation of politics – with the result that, instead of politics, a moralistic utopia came to predominate in modern society. According to Habermas, both the reduction of morality to private convictions and the discrediting of discussion in the public sphere as civil war are completely unjustifiable. For as the institutionalisation of the constitutional state and organs of public political discussion demonstrated, however contradictory that might have been, it was by no means a moralisation of politics that had been implied by Enlightenment critique, but rather the rationalisation of politics.[5] In the context of the public sphere, the activities of the state are through public discussion brought into relation and agreement with the citizens. In the medium of public discussion, political force and violence are rationalised or civilised by being rendered open or public and thus transformed into legitimate power and political authority.

The relation that Habermas perceives to hold between critique and crisis, then, is very different from the one postulated by Koselleck. Rather than the crisis of state-centred society having been caused by moralising, utopian critique and hence the obliteration of politics, Habermas (1973, 358–59; 1989a; 1992b) sees critique as arising from society in the sense of the public sphere in response to the unrationalised exercise of political power by the state. Its political motive is to rationalise state activity through publicity. Drawing its cultural resources from the future, it involves the projection of the possibility of a fully rationalised, i.e. open or public, exercise of power. Given the discrepancy between the present and the future, however, it is at the same time based on the assumption that human beings are able to make their own history. As such, critique does not only have the same origin as utopia, but it is from the start also bound to the philosophy of history.

Here we arrive at a crucial point. However much Habermas is able to point out Koselleck's failings and to reverse the relation between critique and crisis, he himself, to be sure, took a route in his critique of Koselleck that led the diagnosis of the crisis of early modern society and hence the pathogenesis of modern society astray. As the analysis of the construction of Enlightenment sociology suggests, the problem lies in his retention of the philosophy of history and of his particular version of utopianism.[6]

Enlightenment Sociological Critique

A step beyond such problems, to begin with, lies in not confusing the critique associated with Enlightenment sociology in the course of its discursive construction with Enlightenment critique in the sense either of Koselleck or of Habermas. Indeed, corresponding to the need argued for above to maintain a differentiated concept of the Enlightenment, there is no such thing as Enlightenment critique per se. Various culturally and institutionally different collective actors representing distinct cognitive frames advanced their own particular notions of critique. Koselleck's conception of critique as the cause of the crisis of early modern state-centred society is only one of these notions, just like Habermas' conception of critique as the means for realising the utopia of open or public political power. Both of these forms of critique were present in the eighteenth century. Yet neither of them exhausts Enlightenment critique. On the contrary, the former amounts to an authoritarian attempt to snuff out critique. The latter, in turn, is a combination of the respective critical orientations of the reform movement towards enlightened despotism and the classical republican or revolutionary Jacobin striving towards the radical self-organisation of society (see Habermas 1989a, 99).[7] That this combination is an ambiguous one, however, is suggested by the adoption not only of the philosophy of history common to both the reform movement and the republican movement, but also of their respective, quite distinct utopian visions. Besides the strands of critique perpetuated by Koselleck and Habermas, however, there still remains the critique characterising Enlightenment sociology. It embraces a variety of objects. It stretches from the critique of enlightened despotism or the authoritarian ideology of the state, through the critique of hyper-rationalism and of the belief in the limitless ability of human beings to make their own history and society, to the critique of populist and revolutionary excesses.

This Enlightenment sociological critique had originally been formulated by participants in the rights discourse who, rather than being centrally placed either in the state or among the mass of the people, occupied positions between these two extremes.[8] From the outset, therefore, it had been linked to a political orientation committed to liberty, rights, humanitarianism, a constitution, a division of sovereignty and a balance of powers that in the form of constitutionalism later became a component of liberalism and today provides for a step beyond the latter. The fact that it was increasingly appreciated that the development of society takes place in the medium of conflict and contestation, however, brought pressure to bear on the direct relationship between a social scientific orientation and a movement or political ideology. In the course of the discursive construction of Enlightenment sociology, therefore, we observe a tendency towards the withdrawal of critique from direct political engagement, without becoming morally and politically indifferent, and its recasting in the form of a more distanced consideration of all the different culturally and socially distinct collective actors and their respective political strategies as well as their cultural and social characteristics and embeddedness. Rather than identifying directly with any particular political direction, Enlightenment sociology aimed its critique at the ideology and utopian projection of all the different orientations, including the one from which it originally stemmed most directly. For this purpose, it located all these political orientations within the larger structured context of society and the process of its constitution, organisation and development.

This does not mean that Enlightenment sociology entertained the misleading idea of being able to assume the objective position of a disinterested observer, or the belief that society is an external reality that admits of objective description and approximation of its truth. It understood itself as part of society, as part of the relations whereby society is produced and reproduced, and instead of pursuing full and complete knowledge about social reality as such, it set out to expose the self-deception or illusion about society nurtured by each of the collective actors involved in the production and reproduction of society, including itself. Examples of such self-deceptions or illusions included: the belief of the absolutist state, reformist administrators, Physiocrats and some *philosophes* that enlightened despotism is rational, while overlooking the fact that it is actually a form of despotism; or the belief of classical republicans that society can organise itself in the form of a state with virtuous citizens who legislate for themselves through their general will, while failing to appreciate the compulsion and coercion actually required to approach such a goal; or the belief of some representatives of the aristocracy and bourgeoisie that the diffusion of liberty making possible strategic struggle and the benefits flowing from it would lead to the desirable society, while losing sight of the actual social costs of naked competition; or, finally, the belief of some Enlightenment authors in progress and perfection, while ignoring the real possibility of falling back into barbarism. By exposing the self-deceptions or illusions of these various social actors, Enlightenment sociology advanced a socio-cognitive critique in the sense of a critique of cultural frames and the social implications and effects of the ideals different social actors claimed to pursue in society. By drawing from a broad base yet focusing sharply, it ultimately approached a critique of the crisis that such frames and their concurrent ideals generated in early modern society.[9]

The socio-cognitive critique exemplified by Enlightenment sociology may at first sight seem to be some version of realism, since it involves a distancing from moralisation and the exposure of the implications and effects of normative positions, whether that of enlightened despotism or of undivided popular sovereignty, or even of some form of liberalism between the two. It should be emphasised, however, that Enlightenment sociology was by no means morally indifferent. It did not simply reduce the normative content of the different positions to functional mechanisms. On the contrary, while it located the different groupings taking moral-political positions within the context of society as a structured setting and analysed the relations among them in the rights discourse, it throughout kept in mind their common, albeit partial, reference to liberty and rights – or what we would today refer to as democracy. It cannot be denied, indeed it must be explicitly acknowledged, that Enlightenment sociology, despite being constructed at the macro-level and being normatively oriented and critical, did not completely transcend the limitations that characterised the early modern practical discourse from which it derived. The true social costs of its peculiar articulation of freedom became apparent and were fully appreciated only later when the question of rights was supplemented by the social question that arose in the wake of the new problem complex of poverty. This identification of the limits of Enlightenment sociology leaves out of account, of course, the contemporary problem complex of risk and the question of nature, not to mention those that sociologists will have to come to grips with critically yet modestly in the future.

The sharp contrast between Enlightenment sociological critique and the opposing forms of critique defended by Koselleck and Habermas suggests a new way of understanding the crisis of early modern or state-centred society and the consequent pathogenesis of modern society.

For Koselleck, the chronic pathology of modern society, manifested in a pervasive depoliticised utopian orientation, can be traced to the moralising assault of Enlightenment critique against the political element embodied by the monarch and state in the early modern period and its subversion and erosion up to the point where moralistic utopianism came to displace politics. For Habermas, the endemic crisis of modern society, taking the form of an insufficient rationalisation in the sense of the communicative openness or publicness of political power, arose in the early modern period on the basis of an involved dominational structure in which political and economic interests became inextricably intertwined. He will regard the project of modernity as being unfinished until such time as political power has been fully rationalised through bringing moral universalism to bear on it in the medium of communication or, better, discourse. Whereas Koselleck thus leads the crisis of early modern society back to Enlightenment critique and Habermas to absolutist-mercantile capitalist domination, the analysis of the discursive construction of sociology shows that neither of these two interpretations is tenable. If one looks

264

beyond these two opposed yet complementary positions towards the process of the production and reproduction or, rather, the construction of society instead, then it immediately becomes apparent that the crisis of early modern society was generated by more than either Enlightenment moralistic critique or absolutist-mercantile capitalist domination.

Rather than being attributable to either the Enlightenment or absolutism alone, it arose from the relations among the different groups or collective actors participating in early modern society, or from the relations through which society is produced and reproduced. The fact that the crisis of early modern society had been carried by social relations explains why it admitted of being perpetuated beyond both the dominational and moralising intentions of absolutism and the Enlightenment respectively and, indeed, to such a degree that we can justifiably speak of the endemic crisis of modern society. Being generated by social relations, the crisis can only be understood with reference to the interrelation of the different ideals that the various groupings claim to pursue in society and the combined social effect of the self-deceptive or illusory components of these ideals.

Modern society came into being three centuries or so ago as a set of relations that was understood as requiring collective action to solve collective problems and, indeed, as itself having to constitute such action to gain and maintain autonomy and sovereignty. When the required action is not forthcoming, when it does not constitute or is incapable of constituting such action, when it cannot solve its own collective problems, then modern society finds itself in the throes of a crisis. In the early modern period, a crisis of this kind arose for the first time. It resulted from the fact that the conjunction of illusory claims advanced by the principal social actors impeded or blocked the channel necessary for the full mobilisation and taking of the required collective action.

Most important among these claims were, on the one hand, those of the absolutist state and its supporters and sympathisers and, on the other, those of the republicans and Jacobins. The claims of the constitutionalists were by no means without importance, yet they were nevertheless subordinated to the former two in both the late eighteenth-century American and French constitutional arrangements.[10] Whereas the first group claimed to pursue the ideal of a fully rational society, they brought a despotic regime into being. The second group's compulsive civic moralism of virtue, frequently followed by bloody consequences, in turn did not prevent them from claiming that they represented a self-organised society. The inherent ambiguity of the third group's frame allowed them to hide from themselves the naked strategic struggle that was being advanced in their own ranks under the cloak of liberty, rights, the division of sovereignty and the separation of powers.[11] Together these more or less important yet equally illusory ideals foreclosed the recognition of the existence side by side of ineliminable cultural and social differences and contradictions, not to mention the need to accommodate them as differences and contradictions under the same roof, as it were. Despite the fact that constitutional, legal and political arrangements had been institution-alised, various culturally and socially distinct groups were not allowed any room for manoeuvre, not to mention participation. Certain class-specific, sub-cultural groups were simply overwhelmed and suppressed by a hegemonic public sphere and discourse, and others such as ethnic minorities (e.g. the Jews) and women[12] were excluded in a manner which left its scars on the very structure of modern society.

Sight was lost of the contradictory and conflictual process of the con-stitution of society. An impediment was placed in the way of the basic type of social conflict that is essential for the production and reproduction of cultural differences and social groups or classes. A politics of administered public opinion, a politics of popular collective decision-making, and a politics of power elites locked in battle and obliterated a participatory politics, a politics of conflict, contestation and compromise. This dearth of politics, this lack of a sufficient level of politics, not only constituted the crisis of early modern society, but also provided the point of departure for the pathogenesis of modern society. For the core of the persistent crisis of modern society has been and remains to this day the absence of a participatory politics of conflict, contestation and compromise and, supporting it at a more fundamental level, a culture of contradictions.

Notes

1. Introduction: Discourse and Sociology

1. See also Anderson (1980, 22) who points out that all the critical innovations of the period related to communication. This is the sense, moreover, of referring to early modernity as 'commercial society' (Heilbron et al. 1998, 77–106).

2. Toulmin (1992, 6–9) puts forward various suggestions for the interpretation of modernity.

3. Cherkaoui (1997, v) also points out that 'the social and political problems, thought to be consequences of the French Revolution, are in fact prior to it... Those problems emerged under the Old Régime.'

4. In this respect, Touraine (1988) is correct when he says that '... sociology, at once evolutionist and functionalist, was destroyed...more by historical transformations than by intellectual critiques' (5). But when he extends this insight into the categorical statement that 'Sociology was constituted as the ideology of modernity' (3), then he commits the same error as Habermas, namely interpreting sociology in its original form from an anachronistic nineteenth- and twentieth-century point of view.

5. Starting from a Habermasian base, this approach is related to the proposals put forward by Honneth (1991), Miller (1986), and Eder (1993a; 1996).

6. See also Goldmann (1964; 1975), and Berger and Luckmann (1971). To these names should be added that of Elias (1973; 1982), one-time assistant of Mannheim in Frankfurt, who took up the latter's (Mannheim 1972, 278) idea of a broadening basis of knowledge which is accompanied by a higher degree of abstraction to construct a wide-ranging social theory, the theory of the civilising process.

7. On the problem of imputation, see Bürger (1978, 39–54).

8. Despite many very interesting features, this is true even of Luhmann's autopoietic version of systems theory introduced in the 1980s. According to him (1985, 141): 'It is completely misguided to search for a carrier of meaning. Meaning carries itself in that it self-referentially makes possible its own reproduction' (my translation). See also Miller's (1987, 197–202) critique in which he proposes to conceive of meaning neither objectivistically nor subjectivistically but rather in terms of 'collective reflexion and learning processes'; and Hahn (1987) and Lohmann (1987), both of whom demonstrate the untenability of Luhmann's thesis that the loss of meaning (and hence crisis) is impossible in the context of meaning systems.

9. I prefer to call it the theory of sociation. This terminology derives from the

Notes

German *Vergesellschaftung* and is intended to give expression to a constructivist-structuralist theory of the collective production and reproduction of society. Instead of either 'system' (Luhmann) or 'lifeworld' (Habermas), sociation is chosen as the basic theoretical concept in order to indicate that the preceding process both generating and structuring social reality is at the centre of attention. Instead of the rather abstract 'structuration' (Giddens), the concept of sociation suggests more directly what is at issue. It is not concerned merely with a process of structuration but rather with a process, involving both construction and structuration, that relates or divides and brings together people and things in a way that is constitutive of their social reality. In the present context, it is not possible to give an outline of the theory of sociation. It owes something to authors such as Lukács, Adorno, Piaget, Goldmann, Habermas, Touraine, and Bourdieu. Interesting comparable reflections are to be found in, for example, Unger (1987a, 144–69).

10. In his final years, Parsons (1977b, 69) admitted that he had 'always assumed that social order *existed*' (his own emphasis).

11. See now, however, Eder (1993a) for a different position.

12. While Giddens (1986, 139–44) is critical of the micro-macro scheme and Eder (1993a, 45) adopts it instead of the agency-structure scheme, Ritzer (1992, 537–96) draws a sharp distinction between the two theoretical models in that he identifies the micro-macro distinction with the American approach and the agency-structure distinction with European social science. This evaluation is not convincing, though.

13. Compare Eder (1993a, 14, 60, 187).

14. On the role of the public and the level of contingency it represents, see Strydom (1999a).

15. These cognitive structures will later be considered as micro-level framing devices employed by actors to construct frames that go into the make-up of an emergent macro- or master frame which becomes collectively accepted on the basis of the response of the public. They are all carried by communication and are given their structuring – whether coordinating or controlling – force by discourse.

16. Swidler (1986, 278, 280) discusses these two moments under the title of 'unsettled lives' and 'settled lives'. In his sociology of knowledge, Bloor (1991, 78) adopts a comparable distinction.

17. As regards these three dimensions, different but comparable positions are put forward by Touraine (1977; 1981; 1988), Giesen (1991b), and Eder (1993b). Of particular importance is Touraine's concept of the cultural model.

18. The first occurred in the wake of the Reformation, Counter-Reformation and the Thirty Years War at the end of the sixteenth and the first part of the seventeenth century and eventually led to the establishment of the constitutional state. The second occurred in the wake of the division of society by the industrial capitalist market economy in the second half of the nineteenth century and eventually led to the establishment of the welfare state.

19. I have in mind here in particular the individualisation thesis (Beck 1992, 91–154; Beck and Beck-Gernsheim 1996) taken in the sense of a release from structure. The answer, on the other hand, does not lie in the structural determinism of Bourdieu's (1986, 169–225) habitus either.

20. Bourdieu (1997), one of the major late twentieth-century theorists of language use and power, is also relevant here. Besides the concept of 'field', he does not have a theoretical concept of discourse comparable to that of Foucault and Habermas, but he criticises both: the former for his structuralist or semiological discourse analysis, and the latter for his appropriation of pragmatics or speech act theory. As against Foucault, he introduces a reflexive epistemology, and as against both Foucault and Habermas, he stresses a more specific sociological approach to context and power. However, his

characteristic over-emphasis of cultural domination, the economics of practice, and status politics, which finds its affirmation in his misunderstanding of Habermas, clearly displays the limits of his own sociological approach. It is not possible, therefore, to adopt his position instead of a synthesis of Habermas and Foucault. One could, of course, consider replacing Foucault with Bourdieu. While I shall continue to draw on the fruitful aspects of Bourdieu's work, however, the specific intention here is to make a contribution not to the well-developed Bourdieu debate but rather to the Habermas-Foucault debate which has hardly come off the ground (for example Honneth 1991; Hoy 1987; Poster 1991; Calhoun 1992; Kelly 1994; Hoy and McCarthy 1994).

21. By contrast with Habermas' emphasis on the reflexive dimension of communication, Foucault takes a position that is comparable with Bourdieu's focus on the taken-for-granted doxa.

22. For example, below three historically specific discourses, each with its own cultural logic, are distinguished from one another: the rights, the justice and the responsibility discourses.

23. For example, the justice discourse of the nineteenth and twentieth century simultaneously made possible the deconstruction of the classical emancipation movements and the construction of the labour movement, in the same way that in the context of the contemporary responsibility discourse we witness both the deconstruction of the labour movement and the construction of the new social movements.

24. Theoretically, it should be pointed out, the theory of social evolution is of importance as an assumption informing this book, yet social evolution in a very specific and decidedly non-traditional sense (Strydom 1987; 1992a; 1993; compare Eder 1988, 285–387; 1993a, 17–41). But this is not a topic for discussion in its own right in the present context.

25. See, for example, Schmidt (1987; 1992) and Luhmann (1992) on constructivism rooted in cybernetics, developmental and language psychology, and biology. Against a Kantian-inspired structuralist and phenomenological foil, the sociology of science has played a leading role since the 1970s in placing constructivism on the sociological agenda (for example Bloor 1991; Van den Daele 1977; Latour and Woolgar 1979; Knorr-Cetina 1981a; Fuller 1993). For general overviews, see Sismondo (1993) and Delanty (1997). Particularly interesting about the latter is that Delanty gives a central place to the relationship between social science as a professional culture and the public culture of debate on society.

Part I: Theory of Discourse and Discourse Analysis

Introduction: From Presentism and Historicism to Discourse

1. See also, for example, Giddens (1976), Lepenies (1977b; 1981; 1988), Jones (1977), Kuklick (1979), and Hawthorn (1987). One of the most important general theoretical works dealing with the problems encountered in this field is Heller (1982).

2. Rather than a historical approach tied to the assumptions of the consciousness of world history – Heller's (1982, 23–27) 'consciousness of reflected universality' – typical of the modern period (i.e., late eighteenth to the mid-twentieth century), both historicism and the discourse approach are informed by the new late twentieth-century historical consciousness – Heller's (1982, 28–35) 'consciousness of reflected generality' – that appreciates the generality of humankind, the globalisation of human history, the plurality of cultural orientations and interests, and above all the fragility of our civilisation. Whereas historicism as a radical form of contextualism discredits itself by appealing in vain to the normative force or validity of the factual (Habermas 1996, 2), however, the discourse approach focuses on the historical present while retaining a

Notes

normative reference point: neither facticity as in contextualism, nor a projected counterfactual as in Habermas, but the contemporaneous and simultaneous being together or 'Togetherness' in the sense of the 'absolute (present) now' (Heller 1982, 41) which demands 'solidary or planetarian responsibility' (Apel 1988; 1990; 1991b; Heller 1982, 47).

3. Also cited in Baehr and O'Brien (1994, 73–74).

4. In terms of the presupposed theory of time or, more specifically, of history (for example Heller 1982, 36–50), Turner can be interpreted as identifying the present with the present historical age –i.e., the nineteenth century –while abstracting from the historical present and thus ignoring the cultural structure or the socio-cultural world of the authors involved.

5. Also referred to in Baehr and O'Brien (1994, 18–19).

6. This is one of the most acute theoretical insights gained by the social sciences in the recent past, yet one that is not yet adequately appreciated and understood. It turns on the recognition of the significance of the cultural dimension of social action and the consequent opening of the relational and structured context to constructivist treatment. See Eder (1993a, 14) and Strydom (1999a, 18).

2. Theory of Discourse

1. For its part, the linguistic or pragmatic turn of course depends on the fundamental change of historical consciousness that has taken place in the twentieth century, entailing – in Heller's (1982) terms – a shift from 'consciousness of reflected universality: world-historical consciousness' to 'consciousness of reflected generality: the task of planetarian responsibility', the latter of which includes the recognition of language or communication as a human universal.

2. See, for example, Apel (1967; 1967/70; 1973; 1976; 1980; 1981).

3. I approach the theory of discourse here from a Habermasian point of view, but also seek to incorporate aspects of Foucault's work. In so doing, I draw inspiration from Honneth's (1991; 1995, 1) suggestion that Foucault's social theoretic achievement can be taken up meaningfully in a communication theoretic framework.

4. See also Frank (1990a, 409).

5. While Foucault is here placed against his French background, one should not lose sight of the impact of Heidegger on post-structuralism, including Foucault's theories of discourse and power. See, for example, Habermas (1987b), Apel (1991a, 131–35) and Brunkhorst (1991). An important aspect of Heidegger's contribution which is neglected by the German authors yet plays a central role in the works of the French authors, although not necessarily acknowledged as such, had been brought to the fore long ago by Mannheim (for example 1993, 404–06):

> It appears that the different parties are all competing for the possession of the correct social diagnosis... the competing parties are always struggling to influence what the phenomenologist Heidegger calls the 'public interpretation of reality'... The nature of the generally accepted interpretation of the world at any given time is of decisive importance in determining the particular nature of the stage of historical evolution reached at that time... this public interpretation of reality is not simply 'there'; nor, on the other hand, is it the result of a 'systematic thinking out'; it is the stake for which men fight.

6. See also Rorty (1989).

7. For the acknowledgement of Apel's critique, see Habermas (1974a, 15 and 284, note 27).

8. See Dreyfus and Rabinow (1982, 102–03), Honneth (1991, 150), Rabinow

(1987, 9–10), Hoy (1987, 4), Fink-Eitel (1989, 67–70) and Merquior (1991, 84).

9. Dreyfus and Rabinow (1982, 79–125), Honneth (1991, 146–48), Hoy (1987, 3–6), Fink-Eitel (1989, 57) and Frank (1990a, 417, 420, 421, 425).

10. See also Bernstein (1989).

11. See also Rabinow (1987, 10) and Hoy (1987, 4).

12. See also Honneth (1991, 144, 169–70).

13. See also Gordon (1980, 244–45), Dreyfus and Rabinow (1982, 104–05) and Honneth (1991, 144, 151).

14. See also Gordon (1980, 245).

15. Foucault writes:

We can now understand the reason for the equivocal meaning of the term *discourse*, which I have used and abused in many different senses: in the most general, and vaguest way, it denoted a group of verbal performances; and by discourse, then, I meant that which was produced (perhaps all that was produced) by the groups of signs. But I also meant a group of acts of formulation, a series of sentences and propositions. Lastly – and it is this meaning that was finally used (together with the first, which served in a provisional capacity) – discourse is constituted by a group of sequences of signs, in so far as they are statements, that is, in so far as they can be assigned particular modalities of existence.

See also Honneth (1991, 136–37) and Frank (1990, 421).

16. See also Honneth and Joas (1988, 129–50).

17. Foucault (1980, 91) speaks of the view of power as a relation emanating from the hostile engagement of forces as 'the Nietzsche hypothesis'.

18. See Habermas (1992a; 1996) for his latest systematic statement.

19. See also Münch (1984, 77–126) and McCarthy (1992). Bourdieu's (1997, 107, 257) critique of Habermas could also be mentioned here. However, from its brevity one gains the impression that Bourdieu neglected to study Habermas in any depth, which would explain also his apparent inability to comprehend what Habermas did achieve.

20. See also Münch (1984, 90–91, 112–13).

21. In *Between Facts and Norms* (1996, 108–09) Habermas admits that he has hitherto not differentiated sufficiently between discourse and moralisation. The introduction of this distinction then allows him (1996, 159–62) to put forward a typology of discourse embracing pragmatic, ethical-political, moral and finally juristic discourse. This typology was developed some years earlier (Habermas, 1991, 100–18).

22. In terms of Habermas' new position, this would mean that discourse concerns not just moral questions but also ethical ones concerning identity and form of life as well as pragmatic ones.

23. Power has a number of different connotations. On the one hand, power relations that cannot be neutralised are manifest in discourse. To deal with this aspect, Habermas (1996, 165–67) recently introduced the concept of negotiation or bargaining. Simultaneously, he also developed (1996, 133–51) a differentiated concept of power embracing communicative, social and administrative power. On the other hand, power is present in discourse in the form of hidden or latent power structures and asymmetrical relations. It is this aspect, which Habermas does not deal with, that is covered by Foucault – as is made clear in the next note. Bourdieu (1997, 107, 257) has this same dimension of power in mind in his critique of Habermas.

24. Waldenfels (1991, 112–13) has convincingly argued that the fact that no order admits of complete justification opens the door for the problem of power. In the meantime, Habermas (cited in Calhoun 1992, 78–79) himself has explicitly stated that it is judicious 'to suppose that most discourses…imply power structures that are not only hidden but systematically latent, that is, structurally concealed from their

participants'. At the same time, he admitted that Foucault's conception is essential in discourse analysis for the purposes of exposing hidden asymmetries and power structures. He is hesitant to follow Foucault in accepting that discourses are in principle power-discourse formations, however, since he is convinced that discourse incorporates also a self-corrective tendency in that it exhibits a critical sensitivity towards systematic exclusionary mechanisms. Public discourse, for instance, can be said to be an attempt to exclude violence that again reproduces violence internally. Crucial for him, however, is that this internally reproduced violence is cast in a criticisable form. The position Habermas takes here provides sufficient ground to search for a complementary theoretical-methodological structure embracing both his and Foucault's conceptions. In the 1980s and early 1990s, various members of the younger generation of critical theorists appreciated this possibility: Honneth (1991) cleared the way in 1985, Benhabib (1992, 94) mentioned Habermas and Foucault in one breath, Cohen and Arato (1992, 257) regarded the incorporation of Foucault as essential for social theory if it is to avoid apology, Eley (1992, 331) saw Habermas' position as being in need of extension by means of Foucault, and McCarthy (1993) searched for continuities and even saw fit to submit (McCarthy 1994, 230) that 'Foucault's powerful insights do not require, and indeed are not even compatible with, either his ontology of power or his totalistic conceptions of society, and...can be developed more fruitfully as a continuation of, rather than an alternative to, critical social theory'.

25. That is, a basic mutual understanding that is nevertheless accompanied by disagreement (Miller 1992, 14). In this respect, Bourdieu's position is similar to Foucault's.

26. Lyotard has criticised Habermas for not being able to incorporate dissensus into his consensus-oriented approach (Frank 1988; 1990b), but Apel (in Rötzer 1987, 70) has insisted that dissensus can without difficulty be integrated into their discourse ethical position: 'The central idea of the consensus theory of discourse ethics is after all precisely that consensus is pursued under completely free conditions, so that dissensus anyway enters as a matter of course. Dissensus and consensus belong together. If one wants to organize discourses that are oriented towards the establishment not of consensus but of dissensus, however, then they would not be genuine discussions of arguments' (my translation). For a brief statement of his position on communicatively irresolvable conflict or 'differend', see Lyotard (1993, 8–10).

27. Given its lack of theoretical foundation or, rather, the implication of a sociologically indefensible systems theoretical concept of society (Honneth 1991, 173–75), Foucault's (1981, 139–43) conception of the institutional control of the body and the population, based on the threefold scheme of norm-body-knowledge, cannot be endorsed here, yet this does not mean that his innovative idea of a rationalized modality of power characteristic of modern society has to be surrendered. However, this concept needs to be incorporated into a broader theoretical framework. If this is done, it can be related to the normatively informed complementary concept of 'communicative power' proposed by Habermas (1996, 151).

28. Compare Habermas (1990, 15; 1992b, 424–30) correcting himself in meeting Foucault's challenge more generally and criticisms articulated by Eley (1992) more specifically. See also Baker (1992), Fraser (1992) and Kramer (1992). Bourdieu's (1997) concern with causally effective social structures such as the state and the dominant class is accommodated here, as are Foucault's hidden exclusionary power structures, but the latter's all-pervasive microcosmic capillary power structures are more difficult to accept sociologically, unless one is willing to countenance a bland functionalism.

29. See also Habermas' (1979, 148–49) related distinction between the descriptive level of social conflict and the analytical level of learning.

3. Sociological Theory of Discourse

1. This is the model that Parsons developed in the 1950s to assign functions to each of the four subsystems making up society as an action system maintaining itself in relation to its environment. Later Parsons (1966, 7) summarised these four functions as follows: 'Within action systems, cultural systems are specialised around the function of *pattern-maintenance* [earlier called 'latency'], social systems around the *integration* of acting units (human individuals or, more precisely, personalities engaged in roles), personality systems around *goal-attainment*, and the behavioural organism around *adaptation...*' (my italics).

2. Habermas' (1996, 157–68) recently introduced ethical-political and pragmatic discourse types obviously go a long way toward meeting these demands.

3. Compare also the analysis of social conflict in modern society in Miller (1992, 28–35).

4. It is of course the case that, whereas Habermas is more interested in reflexivity, Foucault favours unquestioned assumptions and conceptions that have acquired the force of nature. Bourdieu's emphasis on 'doxa' possesses the same strategic sense as Foucault's concern with the 'never-said' (see also Fowler 1997, 92).

5. See, for example, Habermas (1974a, 13; 1987b, 357–67) and Eder (1991; 1993a, 42–62).

6. For a penetrating critique of Luhmann, see Miller (1987).

7. Miller (1987, 187–88) and Eder (1993a, 8, 60) similarly build on this important theoretical insight. See also Calhoun (1993).

8. The feedback loop between the two phases of discourse can be clarified by means of an interpretation of C. A. van Peursen's (1970, 160–86) threefold model of the development of knowledge. Once a problem is collectively circumscribed and common ground appears between the participants, the first two steps in the trajectory of the development of knowledge take effect. Foundational knowledge is explored and established up to the point where it is sufficiently articulated to allow transition to the next stage which takes the form of the application of the knowledge through technology. This primary or simple development, which largely coincides with the re-establishment of certainty and is increasingly carried by specialists or experts, is followed by the ethical phase in the development of knowledge which involves the public and the movements and organisations emerging from it. It consists of a confrontation with the consequences engendered by the application of knowledge and the concomitant inducement of reflection on those consequences and their implications. The circle is complete: the ethical reflection chips away at the crust of self-evidences and lays bare the taken-for-granted assumptions, thus in a shift from expert discourse to societal discourse transforming certainty once again into uncertainty.

9. It is at turning points of this kind that the concept of crisis, strictly speaking, becomes applicable, i.e., crisis informed by the medical sense of the word of a critical turning point or decisive moment in an illness that determines the final outcome, whether recovery or death. Both Habermas (1976, 1) and Rabb (1975, 31) introduce their sociological and historiographic uses of the concept of crisis with reference to this medical sense.

10. According to Habermas (1976, 3), only subjects can be involved in crises: 'only when members of a society experience structural alterations as critical for continued existence and feel their social identity threatened can we speak of crises'.

11. See also Evers and Nowotny (1987, 20–21).

12. For an instructive discussion of the make-up and resolution of objective problem situations with some reference to Popper's 'three-world theory', see Miller (1986, 306–20).

13. See also Eder (1993a, 64, 52).

14. This is a crucial theoretical point given the contemporary obsession with an unmediated processual view, from Giddens' structuration theory to post-structuralist and postmodernist Nietzschean vitalism.

15. These include Habermas' old theoretical and practical discourses and his new pragmatic and ethical-political types as well as negotiation or bargaining.

16. Meta-theoretically, for example from the point of view of the theory of time or history, this level could be regarded as a particular manifestation of historical awareness. In the modern period, this could be either the early modern 'consciousness of generality reflected in particularity', or the modern 'consciousness of reflected universality or world history', or finally the nascent 'consciousness of reflected generality' – to employ Heller's (1982, 16–35) terms.

17. For example the three distinct semantic worlds centred on the early modern democratic revolutions, the modern industrial and scientific-technological revolution, and events such as the Chernobyl disaster respectively.

18. For example the shift from the early modern rights frame to the modern justice frame, or from the latter to the contemporary responsibility frame, as will become apparent below.

19. See also Gamson (1992a, 67) and Eder (1992c, 2–3).

20. For example Nowotny (1973), Nowotny and Schmutzer (1974), Cicourel (1973), Touraine (1977; 1981; 1988), Habermas (1979), Knorr-Cetina and Cicourel (1981), Moscovici (1982b), Fuller (1984), Bourdieu (1986), Miller (1986), Knorr-Cetina (1988; 1994), Eder (1988; 1993a; 1996), Eyerman and Jamison (1991), Holland and Quinn (1991), Shweder and LeVine (1993), Van Dijk (1997), Strydom (1999b) and Delanty (1999a).

21. Drawing on phenomenology, particularly Heidegger (1967), Mannheim (1993, 405) already in the 1920s gave a clear circumscription of the cognitive order:

> The nature of the generally accepted interpretation of the world at any given time is of decisive importance in determining the particular nature of the stage of historical evolution reached at that time. This is not merely a matter of the so-called 'public opinion' which is commonly recognized as a superficial phenomenon of collective psychology, but of the inventory of our set of fundamental meanings in terms of which we experience the outside world as well as our own inner responses.

Heller (1982, 41) speaks of a 'cultural structure'; Bourdieu (1986, 468, 471) insists that '[a]ll agents in a given social formation share a set of basic perceptual schemes... [a] system of classificatory schemes...'; and Habermas (1996, 286) accepts 'the intersubjectivity of a prior *structure* of possible mutual understanding'.

22. See also McAdam et al. (1996). For a critique, see Strydom (1999a).

23. See also William Gamson's (1992a, 6–8, 29–114) analysis of 'collective action frames' as well as Capek (1993). Earlier, the South African political scientist Peter Du Preez (1980) made very interesting use of Goffman's concept of frame in the context of identity politics.

24. Interestingly, the concept 'cognitive praxis' is clearly informed by what may be called a genetic-structuralist or constructivist-structuralist position.

25. Although apparently influenced by Gamson, Eder's position is built on theoretical insights drawn from Habermas, Touraine and Bourdieu – for him the three most important social theorists. The present author (Strydom 1992b; 1994, 19–25) has clarified and developed further aspects of Eder's position that are relevant here. This will be taken up below.

26. Bourdieu's concern with deeper-seated cognitive structures might be attributable to his anthropological orientation which apparently does not always benefit his sociology.

27. See also Gamson (1992a, 69–70) and McAdam et al. (1996).

28. Besides Piaget (for example 1973, 207–09), the work of the Uppsala school on social rule system theory contains suggestions toward ways of theoretically and methodologically conceiving and operationalising such rules. See, for example, Burns and Flam (1990).

29. This position stems from a critique and development of Eder (1992b, 18) presented in Strydom (1994, 23).

30. A similar critique is put forward also in Strydom (1994, 23). On the responsibility frame, see Strydom (1999c; 1999d).

31. While this conceptualisation leans on Piaget (1969; 1970; 1973), it obviously has certain affinities with Thomas Kuhn's (1970) concept of 'paradigm'. This equivocal concept is avoided here, however, in favour of the more analytical one of a frame consisting of intellectual, moral and conative dimensions.

32. Compare also Oser's (1981) earlier attempt, standing in Piaget's cognitivist tradition, to analyse the generation of cognitive structures. Du Preez (1980, 49) draws on Alisdair MacIntyre's analysis of ideology to give content to his Goffmanian frame analysis. Crucial are three key components: (i) the delineation of general characteristics of nature or society or both; (ii) an account of the relation between what is the case and how we ought to act; and (iii) beliefs that define for a given social group their social existence.

33. A systematically developed position drawing on a range of sociological authors, including Goffman's frame analysis, and operating with a threefold distinction of descriptive, evaluative and prescriptive rules, is the social rule system theory of the Uppsala school (e.g. Burns 1986; Burns and Flam 1990). A different yet interesting proposal that starts from Popper's (1972, 106–90, here 155) 'three-world theory' and employs Parsons' (1977b, 113, 281) concept of symbolic codes, which differs sharply from Luhmann's (1986a) binary codes, is put forward in Giesen (1991a), Giesen and Junge (1991) and Eisenstadt and Giesen (1995). For a critique of Popper's three-world theory, which could serve as a starting point for a critical assessment of Giesen, see Habermas (1984, 76–79).

34. For his position on knowledge or cognitive interests, see Habermas (1972).

35. For his position on validity claims, see Habermas (1979, 1–68; 1984, 8–53).

36. Habermas' (1992a, 346) latest proposal is to think in terms of 'the deepgrammatical distinctions among the pragmatic, ethical and moral uses of reason' (my translation). For the less revealing English translation, see Habermas (1996, 285).

37. These devices are the tools that social actors take from the toolbox of culture (Swidler 1986) or from what Schutz (1976, 80–81) much earlier called the 'stock of knowledge at hand'.

38. See also Fisher (1984), Wuthnow (1989) and Somers (1994; 1995).

39. Habermas (1996, 364) makes a distinction between 'actors who…emerge from the public and take part in the reproduction of the public sphere itself' and 'actors who occupy an already constituted public domain in order to use it'.

40. Burns and Flam (1990, 42–43) speak of the 'struggle' of frames. Here Karl Mannheim's (1993, 399–437) essay on competition as a cultural phenomenon, although from the 1920s, still makes compelling reading.

41. Instead of 'double contingency', which has been placed at the centre of social theory by Mead, Schutz, Parsons, Luhmann and Habermas, the level relevant here is what may be called 'triple contingency' (Strydom 1999a).

42. It is interesting to note that whereas Foucault (1980, 108) in a lecture dating from 1976 insisted that '[p]ower must be analysed as something which circulates', Habermas (1996, 354) in 1992 undertook to inquire into the 'circulation of power' and to make it central to his account of the public sphere. There is no evidence to suggest that he was following Foucault's proposal, though.

Notes

4. Discourse of Modernity

1. See also Habermas (1987c, 105).

2. See also Castoriadis (1991, 187).

3. In the historiography of the early modern period, the concept of the 'general crisis' has become firmly established since the Marxist Eric Hobsbawm (1954) first proposed it some forty years ago and the conservative Hugh Trevor-Roper added a political dimension to the former's economic account. See, for example, the collection of essays on the crisis from the journal *Past & Present* in Trevor Aston (1980) as well as Theodore Rabb's (1975) interesting synthetic endeavour based on a clarification of the concept of crisis with reference to its medical usage. According to the latter's interpretation, it is possible to distinguish (i) a phase of bewildering change and fragmentation starting around 1500, which came to a head in (ii) a period of crisis between the early seventeenth century and approximately 1660, followed by (iii) a phase in which the crisis was resolved.

4. In his recent work, however, Habermas (1996, 37) takes a more sociological position in so far as he maintains that under modern conditions complex societies require discourses to be conducted permanently.

5. This problem is the focal point of Habermas' (1996, 329–87) sociological concern in his latest major work. See also Moscovici (1990, 9), Bloor (1991, 65–66) and the French 'regulation school' (Amin 1994).

6. While Marshall's (1973) citizenship complexes of 'civil', 'political' and 'social' rights are clearly relevant here, they are neither strictly parallel to nor exhaustive of the three discourses. His civil and political rights both fall within the framework of the rights discourse, and his social rights belong to the context of the justice discourse. The responsibility discourse concerns a new issue not covered by his work – indeed, one that goes beyond his problem, citizenship. See, for example, Touraine (1995) who raises the question of a 'politics of recognition' vis-à-vis a 'politics of citizenship'. Interesting discussions of Marshall are to be found in Parsons (1977b, 333–40) and Giddens (1987a, 200–09). Although going in various ways beyond Marshall, none of these authors captures the sense of the issue at stake in the responsibility discourse, however. Parsons' extension of Marshall's scheme by culture is interesting but not yet sufficiently fleshed out. Giddens' reduction of Marshall's social rights to economic rights is curiously one-sided, as Parsons already clearly sensed, but his insistence on arenas of contestation rather than phases of development and hence on class conflict is highly relevant. In this latter respect, see also Eder (1993a, 191). Although it includes no reference to him, the last three moments in Habermas' (1987a, 357–61) sketch of 'epochal waves of juridification', running from the bourgeois state via the constitutional and the democratic constitutional state to the democratic welfare state, would seem to be comparable to Marshall's scheme. Habermas' concern with 'the colonisation of the lifeworld' of course indicates that he is motivated more by developing a critical response to the problem of the relation between democracy and capitalism-cum-bureaucracy than is Marshall. See also Habermas (1996, 77) and Turner (1993). In contradistinction to Marshall's emphasis on rights throughout and Habermas' focus on juridification (i.e. the constitutionalisation, democratisation and socialisation of the state), the distinction among three discourses is informed by a broader view deriving from the theory of sociation. Rather than citizenship or juridification, the reference point is provided by the construction of society in relation to distinct problem and issue complexes. Whereas the first of these complexes turned on the juridification of society, the second and the third involved the industrialisation and the culturalisation of society respectively.

7. On the political or constitutional question at the core of the rights discourse, see, for example, Skinner (1978) and Tuck (1979; 1993).

8. For example, Locke (1978; 1970), Paine (1954), Gouges (1987) and Kant (1965). For contemporary statements see: Bloch (1961), Dworkin (1978), Alexy (1986), Unger (1987b, 508–39) and Habermas (1996, 82–131).

9. On the social question at the core of the justice discourse, see, for example, Arendt (1971, 68–135; 1984, 59–114) and Heller and Fehér (1988, 106–18). It is because historians of the social sciences have neglected to trace sociology back to the early modern period that Arendt (1971, 298, 38–49), who is admittedly correct that we need a political philosophy rather than a philosophy of history, sees fit to discredit sociology.

10. Bentham (1948), Mill (1867), Sidgwick (1884; see Schneewind 1986). For contemporary statements, see Rawls (1985) and Habermas (1996, 42–81).

11. On the question of nature at the core of the responsibility discourse, see Moscovici (1982a, 13–32; 1990). See also Luhmann (1986a), Halfmann (1986), Eder (1988, 253–55), and Van den Daele (1992).

12. For example, Van Peursen (1970), Jonas (1973; 1976; 1982; 1984), Lenk (1992), Melucci (1985, 806, 809; 1996, 170), Apel (1988; 1990; 1991b), Beck (1988), Offe (1989), Dower (1989), Kaufmann (1992), Bernstein (1994), Strydom (1999c; 1999d) and Delanty (1999a; 1999b).

13. For example, Jonas (1984, 7, 8) writes that 'Finally unbound, Prometheus, to whom science gives unprecedented powers and whom economics furnishes with a restless drive, cries out for an ethics that through voluntary restraint would prevent his power from becoming an evil…[i.e., an ethics of] responsibility'. Apel (1991b, 264) in turn submits that: 'Thus it appears that in both dimensions of cultural evolution, namely, that of technological interventions in nature and that of social interaction, a global situation has been brought about in our time that calls for a new ethics of shared responsibility, in other words, for a new type of ethics that, in contradistinction to the traditional or conventional forms of ethics, may be designated a (planetary) macroethics'. See also Strydom (1999d).

14. For a comprehensive overview of new social movement theories, see Buechler (1995). For the theoretical and methodological discussions taking place among social ecologists, deep ecologists, eco-Marxists and others, see, for example, the issue of the journal *Society and Nature* (1 [2] 1992) dealing with the philosophy of ecology, edited by Fotopoulos. The formation of new identities is also observable among political as well as business or industrial actors – for example, Margaret Thatcher's green speech of the mid-1980s has been paralleled by the greening of industry.

15. Melucci was one of the first sociologists to focus the problem of risk and culture, particularly in 'The Symbolic Challenge of Contemporary Movements' (1985), but see also 'The New Social Movements' (1980) and 'An End to Social Movements?' (1984). For his latest statements, see Melucci (1989; 1995). For Beck, the 'risk society' is one in which the collective dangers and threats generated by culturally defined social activities and processes are transformed, through a disavowal of responsibility by experts, business and politicians, into risks – the risk society thus being comparable to a drug addict. For Moscovici, post-civilisation or 'culture' is a state in which people understand their society as a form of nature. Lash shows, under the impact of Luhmann (and Parsons?), that society is today increasingly understood as being characterised by a fully differentiated cultural sphere, with the result that value pluralism and multiculturalism lead to a struggle over the cultural creation of reality.

16. For Willke, 'neocorporatism' refers to a new set of cooperative relations among the subsystems of society taking the form of a polycentric architecture mediated by intersystemic negotiation which came about as a result of the threefold refraction of state politics by ungovernability, implementation deficits and subsystem autonomies. Far from having been weakened, however, the state has simply changed its form from a directly interventionist 'Leviathan' operating according to the logic of power to a

'preceptor' engaging in indirect steering through persuasion and instruction. Wilson (1990) provides an overview of theories of neo-corporatism. For Eder, 'postcorporatism' refers to the nascent fluid arrangement, beyond the corporatist relations of the state, employers and the unions and their normative conflicts over the distribution of goods, that takes the form of a struggle fought out in the mass media among environmental protest, business and political actors over the cultural and social construction of reality.

17. Considering the structuration of the crisis discourses, the position taken here correspondingly does not imply that there is only one frame operative at any one time. In any and every social situation, a multiplicity of frames is available for activation and application. The choice is here made to focus on macro-frames identified in relation to societal problems and within each to consider contradictory, competing and hence conflicting meso-frames.

5. Sociological Discourse Analysis

1. For overviews of these traditions of critical discourse analysis, see, for example, Fairclough and Wodak (1997) and Wodak et al. (1998, 42–43).

2. The contradiction entailed by accepting both these positions on Foucault's theoretical premises should have become clear from the analysis of his contribution to the theory of discourse in Chapter 2 above.

3. A comparable position is taken by Bourdieu (1986, 477) when he submits that 'classificatory systems are the stake of struggles between the groups they characterize and counterpose, who fight over them while striving to turn them to their own advantage'.

4. The present author was principal investigator of the Irish part of this six-country research project which was funded by the Commission of the European Union within the context of its Environment Programme.

5. Unlike Eder, who has recently begun to emphasise narrative analysis, the present author some years ago embarked on bringing out the cognitive dimension of sociology. See Strydom (for example 1999b) and Delanty (1999a).

6. In the course of a discussion at a conference on his book *The Structural Transformation of the Public Sphere* held in 1989 at the University of North Carolina, Chapel Hill, Habermas gave the following interesting off-the-cuff sketch of 'empirical research...of social movements...[and]...new crystallisations' which may be taken as a rough outline of the methodology presented in a more systematic form and in more detail here:

> First, you go into this analysis with a seemingly abstract frame, mainly an organisational model. This is designed so that you can identify, say, the stage of a certain process of organisational stabilisation. The function and declared purpose of the organisation is now moving away from the participants' orientations, even those orientations on which the participants can, to a certain degree, gain consent. Second, there is an evaluation of the wheeling and dealing, the interactions, particularly the will-formations within this group. I find it telling to look into these mixed up, lively, bodily expressive, elliptic, noisy discussions where some issue is at stake, with a certain analytical tool to see which issues are at stake, which argument is finally brought up, and where it changes and can be abstracted. And how they evaluate it in ethical, moral, practical, and legal terms. This abstraction, I think, is adequate for what we are interested in, for what I would be interested in if I were to study processes of opinion formation. In fact, opinions are going into a communicative process, from which the agents are in a way disowned. From this context, finally,

arise topics and designs, which mean programs and arguments, which mean reasons, that are then translated into communicative processes in which this very collective cannot, in bodily presence, participate at all (Habermas 1992a, 472–73).

7. From this point of view, it does not make sense to oppose micro-discourse analysis and macro-discourse analysis as alternatives between which one has to choose, as does Johnston (1995, 219).

8. See Eder (1992c; 1996, 166) for this distinction.

9. See also Bourdieu (1997) and Eder (1996, 169).

10. Bourdieu (1997, 230) speaks in this case of 'cultural' and 'symbolic capital'. Apparently following Bourdieu, Eder (1996, 169) refers to 'frame capital', although analysis along these lines is not pursued.

11. This is particularly the case in the debate about the relation of the micro- and macro-dimension. On this, see, for example, Knorr-Cetina (1981a; 1981b; 1988), Alexander et al. (1987), Mayntz (1990; 1992), Ritzer (1992, 535–96) and Eder (1993a, 8, 45).

12. Rather than following the traditional mechanistic and causalistic lead, the theoretical and methodological approach appropriate here is perhaps better conceived in terms of the laser metaphor – i.e., 'the splitting of light-waves that are in phase, thus creating both a reference beam and another beam carrying multiperspectivist inform-ation' (Adam 1990, 160) – as being based on holographic or hologrammatic principles.

13. The following arguments were developed at more length in Strydom (1999a, 15–20).

14. See Condor and Antaki (1997) for an overview of the alternative mentalistic and social traditions in cognitivism. Here, needless to say, the emphasis is on socio-cognitivism.

15. The legitimationist position proceeds from the moral criterion of good and bad, evaluates the social actors according to it, and finally identifies with the one it judges to represent the good and hence as being legitimate. See Strydom (1999a, 22).

16. This is the epistemological problem with which feminists, critics adopting a Third World point of view and others are faced today. That it urgently needs to be addressed has been clear for some time. See, for example, Gulbenkian Commission (1996, 88).

17. In developing this concept of critique, I start from the concept of critique put forward by Eder (1988, 319–20; 1993a, 99), following Bourdieu in certain respects, but whereas he conceives of it in opposition to Habermas as a negative procedure that requires no reference to a positive normative standard, I adopt a middle position instead. Both positive and negative reference points for critique can be gained from cultural models, or the objective structural features of social situations, and the practical use that is made of such cultural models in particular situations. Whereas Eder defends a concept of 'social critique', I am proposing a concept of 'socio-cognitive critique'.

Part II: Discourse of Modernity and the Construction of Sociology

6. The Early Modern Problem of Violence

1. On humanism, see also Cassirer et al. (1975), Mandrou (1978) and Eder (1985, 88–89).

2. On the scientific movement, see also Merton (1970), Toulmin and Goodfield (1968), Losee (1972), Needham (1972), Webster (1975), Knowles (1976), Fichant and Pêcheux (1977), Heidegger (1972; 1978, 265–71), Mandrou (1978), Moscovici

Notes

(1982a), Münch (1984), Hill (1988), Merchant (1989), Groh and Groh (1991) and Jacob (1994).

3. See also Poggi (1978), Anderson (1980), Skinner (1978, I, 113–38), Giddens (1987a, 103–16) and Mann (1987, 416–99).

4. Since historians such as Michelet and Burckhart in the mid-nineteenth century stylised the concept of the Renaissance as an ideological weapon of liberalism against the spread of the romantic nostalgia for medieval culture (Hauser 1951, II, 4–5; Koselleck 1985), it has come to be generally regarded as the beginning of modernity, the flowering of modern culture and civilisation. This general view has been criticised on numerous occasions. Hauser (1951, II, 3) has proposed to push the beginning of the modern period back to the end of the twelfth century 'when money economy comes to life again, the new towns arise, and the modern middle class first acquires its distinctive characteristics'. Braudel (1985) of the French *Annales* school of historiography similarly traces the beginning of the modern world back to the emergence of the European world economy. Nisbet (1980, 78–81, 101–03), who regards it as a myth, sees the Renaissance as being preceded by a twelfth-century renaissance and possibly even linked to a continuous process of renaissance since the tenth century. In the meantime, however, all of these points of view have themselves in effect been relativised by the argument, summarised by Nederveen Pieterse (1990, 87–89), that they are all Eurocentric in so far as they understand world history as beginning with the flowering of European history. What needs to be taken into account to circumvent 'European narcissism' (Nederveen Pieterse 1990, 87) is the formative processes of Europe itself, and no sooner is this done than it becomes clear just what a crucial role had been played by the Islamic world and Byzantium as well as by the Ottoman Empire (Delanty 1995a). As regards the Renaissance, what is hailed as the magnificent flowering of European culture and civilisation actually took place on the basis of the ninth- and tenth-century renaissance of Islam and Byzantium, a synthesis of Indian, Persian, Chinese, African, Semitic and Hellenic contributions (Nederveen Pieterse 1990, 89–90, 103–04). While the narcissistic or Eurocentric view of the Renaissance is obviously one that we can no longer afford to perpetuate naively, the question arises as to precisely what the thrust of all these criticisms is. The point, surely, is not and cannot be that the Renaissance as an important event in European history should be ignored and forgotten. It could even less be that there never had been an event such as the Renaissance. What the criticisms seek to achieve is a certain relativisation or decentring of the European or Western view so as to create a more contextually sensitive understanding of world history. This is taken on board here.

5. While the Renaissance or, rather, the humanistic phase of the Renaissance displays certain motifs that could be taken as characteristically modern, it is not quite correct to assume, as is often done (for example Neederven Pieterse 1990, xi), that this first phase was actually the beginning of the modern world. As Hauser (1979, 6–11, 23–43) has convincingly argued, this was accomplished for the first time only in the wake of the crisis of the Renaissance. This occurred in the mid-sixteenth century when the questioning of the validity of the synthetic worldview of the Renaissance centred on human beings and hence on such values as individualism, naturalism, objectivism and rationalism induced reflection on its foundations, with a general cultural crisis consequently taking Europe in its grip for the first time since the dissolution of antiquity. It is the generalisation of this same crisis that allows Mandrou (1978, 284), with reference to Paul Hazard, to speak of 'the crisis of European consciousness' that persisted all through the sixteenth and seventeenth centuries. Rather than Europe, of course, it was more correctly a matter of Christendom in the process of traumatically being transformed into Europe (Delanty 1995a, 66–69). While its cultural dimension is of crucial importance in the present context, this crisis also had economic, political and

social connotations. Not only did the humanistic worldview, which was itself tied to the collapse of the cosmology of the previous period, start to waver, but economic, political and social relations were all in disarray (Aston 1980; Rabb 1975; Merchant 1989, 192).

6. As regards the period relevant to this book, this increase in the population of Europe would continue to 103 million in 1650, 144 million in 1750 and 187 million in 1800, according to figures cited by Braudel (1985, I, 42).

7. The development of economic structures is based on the general yet weak positive probability that knowledge of innovations that reduce toil and increase productivity will not only be preserved but under certain conditions also be enhanced (Wright 1989, 94–96). It involves cognitive learning processes (Moscovici 1982a; Eder 1988, 329–45) that run, not without failures and regressions, from everyday routines through systematised knowledge to theoretical reflections. The effect of these learning processes can be found in the increased complexity of the experience of reality, the hastened tempo of learning, the extent of knowledge, and the differentiation of inventive practices (for example hunting-gathering, agriculture/crafts, engineering, science). Concomitantly, economic structures have slowly developed over thousands of years. At the time of the transition from feudalism to modernity, the state of the art was indicated by such phenomena as the increasing importance of technical engineering knowledge, its linking with new experimental finance and merchant capitalist practices, the emergence of the commodity market, the stimulation of free competition and information exchange (Habermas 1989a, 14–26). Initially, this was concentrated in the Mediterranean area, but a shift occurred both northwards and westwards (Braudel 1985, III, 89–385), with the result that England became the heart of the world economy (Braudel 1985, III, 353–56). From the late fifteenth to the eighteenth century, economic development here took the form of the transformation of subsistence into commercial farming oriented towards the export of wool to manufacturers on the Continent. In this context we encounter the 'enclosure movement'. At the same time, both England's trade radius and her commercial fleet expanded, gradually taking the place previously occupied by the Portuguese, the Spaniards and the Dutch. In this context we encounter the phenomenon of 'primitive accumulation' in its wider reaches, such as overseas exploration and expansion, conquest, imperialism and colonialism.

8. For a general discussion, see, for example, Nederveen Pieterse (1990). On slavery, see Wirz (1984).

9. The development of political structures is based on the general, quite strong probability that human beings form figurations in the sense of defence-and-attack or survival units that give reality to their interdependence and increase their ability to use and control power and violence more effectively for the purposes of preventing their subjugation or annihilation (Elias 1978, 72–76, 138–39; 1982). Although the development of such survival units, both internally and externally, could involve relationships totally unregulated by norms, for example, Elias' (1978, 75–80) so-called 'primal contest', it most typically does implicate normative or moral learning processes (Habermas 1979, 95–129; Eder 1988, 352–70). These processes run, not excluding failures and regressions, from everyday rules of interaction through systematised legal norms to ethical principles. The effect of these learning processes can be found in the degree of complexity of the social environment, the tempo of moral learning, and the extent and relevance of moral representations in social life. Parallel to moral learning processes, political structures have slowly developed over an extended period from kinship or tribal survival units through state defence-and-attack units of various kinds to the modern form of the nation-state, which itself may (Jessop 1994, 264, 269–75; Peck and Tickell 1995, 297–307) or may not (Giddens 1987a, 291) be in decline today. At the time of the transition from feudalism to modernity, the level of the development of political structures was indicated by such phenomena as the intensification of

competition between central rulers, the centralisation of military, financial and administrative power, and the emergence of the absolutist or near-absolutist state as the early political form of modernity (Elias 1982; Giddens 1987a; Eder 1988, 206; Eisenstadt 1991, 29).

10. See also Tilly (1975) and Mann (1987, 416–99).

11. This typology is useful, but if the historical dimension is added to it an awareness of the variability of specific cases can be retained. For example, during the phases dominated by the Tudors (1485–1603) and Stuarts (1603–1649), England had been quite close to absolutism.

12. See, for example, Parsons (1977a, 141–45), Mandrou (1978, 133–37, 165–68), Koselleck (1985; 1988, 41–50), and Williams (1988, 29).

13. See also Williams (1988, 29, 31) and Giddens (1987a, 86).

14. A significant presupposition of this development, as will become clear later, was the establishment of the rights frame in the critical period between 1572 and the 1640s in the early modern discourse.

15. See also Skinner (1978, I, 118–38), Williams (1988, 192), and Nederveen Pieterse (1990, 195–206).

16. Rabb (1975, 19) provides an illuminating clarification of the background against which the recent interest in military matters and war (for example Mann 1987; Giddens 1987a; Joas and Steiner 1989) arose: in response to problems raised by Hobsbawm and Trevor-Roper's thesis of the 'general crisis' of the seventeenth century, some continued with research into economic and demographic slowdown while others, such as Michael Roberts, sought to shed light on the subject by inquiring into the early modern 'military revolution'.

17. See also Mann (1987, 484–86).

18. See also the critique of Honneth and Joas (1988, 119–29).

19. On printing, reading and writing, see, for example, Eisenstein (1980; 1993) and Furet and Ozouf (1982).

20. In the case of the Jews, other considerations such as religion, ethnic purity (*limpieza de sangre*) and national unity undeniably also played a part, but it was in particular their central position in the finance and economic sector and especially in the sensitive area of culture that led to the decisive renewal of the pogrom in Spain in 1391 (Geiss 1988, 116–21). Parker (1990, 297–99) leads the European witch-craze of 1580–1640 back to a superstitious movement in popular culture that had been eradicated by the ruling elite through the introduction of the written culture, but important here is precisely the exclusion of knowledge carried by women, for example knowledge of medicinal plants, by this very monopolisation of culture.

21. By no means only women had been accused of witchcraft, but according to Parker (1990, 299) 75 per cent of all those accused were women.

22. As long ago as 1928, Mannheim (1993, 412), writing as follows, recognised science as a state-monopolised form of knowledge: 'The Church was met by a formidable opponent in the rise of the absolutist state, which also sought to monopolise the means of education in order to dispense the official interpretation of reality; this time, however, the chief educational instrument was to be science'.

23. Mandrou's (1978, 21–27) appreciation of the insecurity of early modern intellectuals and the oppression they suffered contrasts sharply with Parker's (1990, 320) emphasis on the unity of the European intellectual community and the freedom of movement of its seventeenth-century representatives.

24. See also Benjamin (1978, 248).

25. This is the background against which Foucault's (1970; 1972) interpretation of the human and social sciences as a new conceptual means belonging to a new disciplinary order must be understood. That this is a one-sided view that cannot simply

be applied to sociology becomes clear as soon as one appreciates that it did not derive exclusively from forms of knowledge monopolised by the state. This is a topic of the following chapter.

26. Drawing on German Baroque literature, Benjamin (1978, 236) mentions examples such as 'Großtanz' and 'Großgedicht'.

27. See also Luhmann (1980, 72–161; 1986b, 76–83).

28. Eder (1988, 207) speaks of an 'evolutionary experiment'.

29. Habermas' (1989a, 5–12) account of 'representative publicness' clarifies the relation involved here: the monarch 'is' the state, and hence he represents it not on behalf of but in front of the eyes of the people, displaying himself in his personal, concrete existence as the embodiment of some sort of higher power.

30. For a critique, however, see Habermas (1987b, 238–326).

31. This analysis also applies well to the typical public ceremony of the burning of a heretic known as *auto da fé* staged by the Spanish Inquisition.

32. For an overview of the major events, see Table 7.1. The question of precisely how the Protestant Reformation of the sixteenth century is to be interpreted has for long been a matter of conflict among social scientists. For example, the Parsonian Bellah (1973, 289–94) offers a positive interpretation of the Reformation as a progressive evolutionary stage in its own right. As against him, the Habermasian Döbert (1973, 311) draws attention to what he conceives as the regressive features of the Reformation. Although not in evolutionary theoretic terms, Weber (1976) originally provided the positive starting point from which Bellah departs, yet one of the leading Weberians of our time, Schluchter (1981, 156), not uninfluenced by Habermas and Döbert, takes issue with the master by presenting the significance of the Reformation as being highly ambivalent. Despite these conflicting interpretations, there is nevertheless general agreement among sociologists that the Reformation was one of a small number of momentous historical events possessing a varied yet constitutive significance for modern society. That it provided one of the most fecund contexts of violence in the early modern period is beyond dispute.

33. See, for example, Mandrou (1978, 100–17, 171–83), Anderson (1980), Labrousse (1983, 1–10), Mann (1986, 463–68), Koselleck (1988, 15–22), and Williams (1988). It should be borne in mind, of course, that while the Catholics and Protestants engaged in mutual conflict, they nevertheless represented a united front in the contemporaneous struggles of Europe against non-Christians (for example Elton 1985, 242–43; Elliot 1985, 175–200; Parker 1990, 76–94; Delanty 1995a, 48–64, 84–99).

34. While various tensions in Europe played a part in bringing about and sustaining the Thirty Years War, it was in an important sense the last attempt of Catholic Europe to stamp out the Reformation.

35. Rabb's (1975, 117–18) explanation of 'the fundamental shift from turbulence to calm' in the wake of this war is interesting yet inadequate in so far as he ascribes it to the aristocracy.

36. See, for example, Elliott's (1985, 107–15) discussion of the question 'Wars of religion?' His conclusion is that whether a given conflict counts as a war of religion depends to some extent on whose war is under consideration. Mann (1986, 467), speaking of 'religious-political wars', also stresses the dual nature of these conflicts.

37. On the Thirty Years War, see, for example, Elton (1985), Elliott (1985), and Parker (1990).

38. What should be borne in mind, of course, is that the characteristic violence-saturated abuse of power of the early modern state was in time confronted by an oppositional force that itself owed something to the dynamics within and between the conflicting religious communities. This theme will be taken up in the next chapter.

39. The frontispiece of the first edition of Thomas Hobbes' *Leviathan*, published in

1651 in London, carries a picture of a sovereign monarch, ruling over his realm with sword and staff in hand, whose body is composed of the bodies of his subjects.

40. For an extended contextualist history of the idea, see Tuck (1993, 36–119).

41. Francesco Guicciardini, whose language strongly influenced late sixteenth-century theorists, in the 1520s spoke of *la ragione ed uso degli stati*, translated by Tuck (1993, 39) as 'the reason and custom of states'.

42. See also Eder (1988, 100, 207–08).

43. Weber introduced the concept in the economic context but also applied it in such areas as bureaucracy and particularly law. For a critique and development beyond Weber, see Habermas (1984, 243–71).

44. In this respect, Habermas (1987a, 358) writes: '...public law authorises a sovereign state power with a monopoly on coercive force as the sole source of legal authority. The sovereign is absolved from orientation toward any particular policies or from specific state objectives and becomes defined instrumentally, that is, only in relation to the means for the legal exercise of bureaucratically organised domination. The means of effectively allocating power become the only goal.' Maravall (1986, 63) points out that for Machiavellians and Tacitists, both of whom made a strong impact on Baroque culture, it was not a matter of 'the virtue of doing something good' but rather of 'the art of doing something well'.

7. The Rights Discourse

1. A well-known historian has the following to say about the sack of Rome of 1527: 'the veterans stormed the city and sacked it amid such scenes of violence, murder, rape, looting and destruction that the *Sacco di Roma* has remained in the European memory even after many still more frightful events' (Elton 1985, 83).

2. See Tuck (1993, 45–64; 39–45) on Montaigne and Lipsius and on the new late sixteenth-century breed of austere humanism based on the classical Tacitus and the humanists' relation to Machiavelli. See also Maravall (1986).

3. It is noteworthy that Foucault (1970) locates the epistemic mutation leading from Renaissance correspondence to the classical modern system of representation in the literary masterpiece of Cervantes. See also Fink-Eitel (1989, 40) and Merquior (1991, 45).

4. On mannerist art and its significance, see Hauser (1951, II, 97–105; 1979). On Brueghel, in addition to Hauser, see Deinhard (1970), Stechow (1990), Roberts (1992) and Gibson (1993).

5. To this intra-state aspect could be added the destruction of the constitutional order within states, as foreseen by Justus Lipsius at the end of the sixteenth century in the light of the emergence of the Tacitist vision and the new culture of *raison d'État* (Tuck, 1993, 65). On Tacitism, see also Maravall (1986).

6. While renowned theorists such as Hobbes, Weber, Elias and Koselleck proceeded from the assumption of the centrality of violence in the early modern period and the need for its resolution, further confirmation is provided by more recent authors such as the historians Neff (1960, 68–82), Rabb (1975) and Maravall (1986) as well as the sociologist Willke (1992, 216–39). Needless to say, registering this does not necessarily entail agreement with the respective interpretations of these authors.

7. Rabb (1975, 33–34) proposes conceiving of the early modern crisis as a crisis of 'the location of authority'. While this is formally correct, it is too abstract, even from a sociological point of view. The discourse accompanying this crisis at a certain level indeed dealt with 'authority' or, rather, 'sovereignty', yet at its deepest level, as we will see later, it was concerned with rights. The present proposal to locate it within the context of the rights discourse, which is organised by the rights frame, allows one to

conceptualise it in a more historically specific yet comparatively meaningful way. The rights discourse itself had its starting point in the problem of violence.

8. Primary concepts such as sovereignty and particularly rights were of course supported by concerns with truth, reliability and order associated with the philosophical revolution of the seventeenth century and the institutionalisation of science. Toulmin (1992) focuses on the latter concerns.

9. Tuck (1993, 65) writes: '...by the 1590's, Europe *as a whole* could now be seen as a society broken by civil war between nations...' Similarly, Maravall (1986, 20–21) argues that during this period individuals acquired the modern competence to perceive and articulate the wider reaches of social reality.

10. The essential historical information on the different phases is provided, for example, by Elton (1985) and Elliott (1985).

11. On the period from 1598 to 1648, including the Edict of Nantes, the so-called Twelve Years Truce (1609–21), and armed neutral Europe (1598–1618), see, for example, Parker (1990).

12. On the Thirty Years War, see, for example, Parker (1990).

13. On the English revolutionary period, see, for example, Hill (1969; 1988; 1992).

14. On seventeenth-century science, see, for example, Webster (1975) and Van den Daele (1977).

15. Of this Koselleck (1988, 15) says: 'It was from Absolutism that the Enlightenment evolved – initially as its inner consequence, later as its dialectical counterpart and antagonist, destined to lead the Absolutist State to its demise.'

16. According to Koselleck (1988, 64–65):

an outright object and victim of Absolutist policies: the 400,000 *émigrés* whom the revocation of the Edict of Nantes in 1685 had forced to leave France and pour into Northern and North-Eastern Europe. Eighty thousand of them went to England, where they sided with the Whigs and became ardent defenders of the parliamentary constitution. In the Rain-Bow Coffee-House, a Masonic rendezvous in London, they founded an information centre; from there, via Holland (the intellectual trading post of those days), they flooded all of Absolutist Europe with propaganda in support of the English spirit, English philosophy and, above all, the English Constitution. Desmaizeaux, the biographer of Pierre Bayle, Pierre Daude, and Locke's friend Le Clerc belonged to this particularly active group.

17. More than twenty years ago, the South African sociologist Dian Joubert (for example 1972) developed a path-breaking 'sociology of flash-points' (*brandpunte*) concentrating on discourse moments in the sense of symbolically charged or dramatic historical events that increase communication. His particular interest was in liminal moments in which values were exposed and graphically articulated.

18. Marshall McLuhan's (1971) older work on 'the making of typographic man' is still of interest. See also Eisenstein (1980; 1993), Zaret (1992) and Furet and Ozouf (1982) on printing and literacy in the early modern period. For a contemporary reconsideration of typography in the context of the electronic media, consult Giesecke (1992).

19. Accounts of these formal institutional forums are to be found in, for example, Elton (1985), Elliott (1985) and Parker (1990).

20. One aspect of much interest in Labrousse's account is the complex relationship between Bayle as a leading theorist and spokesman and the *Refuge* as a public.

21. See, for example, Mandrou (1978, 252, 256), Saage (1981), Elton (1985, 255), Elliott (1985, 223, 290, 294), Parker (1990, 138, 143, 159, 198, 303), Hill (1992), and Zaret (1992).

22. Grotius was by far the most important of these authors in that he not only formulated the first mature modern rights theory but also laid the foundation for both

seventeenth- and eighteenth-century political theories. Although his rights theory was predominantly absolutist, it proved to be ambivalent enough to have been fruitfully taken up also by a whole range of radical rights theorists, such as the seventeenth-century English radical pamphleteers. See Tuck (1979, 58–81; 1993, 154–201). Materials by various of these authors are contained in Englander et al. (1993).

23. See also Skinner (1978, II) and Mandrou (1978).

24. Retrospectively, this has become known as the tradition of 'liberal constitutionalism'.

25. In this subsection an attempt is made to create the presuppositions for a reinterpretation of the widely accepted distinction between state and society from a constructivist point of view. This is the first necessary step towards recognising sociology in the early modern period.

26. In his famous paper on competition as a cultural phenomenon first read at the Sixth German Sociological Conference in 1928, Mannheim (1982; 1993, 399–437, particularly 419) made some incisive remarks on this theoretical problem. The enlightening discussion that followed the original paper is contained in Meja and Stehr (1982, 371–401). For a contemporary statement of the logic of separation and coordination accompanying social conflict, see, for example, Miller (1986; 1992) and Eder (1993a, 191). From the point of view of historiographical practice, see the interesting statement by Pocock (1985a, 1–34).

27. A comparative perspective on the societal semantics of three distinct historical periods is illuminating:

16th–18th century	late 18th–20th century	late 20th century
violence	poverty	risk
state	economy	ecology
order	growth	sustainability
constitution	the social	nature
rights	justice	responsibility
law	money	knowledge

28. This is of course the basic societal issue at the root of sociology that Parsons (1977b, 69–70) sought to capture under the title of 'the Hobbesian problem of order'. That it is a more complex matter than intimated by this title, however, becomes apparent when one adopts a constructivist view which gives recognition to all the major collective agents who had been involved in its identification, definition and resolution.

29. On Tacitism as a realistic etatist ideology which harks back to Tacitus and stresses a well-organised state, *raison d'État*, *arcana imperii*, arms, money, severe discipline, and the overriding of ethical, moral and legal norms, including all constitutional niceties, see Tuck (1993, 39–119) and Maravall (1986, 63, 90, 100, 217–18).

30. For example, the late sixteenth- and early seventeenth-century Calvinists, Jesuits and constitutionalists (for example Althusius), and Locke in the late seventeenth century.

31. For example, the republicans as anti-statist, and the Levellers and other extreme radical groups and movements as fundamentalist.

32. It is customary to interpret the early modern period in terms of the priority of the political (in the narrower sense of the state), the projection and triumph of a political vision of social life that subordinated the social dimension to political categories. It is this view, which is strengthened by the fact that absolutism spectacularly succeeded in the mid-seventeenth century, that in the past led historians of the social sciences, sociology in particular, to deny the relevance of going back behind the nineteenth

century. From a constructivist point of view, by contrast, it is clear that the question of society already posed itself in a differentiated way in the early modern period. It certainly was not in the form of the issue of the survival of society in its social environment as in the nineteenth century, but why should it be excluded in the more subtle form of the issue of the survival of society in its political environment? Manicas (1988, 27–28, 32) refreshingly regards the early modern period as having witnessed society as 'a dominant background assumption' and even 'the emergence of society as a framing notion', as 'a framing concept for the new kind of political order'.

33. Giddens takes on board the notion of the 'discourse of sovereignty', with an unspecific reference to Hill (1988). He conceives of it as being associated with the organs of government, either the monarch or the bureaucratic state. The shift to popular sovereignty is not envisaged. This may be accounted for by the fact that he adopts a theoretical and methodological approach that seems to preclude an appropriate analysis of the phenomenon. He avoids facing the problem of culture in sociology. Sociology indeed needs to be defended today, yet this does not require the rejection of a culturally sensitive approach.

34. Tuck (1979, 6–7), for example, argues that 'active rights are paradigmatic' and that 'to attribute rights to someone *is* to attribute some kind of liberty…[or]…sovereignty…to them'. Rights in the sense of active rather than passive rights are on a par with sovereignty. On a similar assumption, Habermas (1989b, 21) criticises liberals and communitarians, both of whom see, but of course from contrary points of view, popular sovereignty and human rights as competing with one another. According to him: 'Human rights do not compete with popular sovereignty; they are identical with the constitutive conditions of a self-limiting praxis of public-discursive will-formation' (my translation). See also Habermas (1996, 84, 100, 127).

35. On rights theory in the early modern period, see Skinner (1978, II) and Tuck (1979).

36. An author who persuasively advanced the conceptual strategy of sovereignty is the Nazi political theorist Carl Schmitt (1970). Even Walter Benjamin's (1978, 245) analysis of the background of the Baroque tragic drama attests to his immense impact. For a critical analysis of Schmitt's legacy, see Habermas (1997, 105–17; 1998, 134–38, 193–201).

37. Rabb's interesting attempt to make sense of the literature on 'the crisis of the seventeenth century' by developing a synthetic view on the crucial transformation from turmoil to relative tranquillity between 1500 and 1700 came to my attention only after I had substantially finished writing the present book. I was surprised by the degree to which it historically supports the proposed analysis. Whereas Rabb approaches 'the great shift' from a historical angle, the analysis in this book is guided by a theoretical point of view, i.e. a cognitivist communication theory of society entailing a concept of discourse possessing a two-phase structure. The correspondence is encouraging, but Rabb encounters certain difficulties. While undeveloped communication theoretical assumptions are apparent in his work, he lacks not only a theory of discourse but, still more crucially, also a theory of cognitive structures. The latter would have allowed him to develop a clearer understanding of the 'structure' that became established in the late sixteenth and early seventeenth century, while the former makes it possible to adopt a still wider view – admittedly a difficult thing for a historian to do – which includes also the eighteenth century. This is what the notion of the rights discourse has been designed to achieve. What is interesting is that Rabb's conception of a development through phases separated by a turning point is derived from the concept of 'crisis' in its medical sense: an illness, a decisive moment occurs, and a resolution is achieved. See also Habermas' (1976, 1–8) discussion of a social scientific concept of crisis.

Notes

38. Hauser (1951, II, 106) circumscribes it as follows: 'Mannerism is the artistic expression of the crisis which convulses the whole of Western Europe in the sixteenth century and which extends to all fields of political, economic, and cultural life'.

39. Since most historians work with shorter rather than longer time periods, they tend to identify the resolution of the general crisis of the seventeenth century with the political stabilisation that had set in during the latter part of the century. This is clearly the case in Rabb's (1975, 63–73, 117–18) account. This raises the problem of seeing the absolutist state or, more generally, the *ancien régime*, as part of the solution. A broader view that includes the American War of Independence and the French Revolution suggests, by contrast, that the state was actually, although not fully, part of the problem. Historians like Rabb are given to interpretations that are too concretistic. The new structure of the seventeenth century that brought stability was not the state as such but more broadly and more profoundly a new cultural cognitive structure, here called the rights frame. It for the first time made possible the formation of new identities as well as mobilisation and action. This conceptualisation allows the recognition of a variety of different agents and, hence, the overcoming of the unhistorical explanation that bureaucracies and aristocracies alone were responsible for the 'luxury' of a new framework (Rabb 1975, 63, 117–18).

40. Tuck covers exactly this period in his book, *Philosophy and Government 1572–1651* (1993), which in turn is a much more detailed coverage of the same material presented in an earlier book (1979). The period is characterised, in his view, by the emergence of a new culture of scepticism, Stoicism and *raison d'État*, on the one hand, and resistance to this development on the basis of constitutionalism, on the other.

41. The book in question here is his famous *Six Books of the Commonwealth*. For his argument about sovereignty, see Bodin (1993), and for a contextual review, see Skinner (1978, II, 284–301).

42. In the Habermasian tradition, this problem is dealt with in terms of the transition to a post-traditional morality. See, for example, Eder (1985, 67–86) for a meticulous analysis. Habermas (1988) speaks of a 'post-metaphysical' position.

43. Tuck (1979, 177) identifies 'two great *floruits* of rights theories: the first *c.* 1350–1450, the second *c.* 1590–1670'. The more important second one forms the historical basis of the argument developed here.

44. See, however, Pocock's (1985a, 218–30) and Dunne's (1985) interpretations of Locke.

45. The Calvinist constitutionalists, emphasising as they did pacts between kings and people, were less inclined to conceive of rights as preceding natural principles than as civil principles (Tuck 1979, 40, 42). In the context of the English Civil War, however, they were defended as 'inalienable rights' on the basis of the modern theory of right developed by Grotius (Tuck 1979, 143, 147–49).

46. It is of course the case that Henry of Navarre, then King Henry IV of France, was assassinated in 1610, and that although the details were never clarified, as in the case of John F. Kennedy, some believe that Catholic forces were behind it. For an interesting account, see Toulmin (1992, 45–56).

47. On these authors, see Skinner (1978, II, 310, 340, 345).

48. In his provocative historical analysis of the discontinuity marked by the crisis of the seventeenth century, Rabb (1975) speaks of 'a new framework' (62) or 'structure' (64, 72, 77) that became established which brought stability to the early modern period. He thinks of it as 'the location of authority' (33) and associates it with the 'decline of religion' and the ascendancy of 'politics' (64) and more specifically the 'state' (72). In fact, he regards the modern state as representing the conclusive establishment of the new structure that brought stability with it. That he is dissatisfied with this all too concretistic position, however, is indicated by his repeated assertion that this structure

was not something real, some definable objective circumstance, but rather a matter of 'perception' (79, 116–17). What he obviously lacks is a cognitive concept of structure or frame. Fragments of such a frame are actually to be found in his account, for example: 'a willingness to stop pressing dissensions to their logical conclusion' (72), the belief that 'the world was harmonious and sensible' (114) and that 'human beings were marvellously capable, endowed with orderly Reason that could solve all problems' (114).

49. An interesting example of the conceptual analysis of a frame is to be found in Capek's (1993) work on the 'environmental justice frame', but it is not yet sufficiently thought through. It certainly makes sense to see 'the residents' ability to mobilise for social change [as being] linked to their adoption of... [a]...frame', but it is misleading to identify a frame – i.e., a structure – directly with claims-making activity.

50. To fill it out substantively, I draw on Habermas' (1996, 82–193) work on law and the constitutional state.

51. As regards a further analysis of the rights – or, for that matter, any other – frame in the sense of a set of rules constituting the cognitive order, which cannot be undertaken in the present context, the work of the Uppsala school (for example Burns 1986; Burns and Flam 1990) on social rule system theory could be useful.

52. 'Liberalism' as a designation of an ideological current was first coined in 1820 with reference to the so-called *Liberales* in the Spanish Cortes (Bramsted and Melhuish 1978, 3).

53. Bellamy (1992, 1–4) refers rather narrowly to the early modern variety as 'ethical liberalism', whereas what is really at issue, in addition to the ethical, is its moral-legal dimension.

54. Habermas (1996, 125–26) speaks of 'the general right to equal liberties...[or]... individual liberties'.

55. For example: Habermas (1974a, 67; 1996, 90), Manicas (1988, 28) and Touraine (1995, 258).

56. It should be borne in mind that the scientific revolution proper occurred only in the late eighteenth and nineteenth centuries, with the implication that seventeenth-century science should not be overburdened with an anachronistic interpretation. See, for example, Toulmin and Goodfield (1968, 152, 208, 225, 269) and Moscovici (1982a, 325–433).

57. This is the dimension captured by Toulmin (1992) by means of the concept of 'the scaffold of modernity'. Since he neglects the normative and aesthetic or conative dimensions, with the result that he remains close to the traditional conception, despite his appeal to humanism, it is necessary to complement his analysis by the addition of what is here called the rights frame. Only then can the cognitive order of early modernity be understood adequately.

58. The widespread yet misleading voluntarist view of the institutionalisation of science, according to which a handful of scientists had coalesced around a new and firm approach to knowledge and thus decisively triumphed, must be resisted. As argued earlier, the truth is rather that science was institutionalised in both England and France by absolutist fiat (Van den Daele 1977; Mandrou 1978, 213–27, 265–83), and that it was therefore from the outset a 'state-monopolised form of thought' (Mannheim 1993, 412). See also Merchant (1989).

59. The case of Germany, where a reading revolution occurred and a patriotic identity was constructed, is a very interesting one, too. Giesen and Junge (1991) and Eisenstadt and Giesen (1995) have subjected it to a penetrating analysis – although one might not fully agree with their Popperian theoretical foundations.

60. That is, authors such as Beza and Du Plessis-Mornay who adopted a radical theory of popular sovereignty and, indeed, regarded the tyrannicide of a legal monarch as justified (Skinner 1978, II, 339).

Notes

61. On the eighteenth-century debate, the American Revolution and republican tradition, see Pocock (1975, especially 462–505). There is some disagreement about whether the American War of Independence, also called the 'American Revolution', represents a revolution in the same sense as the French event. As against Hannah Arendt (1984), Habermas (1973, 365–70; 1974a, 82–120; 1989b, 10) argues that, strictly speaking, it was not a revolution. Essentially, in contrast with the Americans and related Europeans such as the Englishman Thomas Paine who, despite appearances, developed a liberal understanding of their political activity and remained attached to the classical tradition of natural law, the French made a transition to modern rationalist natural law which allowed a revolutionary self-understanding. Rather than continuing an old tradition, rather than affirming age-old rights, they laid claim to the principles of modern rationalist natural law and undertook to realise them in the form of a constitution that founds and organises a completely new society and its government or state; rather than letting a revolution result from the events, the French protagonists consciously made a revolution. Taylor (1990, 111) also points out that the American decision to rebel was taken by political authorities in terms of the early modern right to resist a tyrant ruler.

62. On George III, see Hibbert (1998).

63. It is this reference to the early modern theory of resistance and popular sovereignty that leads Habermas to maintain that the American War of Independence does not qualify as a revolution in the proper sense of the word.

64. On the French Revolution and Enlightenment, see, for example, Hufton (1985), Rudé (1988), Williams (1988, 157–242), Furet (1981; 1992), Fehér (1987), and Baker (1987). Authors dealing specifically with the Enlightenment include Cassirer (1951), Gay (1967; 1969), Porter and Teich (1981), Hampson (1984), Eder (1985), and Koselleck (1988).

65. Due to the world historical impact of the French Revolution, it is a singular and virtually incomparable historical event. It is the paradigmatic revolution, the one that imbues the modern idea of revolution with its very meaning (Touraine 1994, 121–23), in that it was a struggle against an old order by a popular sovereign force seeking to emancipate itself from the traditional fetters of power and domination. It is not surprising, therefore, that such historical events as the Renaissance, the Reformation, the achievements of the scientific movement, the Dutch, English and American revolutions and later the industrial revolution became more generally understood as revolutions only in relation to the French Revolution, either in the run up to it (Groh and Groh 1991, 76) or in its wake (Braudel 1985, III, 537). This understanding, which developed slowly between the mid-eighteenth and the mid-nineteenth centuries, found explicit expression for the first time only in the writings of Adolphe Blanqui and Friedrich Engels. It is the characteristic nineteenth-century idea of revolution informing all these events, paradigmatically expressed by the French Revolution, that resides at the core of the dominant Western understanding of modernisation as a process driven by reason and as eventuating in a universal modernity. The connection between revolution, on the one hand, and reason, modernisation and universalism, on the other, explains why questions are today asked about the French Revolution (Habermas 1989b, 8–16; Touraine 1994, 121–22). By the time of its bicentenary, a controversy has erupted about whether the French Revolution has come to an end, whether it has lost its actuality, its ability to influence and orient action in the present (Furet 1981; 1992; Habermas 1989b), and even whether we should not speak of a number of revolutions rather than of a single homogeneous one (Fehér 1987). While this controversy is pregnant with implications for the current period and its interpretation, it does not call into doubt the significance that this historical event had for the constitution of modern society. More importantly in the present context, however, is that it underlines the need

not to impose nineteenth- and twentieth-century concepts on the interpretation of the early modern period, particularly the eighteenth century up to the end of the first phase of the French Revolution, i.e. 1793.

66. On Turgot, see Manuel and Manuel (1979, 461–86) and Furet (1992, 21–26), and on Necker see Furet (1992, 35–41).

67. To the extent that the establishment of classical liberal rights made possible the institutionalisation and efflorescence of the capitalist market economy, the late eighteenth and particularly the nineteenth century were compelled to confront the negative consequences and side-effects of capitalism in the new form of proletarianisation, immiserisation and poverty.

68. For advanced recent analyses, see Habermas (1996) and Held (1996).

69. See Habermas (1987b, 286–91), Honneth and Joas (1988, 129–50), and Dreyfus and Rabinow (1982, 200–01).

70. Compare Habermas' (1996, 359–87) concept of a 'constitutionally regulated power circuit'.

71. See, for example, Habermas (1984, 267–70) and Eder (1988, 100).

72. For an overview, see Held (1980, 148–74). For a comparison of Foucault with Adorno, see Honneth (1991).

73. It is crucial to note that this concept refers not merely to conventional institutional politics but at the same time also to what has come to be called 'identity politics' (for example Du Preez 1980; Cohen and Arato 1992, 526, 548–55). Over and above conflicting political perspectives, it is necessary to bring into purview the generation and interrelation of contradictory and potentially conflicting perspectives at the deeper and more pervasive level of the process of the cultural and social construction of reality. It is in this latter sense that Eder's (1993a, 194) concept of 'a culture of contradictions' should be understood.

74. This position is developed from different points of view by, for example, Koselleck (1988), Eley (1992), Fraser (1992), Eder (1993a, 191–92, 194), and Touraine (1995). This question, which provides the guideline for the interpretation of Enlightenment sociology, is taken up again in the last section of Chapter 9 and in the Conclusion.

8. Contributions to Enlightenment Sociology

1. The reconstitution of the cognitive order was accompanied by a change in historical consciousness. Following Heller (1982, 16–19), the form of historical consciousness corresponding to the rights discourse can be said to have exhibited the following features: (i) an awareness of a new beginning in history and (ii) an awareness of generality (i.e. human nature) embodied in particularity (i.e. a historically specific socio-political-legal arrangement). These features entailed a consciousness about history that allowed: the construction of the past as history rather than myth; the understanding of history through re-imagining it; the identification of a plurality of histories each of which at some point collapsed or terminated; the treatment of the past as a source of knowledge; and the comparison of different histories, including that of contemporary civilisation, in terms of their common regularities, patterns or stages (not to be confused with the universal-historical stages of the late eighteenth and nineteenth century). On the one hand, these assumptions made possible the emergence of the social sciences, including sociology. On the other hand, the implied distinction between nature and culture and the concurrent perception of human nature as contradictory led to the emphasis on human freedom and reason.

2. See also Habermas (1974a, 49–50, 56) and Skinner (1978, I, 246–47).

3. See also Pelczynski (1984) and Cohen and Arato (1992).

4. The word 'democracy' was not widely used in the eighteenth century but gained

currency only in the following century. For a general account, see Held (1996); for America and Britain, see Williams (1979, 82–87); for France, see Touraine (1995).

5. On dealing with uncertainty, see Evers and Nowotny (1987), and on a sociological theory of learning, see Nowotny and Schmutzer (1974), Eder (1985) and Miller (1986).

6. See also Horkheimer (1972, 95), and especially Manuel and Manuel (1979).

7. On Hobbes, see Windelband (1958, II, 412–13, 431–36), Randall (1962, 532–59), Koselleck (1988, 23–40), Habermas (1974a, 56–76), Merchant (1989, 206–15) and Sommerville (1992).

8. This approach is rooted in his theory of motion and his concept of man and state as machines. For a collection of relevant writings in addition to *Leviathan*, see Hobbes (1967).

9. See Habermas (1974a, 67; 1996, 90), who suggests that Hobbes is the real founder of liberalism. See also Touraine (1995, 258). Manicas (1988, 28) speaks of 'Hobbes, that recalcitrant liberal'. Sommerville's (1992, 103) objection that the image of Hobbes as a liberal in the sense of being an advocate of the minimalist state is only partially correct does not apply to Habermas, since the latter's argument goes still further.

10. On Vico, see Apel (1955; 1963), Windelband (1958, II, 526–28), Randall (1962, 943–44, 955–60), Fisch (1970), Fisch and Bergin (1970), Habermas (1974a, 41–81) and Berlin (1979a; 1979b).

11. On hermeneutics, see Apel (1955, 153–56; 1963, 336), Palmer (1969), and Outhwaite (1995).

12. See also Habermas (1974a, 73–76).

13. Representatives of the late Enlightenment such as Mercier, Turgot, Condorcet and Kant are discussed by Manuel and Manuel (1979, 453–531).

14. This is an interesting proposal, but while Randall wrote at the time of the revival of neo-evolutionism represented by such authors as Parsons, Habermas and Luhmann, today we are no longer able to understand evolution in the universal historical, developmental-logical terms of these authors, nor did Vico do so. For contemporary sociological views of evolution, see Eder (1988; 1992d) and Strydom (1992a; 1993) as well as Dietz et al. (1990).

15. There is a tendency going back to the nineteenth century to interpret this contribution of Vico's in terms of the philosophy of history, yet it should be resisted. The Vichian programme was, by contrast, a consistently constructivist one. Vico understood history, moreover, as a cyclical process.

16. See, for example, Windelband (1958, II, 437–528), Randall (1962, 803–06, 921–83), Gay (1969, 167–215, 319–95), Seidman (1983, 21–41) and Jauss (1990a, 31–51).

17. On this, however, see Bierstedt (1978, 24), who points out that Montesquieu did know about Vico and his work, had discussions about it in Venice, might even have met Vico there, and might have owned a copy of his book.

18. On Montesquieu, see Randall (1962, 946–55), Gay (1969, 323–32), Berlin (1979a, 130–61), Aron (1979, 17–62), Szacki (1979, 59–61) and Shklar (1987).

19. Aron, who refuses to be misled by the usual positivist interpretation of Montesquieu, which has been given wide currency by Durkheim (1960; 1997), insists on natural law as an inherent component of Montesquieu's position. This is acceptable as long as it is recognised at the same time that Montesquieu was also in the process of transforming natural law. On the relation between sociology and natural law, see the older yet still highly readable essay by Philip Selznick (1961) as well as Habermas (1974a) and Stein (1980). Considering this transformation, Seidman's (1983, 8–9) proposal to divide the Enlightenment into two distinct currents, contractarianism and the science of man, seems to be too strong.

20. On Enlightenment sociology, see Gay (1969, 323–43).

21. See also Aron (1979, 35, 56–57), Berlin (1979a, 151) and Taylor (1990, 105). See also Cohen and Arato (1992, 88–89). Although Montesquieu develops his position here with reference to his preferred form of monarchical government, the thrust of the argument is wider than monarchy.

22. See also Fletcher (1939).

23. Compare Aron (1979, 60), Berlin (1979a, 157–59), Bramsted and Melhuish (1978, 3, 117–21), Seidman (1983, 15–16) and Held (1996, 70–94). On liberalism, see also Mannheim's (1972, 197–206) old yet still interesting account.

24. Early modern liberalism, which was a broad legal-ethical-moral doctrine of freedom with both a philosophical and a social dimension, was displaced in the nineteenth century by a much narrower economic doctrine. See, for example, Bellamy (1992, 1–4) who speaks of 'ethical liberalism' and 'economic liberalism'. At issue in liberalism in the broad sense was first a general right to freedom in the sense of a right to equal subjective freedoms. This general right was then followed by the well-known classical liberal rights (see Habermas 1996, 125). The shift from the broad to the narrower doctrine coincided with the transition in the late eighteenth century from the rights discourse concerning the constitutional question to the justice discourse concerning the social question.

25. Taylor (1990) draws a distinction between two anti-absolutist or liberal doctrines: the more economically oriented 'L-stream' running from Locke via the Physiocrats, Smith and political economy to Marx, and the more politically oriented 'M-stream' running from Montesquieu to Tocqueville (1955).

26. In Book I, Chapter 1 of *The Spirit of the Laws*, Montesquieu (1989, 4) makes this relation unequivocally clear: 'Therefore, one must admit that there are relations of fairness [*equité*] prior to the positive law...' See also Aron (1979, 53–54). According to Seidman's (1983, 8–9, 21) interpretation of natural law, this should have committed Montesquieu in principle to subscribe to contractarianism with its basic assumption of a pre-social natural individual, but it is clear that it did not; as Seidman knows, Montesquieu (1989, 5) proceeded from the assumption that human beings were '[m]ade for living in society'.

27. Seidman (1983, 23) refers to Montesquieu's 'holistic view of society' which is analysed as such.

28. See also Aron (1979, 45). This global conception of society was reinforced by the inclusion of a map of the world in the French edition of *De l'Esprit des Lois*. It was retained in the 1951 edition of Gallimard in Paris, but apparently excluded from the Cambridge edition of 1989.

29. On this tension, see Turner (1994). It has of course a still deeper significance in that it touches on the problem of the relation between cultural relativism and a (normatively relevant) common humanity which had been central to Enlightenment sociology and has come to the fore again in our own time. In any event, the identification of society with the nation-state rather than a global reality was a concomitant of the emergence of nationalism.

30. Although he did not develop the insight at length, Montesquieu (1989, 311) did see that the more communication penetrates society, the more easily it changes.

31. For early moderns living before the late eighteenth century, history possessed a quality of generality (i.e. historically specific manifestations of a common human nature) rather than universality (i.e. a progressive historical form with which others have to catch up). It is interesting to note that the ecology crisis, among other things, is leading us today to exchange the modern stress on universality for a new sense of generality. This is one factor that gives Montesquieu's contribution a new relevance.

32. This is the case not only – quite predictably – with Durkheim (1960; 1997), but even with Gay (1969, 330) and Berlin (1979a, 161).

Notes

33. See also Aron (1979, 57).

34. On the Scottish Enlightenment, see Windelband (1958, II), Lehmann (1930; 1952; 1960), Randall (1962), West (1965), Kettler (1965), Forbes (1966), Schneider (1967), Bryson (1968), Habermas (1969b; 1971; 1974a; 1996), Gay (1969), Rendall (1978), Phillipson (1981), Wuthnow (1989), Eriksson (1993), Swingewood (1991; 1997), and Berry (1997). The renaissance of Scottish Enlightenment studies during recent decades, particularly as represented by the Cambridge school, has made available a whole range of critical perspectives with which it will unfortunately not be possible to engage in detail in the present context. Crucial, however, is the concurrent reflection on interpretative approaches. See, for example, Forbes (1975), Pocock (1975, 462–505; 1985a; 1985b), Meek (1976), Stein (1980), and Hont and Ignatieff (1985). An important contribution of which use will be made is the problematisation of the critical perspectives of classical republicanism, the aristocratic and merchant emphasis on commerce, and natural law or civil jurisprudence.

35. For example: *The Natural History of Religion* (David Hume, 1755); *An Essay on the History of Civil Society* (Adam Ferguson, 1767); *A View of the Progress of Society in Europe* (William Robertson, 1769); *Observations Concerning the Distinction of Ranks in Society* (John Millar, 1771), revised as *The Origin of the Distinction of Ranks* (1779); *An Inquiry into the Nature and Causes of the Wealth of Nations* (Adam Smith, 1776); *View of Society in Europe in its Progress from Rudeness to Refinement* (Gilbert Stuart, 1778); *Essay on the History of Mankind in Rude and Cultivated Ages* (James Dunbar, 1780); and *A Historical View of the English Government* (John Millar, 1786).

36. On Montesquieu as a sociologist in the sense of one who sought to make history theoretically intelligible, see Aron (1979, 18–19). Crucial to appreciate here is that Montesquieu did not operate with a consciousness of universal world history, as would be the case with late eighteenth-century authors, but rather with a consciousness of a plurality of particular histories exhibiting comparable features due to the common characteristics of humankind. For this distinction, see Heller (1982, 11–27).

37. Rather than just a formalism, such as the contract or rational calculus proposed by contractarianism and utilitarianism respectively, the Scots were interested in the more pervasive, spontaneous and informal groupings and processes involved in the construction and organisation of society. Looking beyond formal or rationalistic arrangements, they sought to identify something approximating a 'natural history' or a natural pattern. This does not imply, however, that they adopted a naturalistic approach. Thus Montesquieu (1989, 308) spoke of being 'more attentive to the order of things than to the things themselves'. See Selznick (1961) on sociology's non-naturalistic concern with 'a "natural" order'. Unger (1987a; 1987b) and Habermas (for example 1996) provide contemporary statements of the problem.

38. Forbes (1966, xxiii) speaks of the 'Scottish "philosophical" historians' and Pocock (1975, 498) of the 'conjectural historians'.

39. The interpretation of the Scottish Enlightenment in terms of the civil jurisprudential paradigm – i.e., instead of seeing it as having been caught up in the tension between the civic or classical republican and the commercial or Whig traditions – is characteristic of a relatively new 'Cambridge paradigm' represented by such authors as Forbes, Skinner, Stein, Tuck and Tully. It is related to the twentieth-century linguistic turn as well as the revival of interest in natural law or modernised natural jurisprudence (see Pocock 1985b; 1985a, 1–34, 49). Habermas also exhibits this same dual interest, his latest major work (Habermas 1996) being of special interest in this respect. Nevertheless, it would seem as though Habermas' (1996, 43–44) interpretation of Ferguson and Millar does not reach this level. His work sensitises us to the fact, however, that the Scottish moral philosophers did not latch directly on to natural law as such since they had transformed it in the context of their theory of the natural history of society. This

transformed version is what I take Pocock's modernised natural or civil jurisprudence to refer to. For a critical view, see Murphy (1991).

40. While Eriksson (1993), on the one hand, offers an interesting and useful account of the original formulation of sociology in the context of the Enlightenment, particularly its Scottish variety, his concentration on the 'discursive innovation of the 18th century', in the sense of an epistemological rupture eventuating in the establishment of the 'discourse of sociology' without any attention being paid to the discourse of modernity, leads him to link the emergence of sociology too closely to Smith's social scientific transformation of Newton. Manicas (1988, 24–36, 37–52), on the other hand, appreciates the importance of the issue of society in its political environment, yet instead of dealing with the sociological contributions of Ferguson and Millar he proceeds in conventional manner directly via the contribution of Smith to political economy.

41. The proposal to locate Scottish Enlightenment sociology within the context of the rights discourse signifies that an option is made here against the traditional interpretative approaches in favour of a new one which is suggested by the Cambridge school (Hont and Ignatieff 1985; especially Pocock 1985b) and, I think, is also to be found in Habermas' latest publications, particularly *Between Facts and Norms* (1996). Rather than either the civic or 'civic humanist' (Pocock) paradigm or its opposite, the commercial-liberal paradigm, which in the final analysis shares the republican premises of the former, the Scottish Enlightenment is approached from the point of view of the significance of the civil jurisprudential tradition. The emphasis is then neither on virtue nor on wealth but rather on the social, rights and active participation. It is only from the latter point of view, which brings questions of manners and taste into view, that the Scottish concern with the difference between the 'rude' and the 'polished' makes sense at all. Once this is grasped, it becomes possible to save the Scottish Enlightenment authors from anachronistic interpretations that read a philosophy of history into their writings.

42. It is important to appreciate that Ferguson was as little simply a Tory Jacobite in the classical republican tradition as Millar was merely a liberal Whig on the side of the commercial oligarchy. Their common civil jurisprudential commitment took them beyond both the ancient notion of freedom centred on virtue and the liberal notion of freedom oriented towards power and wealth.

43. Assuming that sociology received its first formulation in the Enlightenment, particularly the Scottish Enlightenment, Eriksson (1993, 253) sees the new 'discourse of sociology' as having emerged on the basis of a new theoretical problem, a conceptual framework, and a major break with the common-sense understanding of social life and history prevalent at the time.

44. Eriksson (1993) makes the interesting proposal that the Scots, inspired by Newton's spectacularly innovative theory of gravity, transposed 'subsistence' into a new conceptual category and thus provided sociology with its basis and framework. Here one should caution against a one-sided emphasis on the link with science, however, and furthermore encourage the author to interpret the following statement by John Millar describing the programme of the Scottish school not just as corroborating his own proposed interpretation but more broadly as in fact exhibiting their civil jurisprudential connection, the context of the rights discourse and the problem of the survival of society in its political environment: 'Smith followed the plan that seems to be suggested by Montesquieu; endeavouring to trace the gradual progress of jurisprudence, both public and private, from the rudest to the most refined ages, and to point out the effects of those arts which contribute to subsistence, and to the accumulation of property, in producing correspondent improvements or alterations in law and government' (cited by Eriksson 1993, 262, as well as by Meek 1971, 12, from Dugald Stewart).

45. On this tradition, see Windelband (1958, II, 500–18), Randall (1962, 741–845), Forbes (1975, 16–58), and Moore and Silverthorne (1985).

Notes

46. On Shaftesbury, see Windelband (1958, II, 488–89, 501, 508–09) and Randall (1962, 741–54).

47. Authors who stress their liberalism include Lehmann (1930, 161–63, 221; 1960, 125, 126–27, 169) and Forbes (1966, xxxviii). While the former tends to link Millar too closely to a narrow Whig notion of liberalism, however, the latter emphasises too strongly Ferguson's attachment to the civic tradition of virtue. To interpret them as precursors of right-wing liberalism, as does Friedrich Hayek (see Berry 1997, 196–98), is even less justifiable. As their notion of civil society suggests, Ferguson and Millar's liberalism combined elements deriving from Locke's more economic and Montesquieu's more political strands. For the distinction between the 'L-stream' and the 'M-stream', see Taylor (1990). Cohen and Arato (1992, 90), who reduce the Scottish – even Ferguson's – model of civil society to an economic one, apparently overlook the impact that Montesquieu had on the Scottish Enlightenment.

48. Recent research has rendered the interpretation of Locke problematic. Pocock (1985a, 218–30) questions the conventional wisdom that assigns great significance to Locke in the context of the Revolution of 1688–89 and the ensuing debate; Dunne (1985) insists that there is a radical break between the theocentric thought of Locke and the social analysis of the Scottish Enlightenment; and Moore and Silverthorne (1985, 80–81) argue that Carmichael imbued Locke with significance for the Scottish Enlightenment by having brought his thought to bear on the natural jurisprudence tradition, particularly as represented by Pufendorf. Fortunately, we do not have to concern ourselves too deeply with this problem.

49. One could regard these latter two as a concern with formally free labour, as does Therborn (1977, 132), but this is too narrow an interpretation in so far as it approaches the rights discourse in a Marxist manner from the nineteenth-century point of view of the social question or the justice discourse. He thus blots out precisely what is of interest here: the constitutional question and the rights discourse.

50. Here I draw not only on Taylor's (1990) distinction between the Lockean and Montesquieuian streams in the conceptualisation of civil society, but in particular also on Calhoun's (1993, 271–73) attempt to distinguish between the self-regulative and self-organisational dimensions of civil society. In so far as Calhoun links Ferguson to Locke and overlooks the former's relation to Montesquieu, however, his position is indefensible and misleading. Cohen and Arato (1992, 90) commit the same error when they claim that Ferguson, among others, reduced civil society by identifying it with its material civilisation rather than its political organisation.

51. It is this concern, based on a new formulation of the fundamental principles of natural law, that they shared in one form or another with their fellow Scots. For Hume's version, see Forbes (1975, 59–90) on 'A Modern Theory of Natural Law'.

52. For a contemporary account of philosophical and historical anthropology with reference to Plessner, Elias, Foucault and Habermas, see Honneth and Joas (1988).

53. For example Lehmann (1930, 80–118; 1960, 99–100, 122, 123, 129); Habermas (1969b, 217; 1971, 36). No developmental-logical evolutionary assumptions could possibly have been implied in their work, however. For a critique of evolutionism in this sense, see Strydom (1992a). See also Dietz et al. (1990).

54. On the eighteenth-century stage-bound developmental theory, see Meek (1971; 1976) and Stein (1980). Although it has under the influence of Meek come to be called the 'four stages theory', this does not apply to Ferguson, who works with three stages, and applies only with difficulty to Millar, who works with a flexible three-four stage concept. These contemporary authors, who read the Scottish authors from the nineteenth-century point of view, thus anticipating what was yet to come, tend to interpret the stadial theory too strongly and, even given that Ferguson and Millar theoretically employ a developmental concept, often give too much weight to it in the

context of the pre-revolutionary Enlightenment. Eriksson (1990) points out that the proposal to connect the idea of accumulated change to evolution in the sense of progress towards something better constitutes 'a somewhat prejudicial simplification... as the Enlightenment could show nearly as much cultural pessimism as optimism...As for the four-stage authors, they were decidedly no optimists for the future...' (212). See also Seidman (1983, 310) who stresses the Enlightenment's characteristic 'dualistic and cyclical viewpoint'.

55. See also Lehmann (1930, 80–93), Kettler (1965, 228–38), and Meek (1976, 150–55).

56. See also Lehmann (1930, 221; 1960, 129) and Meek (1976, 160–73).

57. Ferguson opens his *An Essay on the History of Civil Society* (1966, 1) with the statement that both animals and human beings 'exhibit a progress in what they perform, as well as in the faculties they acquire', but that in the case of humans '[t]his progress...is continued to a greater extent than in that of any animal'.

58. See also Lehmann (1960, 129). Despite the fact that his contributions to the interpretation of Ferguson and Millar date from 1930 and 1960, reference is here regularly made to Lehmann in view of the fact that, as one of the few sociological interpreters (the other major one being Louis Schneider), his overviews and analyses remain the most comprehensive ones available. Needless to say, the interpretative approach adopted here differs sharply from his, while his assumption – pointed out by Ignatieff (1985, 321) – of the availability of modern sociological categories is of course not shared.

59. On these concepts, see Mannheim (1972, 200–01), Williams (1979; 1971), and Manuel and Manuel (1979, 453–531).

60. Forbes (1966, xiv) insists that 'the thinkers of the Scottish Enlightenment are not to be regarded as poineers of this idea', i.e., 'the idea of progress'. Even Meek (1976, 155, 171), who pushes the progressivist view, has to admit in the end that it does not really apply to either Ferguson or Millar.

61. Meek's (1971; 1976) progressivist interpretation of the stadial theory is actually undertaken from a Marxist point of view. His objective, which is not entirely defensible, is to portray the Scottish Enlightenment as a precursor of the materialist theory of history.

62. See also Meek (1971; 1976, 68–76).

63. On the Girondins, see Furet (1992, 120–21, 126–30).

64. See Ferguson (1966, 236–80). Forbes (1966, xv) argues nevertheless that Ferguson did not regard decline as inevitable but rather issued warnings of 'the dangers to which an advanced stage of civilisation is especially prone'. This, according to him, is 'the cutting edge of the *Essay*'. It is this awareness of contingency and vulnerability, linked to history without a script, that is characteristic of Enlightenment sociology and is again assuming significance today.

65. For an overview, see, for example, Lehmann (1930, 126, 129–31; 1960, 134–35).

66. See, for example, Lehmann (1930, 119–21; 1960, 129–30). Interesting from a contemporary point of view is that Millar (1806, 14–108) concentrated in particular on the position of women in society. See also Swingewood (1997, 139–40).

67. See, for example, Lehmann (1930, 129–38; 1960, 135–36).

68. See, for example, Lehmann (1930, 109, 139, 144; 1960, 125–26, 130–31, 136) and Pocock (1985a, 103–23).

69. See, for example, Lehmann (1930, 107–09).

70. See, for example, Lehmann (1960, 132, 140).

71. On Ferguson's political attitude, see Kettler (1965, 82–104). Kettler (1965, 40) calls Millar a 'radical reformer', but Ignatieff (1985, 324) thinks he had been involved only in 'a narrowly political reformism' inspired by a Foxite Whig middle-class and gentry point of view.

72. See, for example, Lehmann (1930, 144, 147; 1960, 125, 139).

73. See, for example, Lehmann (1960, 142).

74. On 'public spirit', see Habermas (1989a, 93–94; 1974a, 77–78), although his interpretation in terms of the philosophy of history is misplaced. The important point is that 'public spirit' should not be read exclusively in terms of the civic tradition but must be seen in relation to 'opinion' or 'public opinion'.

75. See, for example, Lehmann (1930, 119–28, 156; 1960, 129–32, 135–40). Millar took this route in particular in his later work, *A Historical View of the English Government of the year 1786*, which was influenced more strongly by Adam Smith's view of a market society than his earlier masterpiece. See Ignatieff (1985, 321–22).

76. Lehmann (1960, 136).

77. For an overview, see Lehmann (1960, 138–39).

78. For an overview, see Lehmann (1930, 123–25). See also Millar (1806, 236–37).

79. See also Lehmann (1930, 119–20, 131–35, 155–56; 1960, 134–35, 144). Focusing on 'human society', Millar (1806, 2, 4) explicitly surveyed 'the present state of the globe'.

80. In his account of the social theory of the Scottish Enlightenment, Berry (1997, 185–98) makes an interesting distinction between 'explanatory' and 'significatory' interpretations. The former type, which seeks to explain the origins or to delineate the basic ideas of the Scottish Enlightenment, includes ideological, cultural or contextual and intellectual versions; the latter type, by contrast, is interested only in what the work of the Scots signifies and thus seeks to draw out their significance for subsequent developments. He subsumes all attempts to claim the Scottish Enlightenment for sociology or for liberalism under the latter type. The reflexive account given in this chapter and the next, however, cannot be so subsumed, since its cuts across Berry's two categories. The reference to the rights discourse and rights frame gives it an explanatory dimension, while the analysis of the discursive construction of Enlightenment sociology gives an expanded and, indeed, quite different meaning to the significatory dimension.

9. Discursive Construction of Enlightenment Sociology

1. On More in historical context, see Manuel and Manuel (1979, 117–49), Englander et al. (1993) and ancillary materials in More (1989).

2. See also Skinner (1990).

3. See, for example, Goudsblom (1977, 15–16), with reference to Elias.

4. On Hobbes in historical context, see Sommerville (1992).

5. For example, Windelband (1958, II, 526), Randall (1962, 943–44), Berlin (1979a, 119), Szacki (1979, 45) and Jauss (1990, 27).

6. The appropriation of Vico's work within this new context sporting positivistic, political economic and evolutionary points of view entailed a threefold distortion of his basic ideas. It was left to hermeneutics, which developed strongly in opposition to this tendency, to salvage and defend whatever could be saved – on which see, for example, Apel (1955, 166–80; 1963, 20–21, 58–59) and Habermas (1972, 148–49).

7. Chamley (1975) offers valuable insight into this network in his attempt to clarify the relation between Montesquieu's *De l'Esprit des Lois* and Hume's 'Essay on National Characters'.

8. On Montesquieu in historical context, see Berlin (1979a), Shklar (1987) and Cohler (1989).

9. On the Scottish context, see Kettler (1965, 15–32), Rendall (1978) and Wuthnow (1989, 251–64).

10. On the Scottish Enlightenment, particularly Ferguson, in eighteenth-century Italy, see Venturi (1985).

11. See also Swingewood (1991, 18). Szacki (1979, 78) wrongly interprets it as a form of philosophy of history.

12. On the late eighteenth-century reform movement as representing a hegemonic discourse that subsumed forms of popular democratic mobilisation, see Eley (1992, 326–31).

13. On the eighteenth-century debate and its significance for the American Revolution, see Pocock (1975; 1996, 246–317).

14. See also Hawthorn (1987, 30–31), who traces the emergence of utilitarianism and beneficent evolutionism, both of which obliterated the sociological insights of the Scots, to their naturalistic approach, particularly the difficulties it created for their notion of liberty. Swingewood (1997, 136, 148) repeats the question of the 'eclipse' of Scottish sociology but, although recognising the need for a sociological explanation, declines to pursue it.

15. Forbes (1966, xiv) correctly speaks of the 'comparative eclipse' of Ferguson's *Essay*.

16. For example, by Lukács (see West 1965) and Habermas (e.g. 1969b, 216–19; 1996, 43–44).

17. Similarly Bierstedt (1978).

18. One way of pinpointing the emergence of the 'discourse of sociology' in the eighteenth century is exhibited by the work of Eriksson (1990; 1993). A different option is made here, however, one that is still less anticipatory and hence less scientistic. An interesting point of contact between Eriksson's work and the present book is to be found in his notion of a 'pattern of thought' or 'conceptual order' and the notion of 'frame' or 'cognitive order' employed here.

19. Horkheimer and Adorno (1972, xii) recognised this when they bitingly wrote in 1944: 'Ultimately, Comte's school of apologetic usurped the succession to the inflexible Encyclopedists, and joined hands with everything that the latter had formerly rejected'. Nevertheless, and despite the cogency of speaking of 'the dialectic of Enlightenment', they themselves are guilty of a reductionist approach. Following Hegel, Horkheimer and Adorno (1972, 3–42) reduce the Enlightenment to utilitarian positivism. Eriksson (1993, 251) is correct when he acknowledges that Comte is 'the father of the name of sociology' but rejects the corollary that he is the founder of 'the discourse or conceptual frame of sociology'. He insists that 'the first formulation of sociology' be located in the context of the Enlightenment, particularly the Scottish Enlightenment – a proposition, as he observes (Eriksson 1993, 253), that is well known but has not yet become part of the history of the discipline and therefore requires to be defended by the strongest arguments possible. In so far as his concentration on 'the discourse of sociology' entails a screening out of the discourse of modernity, however, the arguments he musters are not yet strong enough.

20. For example, Foucault (1970; 1972), Lyotard (1984) and Bauman (1989a; 1989b; 1990).

21. In accordance with the terminological usage in this book, I substituted the more appropriate term 'frame' for Baker's 'discourse'.

22. Although agreeing with Marx's critical assessment of the Physiocrat doctrine as 'a bourgeois reproduction of the feudal system', Habermas (1989a, 54, 55, 69, 80, 95, 99) repeatedly pays tribute to the Physiocrats for having been not only the first but also the most decisive to establish the concept of the public sphere as the place of critical activity. It could be argued that Habermas' reception of the rationalist frame is not unrelated to the nature of the German Enlightenment, i.e., its identification with enlightened absolutism and the fact that it grew out of administrative, juridical, educational and scientific practices. On the German Enlightenment, see Eisenstadt and Giesen (1995, 85–86).

23. It is of course the case that the major antagonistic interpretations of the Enlightenment in relation to the human and social sciences, such as those of Parsons (1968), Marcuse (1973), Therborn (1977), Collins (1994) or Foucault, which has been taken up by Bauman (1989a; 1989b; 1990), all as a rule operate with an undifferentiated concept.

24. The discontinuity represented by the French Revolution, particularly the break established by the separation of its first and second phases, is made graphically clear by Jauss (1990a; 1990b). According to Fehér (1987) and Heller and Fehér (1988, 106), the social question arose for the first time in the most radical phase of the French Revolution, the Jacobin dictatorship.

25. The necessity of such a distinction has been brought home by a number of different approaches, such as Douglas and Wildavsky's (1982) anthropological theory of culture and the revisionist historians Furet's (1981) and Baker's (1992) culturally sensitive historical approach. On British and French revisionism, see Fehér (1987, 1–29). The contributions of such representatives of the Cambridge school of political historians as Forbes (1975), Skinner (1978), and Pocock (1985a; 1985b) are also relevant here. Habermas' (1987a) later work indeed allows for a comparable distinction in so far as it works with the conceptual triad of solidarity, money, and power. In *The Structural Transformation of the Public Sphere* (1989a, 98, 99), he actually did distinguish different positions (for example those of the Physiocrats, Montesquieu and Rousseau) and recognised competing and polarised uses of *opinion publique*, yet he has conceded the point (1992b, 424–25) that he tended to proceed in an insufficiently culturally-sensitive manner. His latest major work (1992; 1996) goes some way towards correcting this at the theoretical level. For important sociological attempts to bring a pluralistic theoretical view to bear on modernity, see Heller (1982), Linkenbach (1986), Fehér (1987), Eder (1988) and Arnason (1988; 1994).

26. This interpretation goes back to Habermas' problematic tendency, on the one hand, to latch on to the predominant rationalistic normative code and to approach the public sphere in those terms, and, on the other, to regard civil society from the point of view of Locke, the Physiocrats, Marx and a Marxian Hegel. This accounts for his insensitivity to the problem of access to the public sphere and to the significance of enduring differences in civil society. Compare Calhoun's (1993) critique.

27. Once again, the term 'frame' was substituted for Baker's 'discourse' in both these citations.

28. It is interesting to note that while Habermas has given up the original socialist democratic position he borrowed from Wolfgang Abendroth and put forward in *The Structural Transformation of the Public Sphere* (Habermas 1989a; see also 1992a, 443) in favour of a deliberative or procedural one (1989b; 1994; 1996), he has retained the rationalist frame originally derived from such Physiocrats and administrative reformers as Anne Robert Turgot and Chrétien Guillaume Malesherbes. The problem with this is not its rationalist character *per se* but rather his presentation of it as the one and only justifiable position on the assumption of social equality rather than inequality and of the restriction of politics to deliberation about the public good to the exclusion of contestation (see, for example, Benhabib 1989; Fraser 1992; Eley 1992). Despite his concessions (Habermas 1992a, 424–25), it also seems as though he at times nevertheless continues to operate with the notion of one single comprehensive public sphere rather than a network of multiple publics. In so far as Enlightenment sociology involved a step beyond moral and political philosophy and surrendered the tendency towards moralisation, it placed the rationalistic position as one among others within a larger structured context which allowed both institutional arrangements (for example a constitution) and the interrelation of a plurality of culturally different and socially unequal collective actors or publics through deliberation as well as contestation.

29. By politics is of course not meant contestation and conflict over governmental power alone but also over cultural assumptions and institutional arrangements. Over and above politics in the narrow sense, at issue here in particular is the cultural and social construction of society. Under the title of 'biopolitics', Fehér and Heller (1994) point out some dangers inherent in this new kind of politics.

30. Inspiration is drawn here from Rödel et al. (1989), Preuss (1989), Benhabib (1989; 1992), Fraser (1992), Eley (1992), Habermas (1994; 1996), and Touraine (1995).

10. Crisis and Critique: The Relation between Social and Political Theory

1. See also Benhabib (1986) and Touraine (1995). Unger (1987a) discusses this question of politics from the point of view of social theory.

2. See also Calhoun (1992, 463).

3. See, for example, Habermas (1997, 105–17). For a contemporary attempt to rehabilitate Schmitt, see the well-known journal *Telos*. I am astonished that Alexander (1993, 798) could describe Schmitt as an early critical theorist.

4. In his emphasis on a culture of contradictions, Eder is following Touraine (1977; 1981; 1988) as well as Bourdieu (1986; 1990) in so far as they propose to regard cultural orientations or classificatory schemes not as given but rather as being the object of social struggles. See also Eder (1988; 1992d).

5. For a continuation of his defence against the right-wing critique of a moralisation of politics, see Habermas (1998, 193–201). An interesting issue here is humanitarian intervention.

6. Instead of the philosophy of history, Habermas has since the 1970s sought a foothold for a notion of rationality and hence a normative reference point in speech act theory (for example 1979, 1–68; 1984, 8–43) as well as in moral and legal theory (for example 1996). From a sociological point of view, however, even this position of his continues to raise problems since he insists on retaining the point of view of a moral philosopher who measures social reality with a normative yardstick beyond society. Instead of believing that one knows beforehand what such a standard amounts to, it is necessary to proceed more indirectly and more immanently – without, however, becoming normatively indifferent. This can be done by taking account not only of all the normative standards communicated within a given structured context but also of the implications and effects following from the relation of sociological knowledge to such constructions. See Strydom (1999a, 12–20).

7. Despite all the changes that his thinking has undergone, this combination, which he believes had been made by the French Revolution, remains at the centre of Habermas' (for example 1989b; 1996) work.

8. Therborn (1977, 144) registers this but over-interprets it from a Marxist point of view. Collins (1994, 38–39) also appreciates the fact that sociology is a politicised social science but, although thinking of the nineteenth century (i.e., the justice discourse) rather than the eighteenth century (i.e., the rights discourse), more correctly links it to political liberals rather than exclusively to economic liberals. The accounts of both authors would have benefited from a clearer recognition of the difference between the distinct discursive contexts of the eighteenth and the nineteenth centuries.

9. This type of critique was overlooked by Habermas (1969b, 218–19; 1971, 38–39; 1974, 78) in his interpretation of the Scottish Enlightenment according to which Ferguson and Millar engaged in a limited critique of social institutions against the background of a conservative assumption of the natural history of society. This interpretation reflects Habermas' own notion of ideology critique which is based on the acceptance not only of the philosophy of history but also of a normative criterion beyond society. The socio-cognitive critique at issue here, however, is not an aprioristic

Notes

moralising critique that anticipates the perfect or ideal solution to the problems of society, but rather one that seeks to expose the implications of different positions in a structured social context and thus to discover what is both possible and rational in that context.

10. On America or the 'Atlantic republican tradition', see Pocock (1975). Touraine (1995, 259) submits that the standard political form of society established at the beginning of the modern period, namely the republic, was a fulfilment of the visions of Hobbes and Rousseau rather than those of Locke and Montesquieu. Today, however, concerted efforts are under way to incorporate the latter two, Montesquieu or what Taylor (1990) calls the 'M-stream' in particular.

11. This ambiguous liberal constitutionalist frame has gained central importance in the late twentieth century, characterised as it is by the opening up of 'a new liberal era' (Touraine 1995, 266). In opposition to neo-conservatism or neo-liberalism, the search is on for a new form of 'procedural' or 'deliberative' democracy (for example Dryzek 1990; Habermas 1994; 1996; Benhabib 1992) or a 'politics of recognition' (Taylor 1994; Honneth 1995; Touraine 1995). See also Unger (1987a), Lefort (1988), Rödel et al. (1989) and Held (1996).

12. The most graphic example, perhaps, is the failure of the Constituent Assembly to consider the possibility of the inclusion of women's suffrage in the French constitution, and the subsequent execution – albeit for Girondist sympathies – in 1793 of Marie-Olympe de Gouges, author of the manifesto *The Declaration of the Rights of Women* (1987). For a short history and documentation, see Baker (1987, 261–68).

Bibliography

Adam, B. (1990), *Time and Social Theory*, Cambridge: Polity.

Alexander, J. (1993), 'The Return to Civil Society', *Contemporary Sociology*, 22 (3), 797–803.

Alexander, J. et al. (eds) (1987), *The Micro-Macro Link*, Berkeley: University of California Press.

Alexy, R. (1986), *Theorie der Grundrechte*, Frankfurt: Suhrkamp.

Amin, A. (ed.) (1994), *Post-Fordism: A Reader*, Oxford: Blackwell.

Anderson, P. (1980), *Lineages of the Absolutist State*, London: Verso.

Apel, K.-O. (1950), *Dasein und Erkennen: Eine erkenntnistheoretische Interpretation der Philosophie M. Heideggers*, unpublished dissertation, University of Bonn.

Apel, K.-O. (1955), 'Das Verstehen', in E. Rothacker (ed.), *Archiv für Begriffsgeschichte*, Vol. I, Bonn: Bouvier, 142–99.

Apel, K.-O. (1963), *Die Idee der Sprache in der Tradition des Humanismus von Dante bis Vico*, Bonn: Bouvier.

Apel, K.-O. (1967), *Analytic Philosophy of Language and the Geisteswissenschaften*, Dordrecht: Reidel.

Apel, K.-O. (1967/1970), 'Einführung', in K.-O. Apel (ed.), *Charles Sanders Peirce: Schriften*, Vols I–II, Frankfurt: Suhrkamp, 11–153, 10–211.

Apel, K.-O. (1973), *Transformation der Philosophie*, Vol. I: *Sprachanalytik, Semiotik, Hermeneutik*; Vol. II: *Das Apriori der Kommunikationsgemeinschaft*, Frankfurt: Suhrkamp.

Apel, K.-O. (ed.) (1976), *Sprachpragmatik und Philosophie*, Frankfurt: Suhrkamp.

Apel, K.-O. (1980), *Towards a Transformation of Philosophy*, London: Routledge and Kegan Paul.

Apel, K.-O. (1981), 'Charles W. Morris und das Programm einer pragmatisch integrierten Semiotik', introduction to C. W. Morris, *Zeichen, Sprache und Verhalten*, Frankfurt: Ullstein, 9–66.

Apel, K.-O. (1988), *Diskurs und Verantwortung: Das Problem des Übergangs zur postkonventionellen Moral*, Frankfurt: Suhrkamp.

Bibliography

Apel, K.-O. (1990), 'The Problem of a Universalistic Macroethics of Co-Responsibility', in S. Griffieon (ed.), *What Right does Ethics Have?*, Amsterdam: Vrije Universiteit University Press, 23–40.

Apel, K.-O. (1991a), 'Sinnkonstitution und Geltungsrechtfertigung: Heidegger und das Problem der Transzendentalphilosophie', in Forum für Philosophie Bad Homburg (ed.), *Martin Heidegger: Innen- und Aussenansichten*, Frankfurt: Suhrkamp, 131–75.

Apel, K.-O. (1991b), 'A Planetary Macroethics for Mankind: The Need, the Apparent Difficulty, and the Eventual Possibility', in E. Deutsch (ed.), *Culture and Modernity: East-West Philosophical Perspectives*, Honolulu: University of Hawaii Press, 261–78.

Apel, K.-O. (1998), *Auseinandersetzungen in Erprobung des transzendental-pragmatischen Ansatzes*, Frankfurt: Suhrkamp.

Arendt, H. (1971), *The Human Condition*, Chicago: University of Chicago Press.

Arendt, H. (1984), *On Revolution*, Harmondsworth: Penguin.

Arnason, J. P. (1988), *Praxis und Interpretation*, Frankfurt: Suhrkamp.

Arnason, J. P. (1994), 'Nationalism, Globalization and Modernity', in M. Featherstone (ed.), *Global Culture: Nationalism, Globalization and Modernity*, London: Sage, 207–36.

Aron, R. (1979), *Main Currents in Sociological Thought*, Vol. I, Harmondsworth: Penguin.

Ashcraft, R. (1986), *Revolutionary Politics and Locke's Two Treatises of Government*, Princeton: Princeton University Press.

Aston, T. (ed.) (1980 [1965]), *Crisis in Europe 1560–1660*, London: Routledge and Kegan Paul.

Bacon, F. (1965 [1605]), *The Advancement of Learning*, London: Dent.

Baehr, P. and O'Brien, M. (1994), 'Founders, Classics and the Concept of a Canon', *Current Sociology*, 42 (1).

Baker, K. M. (ed.) (1987), *The Old Regime and the French Revolution*, Chicago: Chicago University Press.

Baker, K. M. (1992), 'Defining the Public Sphere in Eighteenth-Century France: Variations on a Theme of Habermas', in C. Calhoun (ed.), *Habermas and the Public Sphere*, Cambridge, MA: MIT Press, 181–211.

Barthes, R. (1967), *Elements of Semiology*, London: Cape.

Bateson, G. (1973), *Steps to an Ecology of Mind*, Frogmore: Paladin.

Bauman, Z. (1989a), *Legislators and Interpreters: On Modernity, Postmodernity, and Intellectuals*, Cambridge: Polity.

Bauman, Z. (1989b), 'Legislators and Interpreters: Culture as Ideology of Intellectuals', in H. Haferkamp (ed.), *Social Structure and Culture*, Berlin: De Gruyter, 313–32.

Bauman, Z. (1990), 'Gesetzgeber und Interpret: Kultur als Ideologie von Intellektuellen', in H. Haferkamp (ed.), *Sozialstruktur und Kultur*, Frankfurt: Suhrkamp, 452–81.

Bauman, Z. (1992), *Modernity and Ambivalence*, Cambridge: Polity.

Bayle, P. (1995 [1682]), 'On Superstition and Tolerance', in I. Kramnick (ed.), *The Portable Enlightenment Reader*, New York: Penguin, 75–81.

Beck, U. (1988), *Gegengifte: Die organisierte Unverantwortlichkeit*, Frankfurt: Suhrkamp.

Beck, U. (1992), *Risk Society: Towards a New Modernity*, London: Sage.

Beck, U. and Beck-Gernsheim, E. (1996), 'Individualization and "Precarious Freedoms"', in P. Heelas, S. Lash and P. Morris (eds), *Detraditionalization: Critical Reflections on Authority and Identity*, Oxford: Blackwell, 23–48.

Beck, U. and Bonss, W. (eds) (1989), *Weder Sozialtechnologie noch Aufklärung? Analysen zur Verwendung sozialwissenschaftlichen Wissens*, Frankfurt: Suhrkamp.

Beck, U., Giddens, A. and Lash, S. (1994), *Reflexive Modernization: Politics, Tradition and Aesthetics in the Modern Social Order*, Cambridge: Polity.

Bell, D. (1978), *The Cultural Contradictions of Capitalism*, London: Heinemann.

Bellah, R. N. (1973), 'Religiöse Evolution', in C. Seyfarth and W. M. Sprondel (eds), *Seminar: Religion und gesellschaftliche Entwicklung: Studien zur Protestantismus-Kapitalismus-These Max Webers*, Frankfurt: Suhrkamp, 276–302.

Bellamy, R. (1992), *Liberalism and Modern Society: A Historical Argument*, Cambridge: Polity.

Benhabib, S. (1986), *Critique, Norm, and Utopia: A Study of the Foundations of Critical Theory*, New York: Columbia University Press.

Benhabib, S. (1989), 'Autonomy, Modernity, and Community: Communitarianism and Critical Social Theory in Dialogue', in A. Honneth et al. (eds), *Zwischenbetrachtungen im Prozess der Aufklärung: Jürgen Habermas zum 60. Geburtstag*, Frankfurt: Suhrkamp, 373–94.

Benhabib, S. (1992), 'Models of Public Space: Hannah Arendt, the Liberal Tradition, and Jürgen Habermas', in C. Calhoun (ed.), *Habermas and the Public Sphere*, Cambridge, MA: MIT Press, 73–98.

Benjamin, W. (1978), *Gesammelte Schriften*, Vol. I.1, Frankfurt: Suhrkamp.

Benjamin, W. (1980), 'Über den Begriff der Geschichte', in *Illuminationen: Ausgewählte Schriften*, Frankfurt: Suhrkamp, 251–61.

Bentham, J. (1948 [1776/1823]), *A Fragment on Government and an Introduction to the Principles of Morals and Legislation*, Oxford: Blackwell.

Berger, P. L. and Luckmann, T. (1971), *The Social Construction of Reality: A Treatise in the Sociology of Knowledge*, Harmondsworth: Penguin.

Berlin, I. (1979a), *Against the Current: Essays in the History of Ideas*, London: Hogarth.

Berlin, I. (1979b), 'Vico and the Ideal of the Enlightenment', in I. Berlin, *Against the Current: Essays in the History of Ideas*, London: Hogarth, 120–29.

Bernstein, R. J. (1989), 'Foucault: Critique as a Philosophic Ethos', in A. Honneth et al. (eds), *Zwischenbetrachtungen im Prozess der Aufklärung: Jürgen Habermas zum 60. Geburtstag*, Frankfurt: Suhrkamp, 395–425.

Bernstein, R. J. (1994), 'Rethinking Responsibility', *Social Research*, 61 (4), 833–52.

Berry, C. J. (1997), *Social Theory of the Scottish Enlightenment*, Edinburgh: Edinburgh University Press.

Bierstedt, R. (1978), 'Sociological Thought in the Eighteenth Century', in

Bibliography

T. Bottomore and R. Nisbet (eds), *A History of Sociological Analysis*, London: Heinemann, 3–38.

Birnbaum, N. (1953), 'Conflicting Interpretations of the Rise of Capitalism: Marx and Weber', *British Journal of Sociology*, 4 (2), 125–40.

Bloch, E. (1961), *Gesamtausgabe*, Vol. VI, Frankfurt: Suhrkamp.

Blok, A. (1998), 'The Narcissism of Minor Differences', *European Journal of Social Theory*, 1 (1), 33–55.

Bloor, D. (1991 [1976]), *Knowledge and Social Imagery*, Chicago: University of Chicago Press.

Bodin, J. (1993 [1576]), 'Six Books of the Commonwealth, Chapter 10: The True Attributes of Sovereignty', in D. Englander et al. (eds), *Culture and Belief in Europe 1450–1600: An Anthology of Sources*, Oxford: Blackwell, 425–32.

Böhler, D. et al. (eds) (1986), *Die pragmatische Wende: Sprachspielpragmatik oder Transzendentalpragmatik*, Frankfurt: Suhrkamp.

Bonss, W. (1982), *Die Einübung des Tatsachenblicks: Zur Struktur und Veränderung empirischer Sozialforschung*, Frankfurt: Suhrkamp.

Bottomore, T. and Nisbet, R. (eds) (1978), *A History of Sociological Analysis*, London: Heinemann.

Bourdieu, P. (1986), *Distinction: A Social Critique of the Judgement of Taste*, London: Routledge and Kegan Paul.

Bourdieu, P. (1990), *In Other Words: Essays Towards a Reflexive Sociology*, Cambridge: Polity.

Bourdieu, P. (1997), *Language and Symbolic Power*, Cambridge: Polity.

Bramsted, E. K. and Melhuish, K. J. (eds) (1978), *Western Liberalism: A History in Documents from Locke to Croce*, London: Longman.

Braudel, F. (1985), *Civilization and Capitalism 15th–18th Century*, Vol. I: *The Structures of Everyday Life*; Vol. II: *The Wheels of Commerce*; Vol. III: *The Perspective of the World*, London: Fontana.

Brunkhorst, H. (1991), 'Adorno, Heidegger und die Postmoderne', in Forum für Philosophie Bad Homburg (ed.), *Martin Heidegger: Innen- und Aussenansichten*, Frankfurt: Suhrkamp, 313–38.

Brunkhorst, H. (1992), 'Gesellschaftskritik von innen? Für einen "covering law"-Universalismus ohne Dogma', in K.-O. Apel and M. Kettner (eds), *Zur Anwendung der Diskursethik in Politik, Recht und Wissenschaft*, Frankfurt: Suhrkamp, 149–67.

Bryson, G. (1968), *Man and Society: The Scottish Inquiry of the Eighteenth Century*, New York: Kelley.

Buechler, S. M. (1995), 'New Social Movement Theories', *The Sociological Quarterly*, 36 (3), 441–64.

Bürger, P. (ed.) (1978), *Seminar: Literatur- und Kunstsoziologie*, Frankfurt: Suhrkamp.

Burns, T. R. (1986), 'Actors, Transactions and Social Structure', in U. Himmelstrand (ed.), *Sociology: From Crisis to Science*, Vol. II: *The Social Reproduction of Organization and Culture*, London: Sage, 8–37.

Burns, T. R. and Flam, H. (1990), *The Shaping of Social Organization: Social Rule System Theory with Applications*, London: Sage.

Calhoun, C. (ed.) (1992), *Habermas and the Public Sphere*, Cambridge, MA: MIT Press.

Calhoun, C. (1993), 'Civil Society and the Public Sphere', *Public Culture*, 5, 267–80.

Campbell, T. D. (1982), 'Francis Hutcheson: "Father" of the Scottish Enlightenment', in R. H. Campbell and A. S. Skinner (eds), *The Origins and Nature of the Scottish Enlightenment*, Edinburgh: John Donald, 176–77.

Capek, S. M. (1993), 'The "Environmental Justice" Frame: A Conceptual Discussion and an Application', *Social Problems*, 40 (1), 5–24.

Cassirer, E. (1951), *The Philosophy of the Enlightenment*, Princeton, NJ: Princeton University Press.

Cassirer, E. et al. (eds) (1975), *The Renaissance Philosophy of Man*, Chicago: University of Chicago Press.

Castoriadis, C. (1991), 'Post-Modernism as Generalized Conformism', in W. Zapf (ed.), *Die Modernisierung moderner Gesellschaften: Verhandlungen des 25. Deutschen Soziologentages in Frankfurt am Main 1990*, Frankfurt: Campus, 185–95.

Chamley, P. E. (1975), 'The Conflict between Montesquieu and Hume', in A. S. Skinner and T. Wilson (eds), *Essays on Adam Smith*, Oxford: Clarendon, 274–305.

Cherkaoui, M. (1997), 'General Introduction', in R. Boudon, M. Cherkaoui and J. Alexander (eds), *The Classical Tradition in Sociology: The European Tradition*, Vol. I, London: Sage, i–xxvi.

Cicourel, A. V. (1973), *Cognitive Sociology*, Harmondsworth: Penguin.

Clark, K. (1967), *A Failure of Nerve: Italian Painting 1520–1535*, Oxford: Oxford University Press.

Cohen, J. L. and Arato, A. (1992), *Civil Society and Political Theory*, Cambridge, MA: MIT Press.

Cohler, A. M. (1989), 'Introduction', in C. L. Montesquieu, *The Spirit of the Laws*, Cambridge: Cambridge University Press, xi–xxviii.

Coleman, J. S. (1990), *Foundations of Social Theory*, Cambridge: Harvard University Press.

Collins, R. (1994), *Four Sociological Traditions*, New York: Oxford University Press.

Condor, S. and Antaki, C. (1997), 'Social Cognition and Discourse', in T. A. van Dijk (ed.), *Discourse Studies: A Multidisciplinary Introduction*, Vol. I: *Discourse as Structure and Process*, London: Sage, 320–47.

Condorcet, Marquis de. (1955 [1794]), *Sketch for a Historical View of the Progress of the Human Mind*, London: Library of Ideas.

Conyers, J. E. (1972), 'Ibn Khaldun: The Father of Sociology?', *International Journal of Contemporary Sociology*, 9 (4), 173–81.

Dahrendorf, R. (1959), *Class and Class Conflict in Industrial Society*, Stanford, CA: Stanford University Press.

Dant, T. (1991), *Knowledge, Ideology and Discourse: A Sociological Perspective*, London: Routledge.

Bibliography

Deinhard, H. (1970), *Meaning and Expression: Toward a Sociology of Art*, Boston: Beacon.

Delaney, C. (1986), 'The Meaning of Paternity and the Virgin Birth Debate', *Man*, 21 (3), 494–513.

Delanty, G. (1995a), *Inventing Europe: Idea, Identity, Reality*, London: Macmillan.

Delanty, G. (1995b), 'The Limits and Possibilities of a European Identity', *Philosophy and Social Criticism*, 21 (4), 15–36.

Delanty, G. (1997), *Social Science: Beyond Constructivism and Realism*, Buckingham: Open University Press.

Delanty, G. (1999a), *Social Theory in a Changing World: Conceptions of Modernity*, Cambridge: Polity.

Delanty, G. (1999b), 'Biopolitics in the Risk Society: The Possibility of a Global Ethic of Societal Responsibility', in P. O'Mahony (ed.), *Nature, Risk and Responsibility: Discourses of Biotechnology*, London: Macmillan, 37–51.

De Mey, M. (1982), *The Cognitive Paradigm*, Dordrecht: Reidel.

Derrida, J. (1972), *La voix et le Phénomène: Introduction au problème du signe dans la phénoménologie de Husserl*, Paris: Presses Universitaires de France.

Dietz, T. et al. (1989), 'Definitions of Conflict and the Legitimation of Resources: The Case of Environmental Risk', *Sociological Forum*, 4 (1), 47–70.

Dietz, T. et al. (1990), 'Evolutionary Theory in Sociology: An Examination of Current Thinking', *Sociological Forum*, 5 (2), 153–334.

Döbert, R. (1973), 'Die evolutionäre Bedeutung der Reformation', in C. Seyfarth and W. M. Sprondel (eds), *Seminar: Religion und gesellschaftliche Entwicklung: Studien zur Protestantismus-Kapitalismus-These Max Webers*, Frankfurt: Suhrkamp, 303–12.

Donati, P. (1992), 'Political Discourse Analysis', in M. Diani and R. Eyerman (eds), *Studying Collective Action*, London: Sage, 136–67.

Douglas, M. and Wildavsky, A. (1982), *Risk and Culture: An Essay on the Selection of Technical and Environmental Dangers*, Berkeley: University of California Press.

Dower, N. (1989), *Ethics and Environmental Responsibility*, Aldershot: Avebury.

Dreyfus, H. L. and Rabinow, P. (1982), *Michel Foucault: Beyond Structuralism and Hermeneutics*, New York: Harvester Wheatsheaf.

Dreyfus, H. L. and Rabinow, P. (1987), 'What is Maturity? Habermas and Foucault on "What is Enlightenment?"', in D. C. Hoy (ed.), *Foucault: A Critical Reader*, Oxford: Blackwell, 109–21.

Dryzek, J. S. (1990), *Discursive Democracy: Politics, Policy and Political Science*, Cambridge, MA: Cambridge University Press.

Dunne, J. (1985), 'From Applied Theology to Social Analysis: The Break between John Locke and the Scottish Enlightenment', in I. Hont and M. Ignatieff (eds), *Wealth and Virtue: The Shaping of Political Economy in the Scottish Enlightenment*, Cambridge: Cambridge University Press, 119–35.

Du Preez, P. (1980), *The Politics of Identity: Ideology and the Human Image*, Oxford: Blackwell.

Durkheim, E. (1960), *Montesquieu and Rousseau*, Ann Arbor: University of Michigan Press.

Durkheim, E. (1964), *The Division of Labor in Society*, New York: Free Press.

Durkheim, E. (1997), 'Montesquieu's Contribution to the Establishment of

Political Science', in R. Boudon, M. Cherkaoui and J. Alexander (eds), *The Classical Tradition in Sociology: The European Tradition*, Vol. I, London: Sage, 105–21.

Dworkin, R. M. (1978), *Taking Rights Seriously*, London: Duckworth.

Eder, K. (1985), *Geschichte als Lernprozeß?: Zur Pathogenese politischer Modernität in Deutschland*, Frankfurt: Suhrkamp.

Eder, K. (1988), *Die Vergesellschaftung der Natur: Studien zur sozialen Evolution der praktischen Vernunft*, Frankfurt: Suhrkamp.

Eder, K. (1991), 'Au-delà du sujet historique: vers une construction théoretique des acteurs collectifs', *L'homme et la société*, 25, 121–40.

Eder, K. (1992a), 'Framing and Communicating Environmental Protest: A Discourse Analysis of Environmentalism', Project No. 42, Research Paper No. 6, European University Institute, Florence: unpublished manuscript.

Eder, K. (1992b), 'Negotiating a Postcorporatist Order in Advanced Societies: An Institutional Analysis of Environmentalism', Project No. 42, Research Paper No. 8, European University Institute, Florence: unpublished manuscript.

Eder, K. (1992c), 'Introductory Remarks to Project Meeting', European University Institute, Florence, December: unpublished manuscript.

Eder, K. (1992d), 'Contradictions and Social Evolution: A Theory of the Social Evolution of Modernity', in H. Haferkamp and N. J. Smelser (eds), *Social Change and Modernity*, Berkeley: University of California Press, 320–49.

Eder, K. (1993a), *The New Politics of Class: Social Movements and Cultural Dynamics in Advanced Societies*, London: Sage.

Eder, K. (1993b), 'Die Natur: Ein neues Identitätssymbol der Moderne? Zur Bedeutung kultureller Traditionen für den gesellschaftlichen Umgang mit der Natur', European University Institute, Florence: unpublished manuscript.

Eder, K. (1996), *The Social Construction of Nature: A Sociology of Ecological Enlightenment*, London: Sage.

Eder, K. and Schmidtke, O. (1998), 'Ethnische Mobilisierung und die Logik von Identitätskämpfen: Ein situationstheoretische Perspektive jenseits von "Rational Choice"', *Zeitschrift für Soziologie* 27 (6), 418–37.

Eder, K. et al. (1995), *Framing and Communicating Environmental Issues: Final Report to the Commission of the European Communities*, unpublished research report.

Eisenstadt, S. N. (1991), 'Die Konstruktion nationaler Identitäten in vergleichender Perspektive', in B. Giesen (ed.), *Nationale und kulturelle Identität: Studien zur Entwicklung des kollektiven Bewußtseins in der Neuzeit*, Frankfurt: Suhrkamp, 21–38.

Eisenstadt, S. N. and Giesen, B. (1995), 'The Construction of Collective Identity', *European Journal of Sociology*, 36 (1), 72–102.

Eisenstein, E. L. (1980), *The Printing Press as an Agent of Change, Communications and Cultural Transformation in Early Modern Europe*, Cambridge: Cambridge University Press.

Eisenstein, E. L. (1993), *The Printing Revolution in Early Modern Europe*, Cambridge: Cambridge University Press.

Bibliography

Eley, G. (1992), 'Nations, Publics, and Political Cultures: Placing Habermas in the Nineteenth Century', in C. Calhoun (ed.), *Habermas and the Public Sphere*, Cambridge, MA: MIT Press, 289–339.

Elias, N. (1978), *The Civilizing Process*, Vol. I: *The History of Manners*, Oxford: Blackwell.

Elias, N. (1982), *The Civilizing Process*, Vol. II: *State Formation and Civilization*, Oxford: Blackwell.

Elias, N. (1983 [1939]), *The Court Society*, Oxford: Blackwell.

Elliott, J. H. (1985), *Europe Divided 1559–1598*, London: Fontana.

Elton, G. R. (1985), *Reformation Europe 1517–1559*, London: Fontana.

Englander, D. et al. (eds) (1993), *Culture and Belief in Europe 1450–1600: An Anthology of Sources*, Oxford: Blackwell.

Eriksson, B. (1990), 'Small Events–Big Events: A Note on the Abstraction of Causality', *Archives Européennes de Sociologie*, XXXI, 205–37.

Eriksson, B. (1993), 'The First Formulation of Sociology: A Discursive Innovation of the 18th Century', *Archives Européennes de Sociologie*, XXXIV, 251–76.

Evers, A. and Nowotny, H. (1987), *Über den Umgang mit Unsicherheit: Die Entdeckung der Gestaltbarkeit von Gesellschaft*, Frankfurt: Suhrkamp.

Eyerman, R. and Jamison, A. (1991), *Social Movements: A Cognitive Approach*, Cambridge: Polity.

Fairclough, N. (1995), *Critical Discourse Analysis: The Critical Study of Language*, London: Longman.

Fairclough, N. and Wodak, R. (1997), 'Critical Discourse Analysis', in T. A. van Dijk (ed.), *Discourse Studies: A Multidisciplinary Introduction*, Vol. II: *Discourse as Social Interaction*, London: Sage, 258–84.

Fehér, F. (1987), *The Frozen Revolution: An Essay on Jacobinism*, Cambridge: Cambridge University Press.

Fehér, F. and Heller, A. (1994), *Biopolitics*, Aldershot: Avebury.

Ferguson, A. (1966 [1767]), *An Essay on the History of Civil Society*, Edinburgh: Edinburgh University Press.

Ferguson, A. (1978 [1792]), *Principles of Moral and Political Science*, New York: Garland.

Fichant, M. and Pêcheux, M. (1977), *Überlegungen zur Wissenschaftsgeschichte*, Frankfurt: Suhrkamp.

Fink-Eitel, H. (1989), *Foucault zur Einführung*, Hamburg: SOAK.

Fisch, M. H. (1970), 'Introduction', in G. Vico, *The New Science of Giambattista Vico*, Ithaca: Cornell University Press, xxi–liii.

Fisch, M. H. and Bergin, T. G. (1970), 'Preface', in G. Vico, *The New Science of Giambattista Vico*, Ithaca: Cornell University Press, xiii-xv.

Fisher, W. R. (1984), 'Narration as a Human Communication Paradigm: The Case of Public Moral Argument', *Communication Monographs*, 51, March, 1–22.

Fletcher, F. T. H. (1939), *Montesquieu and English Politics (1750–1800)*, London: Edward Arnold.

Forbes, D. (1966), 'Introduction', in A. Ferguson, *An Essay on the History of*

Civil Society, Edinburgh: Edinburgh University Press, xiii–xli.

Forbes, D. (1975), *Hume's Philosophical Politics*, Cambridge: Cambridge University Press.

Fotopoulos, T. (ed.) (1992), 'The Philosophy of Ecology', *Society and Nature*, 1 (2), whole issue.

Foucault, M. (1970), *The Order of Things: An Archaeology of the Human Sciences*, New York: Random House.

Foucault, M. (1971), 'Orders of Discourse', *Social Science Information*, 10 (2), 7–30.

Foucault, M. (1972), *The Archaeology of Knowledge*, London: Tavistock.

Foucault, M. (1976), *The Birth of the Clinic: An Archaeology of Medical Perception*, London: Tavistock.

Foucault, M. (1979), *Discipline and Punish: The Birth of the Prison*, Harmondsworth: Penguin.

Foucault, M. (1980), *Power/Knowledge: Selected Interviews and Other Writings 1972–1977*, Brighton: Harvester.

Foucault, M. (1981), *The History of Sexuality*, Vol. I: *An Introduction*, Harmondsworth: Penguin.

Foucault, M. (1987a), 'What is Enlightenment?', in P. Rabinow (ed.), *The Foucault Reader*, Harmondsworth: Penguin, 32–50.

Foucault, M. (1987b), 'Truth and Power', in P. Rabinow (ed.), *The Foucault Reader*, Harmondsworth: Penguin, 51–75.

Fowler, B. (1997), *Pierre Bourdieu and Cultural Theory: Critical Investigations*, London: Sage.

Fowler, R. (1991), *Language in the News: Discourse and Ideology in the Press*, London: Routledge.

Frank, M. (1988), *Die Grenzen der Verständigung*, Frankfurt: Suhrkamp.

Frank, M. (1990a), 'Was ist ein "Diskurs"? Zur "Archäologie" Michel Foucaults', in M. Frank, *Das Sagbare und das Unsagbare: Studien zur deutsch-französischen Hermeneutik und Texttheorie*, Frankfurt: Suhrkamp, 408–26.

Frank, M. (1990b), 'Gibt es rational unentscheidbare Konflikte im Verständigungshandeln?', in M. Frank, *Das Sagbare und das Unsagbare: Studien zur deutsch-französischen Hermeneutik und Texttheorie*, Frankfurt: Suhrkamp, 590–607.

Frankenfeld, P. J. (1992), 'Technological Citizenship: A Normative Framework for Risk Studies', *Science, Technology, & Values*, 17 (4), 459–84.

Fraser, N. (1992), 'Rethinking the Public Sphere: A Contribution to the Critique of Actually Existing Democracy', in C. Calhoun (ed.), *Habermas and the Public Sphere*, Cambridge, MA: MIT Press, 109–42.

Fraser, N. (1997), *Justice Interruptus: Critical Reflections on the 'Postsocialist' Condition*, New York: Routledge.

Fuller, S. (1984), 'The Cognitive Turn in Sociology', *Erkenntnis*, 74, 439–50.

Fuller, S. (1993), *Philosophy, Rhetoric, and the End of Knowledge: The Coming of Science and Technology Studies*, Madison: University of Wisconsin Press.

Furet, F. (1981), *Interpreting the French Revolution*, Cambridge: Cambridge University Press.

Furet, F. (1992), *Revolutionary France 1770–1880*, Oxford: Blackwell.

Bibliography

Furet, F. and Ozouf, J. (1982), *Reading and Writing: Literacy in France from Calvin to Jules Ferry*, Cambridge: Cambridge University Press.

Gamson, W. A. (1988a), 'Political Discourse and Collective Action', in B. Klandermans et al. (eds), *International Social Movement Research*, Vol. I: *From Structure to Action: Comparing Social Movement Research Across Cultures*, Greenwich, CT: JAI, 219–44.

Gamson, W. A. (1988b), 'The 1987 Distinguished Lecture: A Constructionist Approach to Mass Media and Public Opinion', *Symbolic Interaction*, 11 (2), 161–74.

Gamson, W. A. (1992a), 'The Social Psychology of Collective Action', in A. D. Morris and C. Mueller (eds), *Frontiers of Social Movement Theory*, Newhaven: Yale University Press, 53–76.

Gamson, W. A. (1992b), *Talking Politics*, Cambridge: Cambridge University Press.

Gamson, W. A. and Modigliani, A. (1987), 'The Changing Culture of Affirmative Action', in R. D. Braungart and M. M. Braungart (eds), *Research in Political Sociology*, Vol. III, Greenwich, CT: JAI, 137–77.

Gamson, W. A. and Modigliani, A. (1989), 'Media Discourse and Public Opinion on Nuclear Power: A Constructionist Approach', *American Journal of Sociology*, 95 (1), 1–37.

Gamson, W. A. and Stuart, D. (1992), 'Media Discourse as a Symbolic Contest: The Bomb in Political Cartoons', *Sociological Forum*, 7 (1), 55–86.

Gay, P. (1967), *The Enlightenment: An Interpretation*, Vol. I: *The Rise of Modern Paganism*, London: Weidenfeld and Nicolson.

Gay, P. (1969), *The Enlightenment: An Interpretation*, Vol. II: *The Science of Freedom*, New York: Alfred A. Knopf.

Geiss, I. (1988), *Geschichte des Rassismus*, Frankfurt: Suhrkamp.

Gibson, W. S. (1993), *Brueghel*, London: Thames and Hudson.

Giddens, A. (1976), 'Classical Social Theory and the Origins of Modern Sociology', *American Journal of Sociology*, 81, 703–29.

Giddens, A. (1984), *Sociology: A Brief but Critical Introduction*, London: Macmillan.

Giddens, A. (1986), *The Constitution of Society: Outline of the Theory of Structuration*, Cambridge: Polity.

Giddens, A. (1987a), *The Nation-State and Violence*, Cambridge: Polity.

Giddens, A. (1987b), 'Weber and Durkheim: Coincidence and Divergence', in W. J. Mommsen and J. Osterhammel (eds), *Max Weber and his Contemporaries*, London: Unwin Hyman, 182–89.

Giddens, A. (1991), *The Consequences of Modernity*, Cambridge: Polity.

Giesecke, M. (1992), *Sinnenwandel, Sprachwandel, Kulturwandel: Studien zur Vorgeschichte der Informationsgesellschaft*, Frankfurt: Suhrkamp.

Giesen, B. (ed.) (1991a), *Nationale und kulturelle Identität: Studien zur Entwicklung des kollektiven Bewußtseins in der Neuzeit*, Frankfurt: Suhrkamp.

Giesen, B. (1991b), *Die Entdinglichung des Sozialen: Eine evolutionstheoretische Perspektive auf die Postmoderne*, Frankfurt: Suhrkamp.

Giesen, B. and Junge, K. (1991), 'Vom Patriotismus zum Nationalismus: Zur

Evolution der "Deutschen Kulturnation"', in B. Giesen (ed.), *Nationale und kulturelle Identität: Studien zur Entwicklung des kollektiven Bewußtseins in der Neuzeit*, Frankfurt: Suhrkamp, 255–303.

Goffman, I. (1986 [1974]), *Frame Analysis: An Essay on the Organization of Experience*, Boston: Northeastern University Press.

Goldmann, L. (1964), *The Hidden God: A Study of Tragic Vision in the 'Pensées' of Pascal and the Tragedies of Racine*, London: Routledge and Kegan Paul.

Goldmann, L. (1975), *Towards a Sociology of the Novel*, London: Tavistock.

Gordon, C. (1980), 'Afterword', in M. Foucault, *Power/Knowledge: Selected Interviews and Other Writings 1972–1977*, Brighton: Harvester, 229–59.

Goudsblom, J. (1977), *Sociology in the Balance: A Critical Essay*, Oxford: Blackwell.

Gouges, M.-O. de (1987 [1791]), 'Declaration of the Rights of Women', in K. M. Baker (ed.), *The Old Regime and the French Revolution*, Chicago: Chicago University Press, 261–68.

Gouldner, A. (1970), *The Coming Crisis of Western Sociology*, London: Heinemann.

Gourevitch, V. (1988), 'Foreword', in R. Koselleck, *Critique and Crisis: Enlightenment and the Pathogenesis of Modern Society*, Oxford/New York/Hamburg: Berg, vii–x.

Groh, R. and Groh, D. (1991), *Weltbild und Naturaneignung: Zur Kulturgeschichte der Natur*, Frankfurt: Suhrkamp.

Gulbenkian Commission (1996), *Open the Social Sciences: Report of the Gulbenkian Commission on the Restructuring of the Social Sciences*, Stanford, CA: Stanford University Press.

Haakonssen, K. (1990), 'Natural Law and Moral Realism: The Scottish Synthesis', in M. A. Stewart (ed.), *Studies in the Philosophy of the Scottish Enlightenment*, Oxford: Clarendon, 61–85.

Habermas, J. (1966), 'Soziologie', in H. Kunst and S. Grundmann (eds), *Evangelisches Staatslexikon*, Stuttgart: Kreuz, 2108–14.

Habermas, J. (1969a), *Strukturwandel der Öffentlichkeit: Untersuchungen zu einer Kategorie der bürgerlichen Gesellschaft*, Neuwied: Luchterhand.

Habermas, J. (1969b), *Theorie und Praxis*, Neuwied: Luchterhand.

Habermas, J. (1971), 'De Kritische en Konservatieve Taken van de Sociologie', in J. K. M. Gevers and H. Wallenburg (eds), *Sociologie als Wetenschap van de Maatschappij*, Vol. II, Meppel: Boom, 34–53.

Habermas, J. (1972), *Knowledge and Human Interests*, London: Heinemann.

Habermas, J. (1973), *Kultur und Kritik: Verstreute Aufsätze*, Frankfurt: Suhrkamp.

Habermas, J. (1974a), *Theory and Practice*, London: Heinemann.

Habermas, J. (1974b), 'On Social Identity', *Telos*, 19, 91–103.

Habermas, J. (1976), *Legitimation Crisis*, London: Heinemann.

Habermas, J. (1979), *Communication and the Evolution of Society*, London: Heinemann.

Habermas, J. (1984), *The Theory of Communicative Action*, Vol. I: *Reason and the Rationalization of Society*, London: Heinemann.

Bibliography

Habermas, J. (1985), *Der philosophische Diskurs der Moderne: Zwölf Vorlesungen*, Frankfurt: Suhrkamp.

Habermas, J. (1986), 'The New Obscurity: The Crisis of the Welfare State and the Exhaustion of Utopian Energies', *Philosophy and Social Criticism*, 11, 1–19.

Habermas, J. (1987a), *The Theory of Communicative Action*, Vol. II: *The Critique of Functionalist Reason*, Cambridge: Polity.

Habermas, J. (1987b), *The Philosophical Discourse of Modernity: Twelve Lectures*, Cambridge: Polity.

Habermas, J. (1987c), 'Taking Aim at the Heart of the Present', in D. C. Hoy (ed.), *Foucault: A Critical Reader*, Oxford: Blackwell, 103–08.

Habermas, J. (1988), *Nachmetaphysisches Denken: Philosophische Aufsätze*, Frankfurt: Suhrkamp.

Habermas, J. (1989a), *The Structural Transformation of the Public Sphere: An Inquiry into a Category of Bourgeois Society*, Cambridge: Polity.

Habermas, J. (1989b), 'Ist der Herzschlag der Revolution zum Stillstand gekommen? Volkssouveränität als Verfahren: Ein normativer Begriff der Öffentlichkeit?', in Forum für Philosophie Bad Homburg (ed.), *Die Ideen von 1789 in der deutschen Rezeption*, Frankfurt: Suhrkamp, 7–36.

Habermas, J. (1990), 'Vorwort zur Neuauflage 1990', in J. Habermas, *Strukturwandel der Öffentlichkeit*, Frankfurt: Suhrkamp.

Habermas, J. (1991), *Erläuterungen zur Diskursethik*, Frankfurt: Suhrkamp.

Habermas, J. (1992a), *Faktizität und Geltung: Beiträge zur Diskurstheorie des Rechts und des demokratischen Rechtsstaats*, Frankfurt: Suhrkamp.

Habermas, J. (1992b), 'Further Reflections on the Public Sphere', in C. Calhoun (ed.), *Habermas and the Public Sphere*, Cambridge, MA: MIT Press, 421–61.

Habermas, J. (1994), 'Three Normative Models of Democracy', *Constellations*, 1 (1), 1–10.

Habermas, J. (1996), *Between Facts and Norms: Contributions to a Discourse Theory of Law and Democracy*, Cambridge: Polity.

Habermas, J. (1997), *A Berlin Republic: Writings on Germany*, Cambridge: Polity.

Habermas, J. (1998), *The Inclusion of the Other: Studies in Political Theory*, Cambridge: Polity.

Habermas, J. and Luhmann, N. (1971), *Theorie der Gesellschaft oder Sozialtechnologie: Was leistet die Systemforschung?*, Frankfurt: Suhrkamp.

Hahn, A. (1987), 'Sinn und Sinnlosigkeit', in H. Haferkamp and M. Schmid (eds), *Sinn, Kommunikation und soziale Differenzierung: Beiträge zu Luhmanns Theorie sozialer Systeme*, Frankfurt: Suhrkamp, 155–64.

Halfmann, J. (1986), 'Autopoiesis und Naturbeherrschung: Die Auswirkung des technischen Umgangs mit lebenden Systemen auf den gesellschaftlichen Naturbezug', in H.-J. Unverferth (ed.), *System und Selbstproduktion: Zur Erschliessung eines neuen Paradigmas in den Sozialwissenschaften*, Frankfurt: Lang, 192–237.

Hamilton, A., Madison, J. and Jay, J. (1948 [1787]), *The Federalist, or, The New Constitution*, Oxford: Blackwell (edited by M. Beloff).

Hamilton, P. (1992), 'The Enlightenment and the Birth of Social Science', in

S. Hall and B. Gieben (eds), *Understanding Modern Societies*, Vol. I: *Formations of Modernity*, Cambridge: Polity, 18–69.

Hampson, N. (1984), *The Enlightenment: An Evaluation of its Assumptions, Attitudes and Values*, Harmondsworth: Penguin.

Hauser, A. (1951), *The Social History of Art*, Vol. II: *Renaissance, Mannerism, Baroque*; Vol. III: *Rococo, Classicism, Romanticism*; Vol. IV: *Naturalism, Impressionism, the Film Age*, New York: Vintage.

Hauser, A. (1979), *Der Ursprung der modernen Kunst und Literatur: Die Entwicklung des Manierismus seit der Krise der Renaissance*, Munich: Deutscher Taschenbuch Verlag.

Hawthorn, G. (1987), *Enlightenment and Despair: A History of Social Thought*, Cambridge: Cambridge University Press.

Hegel, G. F. W. (1967 [1821]), *Hegel's Philosophy of Right*, London: Oxford University Press.

Heidegger, M. (1967), *Being and Time*, Oxford: Blackwell.

Heidegger, M. (1972), 'Die Zeit des Weltbildes', in *Holzwege*, Frankfurt: Klostermann, 69–104.

Heidegger, M. (1978), 'Modern Science, Metaphysics, and Mathematics', in M. Heidegger, *Basic Writings*, London: Routledge and Kegan Paul, 243–82.

Heilbron, J., Magnusson, L. and Wittrock, B. (eds) (1998), *The Rise of the Social Sciences and the Formation of Modernity: Conceptual Change in Context, 1750–1850*, Dordrecht: Kluwer.

Held, D. (1980), *Introduction to Critical Theory: Horkheimer to Habermas*, London: Hutchinson.

Held, D. (1992), 'The Development of the Modern State', in S. Hall and B. Gieben (eds), *Understanding Modern Societies*, Vol. I: *Formations of Modernity*, Cambridge: Polity, 71–125.

Held, D. (1996), *Models of Democracy*, Cambridge: Polity.

Heller, A. (1982), *A Theory of History*, London: Routledge and Kegan Paul.

Heller, A. (1986), 'The Sociology of Everyday Life', in U. Himmelstrand (ed.), *Sociology: From Crisis to Science?*, Vol. II: *The Social Reproduction of Organization and Culture*, London: Sage, 150–63.

Heller, A. and Fehér, F. (1988), *The Postmodern Political Condition*, Cambridge: Polity.

Hibbert, C. (1998), *George III: A Personal History*, London: Viking.

Hill, C. (1969), *The Century of Revolution, 1603–1714*, London: Sphere.

Hill, C. (1988), *The World Turned Upside Down*, Harmondsworth: Penguin.

Hill, C. (1992), 'Protestantismus, Pamphlete, Patriotismus und öffentliche Meinung im England des 16. und 17. Jahrhunderts', in B. Giesen (ed.), *Nationale und kulturelle Identität: Studien zur Entwicklung des kollektiven Bewußtseins in der Neuzeit*, Frankfurt: Suhrkamp, 100–20.

Hobbes, T. (1967), *Body, Man, and Citizen*, New York: Collier.

Hobbes, T. (1973 [1651]), *Leviathan*, London: Dent.

Hobsbawm, E. J. (1954), 'The Overall Crisis of the European Economy in the Seventeenth Century', *Past and Present*, 5, 33–53.

Hobsbawm, E. J. (1977), *The Age of Revolution: Europe 1789–1848*, London: Abacus.

Bibliography

Höffe, O. (1995), *Kategorische Rechtsprinzipien: Ein Kontrapunkt der Moderne*, Frankfurt: Suhrkamp.

Holland, D. and Quinn, N. (eds) (1991), *Cultural Models in Language and Thought*, Cambridge: Cambridge University Press.

Honneth, A. (1991), *Critique of Power: Reflective Stages in a Critical Social Theory*, Cambridge, MA: MIT Press.

Honneth, A. (1995), *The Struggle for Recognition: The Moral Grammar of Social Conflicts*, Cambridge: Polity.

Honneth, A. and Joas, H. (1988), *Social Action and Human Nature*, Cambridge: Cambridge University Press.

Hont, I. and Ignatieff, M. (eds) (1985), *Wealth and Virtue: The Shaping of Political Economy in the Scottish Enlightenment*, Cambridge: Cambridge University Press.

Horkheimer, M. (1972), *Traditionelle und kritische Theorie: Vier Aufsätze*, Frankfurt: Fischer.

Horkheimer, M. and Adorno, T. W. (1972), *Dialectic of Enlightenment*, New York: Herder and Herder.

Hoy, D. C. (1987), *Foucault: A Critical Reader*, Oxford: Blackwell.

Hoy, D. C. and McCarthy, T. (1994), *Critical Theory*, Oxford: Blackwell.

Hufton, O. (1985), *Europe: Privilege and Protest 1730–1789*, London: Fontana.

Hutcheson, F. (1995a [1726]), 'Ideas of Beauty and Virtue', in I. Kramnick (ed.), *The Portable Enlightenment Reader*, New York: Penguin, 318–19.

Hutcheson, F. (1995b [1755]), 'Concerning the Moral Sense', in I. Kramnick (ed.), *The Portable Enlightenment Reader*, New York: Penguin, 275–80.

Huysseune, M. (1993), 'Masonic Lodges as Utopian Spaces? Parallels between Utopia and Enlightenment Freemasonry', in B. Coppieters (ed.), *The World of the Enlightenment/Die Welt der Aufklärung*, Brussels: Vubpress, 87–105.

Ignatieff, M. (1985), 'John Millar and Individualism', in I. Hont and M. Ignatieff (eds), *Wealth and Virtue: The Shaping of Political Economy in the Scottish Enlightenment*, Cambridge: Cambridge University Press, 317–43.

Jacob, J. R. (1994), 'The Political Economy of Science in Seventeenth-Century England', in M. C. Jacob (ed.), *The Politics of Western Science, 1640–1990*, New Jersey: Humanities Press, 19–46.

Jäger, M. (1996), *Fatale Effekte: Die Kritik an Patriarchat im Einwanderungs-diskurs*, Duisberg: DISS.

Jäger, S. and Jäger, M. (1993), *Aus die Mitte der Gesellschaft*, Duisberg: DISS.

Jauss, H. R. (1990a), 'Mythen des Anfang: Eine geheime Sehnsucht der Aufklärung', in H. R. Jauss, *Studien zum Epochenwandel der ästhetischen Moderne*, Frankfurt: Suhrkamp, 24–66.

Jauss, H. R. (1990b), 'Kunst als Anti-Natur: Zur ästhetischen Wende nach 1789', in H. R. Jauss, *Studien zum Epochenwandel der ästhetischen Moderne*, Frankfurt: Suhrkamp, 119–56.

Jessop, B. (1994), 'Post-Fordism and the State', in A. Amin (ed.), *Post-Fordism: A Reader*, Oxford: Blackwell, 251–79.

Joas, H. and Steiner, H. (eds) (1989), *Machtpolitischer Realismus und pazifistische Utopie: Krieg und Frieden in der Geschichte der Sozialwissenschaften*, Frankfurt: Suhrkamp.

Johnston, H. (1995), 'A Methodology for Frame Analysis: From Discourse to Cognitive Schemata', in H. Johnston and B. Klandermans (eds), *Social Movements and Culture*, London: UCL, 217–46.

Jonas, H. (1973), 'Technology and Responsibility: Reflections on the New Tasks of Ethics', *Social Research*, 40 (1), 31–54.

Jonas, H. (1976), 'Responsibility Today: The Ethics of an Endangered Future', *Social Research*, 43 (1), 77–97.

Jonas, H. (1982), 'Technology as a Subject for Ethics', *Social Research*, 49, 891–98.

Jonas, H. (1984 [1979]), *Das Prinzip Verantwortung: Versuch einer Ethik für die technologische Zivilisation*, Frankfurt: Suhrkamp.

Jones, R. A. (1977), 'On Understanding a Sociological Classic', *American Journal of Sociology*, 83, 279–319.

Joubert, D. (1972), *Teer-en Veer in 1932: Rondom die Lamont-Saak*, Cape Town: Tafelberg.

Kant, I. (1957 [1795]), *Perpetual Peace*, Indianapolis: Bobbs-Merrill.

Kant, I. (1963 [1784–98]), *On History*, Indianapolis: Bobbs-Merrill.

Kant, I. (1965 [1785]), *The Metaphysical Elements of Morals*, Indianapolis: Bobbs-Merrill.

Kaufmann, F.-X. (1992), *Der Ruf nach Verantwortung: Risiko und Ethik in einer unüberschaubaren Welt*, Freiburg: Herder.

Kelly, M. (ed.) (1994), *Critique and Power: Recasting the Foucault/Habermas Debate*, Cambridge, MA: MIT Press.

Kettler, D. (1965), *The Social and Political Thought of Adam Ferguson*, Ohio: Ohio State University Press.

Kiernan, V. G. (1980), 'Foreign Mercenaries and Absolute Monarchy', in T. Aston (ed.), *Crisis in Europe 1560–1660*, London: Routledge and Kegan Paul, 117–40.

Knorr-Cetina, K. (1981a), *The Manufacture of Knowledge*, Oxford: Pergamon.

Knorr-Cetina, K. (1981b), 'The Micro-Sociological Challenge of Macro-Sociology: Towards a Reconstruction of Social Theory and Methodology', in K. Knorr-Cetina and A. Cicourel (eds), *Advances in Social Theory and Methodology: Toward an Integration of Micro- and Macro-Sociologies*, London: Routledge and Kegan Paul.

Knorr-Cetina, K. (1988), 'The Micro-Social Order: A Reconception', in N. G. Fielding (ed.), *Actions and Structure: Research Methods and Social Theory*, London: Sage, 21–53.

Knorr-Cetina, K. (1994), 'Primitive Classification and Postmodernity: Towards a Sociological Notion of Fiction', *Theory, Culture and Society*, 11 (3), 1–22.

Knorr-Cetina, K. and Cicourel, A. V. (eds) (1981), *Advances in Social Theory and Methodology*, London: Routledge and Kegan Paul.

Knowles, D. (1976), *The Evolution of Medieval Thought*, London: Longman.

317

Bibliography

Kolakowski, L. (1972), *Positivist Philosophy: From Hume to the Vienna Circle*, Harmondsworth: Penguin.

Koselleck, R. (1973 [1959]), *Kritik und Krise: Eine Studie zur Pathogenese der bürgerlichen Welt*, Frankfurt: Suhrkamp.

Koselleck, R. (1985), *Futures Past: On the Semantics of Historical Time*, Cambridge, MA: MIT Press.

Koselleck, R. (1988), *Critique and Crisis: Enlightenment and the Pathogenesis of Modern Society*, Oxford/New York/Hamburg: Berg.

Koselleck, R. (1989), *Vergangene Zukunft: Zur Semantik geschichtlicher Zeiten*, Frankfurt: Suhrkamp.

Kramer, L. (1992), 'Habermas, History, and Critical Theory', in C. Calhoun (ed.), *Habermas and the Public Sphere*, Cambridge, MA: MIT Press, 236–58.

Kramnick, I. (ed.) (1995), *The Portable Enlightenment Reader*, New York: Penguin.

Kress, G. and Hodge, R. (1979), *Language and Ideology*, London: Routledge and Kegan Paul.

Kuhn, T. S. (1970), *The Structure of Scientific Revolutions*, Chicago: Chicago University Press.

Kuklick, H. (1979), 'Sociology's Past and Future: Prescriptive Implications of Historical Self-Consciousness in the Social Sciences', *Research in Sociology of Knowledge, Sciences and Art*, 2, 73–85.

Labrousse, E. (1983), *Bayle*, Oxford: Oxford University Press.

Lash, S. (1994), 'Expert-Systems or Situated Interpretation? Culture and Institutions in Disorganized Capitalism', in U. Beck, A. Giddens and S. Lash, *Reflexive Modernization: Politics, Tradition and Aesthetics in the Modern Social Order*, Cambridge: Polity, 198–215.

Latour, B. and Woolgar, S. (1979), *Laboratory Life: The Social Construction of Scientific Facts*, London: Sage.

Lau, C. (1984), 'Soziologie im öffentlichen Diskurs: Voraussetzungen und Grenzen sozialwissenschaftlicher Rationalisierung gesellschaftlicher Praxis', *Soziale Welt*, 35, 407–28.

Lefort, C. (1988), *Democracy and Political Theory*, Cambridge: Polity.

Lehmann, W. C. (1930), *Adam Ferguson and the Beginning of Modern Sociology*, New York: Columbia University Press.

Lehmann, W. C. (1952), 'John Millar: Historical Sociologist', *British Journal of Sociology*, 2, 30–46.

Lehmann, W. C. (1960), *John Millar of Glasgow, 1735–1801: His Life and Thought and his Contribution to Sociological Analysis*, London: Cambridge University Press.

Lenk, H. (1992), *Zwischen Wissenschaft und Ethik*, Frankfurt: Suhrkamp.

Lepenies, W. (1977a), 'Das Ende der Naturgeschichte und der Beginn der Moderne', in R. Koselleck (ed.), *Studien zum Beginn der modernen Welt*, Stuttgart: Klett-Cotta, 317–51.

Lepenies, W. (1977b), 'Problems of a Historical Study of Science', in E. Mendelsohn et al. (eds), *The Social Production of Scientific Knowledge*, Dordrecht: Reidel, 55–67.

Lepenies, W. (1981), 'Einleitung: Studien zur kognitiven, sozialen und historischen Identität der Soziologie', in W. Lepenies (ed.), *Geschichte der Soziologie: Studien zur kognitiven, sozialen und historischen Identität einer Disziplin*, Vol. I, Frankfurt: Suhrkamp, i–xxxiv.

Lepenies, W. (1988), *Between Literature and Science: The Rise of Sociology*, Cambridge: Cambridge University Press.

Lévi-Strauss, C. (1977), *Structural Anthropology*, Harmondsworth: Penguin.

Linkenbach, A. (1986), *Opake Gestalten des Denkens*, Munich: Fink.

Locke, J. (1970 [1690]), *Two Treatises of Civil Government*, London: Dent.

Locke, J. (1978 [1689]), 'A Letter Concerning Toleration', in E. K. Bramsted and K. J. Melhuish (eds), *Western Liberalism: A History in Documents from Locke to Croce*, London: Longman, 182–84.

Lohmann, G. (1987), 'Autopoiesis und die Unmöglichkeit von Sinnverlust: Ein marginaler Zugang zu Niklas Luhmanns Theorie "Soziale Systeme"', in H. Haferkamp and M. Schmid (eds), *Sinn, Kommunikation und soziale Differenzierung: Beiträge zu Luhmanns Theorie sozialer Systeme*, Frankfurt: Suhrkamp, 155–64.

Losee, J. (1972), *A Historical Introduction to the Philosophy of Science*, London: Oxford University Press.

Luhmann, N. (1980), *Gesellschaftsstruktur und Semantik: Studien zur Wissenssoziologie der modernen Gesellschaft*, Vols I–II, Frankfurt: Suhrkamp.

Luhmann, N. (1985), *Soziale Systeme: Grundriß einer allgemeine Theorie*, Frankfurt: Suhrkamp.

Luhmann, N. (1986a), *Ecological Communication*, Cambridge: Polity.

Luhmann, N. (1986b), *Love as Passion: The Codification of Intimacy*, Cambridge: Polity.

Luhmann, N. (1991), *Soziologie des Risikos*, Berlin: de Gruyter.

Luhmann, N. (1992), *Die Wissenschaft der Gesellschaft*, Frankfurt: Suhrkamp.

Lukács, G. (1968), *Schriften zur Literatursoziologie*, Neuwied: Luchterhand.

Lukács, G. (1971), *History and Class Consciousness: Studies in Marxist Dialectics*, London: Merlin.

Lyotard, J.-F. (1984), *The Postmodern Condition*, Minneapolis: University of Minnesota.

Lyotard, J.-F. (1993), *Political Writings*, London: UCL Press.

Maas, U. (1989), *Sprachpolitik und politische Sprachwissenschaft*, Frankfurt: Suhrkamp.

Machiavelli, N. (1975 [1513]), *Machiavelli's 'The Prince'*, New York: Barron.

MacRae, D. G. (1969), 'Adam Ferguson', in T. Raison (ed.), *The Founding Fathers of Social Science*, Harmondsworth: Penguin, 26–35.

Mandeville, B. de (1995 [1714]), 'The Fable of the Bees', in I. Kramnick (ed.), *The Portable Enlightenment Reader*, New York: Penguin, 242–54.

Mandrou, R. (1978), *From Humanism to Science 1480–1700*, Harmondsworth: Penguin.

Manicas, P. T. (1988), *A History and Philosophy of the Social Sciences*, Oxford: Blackwell.

Mann, M. (1986), *The Sources of Social Power*, Vol. I, Cambridge: Cambridge University Press.

Bibliography

Mannheim, K. (1972 [1936]), *Ideology and Utopia: An Introduction to the Sociology of Knowledge*, London: Routledge and Kegan Paul.

Mannheim, K. (1982), 'Die Bedeutung der Konkurrenz im Gebiete des Geistigen', in V. Meja and N. Stehr (eds), *Der Streit um die Wissensoziologie*, Vol. I: *Die Entwicklung der deutschen Wissensoziologie*, Frankfurt: Suhrkamp, 325–70.

Mannheim, K. (1993), *From Karl Mannheim*, New Brunswick: Transaction.

Manuel, F. E. and Manuel, F. P. (1979), *Utopian Thought in the Western World*, Cambridge, MA: Harvard University Press.

Maravall, J. A. (1986), *Culture of the Baroque: Analysis of a Historical Structure*, Minneapolis: University of Minnesota Press.

Marcuse, H. (1973 [1941]), *Reason and Revolution: Hegel and the Rise of Social Theory*, London: Routledge and Kegan Paul.

Mariana, J. de (1993 [1599]), 'Whether it is Right to Destroy a Tyrant', in D. Englander et al. (eds), *Culture and Belief in Europe 1450–1600: An Anthology of Sources*, Oxford: Blackwell, 261–68.

Marshall, T. H. (1973), *Class, Citizenship and Social Development*, Westport: Greenwood.

Marx, K. (1977 [1867]), *Capital: A Critique of Political Economy*, Vol. I, London: Lawrence and Wishart.

Mayntz, R. (1990), 'Naturwissenschaftliche Modelle, soziologische Theorie und das Mikro-Makro-Problem', in W. Zapf (ed.), *Die Modernisierung moderner Gesellschaften: Verhandlungen des 25. Deutschen Soziologentages*, Frankfurt: Campus, 55–68.

Mayntz, R. (1992), 'The Influence of Natural Science Theories on Contemporary Social Science', in M. Dierkes and B. Biervert (eds), *European Social Science in Transition: Assessment and Outlook*, Frankfurt: Campus, 27–79.

McAdam, D., McCarthy, J. D. and Zald, M. N. (eds) (1996), *Comparative Perspectives on Social Movements: Political Opportunities, Mobilizing Structures, and Cultural Framings*, Cambridge: Cambridge University Press.

McCarthy, T. (1992), 'Practical Discourse: On the Relation of Morality to Politics', in C. Calhoun (ed.), *Habermas and the Public Sphere*, Cambridge, MA: MIT Press, 51–72.

McCarthy, T. (1993), *Ideals and Illusions: On Reconstruction and Deconstruction in Contemporary Critical Theory*, Cambridge, MA: MIT Press.

McCarthy, T. (1994), 'Rejoinder to David Hoy', in D. C. Hoy and T. McCarthy, *Critical Theory*, Oxford: Blackwell, 217–48.

McLuhan, M. (1971), *The Gutenberg Galaxy: The Making of Typographic Man*, London: Routledge and Kegan Paul.

Meek, R. L. (1971), 'Smith, Turgot, and the "Four Stages" Theory', *History of Political Economy*, 3, 9–27.

Meek, R. L. (1976), *Social Science and the Ignoble Savage*, Cambridge: Cambridge University Press.

Meja, V. and Stehr, N. (eds) (1982), *Der Streit um die Wissensoziologie*, Vol. I: *Die Entwicklung der deutschen Wissensoziologie*, Frankfurt: Suhrkamp.

Melucci, A. (1980), 'The New Social Movements: A Theoretical Approach', *Social Science Information*, 19 (2), 199–226.

Melucci, A. (1984), 'An End to Social Movements?', *Social Science Information*, 23 (4/5), 819–35.

Melucci, A. (1985), 'The Symbolic Challenge of Contemporary Movements', *Social Research*, 52 (4), 789–816.

Melucci, A. (1989), *Nomads of the Present: Social Movements and Individual Needs in Contemporary Society*, London: Hutchinson Radius.

Melucci, A. (1995), 'The New Social Movements Revisited: Reflections on a Sociological Misunderstanding', in L. Maheu (ed.), *Social Movements and Social Classes: The Future of Collective Action*, London: Sage, 107–19.

Melucci, A. (1996), *Challenging Codes: Collective Action in the Information Age*, Cambridge: Cambridge University Press.

Merchant, C. (1989), *The Death of Nature: Women, Ecology, and the Scientific Revolution*, San Francisco: Harper and Row.

Merquior, J. G. (1991), *Foucault*, London: Fontana.

Merton, R. K. (1970 [1938]), *Science, Technology and Society in Seventeenth Century England*, New York: Fertig.

Mill, J. S. (1867), *Utilitarianism*, London: Longmans, Green, Reader, and Dyer.

Millar, J. (1806 [1771]), *The Origin of the Distinction of Ranks: Or, An Inquiry into the Circumstances which Give Rise to Influence and Authority, in the Different Members of Society*, Edinburgh/London: Blackwood/Longman, Hurst, Rees & Orme.

Millar, J. (1960 [1779]), *The Origin of the Distinction of Ranks*, in W. C. Lehmann, *John Millar of Glasgow 1735–1801: His Life and Thought and his Contribution to Sociological Analysis*, London: Cambridge University Press, 165–322.

Miller, M. (1986), *Kollektive Lernprozesse: Studien zur Grundlegung einer soziologischen Lerntheorie*, Frankfurt: Suhrkamp.

Miller, M. (1987), 'Selbstreferenz und Differenzerfahrung: Einige Überlegungen zu Luhmanns Theorie sozialer Systeme', in H. Haferkamp and M. Schmid (eds), *Sinn, Kommunikation und soziale Differenzierung: Beiträge zu Luhmanns Theorie sozialer Systeme*, Frankfurt: Suhrkamp, 187–211.

Miller, M. (1992), 'Discourse and Morality: Two Case Studies of Social Conflicts in a Segmentary and a Functionally Differentiated Society', *Archives Européennes de Sociologie*, 33 (1), 3–38.

Montesquieu, C. L. de Secondat, baron de la Brede et de (1949/1951), *Oeuvres Complètes de Montesquieu*, Vols I–II, Paris: Gallimard.

Montesquieu, C. L. de Secondat, baron de la Brede et de (1989 [1748]), *The Spirit of the Laws*, Cambridge: Cambridge University Press.

Moore, B. (1987), *Social Origins of Dictatorship and Democracy: Lord and Peasant in the Making of the Modern World*, Harmondsworth: Penguin.

Moore, J. and Silverthorne, M. (1985), 'Gershom Carmichael and the Natural Jurisprudence Tradition in Eighteenth-Century Scotland', in I. Hont and M. Ignatieff (eds), *Wealth and Virtue: The Shaping of Political Economy in the Scottish Enlightenment*, Cambridge: Cambridge University Press, 73–87.

More, T. (1989 [1516]), *Utopia*, Cambridge: Cambridge University Press.

Moscovici, S. (1982a), *Versuch über die menschliche Geschichte der Natur*, Frankfurt: Suhrkamp.

Bibliography

Moscovici, S. (1982b), 'The Coming Era of Social Representations', in J.-P. Codol and J.-P. Leyens (eds), *Cognitive Analysis of Social Behaviour*, The Hague: Nijhoff, 115–50.

Moscovici, S. (1990), 'Questions for the Twenty-First Century', *Theory, Culture and Society*, 7, 1–19.

Münch, R. (1984), *Die Struktur der Moderne: Grundmuster und differentielle Gestaltung des institutionellen Aufbaus der modernen Gesellschaften*, Frankfurt: Suhrkamp.

Murphy, W. T. (1991), 'The Oldest Social Science? The Epistemic Properties of the Common Law Tradition', *The Modern Law Review*, 54 (2), 182–215.

Nederveen Pieterse, J. P. (1990), *Empire and Emancipation: Power and Liberation on a World Scale*, London: Pluto.

Needham, J. (1972), 'Mathematics and Science in China and the West', in B. Barnes (ed.), *Sociology of Science*, Harmondsworth: Penguin, 21–44.

Neff, J. U. (1960), *Cultural Foundations of Industrial Civilization*, New York: Harper and Brothers.

Neidhardt, F. and Rucht, D. (1991), 'The Analysis of Social Movements', in D. Rucht (ed.), *Research on Social Movements: The State of the Art in Western Europe and the USA*, Frankfurt: Campus, 421–64.

Nisbet, R. (1980), *History of the Idea of Progress*, New York: Basic.

Nowotny, H. (1973), 'On the Feasibility of a Cognitive Approach to the Study of Science', *Zeitschrift für Soziologie*, 2 (3), 282–96.

Nowotny, H. and Schmutzer, M. E. A. (1974), *Gesellschaftliches Lernen: Wissenserzeugung und die Dynamik von Kommunikationssstrukturen*, Frankfurt: Herder and Herder.

Offe, C. (1989), 'Bindung, Fessel, Bremse: Die Unübersichtlichkeit von Selbstbeschränkungsformeln', in A. Honneth et al. (eds), *Zwischenbetragtungen im Prozess der Aufklärung: Jürgen Habermas zum 60. Geburtstag*, Frankfurt: Suhrkamp, 739–74.

Onions, C. T. (ed.) (1976), *The Oxford Dictionary of English Etymology*, Oxford: Clarendon.

Oser, F. (1981), *Moralisches Urteil in Gruppen, soziales Handeln, Verteilungsgerechtigkeit*, Frankfurt: Suhrkamp.

Outhwaite, W. (1975), *Understanding Social Life: The Method Called 'Verstehen'*, London: Allen and Unwin.

Outhwaite, W. (1995), *Habermas: A Critical Introduction*, Cambridge: Polity.

Paine, T. (1954 [1791]), *The Rights of Man*, London: Dent.

Paine, T. (1995 [1776]), 'Common Sense', in I. Kramnick (ed.), *The Portable Enlightenment Reader*, New York: Penguin, 442–48.

Palmer, R. (1969), *Hermeneutics*, Evanston: Northwestern University Press.

Parker, G. (1990), *Europe in Crisis 1598–1648*, London: Fontana.

Parsons, T. (1966), *Societies: Comparative and Evolutionary Perspectives*, Englewood Cliffs, NJ: Prentice-Hall.

Parsons, T. (1968 [1937]), *The Structure of Social Action*, Vols I–II, New York: Free Press.

Parsons, T. (1977a), *The Evolution of Societies*, Englewood Cliffs, NJ: Prentice-Hall.

Parsons, T. (1977b), *Social Systems and the Evolution of Action Theory*, New York: Free Press.

Pateman, C. (1988), *The Sexual Contract*, Stanford: Stanford University Press.

Pêcheux, M. (1982), *Language, Semantics and Ideology: Stating the Obvious*, London: Macmillan.

Pêcheux, M. (1988), 'Discourse: Structure or Event?', in C. Nelson and L. Grossberg (eds), *Marxism and the Interpretation of Culture*, London: Macmillan.

Peck, J. and Tickell, A. (1995), 'Searching for a New Institutional Fix: The After-Fordist Crisis and the Global-Local Disorder', in A. Amin (ed.), *Post-Fordism: A Reader*, Oxford: Blackwell, 280–315.

Pelczynski, Z. A. (ed.) (1984), *The State and Civil Society: Studies in Hegel's Political Philosophy*, Cambridge: Cambridge University Press.

Perrolle, J. A. (ed.) (1993), 'Special Issue on Environmental Justice', *Social Problems*, 40 (1), whole issue.

Petty, W. (1719 [1691]), *Sir William Petty's Political Survey of Ireland*, Dublin: Browne.

Phillipson, N. (1981), 'The Scottish Enlightenment', in R. Porter and M. Teich (eds), *The Enlightenment in National Context*, Cambridge: Cambridge University Press, 19–40.

Piaget, J. (1969), *Strukturalisme*, Meppel: Boom.

Piaget, J. (1970), *Genetic Epistemology*, New York: Columbia University Press.

Piaget, J. (1973), *Erkenntistheorie der Wissenschaften vom Menschen: Hauptströmungen der sozialwissenschaftlichen Forschung*, Frankfurt: Ullstein.

Pocock, J. G. A. (1975), *The Machiavellian Moment: Florentine Political Thought and the Atlantic Republican Tradition*, Princeton: Princeton University Press.

Pocock, J. G. A. (1985a), *Virtue, Commerce, and History: Essays on Political Thought and History, Chiefly in the Eighteenth Century*, Cambridge: Cambridge University Press.

Pocock, J. G. A. (1985b), 'Cambridge Paradigms and Scotch Philosophers: A Study of the Relations between the Civic Humanist and the Civil Jurisprudential Interpretations of Eighteenth-Century Social Thought', in I. Hont and M. Ignatieff (eds), *Wealth and Virtue: The Shaping of Political Economy in the Scottish Enlightenment*, Cambridge: Cambridge University Press, 235–52.

Pocock, J. G. A. (ed.) (1996), *The Varieties of British Political Thought 1500–1800*, Cambridge: Cambridge University Press.

Poggi, G. (1978), *The Development of the Modern State: A Sociological Introduction*, London: Hutchinson.

Polanyi, K. (1957), *The Great Transformation: The Political and Economic Origins of Our Time*, Boston: Beacon.

Popper, K. R. (1972), *Objective Knowledge: An Evolutionary Approach*, London: Oxford University Press.

Bibliography

Porter, R. and Teich, M. (eds) (1981), *The Enlightenment in National Context*, Cambridge: Cambridge University Press.

Poster, M. (1991), *Critical Theory and Poststructuralism*, Ithaca: Cornell University Press.

Preuss, U. (1989), 'Was heißt radikale Demokratie heute?', in Forum für Philosophie Bad Homburg (ed.), *Die Ideen von 1789: in der deutschen Rezeption*, Frankfurt: Suhrkamp, 37–67.

Quesnay, F. (1995 [1758]), 'The Physiocratic Formula', in I. Kramnick (ed.), *The Portable Enlightenment Reader*, New York: Penguin, 496–502.

Rabb, T. K. (1975), *The Struggle for Stability in Early Modern Europe*, New York: Oxford University Press.

Rabinow, P. (ed.) (1987), *The Foucault Reader*, Harmondsworth: Penguin.

Radnitzky, G. (1970), *Contemporary Schools of Metascience*, Vol. II: *Continental Schools of Metascience*, Göteborg: Akademiförlaget.

Randall, J. H. (1962), *The Career of Philosophy: From the Middle Ages to the Enlightenment*, New York: Columbia University Press.

Rawls, J. (1985), *A Theory of Justice*, Oxford: Oxford University Press.

Rendall, J. (1978), *The Origins of the Scottish Enlightenment*, London: Macmillan.

Restivo, S. (1991), *The Sociological Worldview*, Cambridge, MA: Blackwell.

Ritzer, G. (1992), *Sociological Theory*, New York: McGraw-Hill.

Roberts, K. (1992), *Brueghel*, London: Phaidon.

Rödel, U., Frankenberg, G. and Dubiel, H. (1989), *Die Demokratische Frage*, Frankfurt: Suhrkamp.

Rorty, R. (ed.) (1967), *The Linguistic Turn: Recent Essays in Philosophical Method*, Chicago: University of Chicago Press.

Rorty, R. (1989), *Contingency, Irony, and Solidarity*, Cambridge: Cambridge University Press.

Rötzer, F. (ed.) (1987), *Denken, das an der Zeit ist*, Frankfurt: Suhrkamp.

Rousseau, J. J. (1966 [1762]), *The Social Contract and Discourses*, London: Dent.

Rudé, G. (1988), *Revolutionary Europe 1783–1815*, London: Fontana.

Saage, R. (1981), *Herrschaft, Toleranz, Widerstand: Studien zur politischen Theorie der Niederländischen und der Englishen Revolution*, Frankfurt: Suhrkamp.

Saage, R. (1990), *Das Ende der politischen Utopie?*, Frankfurt: Suhrkamp.

Schäffer, W. (1985), *Die unvertraute Moderne: Historische Umrisse einer anderen Natur- und Sozialgeschichte*, Frankfurt: Fischer.

Schilling, H. (1991), 'Nationale Identität und Konfession in der europäischen Neuzeit', in B. Giesen (ed.), *Nationale und kulturelle Identität: Studien zur Entwicklung des kollektiven Bewußtseins in der Neuzeit*, Frankfurt: Suhrkamp, 192–252.

Schluchter, W. (1981), *The Rise of Western Rationalism: Max Weber's Developmental History*, Berkeley: University of California Press.

Schmidt, S. J. (ed.) (1987), *Der Diskurs des Radikalen Konstruktivismus*, Frankfurt: Suhrkamp.

Schmidt, S. J. (ed.) (1992), *Kognition und Gesellschaft: Der Diskurs des Radikalen Konstruktivismus*, Vol. II, Frankfurt: Suhrkamp.

Schmitt, C. (1970), *The Concept of the Political*, New Brunswick, NJ: Rutgers.

Schnädelbach, H. (1977), *Reflexion und Diskurs: Fragen einer Logik der Philosophie*, Frankfurt: Suhrkamp.

Schneewind, J. B. (1986), *Sidgwick's Ethics and Victorian Moral Philosophy*, Oxford: Clarendon.

Schneider, L. (ed.) (1967), *The Scottish Moralists: On Human Nature and Society*, Chicago: University of Chicago Press.

Schneider, L. (1972), 'Tension in the Thought of John Millar', *Studies in Burke and his Time*, 13, 2083–98.

Schutz, A. (1976), *The Phenomenology of the Social World*, London: Heinemann.

Schutz, A. and Luckmann, T. (1973), *The Structures of the Lifeworld*, London: Heinemann.

Seidman, S. (1983), *Liberalism and the Origins of European Social Theory*, Oxford: Blackwell.

Seidman, S. (1994), *Contested Knowledge: Social Theory in the Postmodern Era*, Oxford: Blackwell.

Selznick, P. (1961), 'Sociology and Natural Law', *Natural Law Forum*, 6, 84–108.

Shaftesbury, Anthony Ashley Cooper, Earl of (1900 [1711]), *Characteristics of Men, Manners, Opinions, Times etc.*, London: Grant Richards.

Shklar, J. N. (1987), *Montesquieu*, Oxford: Oxford University Press.

Shweder, R. A. and LeVine, R. A. (eds) (1993), *Culture Theory*, Cambridge: Cambridge University Press.

Sidgwick, H. (1884), *The Methods of Ethics*, London: Macmillan.

Sismondo, S. (1993), 'Some Social Constructions', *Social Studies of Science* 23, 515–53.

Skinner, Q. (1978), *The Foundations of Modern Political Thought*, Vol. I: *The Renaissance*; Vol. II: *The Age of Reformation*, Cambridge: Cambridge University Press.

Skinner, Q. (1990), 'Sir Thomas More's "Utopia" and the Language of Renaissance Humanism', in A. Pagden (ed.), *The Languages of Political Theory in Early-Modern Europe*, Cambridge: Cambridge University Press, 123–57.

Snow, D. A. and Benford, R. D. (1988), 'Ideology, Frame Resonance, and Participant Mobilization', in B. Klandermans et al. (eds), *International Social Movement Research*, Vol. I: *From Structure to Action: Comparing Social Movement Research Across Cultures*, Greenwich, CT: JAI, 197–217.

Snow, D. A. and Benford, R. D. (1992), 'Master Frames and Cycles of Protest', in A. D. Morris and C. M. Mueller (eds), *Frontiers in Social Movement Theory*, New Haven: Yale University Press, 133–55.

Snow, D. A., Rochford, E. B., Worden, S. K. and Benford, R. D. (1986), 'Frame Alignment Processes, Micromobilization and Movement Participation', *American Sociological Review*, 51, 464–81.

Sombart, W. (1923), 'Die Anfänge der Soziologie', in M. Palyi (ed.), *Erinnerungsgabe für Max Weber*, Vol. I, Munich/Leipzig: Duncker & Humblot, 3–19.

Bibliography

Somers, M. (1994), 'Rights, Rationality, and Membership: Rethinking the Making and Meaning of Citizenship', *Law and Social Inquiry*, 19 (1), 63–112.

Somers, M. (1995), 'Narrating and Naturalizing Civil Society and Citizenship Theory: The Place of Political Culture and the Public Sphere', *Sociological Theory*, 13 (3), 229–74.

Sommerville, J. P. (1992), *Thomas Hobbes: Political Ideas in Historical Context*, Houndsmills: Macmillan.

Stechow, W. (1990), *Pieter Brueghel the Elder*, London: Thames and Hudson.

Stehr, N. (1996), 'The Salt of Social Science', *Sociological Research Online*, 1 (1) <http://www.socresonline.org.uk/socresonline/1/1/stehr.html#top>

Stehr, N. and Meja, V. (1984), *Sociology and Knowledge: Contemporary Perspectives on the Sociology of Knowledge*, London: Transaction.

Stein, P. (1980), *Legal Evolution: The Story of an Idea*, Cambridge: Cambridge University Press.

Stratenwerth, G (1973), 'Rechtsphilosophie', in A. Diemer and I. Frenzel (eds), *Das Fischer Lexikon: Philosophie*, Frankfurt: Fischer, 280–89.

Strydom, P. (1987), 'Collective Learning: Habermas's Concessions and their Theoretical Implications', *Philosophy and Social Criticism*, 13 (3), 265–81.

Strydom, P. (1992a), 'The Ontogenetic Fallacy: The Immanent Critique of Habermas' Developmental Logical Theory of Evolution', *Theory, Culture and Society*, 9 (3), 65–93.

Strydom, P. (1992b), 'A Cognitivist Theory of Frames: Comments on Eder', European University Institute Project No. 42, Research Paper No. 8, Centre for European Social Research, University College Cork, unpublished.

Strydom, P. (1993), 'Sociocultural Evolution or the Social Evolution of Practical Reason: Klaus Eder's Critique of Jürgen Habermas', *Praxis International*, 13 (3), 304–22.

Strydom, P. (1994), 'Reconstituting the Institutional Order: Environmental Conflict and Cognitive Change in Late Twentieth Century Ireland', paper presented to Research Seminar, Department of Political and Social Sciences, European University Institute, Florence.

Strydom, P. (1998), 'Review of Johan Heilbron et al. (eds), *The Rise of the Social Sciences and the Formation of Modernity*', *European Journal of Social Theory*, 1 (2), 293–98.

Strydom, P. (1999a), 'Triple Contingency: The Theoretical Problem of the Public in Communication Societies', *Philosophy and Social Criticism* 25 (1), 1–25.

Strydom, P. (1999b), 'Hermeneutic Culturalism and its Double: A Key Problem in the Reflexive Modernization Debate', *European Journal of Social Theory*, 2 (1), 45–69.

Strydom, P. (1999c), 'The Civilization of the Gene: Biotechnological Risk Framed in the Responsibility Discourse', in P. O'Mahony (ed.), *Nature, Risk and Responsibility: Discourses of Biotechnology*, London: Macmillan, 19–36.

Strydom, P. (1999d), 'The Challenge of Responsibility for Sociology', *Current Sociology*, 47 (3), 65–82.

Swan, P. (1993), 'Communicative Rationality or Political Contestation in Environmental Rights', in W. Schreckenberger (ed.), *Praktische Vernunft, Gesetzgebung und Rechtswissenschaft*, Stuttgart: Steiner, 197–205.

Swidler, A. (1986), 'Culture in Action: Symbols and Strategies', *American Sociological Review*, 51, 273–86.

Swingewood, A. (1991), *A Short History of Sociological Thought*, Basingstoke: Macmillan.

Swingewood, A. (1997), 'Origins of Sociology: The Case of the Scottish Enlightenment', in R. Boudon, M. Cherkaoui and J. Alexander (eds), *The Classical Tradition in Sociology: The European Tradition*, Vol. I, London: Sage, 135–51.

Szacki, J. (1979), *History of Sociological Thought*, London: Aldwych.

Taylor, C. (1986), 'Foucault on Freedom and Truth', in D. C. Hoy (ed.), *Foucault: A Critical Reader*, Oxford: Blackwell, 69–102.

Taylor, C. (1990), 'Modes of Civil Society', *Public Culture*, 3 (1), 95–18.

Taylor, C. (1994), 'The Politics of Recognition', in A. Gutmann (ed.), *Multiculturalism: Examining the Politics of Recognition*, Princeton: Princeton University Press, 25–73.

Therborn, G. (1977), *Science, Class and Society: On the Formation of Sociology and Historical Materialism*, London: New Left Books.

Theweleit, K. (1987), *Male Fantasies*, Vol. I: *Women, Floods, Bodies, History*, Cambridge: Polity.

Tilly, C. (ed.) (1975), *The Formation of National States in Western Europe*, Princeton: Princeton University Press.

Tocqueville, A. de (1955), *The Old Regime and the French Revolution*, New York: Anchor.

Toulmin, S. (1972), *Human Understanding*, Vol. I, Oxford: Clarendon.

Toulmin, S. (1992), *Cosmopolis*, Chicago: University of Chicago Press.

Toulmin, S. and Goodfield, J. (1968), *The Architecture of Matter*, Harmondsworth: Penguin.

Touraine, A. (1977), *The Self-Production of Society*, Chicago: University of Chicago Press.

Touraine, A. (1981), *The Voice and the Eye: An Analysis of Social Movements*, Cambridge: Cambridge University Press.

Touraine, A. (1988), *Return of the Actor: Social Theory in Postindustrial Society*, Minneapolis: University of Minnesota Press.

Touraine, A. (1994), 'The Idea of Revolution', in M. Featherstone (ed.), *Global Culture: Nationalism, Globalization and Modernity*, London: Sage, 121–41.

Touraine, A. (1995), 'Democracy: From a Politics of Citizenship to a Politics of Recognition', in L. Maheu (ed.), *Social Movements and Social Classes*, London: Sage, 258–75.

Touraine, A. et al. (1976), *Jenseits der Krise: Wider das politische Defizit der Ökologie*, Frankfurt: Syndikat.

Trevor-Roper, H. R. (1980), 'The General Crisis of the Seventeenth Century', in T. Aston (ed.), *Crisis in Europe 1560–1660*, London: Routledge and Kegan Paul, 59–95.

Bibliography

Tuck, R. (1979), *Natural Rights Theories: Their Origin and Development*, Cambridge: Cambridge University Press.

Tuck, R. (1993), *Philosophy and Government 1572–1651*, Cambridge: Cambridge University Press.

Turgot, A. R. J., baron de l'Aulne (1995 [1750]), 'On Progress', in I. Kramnick (ed.), *The Portable Enlightenment Reader*, New York: Penguin, 361–63.

Turner, B. S. (1994), 'The Two Faces of Sociology: Global or National?', in M. Featherstone (ed.), *Global Culture: Nationalism, Globalization and Modernity*, London: Sage, 343–58.

Turner, S. (1983), '"Contextualism" and the Interpretation of the Classical Sociological Texts', *Knowledge and Society*, 4, 273–91.

Unger, R. M. (1987a), *Social Theory: Its Situation and its Task. A Critical Introduction to Politics: A Work in Constructive Social Theory*, Cambridge: Cambridge University Press.

Unger, R. M. (1987b), *False Necessity: Anti-Necessitarian Social Theory in the Service of Radical Democracy: Part I of Politics, a Work in Constructive Social Theory*, Cambridge: Cambridge University Press.

Van den Daele, W. (1977), 'The Social Construction of Science: Institutionalisation and Definition of Positive Science in the Latter Half of the Seventeenth Century', in E. Mendelsohn et al. (eds), *The Social Production of Scientific Knowledge*, Dordrecht: Reidel, 27–54.

Van den Daele, W. (1992), 'Concepts of Nature in Modern Societies and Nature as a Theme in Sociology', in M. Dierkes and B. Biervert (eds), *European Social Science in Transition: Assessment and Outlook*, Frankfurt: Campus, 526–60.

Van Dijk, T. A. (ed.) (1997), *Discourse Studies: A Multidisciplinary Introduction*, Vols I–II, London: Sage.

Van Houten, B. C. (1974), 'Inleiding: Ontwikkeling van de Sociologie', in L. Rademaker and E. Petersma (eds), *Hoofdfiguren uit de Sociologie*, Vol. I: *Klassieken*, Utrecht: Het Spectrum, 9–20.

Van Peursen, C. A. (1970), *Strategie van de Cultuur: Een Beeld van de Veranderingen in de Hedendaagse Denk- en Leefwereld*, Amsterdam: Elsevier.

Venturi, F. (1985), 'Scottish Echoes in Eighteenth-Century Italy', in I. Hont and M. Ignatieff (eds), *Wealth and Virtue: The Shaping of Political Economy in the Scottish Enlightenment*, Cambridge: Cambridge University Press, 345–62.

Vico, G. (1970 [1725]), *The New Science of Giambattista Vico*, Ithaca: Cornell University Press.

Waldenfels, B. (1991), *Der Stachel des Fremden*, Frankfurt: Suhrkamp.

Weber, M. (1976), *The Protestant Ethic and the Spirit of Capitalism*, London: Allen and Unwin.

Weber, M. (1978), *Economy and Society: An Outline of Interpretive Sociology*, Vols I–II, Berkeley: University of California Press.

Webster, C. (1975), *The Great Instauration: Science, Medicine and Reform 1626–1660*, London: Duckworth.

West, A. (1965), 'Adam Ferguson', in F. Benseler (ed.), *Festschrift zum achtzigsten Geburtstag von George Lukács*, Neuwied: Luchterhand, 249–58.

Williams, E. N. (1980), *Dictionary of English and European History 1485–1789*, London: Penguin.

Williams, E. N. (1988), *The Ancien Régime in Europe: Government and Society in the Major States 1648–1789*, London: Penguin.

Williams, R. (1971), *Culture and Society 1780–1950*, Harmondsworth, Penguin.

Williams, R. (1979), *Keywords: A Vocabulary of Culture and Society*, Glasgow: Fontana.

Willke, H. (1992), *Ironie des Staates: Grundlinien einer Staatstheorie polyzentrischer Gesellschaft*, Frankfurt: Suhrkamp.

Wilson, F. L. (1990), 'Neo-Corporatism and the Rise of New Social Movements', in R. J. Dalton and M. Kuechler (eds), *Challenging the Political Order: New Social and Political Movements in Western Democracies*, Cambridge: Polity, 67–83.

Winch, D. (1996), *Riches and Poverty: An Intellectual History of Political Economy in Britain, 1750–1834*, Cambridge: Cambridge University Press.

Windelband, W. (1958), *A History of Philosophy*, Vols I–II, New York: Harper and Row.

Wirz, A. (1984), *Sklaverei und kapitalistische Weltsystem*, Frankfurt: Suhrkamp.

Wodak, R. et al. (1998), *Zur diskursiven Konstruktion nationaler Identität*, Frankfurt: Suhrkamp.

Wright, E. O. (1989), 'Models of Historical Trajectory: An Assessment of Giddens's Critique of Marxism', in D. Held and J. B. Thompson (eds), *Social Theory of Modern Societies: Anthony Giddens and his Critics*, Cambridge: Cambridge University Press, 77–102.

Wuthnow, R. (1989), *Communities of Discourse: Ideology and Social Structure in the Reformation, the Enlightenment, and European Socialism*, Cambridge, MA: Harvard University Press.

Zaret, D. (1992), 'Religion, Science, and Printing in the Public Spheres in Seventeenth-Century England', in C. Calhoun (ed.), *Habermas and the Public Sphere*, Cambridge, MA: MIT Press, 212–35.

Zimmerman, A. D. (1995), 'Toward a More Democratic Ethic of Technological Governance', *Science, Technology & Human Values*, 20 (1), 86–107.

Index of Names

Adam, B. 279
Alexander, J. 301
Alexy, R. 277
Amin, A. 276
Anderson, P. 102, 103, 104, 105, 106, 107, 267, 280, 283
Anjou, Duke of 125, 127, 128, 148
Apel, K.-O. 30, 34, 35, 43, 52, 77, 88, 270, 272, 277, 278, 292, 298
Arendt, H. 277, 290
Arnason, J. P. 32, 173, 300
Aron, R. 205, 207, 208, 211, 212, 251, 292, 293, 294
Aston, T. 276, 281

Bacon, F. 107, 109, 110, 189, 193, 194, 197, 214, 215, 217, 242
Baehr, P. 30, 31, 32, 33, 270
Baker, K. M. 167, 171, 241, 251, 254, 272, 290, 299, 300
Barthes, R. 34
Bateson, G. 59
Bauman, Z. 24, 299, 300
Bayle, P. 129, 131, 259, 285
Beck, U. 15, 20, 75, 268, 277
Bellah, R. N. 283
Bellamy, R. 289, 293
Benhabib, S. 254, 272, 300, 301, 302
Benjamin, W. 107, 108, 112, 139, 282, 283, 287
Bentham, J. 277
Berger, P. L. 267
Berlin, I. 204, 205, 212, 239, 292, 293, 298
Bernstein, R. J. 78, 271, 277
Berry, C. J. 294, 296, 298
Bierstedt, R. 239, 292, 299
Birnbaum, N. 32

Bloch, E. 277
Blok, A. 16
Bloor, D. 268, 269, 276
Bodin, J. 101, 133, 147, 162, 187, 288
Böhler, D. 34
Bonss, W. 238
Bossuet, Bishop 187, 241, 251
Bourdieu, P. 60, 62, 66, 87, 132, 268, 269, 271, 272, 273, 274, 278, 279, 301
Bramsted, E. K. 165, 219, 289, 293
Braudel, F. 98, 280, 281, 290
Brueghel, P. 122, 146, 151, 152, 153, 284
Brunkhorst, H. 270
Bryson, G. 294
Buechler, S. M. 277
Bürger, P. 276
Burns, T. R. 154, 275, 289

Calhoun, C. 254, 269, 271, 273, 296, 300, 301
Calvin, J. 101, 109, 119, 122, 126, 127, 128, 134, 142, 158, 159, 161, 162, 163, 193, 286, 288
Campbell, T. D. 217
Capek, S. M. 274, 289
Cassirer, E. 279, 290
Castoriadis, C. 276
Catherine de Medici 117, 127, 128
Chamley, P. E. 298
Charles II 110, 111, 145, 161
Charles V 101, 117, 121, 125, 126
Cherkaoui, M. 267
Cicourel, A. V. 274
Clark, K. 122
Cohen, J. L. 66, 272, 291, 293, 296
Cohler, A. M. 298
Coleman, J. S. 54

330

Index of Names

Subject Index